15°
0°
15°
30°
60°
45°
30°
15°
0°
ICELAND
REYKJAVIK
Hebrides
BRITISH
ISLES
SCOTLAND
NORTH SEA
IRELAND
Belfast
DUBLIN
Irish Sea
ENGLAND
LONDON
English Channel
Cherbourg
PARIS
FRANCE
OSLO
STOCKHOLM
HELSINKI
ESTONIA
LATVIA
LITHUANIA
BALTIC SEA
DENMARK
NETH
BRUSSELS
BELGIUM
BERLIN
GERMANY
POLAND
Rhine
CZECHOSLOVAKIA
AUSTRIA
HUNGARY
RUMANIA
YUGOSLAVIA
Adriatic Sea
BULGARIA
Istanbul
ITALY
Marseille
Toulon
Corsica
Rome
Anzio
Naples
Salerno
Sardinia
TIRANE
ALBANIA
GREECE
Aegean Sea
Athens
Palermo
Sicily
PORTUGAL
SPAIN
STRAIT OF GIBRALTAR
Gibraltar
Tangier
SP. MOR
Port Lyautey
Rabat
Casablanca
MOROCCO
Oran
Algiers
Bizerte
Tunis
Malta
TUNISIA
TRIPOLI
MEDITERRANEAN SEA
Crete
Madeira
CANARY IS
ALGERIA
LIBYA
EGYPT
SPANISH SAHARA
E VERDE IS
FRENCH WEST AFRICA
ANGLO
EGYPTIAN
SUDAN
Dakar
GAMBIA
PORT.
GUINEA
SIERRA
LEONE
LIBERIA
GOLD
COAST
NIGERIA
CAMEROONS
FRENCH EQUATORIAL AFRICA
BELGIAN
CONGO

Grand Admiral

Erich Raeder

MY LIFE

Grand Admiral

Erich Raeder

MY LIFE

TRANSLATED FROM THE GERMAN BY

HENRY W. DREXEL

ANNAPOLIS

UNITED STATES NAVAL INSTITUTE

1960

Library of Congress Catalogue Card No. 60-9236

Printed in the U.S.A.

BY GEORGE BANTA COMPANY, INC., MENASHA, WISCONSIN

Foreword

GRAND ADMIRAL ERICH RAEDER'S story of his life, from his birth and early days in a small town near Hamburg, through his naval career, which began in 1894 and ended in 1943 with his final break with Hitler, his trial and conviction by the International Tribunal at Nürnberg, and the decade he spent in the military prison at Spandau, is a highly interesting historical document. It covers the days of the Kaiser's expanding navy, the principal surface actions of World War I, the political developments and the rebuilding of the navy between the wars, and the major operations in which the navy was concerned in World War II. It includes interesting characterizations of the Kaiser and Hitler, by one who was close to them both. Raeder attributes German political difficulties and the rise of Nazism to the restrictive influence of the Versailles Treaty.

But this account is more than a valuable historical record. It is a revealing study of the character of a man with deep religious convictions, dedicated to his profession as a naval officer, and devoted to the service of his Fatherland. It is the biography of one who, naturally enough, defends himself strongly against the charges of "war crimes" levelled against him, but who accepts full responsibility for his decisions and does not claim that *he* was always right, and others always wrong. The naval reader, particularly the more elderly one, will find much in Raeder's career with respect to the education of officers and men, and the training of the fleet in general, which parallels his own experience.

That Raeder had a sense of humor is evidenced by his anecdote of the admirals who, day after day, encountered the same luncheon at inspections, served by zealous commanding officers who hoped to ingratiate themselves by offering the inspector's favorite dish.

In many places, Admiral Raeder sets forth his very sound concepts of the importance of sea power, the proper inter-relationship and co-ordination of the different national defense services, correct systems of command, and the responsibilities of a leader. He was firm against the domination of one service by another, as was the case with Germany in World War I. He deplores the landmindedness of German leaders in both World Wars. He believed in, and fought hard for, a separate naval air arm. Denied that, he struggled to obtain adequate Air Force support for German naval operations. His failure—for which we may be thankful—was due to the greater influence Göring exerted over Hitler, and the preoccupation of that burly Air Marshal with objectives *he* felt were more suitable to an air force. One could wish that the lessons of German experience in this connection might be brought home to all those having direct responsibility for our own national defense.

One of Raeder's tenets was that the military services should be entirely divorced from politics. According to his own record, he abstained from political activities himself and endeavored to keep the Navy as a whole clear of them. In this, he seems to have been more successful than the other services, due largely to the fact that the Navy, at sea, was further removed from domestic entanglements. He foresaw the disastrous effect, in 1931, of the then Minister of Defense taking on the additional portfolio of the Ministry of the Interior.

Raeder, whose judgment on matters of strategy and tactics was undoubtedly excellent, shows himself to have strongly warned against involvement with England, to have advised against attempting to invade England after the fall of France, and to have opposed the attack on Russia. He frequently and violently disagreed with Hitler, but was completely loyal to him as the legal head of the German government until he felt forced by Hitler's actions to resign in January 1943. Prior to that, he had several times contemplated resigning, but held on in the hope that he thus might protect the Navy.

The International Military Tribunal at Nürnberg was established with the honest purpose of taking steps to discourage in the future such acts of aggression as the Nazi attack on Poland, and the invasion of the Low Countries and of Norway and Denmark. Punishment of political leaders proved, of themselves, to be responsible for such acts is completely justifiable. But the conviction of military leaders who are shown to have been merely carrying out the directives of higher authority is certainly debatable. If each military commander were required himself to decide the international legality of the orders he receives from above before complying with them, the result would be inefficiency and chaos in any defense establishment. It would appear that the sentencing of such an officer by a military tribunal establishes an undesirable precedent which could well be used by *any* victor to the discomfiture of the vanquished.

I believe that the readers of this history will regret, with me, the lonely years spent by this able officer in Spandau, will be glad that his life sentence was ultimately remitted, and will hope that his remaining years may be spent in peace and comfort.

H. Kent Hewitt

H. KENT HEWITT
Admiral, U. S. Navy (Retired)

Annapolis, Maryland
4 February 1960

Preface

IN THE INTRODUCTION to *The Other Side of the Hill,* the British military writer, Liddell Hart, gives an account of an episode in the life of Field Marshal Lord Wellington. During a trip Lord Wellington and an acquaintance passed the time in guessing what sort of terrain they would find on the other side of every hill. When the acquaintance expressed his surprise at Wellington's correct prophecies, the latter replied: "All my life I have tried to find out what lies on the other side of the hill."

It is difficult enough in ordinary life to get an accurate picture of what lies on the other side of a hill that cuts off our view. But it is a great deal more difficult to see what lies beyond that insuperable mountain that separates the present from the future. We live and act for the future, and we try to sketch for ourselves a picture of it, but it comes out blurred and indistinct. We cannot draw its outlines and colors from anything we actually know, but only from our hopes and wishes. Man is denied to know what Fate will bring him. Thus, all decisions and actions we take on the basis of our concept of the future are marred by deficiencies.

He, then, who later looks back from the other side of the hill will necessarily see things in a vastly different light. That which formerly was hazy now is clear. That which was once a problem now has found its solution. Many things that once seemed firm have turned into a mirage. Things once unimportant or even forgotten now stand forth in all their consequence. The view into the past is entirely different from that into the veiled future.

So now we stand on the other side of the hill. More clearly and frequently, for the first time, do we recognize what was right and what was wrong. Events rearrange themselves in their correct pattern. Yet the most searching backward glances are necessary if we are to clarify some of those circumstances and human influences which must be known to us if we are to gain a true picture of those times and things that lie behind us.

This book had its origin in the desire and the obligation to contribute its share to the knowledge of the past. It does not attempt to supplant those authors who, drawing on sources becoming more and more accessible both here and abroad, write the serious volumes of the last half century of German history. My desire is merely to contribute any little knowledge I have toward the fulfillment of their task.

It can be only a small contribution. An officer who, in accordance with tradition and his personal understanding, always saw himself as a servant of the armed forces and the State, cannot feel competent to discuss the historic events of the times other than within the narrow scope of his own experiences. And I was a sailor and a soldier, not a politician.

Being now on "the other side of the hill," I am conscious of the difference between the former picture and the present one. My numerous notes give me, however, the possibility of recording past events, developments, and thoughts—including the errors which we recognize today—from the point of view of that time. My ten years of seclusion in Spandau prison were probably advantageous in that they spared my memory from the confusion of the outside world.

For the Navy and for me—as its commander in chief—there was no foreign political event between the two World Wars as of great significance as the conclusion of the Anglo-German Naval Agreement in 1935. With it ended the period of Germany's captivity which the Treaty of Versailles had brought. The first part of this book covers my naval experiences up to that time, and my impressions of them; the second half treats of the developments from 1935 on. Both parts are inseparably connected.

With the increase in the size of the Navy, starting in 1935, and the numerous duties assigned to it, it is impossible to depict its expansion and achievements, particularly during the war, with any completeness. This must wait until a time when all the data are accessible and must be a task for men who have more time left than I have.

I have been given indispensable help in writing this book by numerous old comrades and friends. It would be an injustice to distinguish some of them by name, since I owe cordial and deeply felt thanks to all. But I do feel the need of thanking Admiral Erich Förste (Ret.), my old, faithful collaborator of many years, for his time and labor in the final editing. He selflessly kept his own views and interpretations in the background in order to let mine come to the fore. In content and presentation the book is therefore my own, and I bear all the responsibility for it.

A kind fate placed me in a profession in which I was active longer than others. Therefore my life is closely bound with that of the Navy, and any achievements of mine are but the result of the performance of duty of all that Navy. Only a few individuals can be mentioned in this narrative, but the merit of the many others is none the less recognized.

My life has brought me the beautiful and the difficult, the exalting and the tragic in rich, often too great, abundance. It has been a life truly full of labor and toil. But in looking back, I am thankful, in spite of everything, that, from early youth on, I could work in an incomparable community of men whose comrade I was. If, with my book of reminiscences, I can contribute even in a small part to the end that they and their devotion to our common, splendid profession will not be forgotten, I shall be happy to have fulfilled this last official and human duty in the evening of my life.

ERICH RAEDER

Kiel, 1957

Publisher's Note

WHILE ENDEAVORING to maintain complete accuracy in the translation of this work from the original German text, the publisher has necessarily had to use latitude in interpreting terms or words which have no exact equivalent in English or in American naval terminology. To have adhered to rigid word-for-word translation would at times have made for confusion rather than clear understanding. This is especially true in connection with German naval ranks and departmental designations, where there is sometimes no exact equivalent in the U. S. Navy.

The publisher has also taken the liberty of inserting footnotes to explain important references or to add additional details concerning persons or events familiar to German readers but not well known to the American public.

In checking such matters and terms, the publisher had the good fortune to receive the invaluable assistance and suggestions of Admiral Erich Förste, GN (Ret.), Rear Admiral S. H. Engel, GN (Ret.), and Captain Edward Wegener, the Naval Attaché of the German Federal Republic in Washington, D.C., to whom they owe a debt of gratitude.

UNITED STATES NAVAL INSTITUTE

1 February 1960

Table of Contents

List of Illustrations

Grand Admiral

Erich Raeder

MY LIFE

I

Early Days in the Navy

TO ENTER the Navy—or, in fact, to go to sea at all—was the last thing in my thoughts when I was a youngster. My father, Hans Raeder, was a teacher of French and English at the Matthias Claudius High School, in Wandsbek, near Hamburg, where I was born on 24 April 1876. And my grandfather had also been a teacher before that, the owner of a private school. My mother was Gertraudt Hartmann, the daughter of the royal court musician, Albert Hartmann.

The salary of a young high school teacher was not large, and the family finances had to be stretched to cover the education of myself and my two brothers. However, this lesson of thriftiness proved an invaluable asset in our later development, for we learned early how to get along with little and how to make each penny count.

The atmosphere in our home was one of discipline tempered with affection. Fear of God, love of truth, and cleanliness, within and without—these were the principles impressed upon us from childhood. I still remember how painstakingly my father explained to me the importance of attending church, as well as the meaning of the service itself, before allowing me to attend the Wandsbek church with him and my mother for the first time.

As far as school was concerned, my brothers and I gave little worry to our parents, for we all learned easily. Our father gave us instruction in physical exercises, such as swimming and skiing, while Mother, who was an accomplished pianist, saw to our musical education.

Studies were lightened by numerous trips, not only to the cities but to the woods and water as well. We became acquainted with Hamburg and its harbor, as well as with the Saxon Forest, where Bismarck's castle was located. In 1888 and 1889 we went to Timmendorf beach, which had only six houses at the time, and to Travemunde, on the Baltic Sea. It was in Lübeck Bay that I saw my first warship, the training brig *Musquito,* the only warship I ever saw until I entered the Navy. We even went aboard the *Musquito,* but I was completely unimpressed.

In 1889, when I was 13, my father was suddenly appointed headmaster of the Friedrich Wilhelm High School in Grünberg, Silesia. This advancement was in recognition of his scholarly attainments, acquired in part from long study in England and France. But for me the change from the classical high school at Wandsbek to the semi-classical school at Grünberg was fraught with difficulties. For while I was proficient in French and Latin, I was a year and a half behind in English and mathematics. However, four weeks of concentrated tutoring under my father at the beach in the summer brought my English up to the mark, and the mathematics teacher in Grünberg improved my geometry in short order.

The change in environment was even greater than the change in curriculum. Apart from the general cultural differences, there was the change in dialect, which for a time proved a real difficulty. But even that disappeared with time. We became accustomed to our new home, and found walking trips through the Riesengebirge as interesting as the Baltic ports and beaches.

A particular contributor to my education at Grünberg was Dr. Leeder, the young professor who taught us geography and history. He made history come alive, not only in connection with the military campaigns of the Napoleonic period and 1870, but also with constitutional history and modern politics. I valued his teachings and friendship so much that I visited him as late as his eighty-fifth birthday, just before the Second World War, when I made one of my regular visits to the graves of my parents, dead since 1932.

The high point of the school year at Grünberg was always the annual trip to the Odetwald, made by the whole school on the second of September each year. Many former students and their families returned to attend the festivities, which consisted of a speech by the school's top student, games and exercises, and a dance for the students. The outing ended with a torchlight procession back to the city.

After graduation, it had been planned that I would attend a university; I had some vague idea of becoming a doctor, a military surgeon. But this would require extra Latin and Greek, credits in which were then required for the study of medicine. So I began taking private lessons in both Latin and Greek to make up for my deficiencies.

In my last year at Grünberg school, I won a book offered as a prize. The book was one written by Admiral von Werner, describing the round-the-world cruise of Prince Heinrich of Prussia as a naval cadet, and it contained fascinating details of life on board a sailing frigate. I read and reread the book all that year until I knew by heart the shipboard life of cadets in the Navy.

Whether it was the book that did it, or whether it was just fate, I do not know. But in March, 1894, just two weeks before final examination at the school, I marched into my father's office and told him that I did not want to study medicine; what I wanted was to enter the Navy. I asked my father to submit a request to the Oberkommando der Marine (High Command of the Navy) for my admission to the Naval School, and to send along with it a transcript of my scholastic record.

This sudden decision for a naval career would have disturbed most parents, for my temperament did not seem particularly suited to a practical profession demanding such great physical exertion. In gym classes at school I had got good grades only by dint of vast effort. However, my father must have had great confidence in my judgment, for he promptly wrote in to the High Command as I had asked, even though the time for such applications to be submitted had already lapsed on October first of the previous year. Yet, amazingly enough, I received a reply almost immediately, ordering me to take a physical examination at the Lancers Regiment in Zullichau, and then to be prepared to appear in Kiel on 1 April, less than 30 days off.

The physical examination offered no problems, but the trip from Silesia to Kiel, and being thrown together there with scores of other naval candidates who were all complete strangers to me, was an ordeal. I had seldom been away from home alone in my whole life, and these lively young strangers came from all over Germany, a surprising number from Bavaria.

Training in the Imperial Navy, 1894-1897

On arrival at Kiel we were temporarily housed in the attic of the Naval School, and immediately took up our training, the first six weeks of which were devoted primarily to infantry drill. This was conducted by Lieutenant von Oidtmann of the Marines, with the drills actually carried out by noncommissioned Army officers as section leaders. The drill corporals were classmates who had been in the cadet corps of the Army.

This infantry drill period was the hardest, unhappiest time of my entire life as a naval cadet. Not because of the hard drilling, but because of the harsh attitude of the noncoms. The barrages of oaths with which they greeted us although not aimed at us personally, were so crude and vulgar that I sometimes seriously considered whether I could continue to serve in any such atmosphere.

In addition to infantry we learned the intricacies of a sailing ship's rigging from ship models, as well as the rudiments of rowing in the cutters. The high point of the six weeks was the naval parade for the Kaiser who came to Kiel to enter his son, Prince Adalbert, in the Navy on the Prince's tenth birthday. Our parade, with the young prince marching on the right flank as company ensign, went off somewhat raggedly, but our taking the oath of office in the naval chapel, with the impressive sermon by the old Chief of Chaplains Langheld, was very moving.

Our short shore duty ended with an inspection, and in May we new cadets made the eagerly awaited transfer to the training ships. I, with some 34 fellow classmates, was assigned to the schoolship *Stosch;* the other 35 were assigned to SMS *Stein.*

The commanding officer of the *Stosch* was Captain von Schuckmann, but the officer immediately supervising our training was Sub-Lieutenant von Studnitz, whose opposite number on the *Stein* was Lieutenant von Rebeur-Paschwitz. Sub-Lieutenant von Studnitz was assisted by Sub-Lieutenant Saxer and two elderly, experienced petty officers, Chief Petty Officers Knie and Gaetje. Both of these were strict disciplinarians, but never resorted to crude or abusive language such as we had experienced ashore. Whenever a wide-eyed midshipman stared at Chief Petty Officer Knie's daredevil acrobatics in the rigging, the chief would say, "I can tell you one thing, youngster; if I fall, I'll take you along with me!" None of us felt that there was anything brutal or threatening in such a statement; instead, it was a comradely bond in a dangerous situation. The solicitude with which the two looked after us when aloft, and showed us all the tricks of handling yards and sails, gave us an entirely new and favorable impression of petty officers.

Our station as naval cadets was at the mizzenmast, the aftermost of the *Stosch's* three masts. At first, I was stationed on the topsail yard, but later on, with three others, I was assigned to the royal yard, the topmost of all the yards, where the sails could not be reefed but had to be taken in with desperate speed in squally weather.

Before breakfast every morning all the naval cadets had to race aloft to the top of the mizzenmast and down again, until each one could perform the feat within 58 seconds. When I was the fourth among our 35 to do this, I felt very proud. But then we were promptly shifted to the same performance on the much higher mainmast, with one minute and three seconds as the time limit to be mastered.

In addition to handling sail, our training consisted principally of such general seaman's work as rowing and sailing in the cutters, and gun drills on the old 15-cm. guns, along with theoretical work in navigation, seamanship, mathematics, English, and French.

That summer we made a training cruise to the Baltic, but that winter we went on a longer cruise to the West Indies.

Our first days during this cruise were full of excitement, including the loss of a propeller in the North Sea and the carrying away of the jib boom in a sudden squall at night in the Bay of Biscay. As a result of these mishaps we had to go into Wilhelmshaven, and, later, Lisbon, for repairs. But then we coasted along beautifully in the trade winds, via Madeira, to St. Thomas, Jamaica, and Havana. The return voyage, via San Domingo, Bermuda, Plymouth, and around Cape Skagen, was equally pleasant. On arrival at Kiel we had to undergo inspection by Admiral von Knorr, and, immediately afterward, the annual examination.

The tests, both theoretical and practical, were stiff ones, and only 60 of us out of the 70 who had entered managed to survive the rocks and shoals. But after the examinations we were allowed to go home on a month's leave. It was with a high heart that I arrived, unannounced, at the home of my parents and brothers in Grünberg that April of 1895. They received me with great joy. While home, I received notice that I had been promoted to the grade of midshipman and that I had finished at the top of my class.

Further Officer Training

At the end of leave I joined my classmates of the Class of 1894 for our next assignment, which saw our 60 members divided equally among four training ships. My assignment was to the sailing schoolship *Gneisenau,* commanded by the friendly Junior Captain da Fonseca-Wollheim, with an equally considerate executive officer, Commander von Dassel. Here our first indoctrination into leadership began, for each of us was assigned a section of apprentices to train in all branches of the service—truly a challenge to any ambitious young man. Of course we had experienced petty officers to assist us. The apprentices themselves were volunteers of about 15 years of age, who, after two years' training, became ordinary seamen. From these seamen, the select ones would, after special training, eventually qualify as petty officers.

But in addition to teaching we were also taught—additional courses in navigation and gunnery, as well as watch standing under both sail and steam.

That year, 1895, was a momentous one for the German Navy, for June 21 saw the opening of the Kaiser Wilhelm Canal connecting the Elbe and the North Sea with the Baltic, with Kaiser Wilhelm II himself dedicating the canal.

Almost all of the world's maritime nations participated. Foreign ships kept arriving throughout the whole spring. They were greeted with great ceremony by the German naval ships anchored all over the harbor. Our own ship, the *Gneisenau,* lay farthest out, near the Friedrichsort lighthouse, and it was our duty to salute each incoming ship with its national anthem played by our band.

Smart appearance of ship and crew, as well as the punctilious performance of ceremonies, was of first importance, and during those weeks ordinary routine was pretty much neglected. The weighty political and social events which took place around the Holtenau locks barely touched us, away out at our anchorage, but at least we had an ideal seat for the spectacular fireworks displays.

Also, the long days at anchor gave us the opportunity to visit back and forth with the other members of our class, from whom we had been separated almost from the time we went to sea. The renewal of associations helped to build up that shipmate spirit which, in the German Navy as in other navies, forms such a valuable characteristic of the service. Hereafter the Class of '94 was to stick together, come war or peace.

As soon as the canal dedication ceremonies were over, we sailed to Lerwick, in the Shetland Islands, for the fall maneuvers of the fleet. Our four training ships represented one of the divisions in the Tirpitz naval maneuvers, which were conducted annually under one of the senior admirals to test battle tactics as a basis for the future Navy bill. Thereafter we made a winter cruise to the West Indies, again to our considerable professional benefit, since it meant much sail handling and watch standing, apart from liberty ashore in tropical harbors. However, the exertion of tending the old "fire-tube" boilers in the torrid tropical heat often left us panting and worn out.

Along with practical engineering and seamanship, we labored steadily with the theory of these subjects as well as navigation, torpedoes, and gunnery—all necessary for passing the examinations at the end of our second year.

The next six months we spent in special training in gunnery, mines, and torpedoes on special ships provided for that purpose.

The fall of 1896 saw us back in Kiel again, for our final year, which was to be at the Naval School itself. Here all the midshipmen of our class were assembled again under the direct supervision of Commander von Cotzhausen, a strict but fair commander.

The Naval School was located directly on the harbor, with excellent facilities for rowing cutters and sailing, and with a gymnasium, athletic fields, and tennis courts. We had comfortable bedrooms, and excellent classrooms. Classes were held in the mornings, with the afternoons devoted to gym classes, sports, and sailing. In the evenings we were free to visit the city until nine o'clock, with later liberty hours for special occasions such as parties, theaters, and concerts.

During the summer we had the privilege of making private sailing trips on weekends, with Eckenforde Bay a favorite destination. In addition to the scenery, the attraction here was the estate of Windeby, whose hospitable owner had four sons and nine charming daughters. It was no surprise to us when four of these daughters eventually married classmates of ours.

It was a busy but pleasant ending to our midshipman training, despite the stiff final examinations. We all looked forward eagerly to graduation and going to the fleet as full fledged officers.

First Duty Station

Wearing my brand new uniform as a sub-lieutenant, I reported aboard the SMS *Sachsen* on 1 October 1897. My assignment was as signal officer, with responsibility for all ship's signalling as well as the training of the signalmen themselves. I felt unusually fortunate because my duties kept me on the ship's bridge, especially during the maneuvers and training cruises. Here a young officer could best gain experience and knowledge through watching the work of the ship's top officers. At the head of these was the commanding officer, Captain Plachte, with an excellent service reputation, and from him I acquired valuable training in the professional fields of seamanship, navigation, ship handling, and tactics, as well as in my special duty of signalling.

At this period all the world's navies were just beginning to recognize the importance of signalling, hitherto so long neglected. For instance, the great French Admiral Suffren had been badly handicapped in his battles, on which rested the fate of India, because he could not make his orders understood through the complicated signal system of the day. Even Nelson's famous signal at Trafalgar—"England expects that every man will do his duty"—required a complicated flag hoist of twelve separate flags. In the Battle of Skagerrak,[1] shortly to come, Admiral Scheer would re-

[1] The Battle of Skagerrak is generally known to British and American historians as "the Battle of Jutland."

quire only two flags to send his famous order, "Battle cruisers attack the enemy! All-out attack!" throughout the entire fleet. Two flags—*Richard* and the numeral *nine*—along with a simultaneous radio command, sent the battle cruisers instantly out on the daring sortie that was the turning point of that battle.

But all that was still in the future, and on the *Sachsen's* bridge I had no idea what an important part communications duty was to play in my future career.

The Deutschland *and the Far East*

My assignment to the *Sachsen,* and temporary duty on her sister ship, ended within a short time and in an unexpected manner. I suddenly found myself ordered as signal officer to the armored battleship[2] *Deutschland,* and bound for the Far East.

This section of the world had unexpectedly become important to most of the big maritime powers. Under Bismarck's strong leadership a colonial policy for Germany had been inaugurated, and, with the intelligent co-operation of German merchants and colonial pioneers, had resulted in the acquisition of important colonies. The defeat of China by Japan in 1894-1895 seemed to forecast the breakup of China, and the leading European powers were competing for spheres of influence there. German diplomacy had recently effected a lease from China of Tsingtao and the Bay of Kiaochow, on the Shantung Peninsula, and a German cruiser squadron under Vice Admiral von Diederichs had been sent to occupy it. Now a second cruiser division was to be formed of the modern cruisers *Kaiserin Augusta* and *Gefion,* with the *Deutschland* as flagship. The reinforcing units would be commanded by Rear Admiral Prince Heinrich of Prussia—Germany's "Sailor Prince"—who ultimately would supersede Admiral von Diederichs in the command.

For the Navy, the new colonial policy meant an active participation for those ships which were suitable for distant service on foreign stations—frigates, corvettes, and gunboats fitted with sails as well as steam. In the rapid development of world politics, it was evident that the navies would play a prominent part.

Naturally the officers and men of our ship were enthusiastic,

[2] The designation of this class of ships has been changed quite often.

both about the new policy and about our prospective part in it. The fact that Captain Plachte was also to be commander of the flagship *Deutschland* was an added pleasure to me personally.

The appointment of Prince Heinrich, the brother of the Kaiser himself, to the command of a Far East Squadron, was a striking indication, not only of the importance of the Far East in international affairs, but also of the increasing place of the Navy in the German national scheme. Prince Heinrich had entered the Navy as a midshipman in 1877, and had taken to the sea and the stiff training so enthusiastically that at the time his brother came to the throne he had already reached the grade of staff officer. A capable and experienced seaman, he also enjoyed tremendous personal popularity with both officers and men.[3]

Kaiser Wilhelm II also had demonstrated a lively interest in the Navy since his early youth, partly perhaps because of his close personal ties with England. One of Queen Victoria's favorite grandsons, he had often visited her, and could frequently be seen around the navy yards of the world's greatest sea power, admiring the latest ships and developments.

Shortly after he had come to the throne, he had transferred the top administration of the Navy, which until then had been in the hands of Army Generals von Stosch and von Caprivi, to the Navy itself by appointing a naval officer to the post equivalent to today's U. S. Chief of Naval Operations. The great influence that the Merchant Marine had always exerted on naval affairs now came to an end. By subsequent directives the administration of the Navy was divided into the Naval High Command (the Office of the Chief of Naval Operations) and the Reichsmarineamt (the Administrative Authority).

All this had gone hand in hand with a new departure in naval construction. Up until then German naval ships were of diversified types, with the requirements for land warfare being paramount considerations. Such was the case of the "attack corvettes," of which the *Sachsen* was an example. The older armored ships, like

[3] He was so attached to the sea that even as a very old man he could be seen at the helm of his own little sailboat at the Kiel regattas sailing in all kinds of weather.

the *Deutschland,* which had been built in England, still carried both sail and steam. It was not until Rear Admiral Tirpitz became Secretary of State of the Reichsmarineamt in 1897 that a definite and progressive policy of naval construction was adopted.

Admiral Tirpitz might almost be called the father of the modern German Navy. He had made a name for himself as the organizer of the torpedo boat force, and had served as Chief of Staff of the Naval High Command. It was under his intelligent leadership that the fundamental principles of fleet tactics had been laid down as the basis for the organization of the future German Fleet. His theories, tested at the annual maneuvers and formulated in *Tactical Service Publication 9* of the Naval High Command, represented the tactical "bible" of the Navy for many years.

Recommissioning an old ship like the *Deutschland* for long service abroad presented its difficulties, but the enthusiasm with which all hands looked forward to Asiatic duty made light work of the task. Ordered aboard were three others of my class—Schwengers, Wegener, and von dem Knesebeck—who, during the next two years, were to become my intimate friends.

My duties aboard were those of signal officer not only of the ship, but of the admiral's staff as well. As a special assignment I also was in charge of the ship's band, which was led by the well-known musician, Pollinger. With a love of music inherited from my mother, I found this responsibility anything but wearisome.

My part in the general training activities of the ship was to prepare the signal quartermaster and signalmen for warrant officer school. Captain Plachte further gave me the assignment for this particular voyage of lecturing the ship's company on the history and sights of the ports we were to visit. This assignment especially appealed to me as it would give me the opportunity to study the history of the country and the peculiarities of its people for each new port, thus broadening my knowledge immeasurably.

After recommissioning in Wilhelmshaven, the *Deutschland* proceeded directly to Kiel to take aboard Rear Admiral Prince Heinrich. The Kaiser came up personally to see us off, and it was at the farewell banquet at Kiel Castle that the Kaiser, in referring to the directive given to Prince Heinrich for his mission, used the expression "mailed fist." This expression gave considerable offense abroad, especially in England, where it was the occasion for many ironic comments.

The following day, 7 December 1897, the *Deutschland* got underway, with the Kaiser accompanying us as far as Rendsburg. In his retinue were the Princes, his eldest sons, as well as Count von Bülow, the Foreign Secretary; Rear Admiral von Tirpitz; and Count zu Eulenburg, the Lord Chamberlain. Parting company at the Rendsburg bridge, the Kaiser, with von Bülow and von Tirpitz, went to Friedrichsruh to visit Prince Bismarck, the aged ex-Chancellor.

In company with the *Deutschland* was the cruiser *Gefion,* and navigating the Channel in the stormy winter weather kept us fully occupied on the bridge; in fact we had transited the Straits of Dover in the fog without being sighted. The British Navy, which was on the lookout to pay Prince Heinrich honors, considered this a particularly seamanlike feat. Our ships anchored in Portsmouth Roads, while Prince Heinrich went up to London to visit his grandmother, Queen Victoria.

Christmas Eve we celebrated in the Bay of Biscay, amid heavy seas. Prince Heinrich, with his staff, honored the ship's officers by spending the evening in the wardroom. To commemorate the occasion, he presented the wardroom with a silver loving cup, from which he took the first drink. As he lifted the cup, he gave the toast, "North or South, East or West, home is best!" Then he passed the cup on, with the request that each one follow suit when he took a swallow. Naturally the senior officers, who were first in order, used up all the more familiar toasts and sayings, so that we sublieutenants were hard put to it for something appropriate when it was our turn. As the custom became a regular thing in our wardroom, our junior officers wore out the pages of the wardroom magazines and papers, looking for appropriate verses or epigrams to use as toasts.

The relationship between the admiral's staff and the ship's officers, often a matter of tension, was exceptionally cordial on the *Deutschland.* The senior staff officer was Lieutenant Commander Count von Spee, who in 1914 was to be the victorious commander of the German squadron at the Battle of Coronel and to perish with it shortly after at the Falkland Islands. Prince Heinrich's personal aide was Junior Captain George Müller, who later ennobled, was to perform both the functions of court chamberlain and general political adviser as head of the Kaiser's Privy Council. The ship's second doctor was Lieutenant Oloff, who, as a university professor and leading oculist in Kiel, after the First World War, was to achieve national reputation.

But it was Prince Heinrich himself who set the standard aboard. Recognized everywhere as a distinguished seaman, his personal charm won him friends everywhere. In many respects he made the British Navy his model, and liked to associate with the British Navy as well as with British Army officers in the ports he visited. It was because of him that German naval officers had to wear a pointed beard if they wore any beard at all.

Although he could be extremely curt when someone or something failed to come up to his stiff requirements, he was both fair and considerate with his subordinates. The one thing that particularly aroused his ire was for some detail of ship's etiquette or official ceremony to go wrong in the presence of foreign ships or their officers.

The junior officers' quarters on the *Deutschland* could not be described as overly comfortable. We were two to a room, and these rooms were far down below and close to the engines and boilers. The single tiny porthole in the stateroom was so close to the waterline that it could not be opened even in port. As a result, I did all my sleeping in a hammock on the gundeck until we reached Hong Kong.

Incidentally our antiquated engines were subject to frequent breakdowns, which gave the engineer officer, Commander Paasche, a great deal of anxiety, and the engineroom force a lot of hot work in the steaming tropics.

The first of these breakdowns delayed our arrival at Gibraltar for several days, causing considerable anxiety at home as to our safety.

It was at Gibraltar, in conversation with British admirals who were old friends, that Prince Heinrich found out the reason for the somewhat chilly welcome he had received in England, even from the Queen. The British had been both annoyed and disturbed by the Kaiser's "mailed fist" speech.

From Gibraltar we cruised through the Mediterranean, Suez Canal, and Red Sea to Aden. Here I substituted for Junior Captain Müller as personal aide to the Prince on his official visit to the Governor, and also at the state banquet.

In the Indian Ocean we ran into heavy weather, made even more unpleasant by repeated engine breakdowns, so that we had to lay over several days at Colombo for repairs. This, however, gave us the opportunity to see something of the beautiful tropical island of Ceylon.

Upon our departure we were surprised to receive a request from the Russian warships *Ssissoi Weliki* and *Navarin,* then in port, to join our squadron for the leg to Singapore. Obviously they had received instructions from St. Petersburg to make this gesture, so definitely calculated for its effect on the British. Prince Heinrich naturally granted permission. The subsequent trip in company not only gave me and my signalmen unusually interesting duty in maintaining communications with foreign ships with a different language, but also emphasized the extent to which navies were being used in furthering national policies throughout the world. Such experiences impressed us younger officers with the necessity of learning from the unlimited experiences of the senior officers as well as through direct study and reading.

Singapore had a large and hospitable German colony, and our stay there gave us an interesting insight into this center of British world power. These, and other impressions gained in the Orient, were subsequently to help me greatly to understand Japanese psychology and military operations in World War II, decades later.

It was at Singapore that we received news of the adoption of the first "Fleet Regulations" and the reorganization of the Naval High Command. In 1897, in preparing his "Fleet Regulations," Rear Admiral von Tirpitz had been careful to limit the powers of the Naval High Command in order not to prejudice the Reichstag against acceptance of the Regulations. Now an Admiralty Staff took the place of the High Command. Its duties were limited primarily to the evaluation of information about foreign navies—in other words, naval intelligence—and the development of strategic plans and tactics. Actual authority for the administration of the fleet itself, and for its progressive development, rested now in the Secretary of State of the Reichsmarineamt, to which office Rear Admiral von Tirpitz himself was appointed. However, this reorganization brought some danger that the new department would formulate its plans without taking into proper consideration the practical experience of the operating commands at sea. Inasmuch as the Kaiser, though greatly interested in the Navy, had no professional naval education or experience at sea, the counsel of an experienced admiral at close hand would be of vast advantage.

The next leg of our cruise took us to the important British base of Hong Kong, where again we had to use the facilities of the shipyard for engine and boiler repairs.

In Hong Kong we first made acquaintance of the British Far East Squadron, under command of Admiral Sir Edward Seymour.[4] Commander of the British flagship *Centurion,* as well as chief of staff to Admiral Seymour, was Captain John Jellicoe later to be the Commander in Chief of the British Grand Fleet in World War I.

Hong Kong just then was a boiling center of international politics. The Spanish-American War was on the verge of eruption, and assembled in the port was the American squadron under Commodore George Dewey, making feverish preparations even then for the coming conflict in the Philippines. The British and the Russians were in hot competition to lease bases in China as an offset to the Tsingtao leave which Germany had just recently secured.

Our stay in Hong Kong not only included sightseeing trips and visits to German families resident there, but also friendly and official calls on the many foreign warships in the harbor.

A high point for me was a trip up river to old Canton that I

[4] Only a couple of years later Admiral Seymour was to command the combined international naval landing force for the relief of the Peiping Legations, besieged by murderous Boxers. Captain Jellicoe distinguished himself in these operations, as did also the German naval captain von Usedom.

made as a member of Prince Heinrich's staff. The trip up the Canton River took all day, and even at that time there was always a serious possibility of an attack by river pirates.

May of 1898 saw us reach our destination, Tsingtao. Here we could observe the interesting military, naval, and cultural work going ahead vigorously under the energetic supervision of the Governor, Captain Jaeschke.

Tsingtao was more than our base; it was a point of departure for visits to other ports and countries. One of the first and most interesting of these was the one we made in May to the Emperor of China. Again I had the good fortune to accompany Prince Heinrich as one of his aides. After a rough debarkation in Tongku Roads, we made the rail trip to Peking via Tientsin—an all-day trip along a route lined by Chinese troops, whose martial deficiencies, however, did not add to our feeling of security.

At Peking, we transferred to sedan chairs for the trips to the European Quarter. Here the Prince and Junior Captain Müller were the guests of Minister Baron von Heyking and his wife, later famous as the authoress of the well-known book, *Letters That Never Reached Him.*

The following days were filled with sightseeing in Peking, including the Forbidden City with its heavenly temple—a favor accorded only as a special courtesy to Prince Heinrich. I especially remember an official banquet tendered us by the French Minister, Monsieur Pichon, who later became Foreign Minister of France.

Climax of the whole week was the Prince's visit to the young Chinese Emperor and his widowed mother at their summer palace several hours' ride outside the city. It was fortunate that the marine detachment at the Legation was sent along under Lieutenant Robert to assure our safety, as the large crowds we encountered at the palace gates did not seem overly friendly.

Before entering the palace, we all changed from our riding clothes to full dress uniform. Then Prince Heinrich entered the palace enclosure in the court sedan chair, with the rest of us following on foot.

The Emperor received Prince Heinrich standing, then asked him to sit to talk, an honor never given to a foreign representative before. After the Prince had presented gifts and decorations, the

Emperor escorted him personally to call on the Empress Dowager in her gardens—another honor never previously accorded to any European.

That afternoon the Emperor paid his return courtesy call on the Prince. During the ceremonies attending the visit there occurred an incident very characteristic of those periods of stress and insecurity just prior to the impending Boxer Rebellion. A German escort of marines had been drawn up to render the customary honors at the temple in which Prince Heinrich was to receive this return call. As a special courtesy to the Emperor, the Prince directed that the escort perform the manual of arms. The rattle of the bayonets and slap of hands on stocks seemed to startle the guest of honor, but the Prince directed the drill officer to carry on with the customary "Load and lock."

To his amazement, Lieutenant Robert whispered, "Can't be done, Your Highness." Then, at the Prince's annoyed scowl, the lieutenant quickly whispered, *"Live ammunition!"*

After the drill was concluded—to the Emperor's manifest relief—Lieutenant Robert explained to Prince Heinrich that he had taken the precaution of having the escort's rifles loaded in case the milling crowds lived up to their surly looks.

Following Peking, we visited both Port Arthur and Weihaiwei. The Russians were well underway with their base construction at their leased Manchurian port, and staged large official fetes for the German Prince. Weihaiwei, on the other hand, never was really built up, the British having leased it only as an offset to the Russian base just across the narrow channel.

Shortly afterward, Prince Heinrich's desire to visit Japan was gratified. Officers and crews had the opportunity to make the acquaintance of the beautiful Japanese scenery and the delightful Japanese civilization, for at that time the old buildings, furnishings, and customs had not been spoiled by westernization.

Other visits were made to Japan in succeeding months, including the official reception of Prince Heinrich by the Emperor of Japan. I was fortunate enough to gain a deeper insight into the life of the country through several trips into the interior.

We also visited Korea, at that time still independent, and it was in the port of Fusan on 1 August 1898 that we received the news of the death of the old Chancellor, Prince Otto von Bismarck. The mourning minute guns ordered for all German naval ships everywhere reverberated through the green hills around the bay, proclaiming here, in this distant, alien land, the depth of Germany's grief.

Port Arthur was not the only Russian base we called at. We sailed along the extensive Siberian coast, visiting not only the great base of Vladivostok but also the Russian penal colonies of Korsakov, on Sakhalin Island, and Aleksandrovsk, on the East Siberian coast. While these latter places were purely Russian, Vladivostok seemed almost European in comparison. Here Prince Heinrich, evidently under instructions from home, established cordial relations with the Russian military and naval commanders. When the Russians were invited aboard the *Deutschland* I once had to demonstrate the 24-cm. casemate guns to them even though it was then late at night.

Of course we welcomed the numerous trips to Shanghai, with its large international colony and almost European life and character.

The Spanish-American War had already broken out with armed clashes. At its beginning Vice Admiral von Diederichs, the German squadron commander, had despatched several cruisers, including the *Kaiserin Augusta,* to Philippine waters. Their appearance aroused the unfriendly suspicions of the American Commodore Dewey, who assumed that they were there with belligerent intentions. It is true that sympathies of many Germans were on the side of Spain, as the underdog, but there was never any intention of unneutral acts on our part. As proof of this, Admiral von Diederichs shortly withdrew most of his ships from Philippine waters.

On the strictly professional side we could not but be impressed by the overwhelming superiority of the well trained, modern American Fleet over the more antiquated Spanish ships at the Battle of Manila Bay.

Ever since leaving Germany I had been making a detailed study of the Philippines, being stimulated to this through personal acquaintance with Professor Blumentritt, the great German expert on the islands. For this purpose I had taught myself Spanish, and I put down part of my findings in a paper entitled *The Philippine*

Revolt against Spanish Domination. The timeliness of the study brought commendation both from Captain Plachte and the Prince himself. Thus began my activity as a writer.

In the fall of 1898 the periodic reassignment of officers in the Navy made extensive changes in the Far East Squadron. Lieutenant Commander Count von Spee was replaced by Commander Hintze, who later became military plenipotentiary with the Czar, and finally, as a member of the Foreign Service, wound up as Foreign Secretary in 1918. But the most important change to me personally was the promotion of Junior Captain Müller to the command of the *Deutschland,* and my assignment as his aide. I was given both responsibility and latitude by him, and he remained my fatherly friend ever thereafter, even when, as Admiral von Müller, he became head of the Naval Cabinet.

As such, he was intimate adviser to the Kaiser during the difficult days of World War I, and became the subject of considerable criticism from naval officers. I was quick to defend him, and remained on intimate terms with him until his death.

The end of 1898 also brought other excitement, because we went into the shipyard at Hong Kong for overhaul and to await the arrival of Prince Heinrich's consort, the Princess Irene, who was coming out on a German Lloyd steamer.

A whirl of entertainment greeted the arrival of the Princess, with the Governor, the British commanders, the clubs, and the German colony vying to honor her. The wealthy German merchant Siemssen had generously placed his villa at the couple's disposal, and small groups of the wardroom officers were invited daily to lunch at the villa. On New Year's Day of 1899 a most impressive service was conducted in the Lutheran Church in Hong Kong in honor of the Prince and Princess and the crew of the *Deutschland.* As part of the service, Handel's "Largo" was beautifully played on the organ, with a violin accompaniment by Chief Conductor Pollinger.

As one result of Spain's defeat in the Spanish-American War, Spain had sold the Caroline Islands, the Marianas, and her other remaining Pacific possessions to Germany. When Prince Heinrich took over command of the Far East Squadron from Admiral von Diederichs, he added several of the ship's officers to his staff and instituted a series of war games, the main purpose of which was to determine what would be the most effective move for the squadron if it were caught in the Orient by a sudden war with England. As one of the staff of the opposing "British Commander," I advanced the theory that in such a case the German squadron would rendezvous in the Marianas and then lose itself in the wide Pacific for action against the enemy. This war game was the first of the studies on which were eventually based the actual strategy of the German cruiser squadron in the Pacific in 1914.

That fall the schedule of officer rotation struck me. I was slated to return home via the regular Lloyd liner, but with two other officers I received special permission to take passage instead on the French steamship *Sidney,* which was leaving immediately for Marseilles. En route we stopped at Saigon, in French Indochina, and Djibouti, in French Somaliland, at the southern entrance to the Red Sea—places which I found most interesting. I also made friendly acquaintance with several young French naval officers who boarded the ship at Saigon. Even with these stops I arrived home sooner than the Lloyd liner could reach there.

Ashore and Afloat, 1901-1905

After my two years at sea and 45 days leave with my parents in Grunberg, I found myself assigned to the First Sailor Brigade at Kiel, at first as platoon officer and later as second aide.

The Sailor Brigades at that time not only were responsible for the enlistment of the naval recruits but for their infantry training as well. In addition they served as central stations for all enlisted seamen personnel not assigned to ships. The Technical Brigades performed the same tasks for the technical personnel.

Among my duties at Kiel, in addition to the recruits' training, was the preparation of a new training manual. I still had time, however, to attend a course in Russian at the Naval War College at Kiel. This opportunity was to provide me with a good foundation for my later studies in this important language.

In the fleet organization of that time, the so-called reserve ships were put into service for the fall maneuvers and were manned by naval personnel based on shore. Having been promoted to lieutenant, I was accordingly made watch officer on the SMS *Aegir* for these maneuvers. And in the summer of 1901 I received orders to the SMS *Grille* as executive officer. This ship was assigned in the summer season for special cruises for the Admiralty Staff, and served as fleet tender and signal repeater in the fall maneuvers.

This gave me an excellent opportunity to study the coast, particularly around the North Sea islands. I did not miss the significance of the presence on these maneuvers of such naval leaders as Admiral von Koester, Admiral Thomsen, the director of gunnery training, Admiral Breusing, and others. At the conclusion of the 1901 maneuvers, there was a fleet review in Danzig Bay in honor of the Czar of Russia.

The meeting between the two emperors went off smoothly, and Kaiser Wilhelm commemorated it by granting to all German naval officers the right, on undress occasions, to wear the dirk, with black ribbon sword belt, as side arms; previously this Russian Navy style had been uniform only for German naval cadets. In return, the Czar, who had been attracted by the German naval officer's wide cape, decreed this thereafter as part of the Russian Navy's uniform.

After the 1901 fall maneuvers my shore duty ended with my new orders to the battleship *Kaiser Wilhelm der Grosse,* this time as full-fledged watch officer. I welcomed this duty, for two years' qualification on a capital ship or torpedo boat was regarded as an absolutely necessary basic foundation in the training of a naval officer, as well as a prerequisite for assignment to the Naval War College or to staff work in lower or higher staffs. The fact that my new ship was also the flagship of Prince Heinrich, returned from the Far East and now Commander of the First Battleship Squadron, added to my enthusiasm.

Gone now were the old, easygoing days of pleasant cruises and peaceful routine; everyone was on his toes to achieve the utmost. Admiral Tirpitz had outlined our program, and we consecrated ourselves to carrying it out rigorously.

Each training year began on 1 October, at which time that third of the crews which had completed its three-year enlistment was replaced by new recruits. This date synchronized with the shift of officers and petty officers, who, however, were rotated on a two-year basis.

Beginning in 1901, though, the recruits, instead of getting their six weeks of infantry training in the Sailor Brigades ashore, were given this training, as well as their initiation into shipboard life, on board the ships themselves. This new procedure allowed their commanding officers to begin training them at their various battle stations in December, thus fitting them for combat duty earlier.

Thorough and comprehensive battle training, including damage control, with wartime conditions closely simulated, began after Christmas. Rapid, efficient action at his battle station was demanded of everyone, and, in the discussions held after the drills, each officer and man was required to present his ideas and back them up with logic. This intensive training, and the resulting critiques, made every man aboard feel a joint responsibility, and largely accounted for the reliability of our Navy in World War I.

The training period ended with a battle inspection conducted by the squadron commander himself, who rated the ships accordingly. As a result, competition was keen in this, as well as in the gunnery exercises, where the ships competed each year for a prize given by the Kaiser. The purpose of the prize was to improve gunnery performance. In his eagerness to win, however, each gunnery officer tried to do his own shooting under the most favorable conditions—something directly opposed to the whole purpose of the thing—so that eventually this competition was discontinued.

Though individual ship's training ended in April, the gunnery and torpedo exercises lasted until midyear. Summer training aboard ship consisted mostly of division work and ship routine, ending with captain's inspection. This training, including discipline, physical training, care of uniforms, etc., really should have come ahead of combat training, but it was considered more important just then to bring the ship as quickly as possible to battle readiness.

In October, unfortunately, I had the misfortune to injure my knee severely in a fall from a ship's ladder. Sent home on sick leave, and flat on my back for four weeks, I wrote an article, "Army and Navy Cooperation in the Crimean War," which found a place in the *New Military Press*.

Back to duty again, I found that the *Kaiser Wilhelm der Grosse* had been laid up and her crew transferred to the *Kaiser Friedrich III.* This new flagship of the squadron led the summer cruise of 1902 to Pentland Firth and then the Irish ports, where I had a chance to visit the capital, Dublin. The next year's training was like the first, except that the summer cruise took us to Spanish ports.

The rigid program of training, inspections, and cruises, with no ship's captain permitted to deviate in the slightest, did speed up the men's purely mechanical actions, but just as inevitably destroyed any originality or independent thinking on the part of the commanding officers. Eventually a revaluation was made in an attempt to bring about more flexibility and variety in the training program.

In 1902 and 1903 the exercises of the First Squadron were devoted to the further development of squadron battle tactics. The transmission of visual signal commands and the rapid execution of speed and course changes under dire battle conditions formed an important part of these exercises. Needless to say, I followed all these exercises and experiments with special interest, since I had chosen this as the subject for my thesis for entrance to the Naval War College. Along with my thesis, my commanding officer had to send in a detailed report on my technical talents and performance of duty. This must have been satisfactory, for I was ordered to the Naval War College on 1 October 1903.

The Naval War College at Kiel had been founded in the days of General von Stosch, but unlike the Army's War College, was not designed solely for the education of General Staff officers. Instead, Tirpitz had succeeded in turning it into a general and professional postgraduate school for all line officers who had qualified at sea for training for future Admiralty, Naval Directorate, or other high staff duties. Thus no special corps just of "Admiral Staff Officers" was ever allowed to develop—a fact which redounded to the advantage of the Navy: A corps of special command specialists like the Army's General Staff is ill suited to the Navy, where the commanding officer invariably leads the battleline in person. It is absolutely essential that such a commander be thoroughly a seaman, able to size up a situation promptly from the bridge or conning tower, to make a rapid decision, and then to transform this decision into action by the correct tactical commands. Only an officer who has already proved his leadership abilities as a ship commander can succeed in fleet command, or in duty on the Admiralty Staff. For, important as is a knowledge of communications and the technique of giving commands, these are secondary to the great essential of proven character as a leader in practice.

The course at the War College was a two-year course, usually with a class of about 15 officers. Among my classmates were a number of officers who later distinguished themselves in World War I: Commander Karl von Müller, for instance, who later commanded the *Emden;* von Schönberg, who was to die with his ship, the *Nürnberg,* in the Battle of the Falkland Islands; Commander Bauer, who headed the submarine service; and Commander Seebohm, who commanded the *Ariadne,* sunk in desperate combat with an overwhelming force of British battle cruisers on 28 August 1914 in the first real engagement between the opposing forces.

Among the main courses at the War College were naval history, naval science, and naval tactics. Instruction in naval staff duties came under Captain Bachmann, who later was to head the Navy's Admiralty Staff. In international law we were instructed first by a professor of criminal law from the local university, but later we had a regular professor of international law. Higher mathematics and physics were also compulsory studies. Professor Pochhammer of Kiel University, enabled even the dullest student to master the complexities of differential and integral calculus through his brilliant lectures and individual instruction.

For elective courses, we had world geography, world history, and oceanography. Every officer who could squeeze into the great hall of the War College crowded to hear Professor Rodenberg's lectures on medieval and modern history, and Professor Krümmel's distinguished lectures on geography were equally popular.

Courses in English, French, Spanish and Russian were offered, and every officer had to study at least one foreign language. Having a fair knowledge of French and English already, I elected Russian, under the accomplished Professor Zielke. Spanish at this time was considered less important than it is now, but I undertook to perfect myself in this at home.

From 1 July to 30 September of each year we spent abroad, on leave for further language practice. I chose to go to Russia.

Russia had been at war with Japan since February 1904. The Russian press, as well as life in the two capital cities, Moscow and St. Petersburg, offered a most interesting spectacle. Through Captain Hintze, my old shipmate in the Orient, who was now our naval attaché, I was accepted into leading Russian families, which gave me an unequalled opportunity to improve my oral fluency in Russian.

Apart from the Russian newspaper accounts of the war, I was especially impressed by the departure of the Russian regiments for the Manchurian front. The officers often made their farewells in cafes or other amusement places—an environment that seemed scarcely in keeping with the seriousness of the situation.

While I was in Russia, the birth of the long awaited heir to the throne occurred, apparently to the real delight of the people, though the display of festive flags from the houses often seemed speeded up by the police.

Each student officer, throughout the course at Kiel, had to prepare papers appropriate to his studies. As one of my earliest papers, I had chosen the international law topic, "War Without Declaration." No one had been more surprised than myself when, only a few days after I had completed my paper, the Russo-Japanese War had been opened by the sudden, unannounced attack by Japanese torpedo boats on the Russian squadron at Port Arthur. For another paper that year I wrote on the subject, "The Economic and Military-Political Position of the United States in the Pacific," which attracted the attention of Professor Krümmel.

In my second year I based one paper on the problems involved in establishing a naval blockade. I also translated into German the French book, *Study of Naval Tactics,* by Captain René Daveluy, with whom I subsequently carried on a stimulating correspondence.

CHAPTER

II

Peacetime Training

I HAD HAD two highly gratifying years at the Naval War College when, in the winter of 1905-1906, I was ordered to the coastal defense armored ship *Frithjof* as navigating officer. The coastal defense ships were incorporated into the naval reserve squadron of the Baltic, so this new duty was excellent training for my subsequent tours as navigation officer on large cruisers. But on 1 April 1906 I was ordered to the Naval Public Information Section of the Naval Directorate in Berlin.

This section, which had been set up in the nineties in order to help prepare the first Navy bills, had nothing to do with naval intelligence in the broader sense; that is, intelligence agents, espionage, and counter-espionage. In fact its entire staff consisted of a director, Junior Captain von Heeringen, and three reviewers, of whom I was the senior. My duty was to read and summarize foreign newspapers and magazines, and to edit our own professional naval publication, *Marine Rundschau,* as well as *Nauticus,* the annual of German naval affairs. The second reviewer, Lieutenant Commander Boy-Ed, later to be famous as attaché at Washington in 1917, was in charge of public relations with the German newspaper men as well as analyzing the press items themselves. Professor von Halle, the third reviewer, dealt with economic questions important to the Navy.

Admiral von Tirpitz, at the head of the Reichsmarineamt, took a personal interest in the press and its comments on naval affairs, so that it behooved us to keep constantly informed bright and early every day on all important news developments. A part of our duties was also to make suggestions to the press as to the handling of certain topics. Hence we reviewers, though only lieutenant commanders, became well acquainted with all the leading German journalists. Better still, we had close personal contacts with Admiral von Tirpitz, who otherwise associated only with the senior department heads.

One of my first official calls was on Privy Chancellor Hammann, the all-powerful press director of the Chancellery and the Foreign Office. Despite his heavy workload, he took the time to give me, a newcomer, invaluable suggestions as to newspaper relations, and put me in touch with a number of authorities in the field of economics and colonial policy. For instance, Dr. Paul Rohnbach, the internationally known scholar, provided *Marine Rundschau* and *Nauticus* with many excellent articles.

My next call was on Helfferich, of the Colonial Office, who gave me much stimulating information, particularly about the Bagdad railroad and Germany's economic policy in the Near East. Every year, during Kiel Week, in June, it was the custom of Admiral von Tirpitz to present the Kaiser with the latest copy of *Nauticus,* which the Kaiser would read thoroughly on his Scandinavian cruise. Having formed a friendship with Hugo Jacobi, I thought the magazine fortunate when this well-known author and journalist offered to write the introductory foreign policy survey for the 1906 annual. But when Jacobi turned the article in, I realized, to my surprise, that for a number of reasons it did not fit the magazine's requirements. There was nothing to do at that late date but to rewrite this very ticklish article myself, using Jacobi's data as the basis. To my delight he was not only generous enough to offer no objections, but was in thorough agreement with the presentation I had made.

Those were the years when the readers of *Marine Rundschau* and *Nauticus* never lacked for interesting reading matter. The naval events of the Russo-Japanese War were just emerging from the cloak of military secrecy, and the various engagements, with the lessons to be learned from them, were subjects for sharp analysis. The Japanese naval blockade and the rules of international law at sea came up for discussion along with other general problems of the naval war in the Far East. The discussions on the laws of war which took place at the Second Hague Peace Conference, in 1907, also were prime material for *Nauticus.* Further, since I could read both French and Russian, I took over the chore of reporting on the French and Russian navies in the "Foreign Navies" section of *Nauticus* and *Marine Rundschau.*

Editorial work on these two publications carried heavy responsibility, as at that time they were both considered in the nature of official publications. For instance, we never could go into much detail as to our own fleet construction, or engage in controversial criticism, especially in connection with technical matters. On the other hand, without really worthwhile information, our magazines would soon lose the interest of our professional officer readers. The only way out was to discuss such purely technical subjects as they developed in foreign navies, while keeping mum on our own Navy's plans.

So universal was the interest in the discussions in the magazines that Kaiser Wilhelm himself wrote, for publication in *Marine Rundschau,* an article on the debated topic, "Armored Cruiser or Fast Battleship?", signing it with the pseudonym "L." (Lehmann). The Kaiser's observations were quite contrary to the ideas of Secretary Tirpitz, so Captain Hopman wrote an article refuting the Kaiser's ideas—and did not suffer at all for his temerity.

Nauticus was delivered on publication to the Kaiser, to the Princess of the Empire, and to other important personages, to keep them informed on national naval policy. As editor, I sent the proof sheets of my first edition of the publication to Admiral Tirpitz, with a request for approval for publication. The next day I was surprised to receive orders to report to him in Wilhelmshaven to discuss the articles personally. I obeyed with trepidation, since the printer's deadline had already been set and any change now would cause great difficulties. However, during a rigorous three-hour questioning by Tirpitz himself, I was able to explain everything, and got full approval from the Secretary.

The following year I was privileged personally to present the Kaiser with his copy of *Nauticus* in the presence of Admiral Tirpitz. This was done during Kiel Week, aboard the light cruiser *München,* on which the Kaiser had embarked to observe a practice attack by Germany's first submarine. After I had given a detailed report on the annual's contents, the Kaiser decorated me with the Order of the Red Eagle, Fourth Class—my first decoration.

In connection with my work I also had the opportunity of attending the sessions of the Reichstag, and was present at the Center Party's attack on German Colonial Policy and at the defense by the Chancellor, Prince Bülow. It was this political controversy that led to the alliance of the Conservatives and the Liberals and the resulting party politics in the next elections. I also heard Prince Bülow's famous speech which brought on his heart attack on the Reichstag floor.

In 1907 I became acquainted with another phase of parliamentary activity when I attended the delegates' first inspection visit to the fleet. The trip was for the information of the Reichstag and the Bundesrat, particularly the Committee on the Budget, and was headed by Secretary Tirpitz personally. The Commander in Chief of the Fleet, Prince Heinrich of Prussia, received the delegates at the gangway of his flagship, the *Deutschland,* and briefed them on the gunnery exercises and tactical evolutions which were to take place. So successful was this cruise that the German Navy thereafter conducted similar inspection trips for the delegates annually.

During my tour with the Naval Public Information Section I undertook translation of half of the Russian epic on naval warfare, *Rassplata* (Reprisal), and Lieutenant Gercke did the other half. Knowledge of this comprehensive work by the Russian naval captain Vladimir Semenoff was a part of the general education of every naval officer up to the First World War. It was *Rassplata* that provided the author, Frank Thiess, with the basic details for his great book, *Tsuschima.*

The autumn of 1908 completed my three-year tour of duty with the Naval Information Section, and I was ordered as navigating officer to the armored cruiser *Yorck,* of the Scouting Forces. This was invaluable duty as preparation for future command. The navigating officer acts as adviser to the commanding officer, and my station on the bridge gave me unequalled opportunity to observe all the tactical exercises and evolutions. Unlike a battleship, a cruiser on scouting and patrol duty operated independently, and its captain was called upon to make frequent independent decisions.

When, in 1909, the *Yorck* was assigned to special duty, I was ordered temporarily as squadron navigation officer on the SMS *Hildebrand* during the fall maneuvers. The *Hildebrand* was flagship of the squadron commander, Rear Admiral Pohl, who was noted for his tactical skill and masterly handling of ships in squadron formation.

My ambition now was to be sent as navigating officer to one of the new battle cruisers or as fleet navigation officer on the fleet flagship *Deutschland*. To my surprise I found myself ordered in the fall of 1910 to duty as navigation officer of the Imperial yacht *Hohenzollern*. It was not only a surprise but a disappointment, as thus I would be assigned for several years to an activity far removed from the fleet itself.

One reason for my losing out on the fleet navigation officer assignment was that a new Commander in Chief, Admiral von Holtzendorff, had relieved Prince Heinrich, and naturally he preferred to choose his own staff from officers he knew personally.

It certainly would have been ungrateful to consider the responsible position on the *Hohenzollern* as undesirable, but my preference was for duty with the fleet. I had never desired "Court duty," with whose arbitrary social rules and etiquette I was familiar from my Berlin duty. For instance, while I, as a naval officer, was invited to the Court balls, my wife, not being of the nobility, could not attend.

For some years the *Hohenzollern* had been following a regular annual program. After winter overhaul, the yacht would proceed in mid-February to the Mediterranean, where it would pick up the Imperial family at Venice and transport it to Corfu. There she would lie at anchor while the Kaiser and his family and Court attendants lived ashore in Achilleion Castle. Toward the end of April the Imperial family would board the ship again for the trip through the Strait of Messina to Genoa, whence the Imperial party would return to Germany by land.

In mid-June the Kaiser would embark again at Hamburg to

participate in the sailing races on the lower Elbe, after which he would proceed through the Kaiser Wilhelm Canal to Kiel for Kiel Week.

The whole German High Seas Fleet would be assembled in Kiel harbor for this international festival, and generally there would be numerous visiting foreign warships there as well. After the regatta, the Kaiser would proceed on his annual Scandinavian cruise, which would end at Swinemunde around the end of July. In September the Kaiser frequently used the yacht to witness some of the fleet maneuvers.

There were variations, of course, from this set program. In 1911, for instance, the Kaiser took a spring trip from Flushing to Sheerness, in England, and that same summer he used the yacht for the reception of Archduke Franz Ferdinand, heir to the throne of Austria-Hungary. And the next summer he cruised in the yacht to Port Baltic, in the Gulf of Finland, for a meeting with Czar Nicholas II of Russia.

As a ship, the *Hohenzollern* fell far short of what an Imperial yacht would be expected to be. In construction she could almost be called a monstrosity. With abnormally high freeboard, she rolled in rough weather to a point uncomfortable even for old sailors. Her watertight integrity would not have met the safety requirements of even an ordinary passenger ship, much less an Imperial yacht. To my amazement even the navigation equipment was exceedingly antiquated; at a time when the ships of the fleet all had gyrocompasses, the *Hohenzollern* had only magnetic compasses aboard. Yet the captain, the navigating officer, and the watch officers were responsible for the very life of the Head of the State, not to speak of the nation's prestige.

Naturally the captain was chosen from officers well known personally to the Kaiser—in other words, they were close to Court circles. This was true of my first skipper, Count von Platen. But his successor, Captain Karpf, had nothing courtly about him, either as to appearance or mannerisms. Instead, he was a simple Mecklenburger of marked uprightness and honesty, who gave the Kaiser and the Kaiserin his views in a frank, though tactful, manner, and who did not hesitate to give emphatic directions to the royal princes. He was a famous sailor, well known in yachting circles, and had won the complete confidence of the Kaiser and his family. He handled the lumbering *Hohenzollern* just as superbly as he later commanded the battle cruiser *Moltke* in the Battle of Jutland.

Professional studies, however, were not completely subordinated on the yacht to pleasure cruising or state entertaining. Lectures were a regular feature of the day, and the military historian, Colonel Dickhuth, was a frequent speaker. His lectures in the summers of 1911 and 1912 on the Wars of Liberation, and the spirited discussions that followed, were a delight to all listeners. For my part, when we passed the island of Lissa, during the Mediterranean cruise of 1911, I delivered a talk on the naval battle that took place there in 1866, when the Austrian Admiral Tegetthoff had defeated the superior Italian fleet by ramming. My observations, along with the detailed diagrams I had prepared, aroused the keen interest of the Kaiser, who entered the ensuing discussion with animation. His enthusiasm made up in part for the fact that, despite the presence of the Imperial couple, one of the courtiers had snored loudly throughout my lecture!

The Mediterranean cruises were filled with official obligations, which, to my satisfaction, the Court retinue took over completely. During Kiel Week, on the conrtrary, the spirit of sport and naval fellowship dominated. The Kaiser liked to take this opportunity not only to inspect new developments in the Navy, but also to associate with visiting foreigners—principally yacht owners with whom he was already acquainted.

Life on the *Hohenzollern* during the Scandinavian cruises, however, was much more pleasant than on the other trips when the Court was in the foreground. The Kaiser abandoned stiff ceremony and was very human, relaxing like any tourist out for a rest. I always felt that on these cruises he showed his real self—warm hearted, quick of comprehension, interested in everything, and eager to please others. From what I could see and hear, his views on political and military matters were soundly reasoned and aptly expressed. All this was different from his stiff formality on public occasions—the result, perhaps, of a sense of uncertainty as well as a measure of vanity.

In his personal habits the Kaiser was unusually temperate; he drank little spirituous liquors and actually preferred fruit juices. The food on the Imperial table was always plain, even when distinguished guests were present.

Although the normal tour of duty on the *Hohenzollern* was three years, Vice Admiral Bachmann, Commander of the Scouting Forces, asked me if I would be agreeable to earlier detachment, in order to serve as his senior staff officer. This assignment I was most happy to accept, as it would take me back to the fleet again in a field I especially desired—reconnaissance and security duty in addition to signaling and the maneuvering of combatant units.

Yet I departed the *Hohenzollern* with an appreciation of the privilege of having served aboard her. I had been permitted there to meet many of the leading personages of the world, but above all I had been privileged to know the Kaiser as he really was—a human individual quite different from the person the rest of the world has pictured him to be.

Going aboard the cruiser *Yorck,* flagship of the Scouting Forces, in September, 1912, I found Vice Admiral Bachmann on leave. Therefore I reported to Rear Admiral Hipper, the second in command. In addition to this position, Admiral Hipper had direct command of the light cruisers which composed the Light Cruiser Group. Tactical command of the Scouting Forces, consisting of the armored cruisers and battle cruisers, was in the hands of Vice Admiral Bachmann himself, in addition to his over-all command of all the Scouting Forces.

Owing to a variety of causes the Scouting Forces were at this time in a low state of readiness. In the process of modernizing it, the old armored cruisers *Roon* and *Blücher* had been replaced by the battle cruisers *von der Tann, Moltke,* and *Goeben*. The *Seydlitz* would not join until the next spring, and the *Derfflinger* not until just at the start of the First World War. Even so, the *von der Tann* was undergoing overhaul much of the first year, and the *Moltke* was away for weeks, completing her trials, and then on a shakedown cruise to North America. And that very fall of 1912, as a result of the political situation, the battle cruiser *Goeben* had been sent, with two small cruisers, to the Mediterranean. She and the light cruiser *Breslau,* later constituted the Mediterranean Squadron.

When I joined the *Yorck,* Admiral Bachmann's staff[1] consisted of myself, as senior officer, then my close friend, Commander Klappenbach, as next senior. Lieutenant Commander Brutzer was staff mine and torpedo officer, as well as ship's torpedo officer on the *Yorck.* Staff engineer officer was Chief Engineer Lemke; staff medical officer was Medical Lieutenant Commander Scholtz, and Lieutenant Commander Block was staff paymaster. Navigation officer was Commander Prentzel, who was also ship's navigator as well. On the staff also were two Lutheran chaplains and a Catholic priest. These were all young and dedicated men, well suited to naval life, and they did remarkable work aboard, particularly during the war.

Teamwork among the members of the staff of the Commander of the Scouting Forces was splendid, both then and later, when the war's demands doubled the workload. My own labors were materially lessened by the long established rule in the Scouting Forces that, differently from the usual division staffs, the senior member of the staff was the official superior of the other staff members, not merely "the first among equals."

When I joined the Scouting Forces, the important question being discussed everywhere was the proposed reorganization of the fleet.

Until then, all ships had received their year's quota of recruits aboard simultaneously on 1 October. This inevitably impaired the battle efficiency of the fleet as a whole for some time. Now it was proposed that one of the fleet's three squadrons was to receive all the recruits each October, while the other two squadrons, with relatively few changes in personnel, would be able to maintain a high state of readiness. In addition, the commanders of the individual ships were to be given much more independence in the matter of training. Furthermore, there would now be greater opportunities for cruises abroad. The inauguration of the new system in 1913,

[1] Staff changes brought about these later replacements: Commander Franz, and, later, Commander Hansen, as second staff officer; Chief Engineer Diffring as staff engineer officer; Medical Lieutenant Commander Hagenah as staff medical officer. Commander Prentzel later relieved me as senior officer on the Scouting Forces staff.

with the battleships *Kaiser* and *König Albert* and the cruiser *Strassburg* cruising to South America, seemed very promising, but the outbreak of the war shortly afterward prevented any further developments along those lines.

Other problems were presented by the replacement of the old armored cruisers with the new battle cruisers. While the older ships could be risked in the effort to strengthen the scouting and patrol lines, the new battle cruisers, like the battleships, had to be withdrawn from positions exposed to night torpedo boat attacks. As a direct result, the newer torpedo boat flotillas, which now formed the advanced scouting lines, assumed a more important role in those tasks which required swift and precise cooperation with the cruisers. During daylight, of course, the swift battle cruisers could, if occasion arose, carry out reconnaissance missions in any engagement with enemy battle cruisers. Further placing the torpedo boat forces under the command of the Commander of the Scouting Forces guaranteed the unified execution of scouting as well as protection against enemy reconnaissance. Lastly, the battle cruisers took on the additional role of serving as a "fast division" at the head of the main battleship forces in a general engagement.[2]

The soundness of the new plans for the tactical use of the Scouting Forces, and, especially, of the battle cruisers, was emphasized in the 1912 war games where Vice Admiral Bachmann won an unqualified victory over the Commander in Chief of the Fleet, Admiral von Holtzendorff, who commanded the opposing force in the simulated engagement. I still remember the satisfaction with which our esteemed commander received the news. During the winter he always suffered severely from sciatica, as a result of which he had practically to drag himself to the bridge. But this day our staff medical officer, Dr. Scholtz, said to me in astonishment: "What has happened? Our admiral's health has improved miraculously! He doesn't show any signs of pain at all this morning!"

[2] The Battle of Skagerrak was to justify not only the use of the battle cruisers as scouts, in conjunction with the light forces, but also as spearhead of the battle line at the most critical moments of the battle.

The winter maneuvers of 1912 were the last in which the High Seas Fleet was commanded by von Holtzendorff. Vice Admiral von Ingenohl took over the command in the spring of 1913.

While of great personal gallantry, and an excellent squadron leader, the new Commander in Chief was slow in decision and had a tendency to worry over details. In addition he lacked the aptitude for clear, convincing speech that carries conviction as well as arouses enthusiasm. However, he did an outstanding job of training the now greatly enlarged fleet in tactical evolutions, and inaugurated the system of handling the battleline with one, or at most two, flag hoists. These signals were hoisted from a protected signal bridge and were simultaneously duplicated by signals sent out over the radio. The radio was to ensure the signals being received and obeyed simultaneously by the fast battle cruiser squadron, which might be operating independently some distance away. This method of signalling was to prove its worth in the coming war.

Close tactical liaison between the fight cruisers and the torpedo boats was also stressed; in fact, Admiral Bachmann often went aboard individual cruisers during night exercises to check.

The entrance of submarines into the naval scene was also recognized by staging combined training between them and the cruisers in the fall of 1912. The light cruisers had already shown marked capabilities as minelayers, so training in this field also became an important part of the program.

The battle readiness of the individual ships was examined in a series of rigorous inspections during March and April. Part of the inspection consisted of a mock combat which each battleship and cruiser had to carry out with a ship of similar type. All phases, including "constructive" hits received and an assessment of resulting damage, had to be considered. For instance, during the mock battle the inspectors might suddenly shut off certain power or telephone lines, or cut out some of the water mains as having been "put out of action by an enemy hit." This realism grew from exercise to exercise, with actual black powder being set off in "damaged" spaces as representative of smoke and gas which would be the result in actual battle, thus testing both damage control measures and the efficiency of the ventilating system. Even antiaircraft defense began to be included for the first time.

Inasmuch as the conditions for each combat had to be changed, to prevent a "pattern" which could be anticipated by the contestants, the Admiralty Staff was taxed to the utmost to invent new situations.

Needless to say, the captains and crews of the ships being inspected labored night and day to be prepared for anything that could be thought up. And the inspecting admiral did not have it any easier. In the Battle Cruiser Group there were four battle cruisers and eight light cruisers, so that, allowing only one day for each battle cruiser and one-half day for each light cruiser, it kept Admiral Bachmann busy from daylight till dark for eight consecutive days to complete the inspection of the whole group.

Though admiral's inspection was very serious—a captain's entire career might be made by a favorable report or ruined by an adverse one—it nevertheless often had a humorous side. The inspecting admiral and his staff usually ate lunch with the captain of the ship being inspected. It was only natural that the host wanted to serve the admiral's favorite dish, partly out of politeness and partly to get him in a good mood, and it was just as natural that they tried to find out his preferences in advance. At one inspection Admiral von Heeringen got roast veal on every ship he inspected because someone had spread the word that he was fond of it. Admiral Hipper was still more unlucky; since he was a Bavarian, he encountered liver dumplings everywhere. Although these were a Bavarian specialty, it happened that Admiral Hipper detested them. In the same way Admiral Zenker later met Leipzig salmagundi on every ship he inspected!

As the naval rivalry with Great Britain increased, the subject of a blockade began to receive intensive study, and under orders from the Admiralty Staff the autumn fleet maneuvers in 1913 were devoted to war studies invloving the blockade of the Bay of Helgoland. In past years the German Navy, basing its conclusions on a wrong assessment of the traditional British attitude in naval warfare, had expected that at the beginning of any conflict between the two powers, the British Fleet would attempt to attack and destroy the German Fleet even in its home waters, and the German Fleet, being the inferior, would have to count on the Helgoland fortifications and the minefields there to withstand the British attack. This was the consensus of opinion up until 1912, as I remembered from a speech by Prince Heinrich when he was Commander in Chief of the Fleet. It was reckoned that the British would set up a "close" blockade of Helgoland by their fleet, even though the increasing defensive powers of torpedoes, mines, submarines, and even aircraft, would greatly increase the danger to the blockading forces. But the war games of 1913 began to create a doubt in our minds as to the accuracy of the German assumption, and by 1914 we were firmly convinced that the British Fleet would not risk such a "close" blockade, but would, instead, substitute a "distant" blockade. The Admiralty Staff moreover concluded that in such a distant blockade the British Fleet would utilize Scapa Flow as its main base.

Vice Admiral Bachmann's successful tour as Commander of the Scouting Forces ended with the 1913 maneuvers. We all felt a personal loss at his going. He was not only a highly accomplished naval officer, but also a master of tactics and strategy, having received much of his training under Admiral Tirpitz himself. On the personal side, he was friendly and approachable, allowing us on his staff the greatest freedom in our work.

But if we had to lose Admiral Bachmann, we could not have had a replacement more to our liking than Rear Admiral Hipper, who took over command of the Scouting Forces on 1 October 1913.

Our new commander was an energetic and impulsive individual, with quick perception and a keen "seaman's eye." But unlike his predecessor, he had risen exclusively through performance in the fleet, having distinguished himself successively with the torpedo boats, then as captain of the armored cruiser *Gneisenau,* and then as commander of the light cruiser and torpedo boat forces. Sheer theory was not his forte; he hated paper work, and up to this time had never had a staff larger than a chief of staff and a flag lieutenant. Now, as commander of all the Scouting Forces, he had to put up with the reports and suggestions of a large staff.

At first he seemed to think that the staff was putting up to him matters which they could have handled themselves, but as the smooth working group gained his confidence, complete cooperation and teamwork was established. This was expedited by Admiral Hipper's natural politeness and good nature, which soon made amends for any harshness when he lost his temper, as he occasionally did on the bridge. At these times he was likely to tell the offender off in crisp, trenchant Bavarian.

But in discussions of exercises and evolutions, even when obvious errors had been made, he was sympathetic in his criticism, and it was no time before we all became deeply attached to him and would go to any lengths to lighten his labors and make his life aboard as pleasant as possible. For instance, having always lived the lonely life of a bachelor, he demanded absolute quiet in the vicinity of his quarters, so we took turns patrolling at night to see that he was not unnecessarily disturbed. He had a special preference for a certain brand of cigars, so we did our best to see that he had ample supplies on hand—something not always easy to do during the shortages of wartime.

The admiral had a deep love of music, and his personal interest resulted in a high standard for the flagship's band. When he went on leave he was always afraid that his second in command, who was thoroughly unmusical, would lower the band's standards. He would say to me, before departing, "Raeder, above all see that so-and-so doesn't make a mess of the music!"

Another hobby of his was hunting, but when he invited me to accompany him on a hunt, I was wise enough to beg off. Knowing how touchy he was on the sport, I pleaded that I did not want my lack of skill and my abysmal ignorance of even the rules of the sport to spoil our pleasant personal relationship aboard.

On the professional side, Admiral Hipper's outstanding ability as well as his enthusiasm infected everyone throughout the Force. In the maneuvers of 1913 and 1914 the tactical combination of the fast battle cruisers operating with a battleship squadron was practiced and practiced again.

These maneuvers usually began with a reconnaissance sortie by the battle cruisers, after which they fell back to form the lead squadron of the main fleet. Highspeed maneuvers of this sort required a keen understanding of tactics as well as superior handling of the cruisers in formation. Nothing could have been better suited to our admiral's temperament and capabilities for quick judgment and sure execution.

These exercises, simulating war conditions as closely as possible, developed superior tactical skill in the commanding officers as well as in the staffs. Part of our own staff's success, perhaps, was accounted for by our close personal friendship, almost all of us being around the same age and four of us being of the same Naval School class.

In my particular field of responsibility I found myself under the keen appraisal of the admiral's eye, as the transmission of battle signals from the battle signal stations received particular attention during the maneuvers of 1913.

All of our intensive efforts paid off when inspection of the Scouting Forces was held in the spring of 1914. With the Commander in Chief of the Fleet, Admiral von Ingenohl, observing from the bridge, Admiral Hipper took the battle cruisers through complicated maneuvers at full speed, executing battle signals promptly with or without the aid of the radio. Even simulated "action damages" decreased the Forces' efficiency little or none. The result was that Admiral von Ingenohl ordered the signal "Well done!" hoisted before the eyes of the entire fleet.

The scouting duties of the Forces was not neglected during this training, either. Combined night operations, employing torpedo boats and the light cruisers, were emphasized. In the spring of 1914 naval airplanes participated for the first time, but were usually compelled to land after a short time or even had to be rescued when forced down at sea.

With the Admiralty Staff convinced that Britain would not risk a close blockade, the possibility of offensive sorties from the Bay of Helgoland was investigated during the fleet's battle maneuvers in the spring of 1914. Any optimism as to the employment of the older ships and torpedo boats in such offensives was to be dispelled, however, the moment hostilities began. The older craft had been constructed for defense against a close blockade; they simply did not have the endurance to operate against the English coast or up in the northern North Sea.

The German Fleet maneuvers in the summer of 1914 were initiated under the grim shadow of Sarajevo and the political crisis precipitated by the shocking assassination there of the Archduke of Austria and his consort. However, the opening phases in the North Sea were carried out as planned, and, at the end, the ships put into various Norwegian fjords to give the crews a rest. Our Force flagship, the *Seydlitz,* anchored in the inner part of Sogne Fjord, where we coaled from a collier. The next evening, 26 July, we received orders for the Scouting Forces to get underway immediately after all the cruisers had finished coaling, and to proceed to a rendezvous with the rest of the fleet at sea, preparatory to the return home. The Imperial yacht *Hohenzollern,* which had cruised to Balholmen, as it did every year, had hurriedly sailed home upon notification of the Austrian ultimatum to Serbia.

It was an impressive scene, that 27 July sailing of the fleet. In the crystal clearness of late afternoon, ship after ship—torpedo boats, battleships, cruisers—threaded their way out of the fjords, to assemble by squadrons and groups in front of the backdrop of Norway's sun-gilded rocks and cliffs. Then, with the fleet flagship, *Friedrich der Grosse* signalling the start, the fleet got underway.

By a remarkable coincidence the French Fleet was also in northern waters and proceeding homeward. With the French president, Poincaré, aboard, it had been visiting St. Petersburg. The two fleets cleared the northern coast, however, without meeting.

In the High Seas Fleet every officer and man received each news flash with ever-increasing tension. Ultimatums—mobilization—Austria and Russia at war—then France—Germany. And on 5 August, the ominous announcement: "Great Britain has declared war on Germany!"

It was up to the German Fleet now. It had a job to do—a job whose seriousness was fully realized by the whole Navy.

III

Opening of the First World War

As is done in all navies, the German Navy had conducted frequent studies and even war games revolving around a conflict with Great Britain. But in actuality such a conflict had not been considered highly probable, and it had not occurred to anyone that German political leaders, even under the inept Chancellor of that time, would ever allow Austro-Hungarian political leadership to seize the reins and let Germany slither into War.

So, far from planning such a war, the Naval Staff did not even know the plan of the Army General Staff to invade France through Belgium. The Navy had not studied, much less prepared for, the occupation and utilization of Atlantic and Channel bases to further such operations. Hence, the formation of a naval corps for these purposes had to be improvised on the moment.

Nor had any long-range plan for all the details of a naval war with Britain ever been prepared. As an example, in the tense days at the beginning of hostilities, the specter of possible enemy sea and air raids was magnified out of all reason. The main fleet base at Wilhelmshaven, crowded as it was with reservists and naval dependents, was a breeding place for wild rumors.

The result was inevitable. The early August nights were filled with rifle flashes and machinegun chattering as jittery sentries and lookouts fired at imaginary enemy planes. People were sure they saw enemy submarines in the Jade Bay off Wilhelmshaven, and even in Wilhelmshaven roadstead itself. One evening a patrol boat in the outer bay fired a Very light to signal that she had sighted a supposed enemy submarine. In accordance with existing patrol directives, all other craft on patrol immediately passed the alert on by firing their own Very lights, until the whole place looked like a fireworks exhibition. Hurrying to the bridge, I asked my signalman where the submarine had been sighted.

"Everywhere, Captain, everywhere!" he answered, waving his arms at the fiery signals arcing in every direction.

Needless to say, patrol directives for signalling an alert of enemy craft were immediately changed.

The *Friedrich der Grosse,* with the Commander in Chief on board, had gone directly to Kiel from Norway, and did not begin her transit of the Kiel Canal until 31 July. In the meantime Vice Admiral Hipper had decided to keep the Battle Cruiser Group ready for sea immediately for reconnaissance. At that time this group consisted of the battle cruisers *Seydlitz, Moltke,* and *Von der Tann,* and the armored cruiser *Blücher.* In the channel leading out from the inner bay there was a large bar which could not be crossed by large ships except at high tide. Admiral Hipper therefore ordered the group to lie outside the bar, anchored and with nets rigged out to defend against torpedo attack. In this way the ships would be able to put to sea at a moment's notice to aid the light forces patrolling offshore in case the enemy made a sudden surprise attack. It was a great disappointment when Admiral von Ingenohl, the Commander in Chief, ordered all heavy forces back to Wilhelmshaven Roads, where they were to stand by in a three-hour readiness condition. At this time Admiral von Ingenohl also placed under the operational command of the Commander of the Scouting Forces all torpedo boats, minesweepers, and other patrol craft, as well as all submarines, airships, and airplanes.

Admiral Hipper had always wanted the torpedo boats under his command for tactically they and the light cruisers should work together. But to be responsible also for the command of all the additional units, and moreover, the security of the entire Bight of Helgoland, imposed a crushing extra burden on him.

There was also the problem of maintaining an efficient communication network among all the elements of these widespread reconnaissance units. As the officer responsible for security patrol, Admiral Hipper could work best from a shore headquarters where he had unlimited telephone connections. But as Commander of the

Scouting Forces, and especially of the big battle cruisers, he ought to be aboard ship where he could proceed against the enemy any time a favorable opportunity presented.

This conflict of command locations was not resolved until much later, when unrestricted submarine warfare was given the priority in 1917 and sorties of the High Seas Fleet rarely occurred. At that time the Commander of the Scouting Forces was given a headquarters on the old cruiser *Niobe,* which, however, always lay moored in port. Not before August 1918, when Admiral Hipper had become Commander in Chief of the Fleet, was the Commander of the Scouting Forces relieved of the burden of security patrol, which was made the responsibility of a newly created Commander of North Sea Protection.

The communications for security patrol against enemy raids were conducted mainly by radio, aided sometimes by visual signals. Either method put a heavy strain on the admiral's staff, since every important happening in the whole of Helgoland Bight had to be reported to the Commander of the Scouting Forces.[1] The staff then had not only to size up the situation but also to make suggestions for appropriate action, which usually had to be taken immediately. An increase in the staff was an urgent need, so Commander Brutzer was attached, with his main duty being that of chief adviser in connection with the security patrol. The staff was to be further enlarged in 1917 by my promotion to the position of chief of staff, with Commander Prentzel taking over my assignment as senior staff officer.

It was characteristic of Admiral von Ingenohl that although he had placed the security patrol of Helgoland Bay under the Commander of the Scouting Forces, he then proceeded to give detailed orders as to how the light cruisers, torpedo boats, minesweepers, and submarines should operate. According to these instructions, the light forces, during daylight, were stationed in patrol sectors centered on the outermost Elbe lightship and cover-

[1] Unfortunately some patrol units sent in alarming reports without waiting to investigate. One such sent in the following report: "Every morning a submarine surfaces off the coast and later disappears again! Please check!" Admiral Hipper's terse reply was, "Send out a motorboat to check it yourself!" The investigator subsequently advised ruefully that the supposed submarine was only the hulk of a sunken steamer, which showed above water at low tide and then disappeared again when the tide came in.

ing the entire Bight. Upon approach of darkness they would steam to sea to form an advanced picket line against any enemy approach, and then return to their inshore stations at daylight.

Naturally, as the patrolling ships ranged farther and farther from Helgoland, the circles widened and the gaps between the respective patrol craft increased. Consequently the ships had to patrol singly, instead of in pairs or groups as prudence would have dictated in the presence of a strong enemy. Furthermore, the regular pattern of patrolling and of anchoring at night made it easy for the enemy, by using submarines, to study the German patrol system and to plan for the most effective way to breach it. A still further flaw was that using the light cruisers for routine picket line work not only exposed them to enemy submarine attacks, but likewise took them, as it also did the torpedo boat squadrons, away from their correct tactical employment—which was to conduct long-range night reconnaissance.

The Battle of Helgoland Bight

The faulty disposition and employment of the patrol ships led inevitably to the surprise enemy attack of 28 August 1914. Taking advantage of the situation and of low visibility which prevented accurate fire of the Helgoland shore batteries, the British battle cruisers came well into the Bight—much farther, in fact, than we had believed they would dare to do in that heavy weather. As a result, the two light cruisers and ten destroyers of our advanced picket line were suddenly beset by a British raiding force of 32 destroyers and two cruisers, backed by two battle cruisers. But supporting these were still three more battle cruisers under Admiral David Beatty and another squadron of six cruisers. Three more of our light cruisers steamed out from the Ems and Jade rivers to help their comrades, but the fight was too unequal. As a result we lost the light cruisers *Köln, Mainz,* and *Ariadne,* and the torpedo boat *V-187.* The British lost none.

To prevent a recurrence of this disastrous experience two large minefields were now laid to bar the enemy from Helgoland Bight, the pattern of patrol was changed, and a support force of heavy ships was kept in constant readiness in Schillig Roads, a broad stretch of water at the entrance to Wilhelmshaven.

As it happened, Admiral Hipper's original plan to guard against such surprise raids, by keeping the whole force of big cruisers in the outer Jade Bay, would not have been possible on a continuing basis, because under wartime conditions some of these forces were always in port, either coaling or being repaired. However, the light cruisers of the security patrol now were brought back to the mouth of the Weser, where they could put to sea at short notice. The minefields guarding Helgoland Bight were patrolled by the older torpedo boats and steam trawlers, while several U-boats were stationed on picket lines farther out. Later, after they had demonstrated their tremendous offensive capabilities, the submarines were used for the direct offensive.

The few airships and airplanes that Germany possessed at the beginning of the war were of limited range and practically useless in bad weather. As air reconnaissance improved, however, the Fleet Command turned more and more to the view that the fleet should not go out to meet the British Fleet when it advanced temptingly into German waters. It was reasoned that the enemy would take this risk only when superior in strength or preparing an ambush of submarines or mines laid by his own minelayers in the path of the expected German sortie. Instead, the German forces should take the initiative only at times when efficient airship reconnaissance was available, or when, with the cooperation of a submarine line of our own, we held a superior tactical position.

At the beginning there was no chance for a successful offensive against the outnumbering British forces. Hence our operations against the enemy were confined mostly to minelaying off the English coast by our light cruisers and special minelayers. These operations, under the direct command of the Commander in Chief, were gratifyingly successful, except in the case of the Seventh Torpedo Boat Squadron. These four boats, all old ones and of little use except for minelaying, were sent out by Admiral von Ingenohl, without any support, to mine the mouth of the Thames on 17 October. Intercepted by the enemy, all four boats were lost.

Reconnaissance sorties by the regular torpedo boat squadron almost every night never located an enemy. Inasmuch as the U-boat force, now proving its efficiency for long-range scouting, had been taken over directly by the Fleet Command, Admiral Hipper proposed that the battle cruisers make a sortie into the northern part of the North Sea. This proposal was approved by the Fleet Command—but no battle ship squadron was assigned to meet the returning cruisers at Horn Reefs, as originally requested. Since our staff considered such support a necessity, the undertaking was canceled. However, Admiral Hipper continued to argue for offensive operations by the battle cruisers on the English coast and in the upper stretches of the North Sea, but only if support by the High Seas Fleet was provided—a precaution in which the Admiral's staff unanimously concurred.

The Fleet Takes the Offensive

At this time the Fleet Command got a new chief of staff—Rear Admiral Eckermann, who replaced the hospitalized Rear Admiral von Mann. Admiral Eckermann decidedly favored a more offensive policy, so that in November and December 1914 there were staged battle cruiser operations against the British ports of Yarmouth, Hartlepool, and Scarborough. With an inshore minefield laid by our minelayers, it was hoped that bombarding these coastal ports would provoke the enemy to sortie from his various bases to intercept our battle cruisers—which would then lure the pursuers back into the maws of our High Seas Fleet, standing behind Admiral Hipper's forces.

One of the main dangers in thus raiding the English coast was the difficulty of accurate navigation. Britain having extinguished all her coastal lights, there were no navigation aids available at night to determine a ship's position. Consequently, at the most critical moment, when they were approaching firing position off the English coast, our navigators had nothing but dead reckoning and their leadlines to warn them of dangerous shoals.

Our staff navigator, Commander Prentzel, always did a masterful job of bringing us into the desired position, but, once there, we had to turn parallel to the coast and take up bombardment course within bare minutes.

On our first sortie, to bombard Yarmouth, which was guarded by numerous sandbanks and shoals, Admiral Hipper gave the signal to turn the moment the leadline found less than twenty fathoms. This proved to be too soon, as our following bombardment was at too great range. However, if even a single one of our ships had gone aground, it would have placed the whole force in the difficult position of either having to abandon it or else stand by against the overwhelming enemy odds that would quickly assemble. Our light cruiser *Stralsund,* being of much shallower draft, though, ran close in and laid her minefild, as planned, well inshore.

On this first occasion, also, we made a mistake in concentrating our fire on the British gunboat *Halcyon,* the only enemy ship in sight. The command was given, "*Seydlitz* open fire!" But trigger-happy gunners on all our four ships opened fire together. With shells splashing from the guns of the whole force, it was impossible to spot the shooting of any one ship down to the target, and as a result the *Halcyon* escaped practically unscathed.

In war, as in everything else, however, experience is a teacher for which there is no substitute, and this sortie to the English coast proved a valuable test of our battle cruisers' capabilities.

Another similar operation accordingly was planned for the middle of December. By now the *Derfflinger* had joined, strengthening the Battle Cruiser Group signally, and this time it was planned to bombard not only the forts at Hartlepool and Scarborough, but the military installations at Whitby as well.

There were fewer navigational difficulties in these waters than in those off Yarmouth, but the distance to be covered was much greater. The new targets lay much nearer the British naval bases on the Tyne and Firth of Forth, flanked by the strong British forces on the Humber. But we were convinced that we could stage the operation successfully if the main body of the German Fleet would only take position to safeguard us against being cut off from Helgoland on our return. This assurance we received, and a rendezvous point was duly set.

Our own preparations were as careful as we could make them. Twice one of our U-boats was sent to check and recheck the waters off our intended targets. Perhaps we should have also checked the interpretation that Admiral von Ingenohl would give to the Kaiser's standing order for fleet operations—that the High Seas Fleet should not give decisive battle to the enemy beyond a definite distance from the Helgoland forts. But, having agreed to a support rendezvous, the Commander in Chief was duty bound to keep it—

or, if pressing reasons arose to prevent, he was equally bound to inform the Scouting Forces of this, and what his alternate arrangements would be. This information was absolutely necessary to the Commander of the Scouting Forces, for, if he met with superior enemy forces, he had to know the whereabouts and plans of the main body if he was to fall back upon it for support.

Confidently the Scouting Forces left their Jade Bay anchorage early on the morning of 15 December 1914, and steered northwest of the Dogger Bank off the English coast. As we headed through the North Sea we received reports of stormy weather to the north of us, and found the wind already freshening where we were. Accordingly Admiral Hipper decided to detach the light cruisers and torpedo boats, except for the minelaying cruiser *Kolberg,* and send them back to the rendezvous point where the fleet was to be before the following noon.

Turning toward the English coast after dark on the 15th, we reached the separation point before dawn, with the wind still stiffening. Here the group was to separate, with the *Moltke, Seydlitz, Blücher,* and *Kolberg* proceeding to Hartlepool and the *von der Tann* and *Derfflinger* to Scarborough. Just before the cruisers separated, we sighted some British picket boats in the dark and fired at them but did not pursue, as our main mission was the bombardments.

The operations off both ports were tactical successes. At Hartlepool, the British shore batteries opened immediately, hitting the *Seydlitz* in the forecastle and the *Blücher* just below the bridge, with several men killed, but our reply promptly silenced them. Meanwhile the *Kolberg* successfully laid her mines right in the middle of the swept channel the British had made through their own protective minefield off the port.

With the *von der Tann* and *Derfflinger* equally successful off Scarborough, the two forces reassembled for the run home through the perilous British offshore minefields—a peril which we negotiated successfully. Then, about noon, we received news from Captain Harder, commodore of the light cruisers and torpedo boats detached that morning, that they had momentarily glimpsed a British battleship division and scattered cruisers in the thick weather off the Humber estuary.

Admiral Hipper's first thought was to turn immediately to support the *Stralsund* and her consorts against the reported enemy, but a second message from the *Stralsund* on the heels of the first stated that the enemy had already disappeared from sight. Accordingly, Admiral Hipper now turned sharply northward to round the British battleship division, which obviously was in position to cut us off from the rendezvous point with the High Seas Fleet.

No one on the flagship had a moment's worry about the light forces, as these should soon be reaching the agreed-upon rendezvous with the main fleet. However, none of us had any way of knowing that in the morning twilight our main fleet had run into the British advance scouting forces, and, to avoid exposure to enemy night torpedo attacks, had turned away. Further, in strict compliance with the general directive against a major engagement beyond the shelter of Helgoland, Admiral von Ingenohl did not proceed later toward the agreed-upon rendezvous, but returned directly to Helgoland Bight. Worse still, he did not inform Admiral Hipper of this, so that the Commander of the Scouting Forces did not know of the change of plan until he received a position report from the main body, well back toward Helgoland, late that afternoon.

Our immediate worry was the enemy battleship division off the Humber, as it probably would try to take an intercepting position between Hartlepool and Helgoland. To avoid collision with the much stronger enemy forces, Admiral Hipper swung the Battle Cruiser Group sharply north, to work around the flank of the enemy forces. His analysis and consequent maneuver were correct, for later it turned out that during the afternoon our Group and the British battle cruisers passed only a few miles apart, and just out of sight of each other.

Meantime the wind had strengthened to gale force. Because of the older *Kolberg* we could not proceed at full speed, so that it was not until dark that we felt we had worked around the trap and were safe in heading for Helgoland once more.

Our reentry into Jade Bay on the morning of 17 December, however, found us with mixed emotions. Our mission had been completely successful; communications in the Scouting Forces had been excellent, the bombardments had gone as planned, and the morale of the group had risen tremendously. On the other hand we felt deep disappointment at the failure of the main fleet to keep the rendezvous. If, on the morning of the 16th, the main fleet had continued on as planned, they would have collided in overwhelming force with the British battleships and battle cruisers of Admiral David Beatty's force, which then would also have been struck by Admiral Hipper's returning battle cruisers. Such an overwhelming concentration should have resulted in a smashing German victory. But the golden opportunity had been allowed to slip —an opportunity that probably would not occur again.

The Battle of the Dogger Banks

One result that the operation had brought about was the abandonment of the Commander in Chief's defensive psychosis, though at the moment we did not know it.

For, during the rest of the month, we lay our mine and fortress defenses, waiting for the enemy to assault. Secret intelligence had informed us that the British would try to block all our exits from Helgoland Bight into the North Sea with blockships and mine barriers. Extensive precautions against such an operation were taken.

The only thing that materialized, however, was a weak raid by enemy submarines, airplanes, and minelayers. For the first time the antiaircraft guns on our cruisers and ashore at Cuxhaven were in action. Enemy minelayers started laying an anti-submarine minefield at Amrum Banks, off Helgoland.

Again, on 19 January 1915, we were alerted by one of our scouting planes to heavy British forces approaching Helgoland from the northwest. U-boats were promptly ordered out to set up a barrier line in the path of the enemy, and other defensive measures were taken. However, the enemy turned away before any contact was made, and we had had our pains for nothing.

With the end of the enemy threat, the Commander in Chief put the fleet back on the standard condition of readiness, which provided not only for ships going into the yard for routine repairs but also for conducting training exercises in the Baltic. He also personally assurred the Commander of the Scouting Forces that no offensive employment for the battle cruisers was considered in the near future, so Admiral Hipper sent the *von der Tann* to join the Baltic exercises.

It was a complete surprise, therefore, when, only a few hours later, Admiral von Ingenohl ordered Admiral Hipper to take both Cruiser Groups and two torpedo boat squadrons, with the flotilla leader, and put to sea on 24 January for reconnaissance toward the Dogger Bank. This operation, it later appeared, was the idea of Rear Admiral Eckermann, Fleet Chief of Staff.

Aside from the erratic and sudden change of mind, the order was disturbing because it provided no rendezvous with the fleet, whose support the experience of 16 December had proved vitally necessary. But, worse still, the operations order was sent over the radio, despite the fact that the *Seydlitz,* flagship of the Commander of the Scouting Forces, was anchored right in Wilhelmshaven Roads where she could easily be reached by visual signals.

For some time we had suspected that the British were deciphering our radio messages. As a result, our cipher keys were changed frequently, and all important operational messages were sent in special code. However, regardless of the cipher key used, the ultimate meaning could be worked out provided the code breaker had possession of our signal book, around which all our codes were built.

As a matter of fact, the British had gained possession of a copy of our signal book through a most unusual circumstance. The German light cruiser *Magdeburg* had been wrecked in the Gulf of Finland in the first month of the war, and Russian divers had recovered the battle signal book from the wreck and had turned it over to the British. Given a few hours time, the British cipher experts could break any of our coded signals. Now Admiral von Ingenohl's radio order, giving full details of the forces to be employed in the projected sortie, as well as the time and courses, was known in the British Admiralty even before we left our anchorage. All the British had to do was to choose the place they would intercept us, and what superiority of force they would need.

That interception was made the very morning we put to sea, so that we were amazed when at daybreak our advanced scouts suddenly reported contact with British light cruisers. Immediately suspicious, Admiral Hipper reversed course southeastward, toward

Helgoland, to avoid being trapped by the British battleships which were probably supporting the British light cruisers.

Deployment of our forces along the new course was quickly achieved, with our own light forces ahead and on the disengaged side from the enemy. Slowly the sky brightened, revealing Admiral Beatty's five battle cruisers to starboard and astern of our three battle cruisers and the *Blücher.* The light forces of both sides were deployed on the disengaged side and ahead and astern.

Firing began immediately at extreme range, which quickly decreased as the British ships overtook our force, held back as it was by the old *Blücher.* Most of the British salvos we avoided by zigzagging, but presently the *Seydlitz* took a hit aft which put both of her 28-cm. after turrets out of action, with the terrific loss of 159 men. Two other subsequent hits added to the damage, but, owing to the *Seydlitz's* excellent firefighting and damage control measures, the fires were extinguished and the vessel kept under control.

The *Blücher,* however, slower and with much lighter armor, suffered terrific punishment, the British battle cruisers taking her under concentrated fire, as she was the rearmost ship in line. Then, in addition to the tornado of shells, she took a torpedo hit below the waterline which left her out of control and dead in the water.

The enemy had not gone unscathed, for we observed our salvos dead on target. The British flagship at the head of their battle cruiser line slowed down and then dropped completely out of line, smoking heavily. Officers on the *Moltke* also thought they saw an enemy ship go down, but nothing was clear in the smoke and battle haze.

Owing to the extreme distance of the enemy from us, Admiral Hipper had to give up his intention of ordering a sortie of our torpedo boats against them in order to take the pressure off the *Blücher.* In fact, during all this part of the action, only one torpedo boat, from our Fifth Squadron, managed to get torpedoes off, and she optimistically reported that she thought she had got hits on one of the enemy battle cruisers.

The *Blücher's* peril now was extreme. There was no hope that our main fleet, though alerted the moment the enemy was sighted, would arrive in time to render support. Further, the light cruiser *Stralsund* had already reported heavy smoke on the horizon, indicating the approach of still other enemy ships—probably battleships.

The British battle cruisers had now turned almost their entire attention on the helpless *Blücher.* Desperate as the chance was Admiral Hipper had just directed a change of course to the south, to draw the enemy away from the *Blücher,* when Captain von Egidy, commanding officer of the *Seydlitz,* reported that not only were his after turrets and magazines completely burned out, but that ammunition for the forward turrets was running low as well.

To have stood by the *Blücher* longer would have risked losing other ships and perhaps the entire Force. With a heavy heart Admiral Hipper countermanded his order and directed a resumption of the withdrawal southeasterly toward Helgoland. Eyes blurred as the sinking *Blücher* disappeared in the haze astern.

The enemy did not pursue.

Our heartbreak over the *Blücher's* loss was greater because all hands believed that it could have been avoided if the operational order had not been sent by radio in the first place; if the fleet had been properly placed to give support, in the second; and, third and closer to us, if the *von der Tann* had been present to add its powerful guns instead of being absent on routine exercises in the Baltic.

We did not at that time have the consoling knowledge of the damage the British flagship, *Lion,* had received, and that she was left so helpless that she had had to be towed to port. Had the main body of our High Seas Fleet been in position to support the Scouting Forces, not only might the *Blücher* have been saved but the *Lion* in turn might have have been destroyed.

Knowing today that the British, through possession of our signals, had been able to plan a complete and overwhelming trap for our Scouting Forces, it is hard to understand why they achieved as little as they did.

On our own part, we in the Scouting Forces felt the pride of stout performance. Our gunnery had been excellent; our communications had gone through smoothly, and orders had been promptly obeyed. Our admiral had given an inspiring example of unruffled courage, and every officer and man had stood firmly at his post. We had received our baptism of fire, and felt we could do even better next time.

But the repercussions of the engagement of 15-16 December and the 24 January Battle of Dogger Bank were felt unmistakably at the beginning of February, when the Kaiser personally visited the fleet at Wilhelmshaven. One of his first actions was to remove both Admiral von Ingenohl and Rear Admiral Eckermann from their posts. Admiral von Pohl, the Chief of Staff at the Admiralty Staff in Berlin, was made the new Commander in Chief of the Fleet, and Captain Michaelis, the extremely capable commanding officer of the battleship *Thüringen,* was made Fleet Chief of Staff. Rear Admiral Eckermann was shifted to the command of the First Squadron of the fleet, replacing Admiral von Lans.

As Chief of the Admiralty Staff in Berlin, Admiral von Pohl had enjoyed close working relations with the Chancellor of the Empire, von Bethmann-Hollweg. Perhaps influenced by the Chancellor, who was opposed to submarine warfare against merchant ships, Admiral von Pohl had not even submitted for the approval of the Secretary, Admiral Tirpitz, the declaration of forbidden war zones around Britain and France before it was submitted for the Kaiser's signature. This was directly contrary to the Kaiser's own directive, which was that all important decisions as to operations should be submitted to Secretary Tirpitz before they were put into effect. In addition, Admiral von Pohl was said to favor using the fleet with the greatest of caution and only under the most favorable circumstances. None of these things won him the full confidence of the offense-minded Admiral Tirpitz.

During his Wilhelmshaven visit the Kaiser honored both Admiral Hipper and myself with the decoration of the Iron Cross, First Class. On the occasion of the first battle cruiser operation against Yarmouth we had been awarded the Iron Cross, Second Class, but both of us had felt that that operation fell short of its real possibilities, and we had foregone wearing the decoration until after the success at Hartlepool.

In an attempt to lure the enemy into battle close to the German bases, at a time and under circumstances of his own choice, Admiral von Pohl developed a program of sending the whole fleet out on frequent but very short-range sorties. Since these sorties were made in areas where the British surface ships no longer were seen during the daylight, neither officers nor crews felt that they would really result in an engagement with the enemy. Yet the sorties exposed the fleet to serious danger from lurking British submarines and hidden minefields laid by enemy minelayers at night—danger which offered no recompense in the way of actually getting at grips with the enemy.

The only distant incursions permitted in the North Sea were the laying of mines on the Dogger Bank—an operation strongly urged by Admiral Hipper. These minefields were set out by our light cruisers, which laid them at night and then quickly withdrew to the protection of our heavy forces just off Helgoland. These minefields were intended to inflict losses upon the enemy if he approached Helgoland, so even these operations could be said to be defensive rather than offensive.

Under these circumstances we in the Battle Cruiser Group were delighted to get away from the inactivity of the North Sea under orders to cooperate with the Army in the Baltic. The Army at this time was trying to drive the Russians from the Gulf of Riga. To add to our pleasure we would serve again under Fleet Admiral Prince Heinrich of Prussia, in supreme command of the Baltic forces, with Vice Admiral Erhard Schmidt in control of actual operations. Protected by the rest of the Battle Cruiser Group, the *von der Tann* blasted the coastal batteries on Uto Island, at the entrance to the Gulf of Finland, during which action the *Moltke* was hit and damaged by a torpedo from a British submarine. With the end of the bombardments, the battle cruisers and other units of the High Seas Fleet returned to Kiel and the Wilhelmshaven area.

Fleet morale, we found on our return from the Baltic, was worse, if anything, than before. The British Fleet, matching caution with caution, had retreated to the west coast and to its strongly guarded base at Scapa Flow, making it difficult for even our submarines to get at them. A northerly sortie of the High Seas Fleet into the North Sea on 23 October 1915 was cancelled at Admiral von Pohl's orders even before it reached Horn Reef lightship, north of Helgoland, when it was reported that British forces had been sighted approaching.

News of the growing dissatisfaction in the fleet reached Admiral von Tirpitz and Admiral von Müller, the head of the Naval Cabinet. Either Admiral von Müller or Prince Adalbert of Prussia, who was a commander with the fleet, then informed the Kaiser. The Kaiser promptly issued a sharp Cabinet order rebuking all criticism of the kind of warfare he had ordered.

But the feeling in the fleet could no longer be ignored. Captain von Trotha, the universally respected commander of the battleship *Kaiser,* reported the matter frankly in a communication through regular official channels. In January 1916 Captain von Levetzow, the equally respected captain of the *Moltke,* requested a conference with Admiral von Pohl and informed him, in most unambiguous language, of the dissatisfaction in the fleet. Admiral Bachmann, head of the Admiralty Staff in Berlin, was equally in disagreement with the policies of the Commander in Chief of the Fleet.

No one had ever questioned either the personal courage or the tactical ability of Admiral von Pohl—least of all I, who had known him personally when I was navigation officer of his squadron. But matters could not continue as they were. It was perhaps a kind fate, then, that suddenly hopsitalized Admiral von Pohl with acute cancer, from which he died on 26 February, less than a month later.

Admiral Scheer Takes Over the Fleet

The Kaiser could not have delighted the fleet more highly than by his selection in mid-January of Vice Admiral Reinhard Scheer, commander of the Second Squadron of the Fleet, to succeed as Commander in Chief.

Admiral Scheer, a real seadog, not only had great practical common sense and a keen sense of perception, but he also possessed that rare commodity, a delight in responsibility. His nickname "Bobschiess"[2] was indicative of the gruff reception he was likely to accord to pessimists or bores. But the fleet's confidence in him was increased when he promptly appointed Captain von Trotha as his Chief of Staff, and Captain von Levetzow as Fleet Operations Officer. It was a perfect team, because Levetzow, while bril-

[2] This is an untranslatable nickname meaning that he was of an extremely aggressive nature. *Conf.* "Bull" Halsey.

liant, was impulsive, whereas von Trotha was the calm and deliberate adviser.

Recognizing the urgent need of reviving fleet morale, Admiral Scheer called a conference of flag officers and squadron and ship commanders to whom he explained his new program tersely but emphatically. Briefly, while bombardments of the British coasts could not be resumed immediately, they would be staged as soon as possible, and raids against enemy shipping would be extended into the upper North Sea. It was hoped that the pressure of these offensives would then force the British to come out from their bases and accept battle under conditions set up in advance by us. As to the present Berlin restrictions on submarine warfare, which required the U-boats to surface and search merchantmen and get their crews off before sinking them, this exposed the U-boats to too much danger. With these restrictions lifted, the U-boats would operate directly against shipping off the enemy coasts as well as cooperating with the fleet in offensives against the enemy fleet.

Lastly, extensive airship reconnaissance should be made prior to and in conjunction with all High Seas Fleet operations.

This program of resuming the offensive was enthusiastically received by all the listeners, and the cordial relationships were still further cemented by the admiral's sociability over the coffee cups at the end of the conference.

When, the next month, the Kaiser visited his new Commander in Chief, Admiral Scheer outlined his ideas to him—and the Kaiser publicly approved the new program at a conference for all the senior officers immediately following.

With the old defensive spirit completely repudiated, the fleet enthusiastically took to training exercises to bring the ships and men back to top battle efficiency. Tactical evolutions, with ships changing from cruising formation into battleline as well as cruising in battle formation itself, were emphasized. And on 5 March 1916 the fleet made an initial sortie into the Hoofden area, without, however, seeing any signs of the enemy.

Bombardment raids on the English coast were the next step on the program, but the new Commander in Chief had the opportunity to demonstrate his mettle even before then. For, on 25 March, British light naval forces carried out a bombardment of their own against our signal station on Sylt Island, just off the Danish border, and the airship hangars at Tondern. Admiral Scheer immediately ordered all light and heavy units on a sortie to the northward to intercept the enemy, if possible, and especially to try to overtake the damaged British destroyer *Medusa,* reported to have been in collision, as a result of which she was having to be towed away.

The sortie was made in the face of heavy weather, which became even worse as the night passed. Our advance pickets made contact with the enemy, and in the dark our torpedo boat *G-194* was rammed and sunk by the British light cruiser *Cleopatra.* The worsening storm then drove all our light forces back to port, but our Battle Cruiser Group, reinforced by the *Lützow,* which had just rejoined, pressed the pursuit well beyond Horn Reefs and only gave over when a decoded British radio message revealed that the *Medusa* had been abandoned in a sinking condition during the night.

As a matter of fact, we later learned that a British battle cruiser force had been north of Horn Reefs that same morning, and steering on a southerly course, so that a meeting of the two battle cruiser forces would have been entirely possible. Had this occurred, probably no engagement could have ensued, as the storm was so severe that neither side could have used its guns at all. Nevertheless, the whole affair proved that, even in operations initiated by minor forces, it was vitally necessary to have the main fleet in position to come to the support of the light forces, if necessary.

New Raids on the Enemy Coast

Resumption of raids on the British coast had been planned for April, but circumstances delayed the movement until the night of 24 April, when the Scouting Forces sortied for a bombardment of Lowestoft and Yarmouth. By a coincidence this occurred at the same time that the British were staging a mine and net laying expedition off the Flanders coast to bottle up our U-boats working out of bases there.

Rear Admiral Boedicker, Commander of the Light Cruiser Group, was temporarily commanding the combined Scouting Forces in place of Admiral Hipper, who had taken sick leave to cure a serious attack of sciatica. Some of the commanders expressed misgivings about the sortie, but I could not share these. Apart from the danger from both bars and shoals as well as enemy minefields off the English coast, the staff of the Scouting Forces did not see anything exceptionally risky in the operation. The accuracy of my prediction was shortly proved, for the flagship *Seydlitz* unexpectedly struck a mine while leading the Force to the Northwest of Helgoland in waters which had been reported completely free of mines.

Instead of cancelling the operation, however, Admiral Boedicker transferred our staff to the *Lützow,* sent the limping *Seydlitz* back to Wilhelmshaven, and resumed course toward Lowestoft. I was delighted to find that the commanding officer of our new flagship was the same Captain Harder who had been commodore of the light cruisers in the earlier raid against Hartlepool.

In the pre-drawn of 25 April we met up with the two U-boats that were to guide us safely into English coastal waters, and began the bombardment of Lowestoft and Yarmouth at daybreak. In addition to shelling the forts, we sighted and sank a British patrol vessel. Next we encountered enemy light cruisers, which, however, disengaged after a brief skirmish and took refuge in shallow water where we could not follow them.

With mission accomplished, we then started homeward, our screening torpedo boats sinking a number of small British craft on the way. One of these was the steam trawler *King Stephen,* which had refused to rescue the drowning crew of the German Zeppelin *L-19* when that airship had gone down in the North Sea some time before. But now the trawler's crew, whom we naturally rescued, were quick to deny having been aboard at the time of the Zeppelin's sinking.

En route homeward we were dogged for some time by British light forces, but these kept at a discreet distance. Later we found that British battle cruisers had also been trailing us, but that these had left off when we neared the rendezvous point with our main fleet.

By mid-May Admiral Hipper was back again, recovered from his ailment, but distressed at having to shift his flag, temporarily, from the *Seydlitz,* which was undergoing repairs for some time, to the *Lützow.* His spirits rose, though, at being back in time to participate in the planning for a raid on Sunderland, which was to get underway just as soon as the *Seydlitz* was back to duty again.

SMS *HOHENZOLLERN*
Kaiser Wilhelm II's yacht at the Kiel Regatta.

BATTLE OF HELIGOLAND BIGHT
German cruiser SMS *Mainz* sinks near Heligoland.

BATTLE OF DOGGER BANK
German battle cruiser SMS *Blucher* capsizes.

GERMAN BATTLE CRUISERS
Raiding the British North Sea coast, 1915.

Sunderland and the Battle of Skagerrak

As Sunderland lay on the Tyne, and very close to the Firth of Forth and other great northern British bases, every one realized that bombarding it would be far more dangerous than the previous southern raids. To lessen the peril, it was planned to station U-boats in strength off all the British bases, both to give warning if the enemy left base and to attack him when he came out. The U-boats carried enough fuel to stay on station until the end of May.

However, one of the conditions for the operation was that extensive Zeppelin reconnaissance was also to be made, and after 20 May the weather conditions would be such that this would be impossible for some time thereafter. Accordingly, Admiral Scheer determined to give up the Sunderland operation in favor of one against British shipping in the direction of the Skagerrak and the Norwegian coast. This would be much safer than an operation against Sunderland without air reconnaissance.

I remember clearly that Rear Admiral von Trotha, the Fleet Chief of Staff, asked my opinion when the change of program was being debated, and I had emphatically given my preference for the Norwegian sortie if we had to do without Zeppelin reconnaissance.

One special precaution was taken to avoid the enemy's getting word of the sortie. As soon as the fleet flagship, *Friedrich der Grosse,* got underway, she was to observe radio silence, with the radio communications for the Fleet being taken over by the Wilhelmshaven guardship in her place. It was thus hoped that the enemy, monitoring our radio messages, would not suspect that the fleet was at sea, but would think it was still at Wilhelmshaven.[3] In this way the British battle cruisers, in case they got into a fight with our Battle Cruiser Group, might be lured into an engagement with our main fleet—which was exactly what was to happen.

[3] This was the identical deception used by the Japanese to conceal the departure of their carrier attack force for the surprise attack on Pearl Harbor on 7 December 1941.

IV

Skagerrak

THE Battle of Skagerrak—or the Battle of Jutland, as it is better known to British and American readers—has been described and critically analyzed from all points of view, not only by historians everywhere, but also by eminent naval officers who participated in it. Admiral H. C. Groos, in the official German *History of the War at Sea* gives a most able presentation, as does also Commander H. H. Frost, USN, in his *The Battle of Jutland,* an objective and most impartial study of great professional value. However, in the opinion of those who participated in the actual battle, many of these historians and analysts do not take sufficiently into consideration the fact that the information the opposing commanders had at their disposal during the battle, and on which they had to base their decisions, was often very scanty, and frequently based on entirely erroneous deductions. The greatest controversy concerning the engagement has been between those who defend Admiral Sir John Jellicoe, the British Commander in Chief, as being right in his reluctance to risk the whole British control of the sea on a single naval battle, and those who assert that Vice Admiral Beatty was right in wanting to crush the weaker German Fleet even at the risk of greater British losses. As for myself, I shall limit myself to the phases of which I had personal knowledge, which primarily concern the battle cruisers.

As stated in all histories, the German High Seas Fleet put to sea on the night of 30 May, for the proposed sortie toward Norway. Early next morning a report from two German U-boats that British battleship forces had left their bases gave Admiral Hipper and all of us the hope that during the day we would at last make contact with the enemy. The initial encounter was brought on almost accidentally by torpedo boats of our advanced scouting line stopping to investigate a suspicious steamer, which turned out to be a small neutral vessel. Our torpedo boats, however, were sighted by the British light cruiser *Galatea,* scouting on the northern flank of Admiral Beatty's extremely powerful force of 6 battle cruisers, supported by 4 fast new battleships, and screened by 15 light cruisers and 27 destroyers.

In addition, also unknown to us, some seventy miles to the northward of Beatty was the entire main body of the British Grand Fleet of 24 battleships, 3 battle cruisers, 8 armored cruisers, 12 light cruisers, and 51 destroyers.

Further, the British through decoding our messages had the incalculable advantage of having advance information that our fleet was going to sea, and about when. Fortunately, owing to the deceptive shift of our radio signals from the flagship to the guardship in the harbor and the use of visual signals as far as possible, the British had not learned of our last minute change of objective from Sunderland to the Norwegian coast.

The first alert we received on the *Lützow,* now being used as the Scouting Forces flagship, was from our light cruiser *Elbing,* scouting ahead and on the flank with accompanying torpedo boats. The message, received just before 2:30 p.m. on 31 May, was electrifying: "Enemy armored cruiser in sight W by N." Moments later, the *Elbing* reported firing and being fired upon.

Our admiral promptly notified Admiral Scheer, then speeded up and changed course northwestward toward the point of contact.

It was a magnificent sight from the *Lützow's* bridge—the *Derfflinger, Seydlitz, Moltke,* and *von der Tann* following in perfect order, rising and plunging in the gray swell, with the smoke of their haste pouring from their stacks. There was a slight breeze out of the west, and a light mist rode in the air.

But the first glimpse we had of the actual enemy was of half a dozen moving blobs on the southwestern horizon about 17 miles away.

Admiral Hipper promptly swung the Battle Cruisers Group around on a reverse course toward the south and east and on a converging angle with the enemy. Almost immediately the enemy, who had been heading northerly, swung southeastward also, and the range began to shorten.

As the distant blobs grew nearer, they took on the appearance of battle cruisers. Our admiral, watching through his glasses, calmly gave orders for the distribution of our fire: ship by ship our battle cruisers were to pair off with the enemy, beginning from the left. This would leave the sixth and last enemy ship unfired upon, but it would be the one farthest away and hence the least dangerous.

There was a moment of supreme tension as the great turrets rotated and the gray gun muzzles elevated. The imminence of a great naval engagement was unmistakable, and on the *Lützow's* bridge we felt a sense of elation at the orderliness with which decisions were being made and signals sent and executed. Our second staff officer, Commander Hansen, who had only recently joined, exclaimed enthusiastically, "Why, it's as calm as if it were nothing but a drill!"

An equal cause for elation was our knowledge that the course on which the battle was developing was leading it surely and rapidly toward our main body, now only 50 miles away.

The range finder operator was calling the ranges steadily: "25,000 yards—23,000 yards—20,000 yards." As he reported "16,500 yards," our admiral nodded with satisfaction. "Open fire!" Simultaneously he sent another signal to Admiral Scheer, detailing the situation, including location, enemy strength, and course of both forces.

The deck shook and thunder pounded our ears as the *Lützow's* 30.5-cm. guns hurled their missiles into the air. Astern the *Derfflinger's* 30.5-cm. battery, and the 28-cm. guns of the *Seydlitz* and *Moltke,* and the 28-cm. guns of the *von der Tann* joined in, firing salvos of one gun from each turret. A minute later we saw the distant flashes to the southwest and knew the enemy had opened fire also.

But instead of the deadly crash of enemy shells striking, we saw only futile splashes a couple of thousand yards to port. It was not until seven or eight minutes later that we received our first hit —not on us, but on the *Seydlitz,* fortunately without material damage. The second hit, also on the *Seydlitz,* was more deadly, wiping out her entire "C" turret. Our own *Lützow* also was hit, and the *Derfflinger* in turn, but fortunately neither hit was disabling.

The effectiveness of our own shooting was difficult to appraise, what with the mist and the smoke from the enemy's guns and stacks blowing between the lines, but our turrets were firing with almost machinegun rapidity, and the enemy, though outnumbering us, suddenly made an unmistakable turn away. Our shells must have been getting home, and the enemy didn't like it. He turned away still farther. And our admiral promptly changed course more toward him, to keep him within the range, which at time had been as short as 13,000 yards.

Equally cheering was the news received just then from Admiral Scheer, locating his main body just 11 miles away and lessening the interval at 15 knots speed.

It was at this exhilarating moment that our rearmost ships, the *von der Tann* and *Moltke,* came under heavy fire from a different direction—four enemy capital ships coming up from the starboard quarter. Our admiral decided it was time to disengage our battle cruisers and leave the situation in the hands of our oncoming main body. A turn away of a couple of points to the east and an increase of speed quickly lengthened the interval between us and the enemy to beyond battle range, and our guns hushed completely.

Th enemy must have just become aware of our main body coming up at this time, for his four battleships reversed course and fell in astern of his remaining battle cruisers which, already beaten, were withdrawing to the northwest.

Our admiral was of no mind to allow them to escape, however, and swung our Battle Cruiser Group about to its long planned position as head of our main battleline. It had been only about one hour since we had first opened fire.

The four enemy battleships which had harassed the *von der Tann* and *Moltke* now received some of their own medicine, not only from the van squadron of our main fleet but also from our Battle Cruiser Group, which divided its attention between them and our original target, the battle cruisers.

The fight now was not only between the opposing heavy units, but between the screening light forces as well, as torpedo boats on each side attempted torpedo attacks, only to be met by counter-attacks from the opposing torpedo boats and light cruisers. Out of this melee between the opposing lines there now came an enemy torpedo which opened the *Seydlitz's* hull to the sea. However, our long practiced damage control measures minimized the damage so that the *Seydlitz* did not even fall out of our speeding formation.

In the pursuit of the enemy, now withdrawing to the northwest, our gunners found themselves severely handicapped by the setting sun into whose glare they were obliged to fire. In fact so great was the handicap that at times the enemy was all but blurred from sight, and our fire had to be held until the target could be located again. In this phase of the action our Battle Cruiser Group was severely pounded, the *Lützow* alone receiving a number of damaging hits.

Up to this time we had had no intimation that the British Grand Fleet was also on the scene. But at 5:40 p.m. another division of British battle cruisers suddenly emerged out of the mist to the north and east, at a distance of little over 11,000 yards. Our screening light cruisers, *Frankfurt, Pillau, Elbing,* and *Wiesbaden,* ahead of us, mistakenly signalled back, "Battleships in sight." Under the impression that it was the van of the British Grand Fleet coming on the field, our admiral swung to the east and then south to close our main body again. The maneuver brought us even closer to the new enemy battle cruiser force—which we were later to learn was the British Third Battle Cruiser Squadron—and in the ensuing exchange of fire the British battle cruiser *Invincible,* flagship of Admiral Hood, was blown to bits under the accurate fire of Commander Paschen, gunnery officer of the *Lützow.* In the accompanying melee, the British armored cruiser *Defence* also went down, and a companion ship was forced out of line. On our part we had also left our light cruiser *Wiesbaden,* crippled and helpless, adrift between the lines where she would fight the full strength of the Grand Fleet before finally going down that night with all hands but one.

By now it was evident that the whole of the British Grand Fleet was to the north and east of us and across our bows in a deadly capping position. It was at this time, about 6:35, that Admiral Scheer signalled for the *Gefechtkehrtwendung,* or simultaneous countermarch by individual ships which had been so often practiced under his critical eye. Immediately, and as smoothly as they had ever done in drill, the 16 ships of his two leading squadrons each turned 180 degrees, and the whole fleet took up the new reverse course to west. So smoothly was this done that the British, who had not believed such an evolution possible, especially under hot fire, were not aware of it until our ships had completely lost themselves in the increasing mist. The six old pre-dreadnoughts of the Second Battle Squadron which Admiral Scheer had brought along only because of the pleading of their commander, Rear Admiral Mauve, did not have to make the ship's rightabout as they were already in the rear and could turn in normal fashion.

As the gunfire died down, however, we in the Battle Cruiser Group could take the reckoning of our own injuries. These were severe. The *Lützow* had been hit by no less than 10 heavy shells and one torpedo, the *Derfflinger* 7 times, the *Seydlitz* 14 times, plus the torpedoing. The *von der Tann's* entire main battery had been put out of action.

It was evident that we could no longer command the Scouting Forces from the *Lützow*. Her bow was low in the water; and her whole forward part afire from her battle injuries. Captain Harder had already cut her speed to a bare five knots, and she could no longer keep up with the line.

I suggested that we should transfer the flag to another of our battle cruisers, but at first Admiral Hipper would not think of leaving her. Only after I pointed out to him that in addition to the *Lützow's* inability to keep up, her radio had been completely put out of commission, would he consent to have a torpedo boat brought alongside.

The leader of the First Torpedo Boat Squadron, commanded by Commander Albrecht, was called alongside to take off the admiral and his staff, while four ships of the squadron were detailed to stay with the *Lützow* and cover her with a smoke screen. The *G-39*, under Lieutenant von Loefen, maneuvered into position perfectly, despite the heavy enemy fire and the violent rolling. As fresh and cool as if he were merely leaving his breakfast table, Admiral Hipper climbed from the quarterdeck of the battle cruiser to the forecastle of the torpedo boat, and quietly gave the order to follow the Battle Cruiser Group, who were already speeding to the west to retain position with the main body. By signal Admiral Hipper had meanwhile placed command of the Group in the hands of the *Derfflinger's* commander, Captain Hartog, until he himself could take personal control again. Just as we were transferring to the *G-39,* another shell hit on the *Lützow* blasted into a turret, and set off the powder in high, leaping flames.

The next two hours spent on the *G-39* were the most miserable of the whole war for us, for despite the warm welcome by the torpedo boat's officers, we could see the battle without taking our rightful part in it. Despite every effort to carry out the admiral's order to overtake the battle cruisers, the *G-39* not only had to avoid collision with our own torpedo boat squadrons in their attacks on the enemy, but also had to dodge the enemy gunfire. Thus it was that we missed the eastward turn of the High Seas Fleet at 6:55 p.m., and the desperate sortie of our battle cruisers and torpedo boats to take the pressure off our main fleet at the crucial moment of the battle.

It was surprising to us when Admiral Scheer, after successfully extricating the High Seas Fleet from the deadly trap of the capping Grand Fleet, and attaining a position where he could have probably safely worked his way home, should have turned to the east again and placed himself in an even more dangerous situation. Those who knew his unconquerable nature could understand his explanation afterward, that he could not refuse to go to the *Wiesbaden's* assistance, but only a miracle could have saved her. And the additional explanation that it was still too light to throw the enemy off his track, and hence that he took the offensive in a bold attempt to disconcert the enemy, is also characteristic.

But when, having once again found the Grand Fleet in overwhelming strength directly across his course, he ordered the sortie of the battle cruisers and torpedo boats against the enemy's main body, it did not seem to us to recognize the true situation. The battle cruisers had already suffered terrific damage, and the remaining guns they had fit to operate could have little effect against the whole British Grand Fleet. But in order to cover still another countermarch directly under the concentrated fire of the British battleships, he had to order a torpedo attack, and he sent the battle cruisers along to support this.

The success of that sortie is now well known. In the face of 31 torpedoes, fired at 10,000 yards from the 14 torpedo boats still available to us, the cautious Admiral Jellicoe turned away, and by the time he was on course again the High Seas Fleet had completed another successful countermarch and lost itself in the gloom to the west again.

Our battle cruisers came out of that inferno only by a miracle. At times they were under concentrated fire of almost the whole Grand Fleet, and at ranges as close as 8,000 yards. Shell after shell ripped into them wiping out turret crews, setting fire to compartments, opening holes through which the water poured. But come out they did, to resume position in the main High Seas Fleet as it slipped away to the south and west.

Meanwhile Admiral Hipper had been ascertained by semaphore signal which of the the battle cruisers was least damaged and offered the best facilities for a command post. The *Moltke* seemed the best suited, so she was ordered to halt and wait for us as the fleet formed for its withdrawal. But just as the *G-39* went alongside of her, the enemy salvos reached for her again and she had to resume speed and leave us behind. Only after this last threat of Beatty's battle cruisers in the deepening twilight had been avoided did we succeed in transferring to the *Moltke* and once more assume position at the head of the Group. But once we were aboard we found that the *Moltke's* radio was likewise badly damaged, so Admiral Hipper directed the *G-39* to remain close by in order to make use of her radio.

The story of the rest of that night is well known: how Admiral Scheer boldly swung to the eastward and crossed through the very rear elements of the enemy fleet itself; how in the darkness torpedo boats found themselves suddenly fighting at pointblank range with cruisers and cruisers with battleships.

In case he found the enemy still between him and home the following morning, Admiral Scheer had ordered the battle cruisers to take station as rear guard of the main fleet. But this message had not reached us on the *Moltke,* and consequently our admiral spent most of the night trying to reach his usual position at the head of the line. Only at dawn, in the vicinity of Horn Reefs, was the *Moltke* able to fall into her assigned position in the fleet.

During the night, however, we were able to give the Commander in Chief information about battle details and the damage our battle cruisers had received. We believed that we had inflicted very heavy losses on the enemy, though we had no idea yet how heavy these really were. As against them we had lost only the *Lützow,* which, in an unmaneuverable condition, had been sunk by our own torpedoes after her crew had been taken off by the escorting vessels.

All our other battle cruisers had been able to make port under their own steam and steerage, though the *Seydlitz,* worst hit of all, had to wait several hours to get across the bar because of the water she had taken in through the torpedo hole and shell holes. Only the excellent seamanship of her commanding officer, Captain von Egidy, and his crew, brought her through at all. For that matter, the superior construction and damage control measures of our cruisers had brought them home afloat after suffering almost identical injuries that had blown three British battle cruisers into bits.

It was the duty of the staff to prepare the detailed combat report, with necessary diagrams, so we began work on this as soon as we were aboard the *Moltke.* It was not a simple job because of the innumerable and rapid changes of course, speed, and orders during the engagement. Nevertheless, by the time we came into port, on 1 June, we had a clear picture of the various phases of the action, and I expected to give our admiral a rough draft for his use in preparing the oral report the Commander in Chief had directed to give to all the senior officers, squadron leaders, and ship commanders. But it was typical of our admiral at first to refuse the offered briefing.

"I won't give any oral report! I led the battle—and that is that!" were his emphatic words.

And it required a lot of persuading before he would make use of the prepared material so that he could explain in detail all his reasons and actions when he reported on the fleet flagship.

As for us of the staff, we felt that we had never had so fine a leader. Despite the turmoil of battle, the weighty decisions to be made, and his own impulsiveness, he had always taken time to listen to the suggestions of the responsible members of his staff. We—the Admiral and I—had used the same telescope on the command bridge and had exchanged views on every situation, and not until this was done had a command been given. In the same way, if a question of courses or positions came up, it was the staff navigation officer, Commander Prentzel, who was consulted. The gunnery officer, Commander Hansen, was questioned in all decisions concerning distribution of fire or opening fire and ceasing fire. In every matter involving torpedo attacks either by our own squadrons or enemy craft, our staff torpedo officer, Commander Brutzer, was called in.

As to communications, I personally gave the Admiral every tactical message that came in, along with suggested action in conformity; this was just the procedure we had used in all our previous wartime maneuvers and engagements. But suggestions alone were not enough; they had to be presented in a logical manner that carried conviction. However, Admiral Hipper was correspondingly appreciative, and on the tenth anniversary of the Battle of Skagerrak he wrote expressly to thank us again.

Kind and appreciative as Admiral Hipper always seemed to be in connection with our suggestions, it was always clear to me that in the final analysis the responsibility for decisions is the leader's alone. Twelve years later, when I was called to head the Navy, I came to realize how heavy this responsibility could be.

After every engagement a careful evaluation is made to ascertain what lessons have been learned and what changes, if any, should be made. In the case of the Scouting Forces, this inquiry centered naturally around reconnaissance, their main duty. The Light Cruiser Group, under Admiral Boedicker, had detected the sudden appearance of the British Third Battle Cruiser Squadron immediately, but had mistakenly reported them as battleships. Once our battle cruisers had joined the main fleet, they had of necessity lost much of their value for scouting. For in the engagement with the enemy's Fifth Battleship Division and his battle cruisers, their assigned position at the head of the Fleet was not well adapted to reconnaissance. However, as we were leaving the *Lützow* our admiral had sent a radio message to the Commander in Chief in which he reported, "The van of the enemy's main body is bearing east to south." This was an error, for it was the enemy battle cruiser *Invincible* that should have been reported, and not "the enemy's main body."

As a result, in order to improve our reconnaissance in the future, at the suggestion of Admiral Hipper the Commander in Chief directed that action reconnaissance be made the duty of the Second Torpedo Boat Squadron, which, on account of the size and speed of its units, was well suited to the task.

Looking at it in retrospect, I believe now that if we had been able to give Admiral Scheer definite information as to enemy losses promptly upon joining the main fleet, this would have given him a better idea as to the enemy's remaining capabilities. Also, after the enemy's further loss of the *Invincible,* a knowledge of this would have made it easier to break away from the enemy.

That the British Commander in Chief also was deprived of valuable information is shown by his loud lament concerning Beatty's failure to report on the position of the German main body. Yet, at the time the report was made, Beatty not only had the van of the High Seas Fleet in plain sight but was actually exchanging shots with it.

That Vice Admiral Beatty was a man of dashing courage is shown by his plea to be allowed to lead the Grand Fleet in a direct thrust at the German main body when the two forces had become disengaged after Admiral Scheer's last turn away. But the American historian, Commander Frost, is more than a little critical of Beatty in the battle, and emphatically called Admiral Hipper the greatest of all the leaders at the Skagerrak. Admiral Hipper modestly waived the accolade in favor of Admiral Scheer, pointing out that Commander Frost was not in a position to appreciate fully the great responsibility of the fleet's Commander in Chief. Certainly Admiral Scheer proved his quality to command by the way in which he initiated the Battle of Skagerrak and then carried it through to its successful conclusion.

For the High Seas Fleet had not only boldly given battle to the outnumbering British Grand Fleet, but had tactically worsted it with a loss to the British of 3 battle cruisers, 3 armored cruisers,

8 destroyers, and 6,995 men, as against the German loss of 1 battle cruiser, 1 old pre-dreadnaught, 4 light cruisers, 5 destroyers, and 2,921 men.

Most of our own losses were among the battle cruisers and light forces. Of the *Wiesbaden's* crew, only one man, First Class Stoker Zenne, was saved. The light cruiser *Frauenlob,* sunk by enemy torpedo in night battle with outmatching forces, took down with her all but five of her crew, her commanding officer, Junior Captain George Hoffman, being lost, just as had been the *Wiesbaden's* commanding officer, Captain Reiss. On the *Lützow,* the chief radio officer, Lieutenant Gaede, had been killed at his station in the first day's fighting.

Our beloved Lutheran chaplain, Fenger, who had borne a charmed life in previous action, was badly but not fatally wounded. In the Hartlepool operation, while he was busy elsewhere, his stateroom on the *Seydlitz* had been wrecked by an exploding 15-cm. enemy shell. The stateroom to which he had been shifted later was similarly wrecked when the *Seydlitz's* after turret was half disabled by a heavy hit. The chaplain himself, peering through an eye slit in a 15-cm. casemate, had his face badly gashed and was hurled bodily through the casemate door when a 38-cm. shell penetrated the armor and killed the crew at the gun.

A chaplain's duties aboard a fighting ship are varied and demanding. He must be understanding and tactful, avoiding both the dangers of frosty dignity and the other extreme of undue officiousness. In bearing he must be beyond criticism, in religion and morals a leader. Though he cannot be an active participant in combat, he has the duty of comforting the wounded and encouraging them by his words and his attitude.

The Germany Navy has always been blessed with exceptionally splendid men as chaplains. Chaplain Fenger was of this type, and when he received the order of the Iron Cross, First Class, after the battle, we all thought it more than merited.

It was only natural that the Kaiser should wish to thank the fleet personally after Skagerrak, and to distribute the decorations that had been awarded. Admiral Scheer and Vice Admiral Hipper each received the decoration Pour le Merite, and Admiral Hipper, as a

Bavarian, was also given the Bavarian order of Max-Joseph, which entitled him thereafter to prefix his name with the "von" of knighthood. I had the honor of receiving from the Kaiser the Knight Cross of the Order of Hohenzollern, with swords.

Representatives from all the ships' crews were also assembled on the pier abreast the flagship to hear the Kaiser's speech of appreciation. Everyone of course expected that the Kasier would pay respect to Admiral of the Fleet von Tirpitz, who was the one man most responsible for the creation of the German Fleet. However, the Kaiser mentioned only Fleet Admiral von Koester, the former tactician of the fleet, who had developed the countermarch by individual ship turnabouts and other tactical maneuvers which had been so successful at Skagerrak. The slight was probably due to the personal disagreement between Admiral Tirpitz and the Kaiser's Chancellor over the restrictions on submarine warfare, as a result of which Admiral Tirpitz had resigned his office at the beginning of the year.

In his written report to the Kaiser on the Battle of Skagerrak, Admiral Scheer had stated that in his opinion the naval war with Great Britain could not be brought to a successful conclusion except through unrestricted submarine warfare. In view of the British arming of merchantmen and other counter measures, he did not believe he could take the responsibility of ordering his submarine commanders to risk their ships and their crews by abiding by the government's present directive requiring searching of merchant ships before taking offensive action against them. Since the government had not abandoned its position, he considered that the only practical employment for the U-boats would be against military targets only.

Meantime, from the moment of the return to port, the Commander in Chief had been employing every possible means to have the damaged ships back in fighting shape at the earliest possible minute. He hoped to do this by August, at least, before the British could repair their damaged ships. He gave it as his belief that the Grand Fleet's greater losses, despite their numerical superiority, had so worried Admiral Jellicoe that he had avoided continuing the battle the second day, though he had been in position where he could have forced such an action. In fact, Admiral Scheer was firmly convinced that, with proper cooperation from our airships and submarines, we could expect even greater success in any future well prepared operation.

With all the battle cruisers undergoing repairs, Admiral Hipper temporarily set up headquarters on the old battleship *Schwaben,* berthed in the inner harbor of Wilhelmshaven. While we were here, Pastor Gustav Frenssen spent several days with us gathering information about all the phases of the action. His novel, *The Brothers,* presents the Skagerrak episodes so colorfully and at the same time so accurately that the reader could almost recognize the living characters even under their fictional names, and could almost feel that he was witnessing the actual combat instead of merely reading about it in the pages of a printed book.

Our Assistant Chaplain Ronneberger also published a special magazine, *On Outpost Duty,* covering the Skagerrak battle, with the contents made up of contributions by crew members as well as petty officers and officers. This publication advanced the morale of the Scouting Forces immeasurably.

Already our Commander in Chief was planning another operation against Sunderland, with the primary purpose of showing the enemy that the German Fleet was eager for another test. With the exception of the *Seydlitz* and the *Derfflinger,* the whole fleet was expected to be ready by the middle of August. To rebuild the Battle Cruiser Group up to strength, the battleships *Bayern, Grosser Kurfürst,* and *Markraf* were added to it. When the original Sunderland operation had been planned in May, our submarines were stationed off all exits from the British Fleet's bases. The same deployment would be made again, and reconnaissance by Zeppelin airships would be a prerequisite.

The German forces put to sea the night of 18 August as planned. At dawn the *Moltke,* serving as flagship of the Scouting Forces, sighted an enemy submarine just as it dived, but the enemy craft managed to place a torpedo in the *Westfalen,* at the rear of the line, so that the battleship had to return to Wilhelmshaven. But the British Fleet, also putting to sea, had run into our own submarine line, as a result of which Admiral Jellicoe reversed his course, delaying his sortie by hours.

That same afternoon our Zeppelin *L-13* reported a heavy enemy force approaching from the Hoofden area. Admiral Scheer promptly swung the High Seas Fleet in that direction, hoping to trap this new enemy force with superior numbers. However, the *L-13* shortly sent another message stating that their first message was in error, and that only enemy "light forces" and not "heavy forces" had been sighted.

As a result of the delayed sortie of the Grand Fleet and our own fleet's diversion through the Zeppelin's erroneous report, the expected battle did not take place. Unrestricted submarine warfare thereafter held priority in the German naval operations, and the last offensive sortie of the High Seas Fleet before the beginning of unrestricted U-boat warfare had ended without the success every one had so fondly anticipated.

V

From Unrestricted Submarine Warfare to Revolution

WITH THE LAST SORTIE of the High Seas Fleet, a complete change in the High Command structure and the conduct of the war occurred. At the end of August, Field Marshal von Hindenburg and General Ludendorff were appointed to head the Supreme Army Command. The enemy's great offensive on the Somme had been checked, and our own disastrous Verdun campaign with its tremendous casualties had been given up.

The shift of objectives brought about the crushing defeat of Russia in 1916, and the way was prepared for the outbreak of the revolution there in 1917.

Also, much to the surprise of the fighting forces, the Kaiser had suddenly made a peace offer to England and France—an offer which we all thought was a last attempt by our government to end the war without resorting to unrestricted submarine warfare. When the peace offer was promptly rejected, we considered that the introduction of unrestricted submarine warfare was both justified and unavoidable, even at the risk of bringing the United States into the war against us.

Admiral Bachmann, the Chief of the Admiralty Staff, had resigned because he had sided with Admiral von Tirpitz in opposition to the Chancellor's restrictions on our U-boats, and had been succeeded by Admiral von Holtzendorff. But Admiral von Holtzendorff had in turn become convinced of the necessity for giving the U-boats a free hand, and after numerous conferences in Supreme

Headquarters, had succeeded in obtaining the Kaiser's and the Army's approval for unrestricted submarine warfare, announced early in February of 1917.

That the declaration should have been made just at the time that "promising" peace talks with the United States were pending was something unheard of by us until later. If the political government had given the Navy its reasons for vetoing unrestricted warfare at this time, the Navy would have been better able to understand its orders.

But once all-out U-boat warfare was decided upon, it took priority over everything else in the Navy. The fleet's main duty then became the task of keeping open mine-free channels in and out of Helgoland Bight for the U-boats and their escorts. Such channels had to be kept open, and since the British were persistent in laying their own mines across them, our augmented minesweeping forces were kept continuously busy. The enemy minefields were steadily extended offshore, so that our minesweepers had to operate farther and farther into the open sea, and hence were more vulnerable to surprise attacks by the British. Due to weather conditions, air reconnaissance was not a complete safeguard. We had to screen our minesweepers with light cruisers, themselves in turn supported by some of our heavy ships.

With so many of our ships diverted to this activity, it was impossible to stage real offensive sorties by the fleet as a whole, and its surface activities were restricted to minor operations designed prtmarily to reinforce the campaign against the enemy's shipping.

For instance, our new light cruisers *Brummer* and *Bremse* made a surprise attack on a British convoy routed between England and Norway. That same night one division of Commander Heinecke's Second Torpedo Boat Squadron attacked a British convoy off Norway while a second division raided enemy shipping on the English coast itself.

Torpedo boat squadrons were also based in Flanders ports, from where they not only escorted our U-boats through the enemy pickets but also raided his shipping as well. The Second Torpedo Boat Squadron once succeeded in driving off the whole of the British guard forces protecting the great antisubmarine net stretched in the English Channel.

In passage to and from Flanders, our torpedo boats generally met no opposition, but, on the night of 22 January 1917, the Fourth Torpedo Boat Squadron unexpectedly encountered strong enemy light forces. My friend and classmate of 1894, Commander Max Schultz, who commanded the squadron was killed on his command bridge. Lieutenant Commander Boehm, although badly wounded, brought the crippled squadron leader into the Dutch port of Ijmuiden and made emergency repairs within the time limit allowed by the neutrality laws, and so brought the ship safely home.

In escorting our U-boats to sea and keeping the channels through the minefields open for them, our torpedo boats made short sorties almost nightly. The battle cruisers and the battleships were assigned as security support for the various minesweeping units. Under these circumstances it was no longer necessary for the Commander of the Scouting Forces to remain with the flagship, so, at the suggestion of the Commander in Chief, Admiral Hipper shifted with his staff to a station ship with superior communications facilities, where he could more efficiently supervise the work of the minesweepers, torpedo boats, and air reconnaissance. Here, instead of on a ship often at sea, he could not only see to the escorting and the minesweeping, but could also hold the necessary conferences with his subordinates. Although the flag quarters on the old light cruiser *Niobe* were very cramped and antiquated, this was a small price to pay for the better radio, increased efficiency, and improved facilities for planning.

All during the war the ships of our fleet had been assigned regular overhaul periods in the navy yard, at which time their personnel had been allowed leave in successive groups. This privilege had not applied to the staff officers, however, as our admiral had simply shifted from one ship to another in order to keep his headquarters at sea. Now, at last, we had opportunity to go on leave ourselves. My July visit to my family at Ahrenshoop, on the Baltic, was the first leave I had had since the outbreak of the war.

When I returned from this leave, my assistant, Commander Prentzel, gave me a confidential report that was staggering. Discipline in the battleships had deteriorated sadly, the overstaying of liberty on the *Prinzregent Luitpold* was especially serious. Up until then I had considered such things impossible in the Germany Navy.

For an understanding of these so-called "mutinies" of 1917, a number of things must be considered.

The discontinuation of real offensive sorties of the fleet upon the introduction of the U-boat campaign had placed the Navy in a difficult situation quite different from the Army's. Patrol duty just offshore was dull and monotonous, and the transition to the temptations of shore life, when the ships came in to coal or for their yard overhaul, was explosive. Ashore the sailors could visit dubious bars and dives of every sort, something entirely disruptive of military discipline. In the Wilhelmshaven yard, in the first years of the war, there had been a fine breed of workmen, truly patriotic. But with the vastly increased work force, due to the heavy wartime workload, there had come an infiltration by many undesirable characters, whose political propaganda was not without effect. Owing to the concentrated area of Wilhelmshaven, this agitation also reached the fleet personnel. The larger the ship, and the less battle activity it had, the more fertile was the soil for sowing dissatisfaction.

One reason for the deterioration of discipline on some ships was that, as the war continued, some of the finest officers in the middle grades—lieutenant commanders and lieutenants—were promoted to more responsible positions elsewhere, and their less experienced replacements were not of the same high caliber. And these officers, who were the division officers, comparable to company officers in the Army, were the chief disciplinary officers in the ship. The effect was worse on the larger ships, with large crews, than in the light cruisers and small ships where the commanding officer and executive officer lived in closer touch with their men. It is notable that in the torpedo boats and submarines, morale remained high to the very end, particularly because of the close relationship between officers and men and because of the stimulus of action against the enemy.

However, the 1917 insubordination and the rioting ashore brought the danger into the light. By correction of the few real grievances and by swift punishment of the agitator ringleaders, discipline was restored, and maintained until the general collapse in 1918, despite continued socialistic agitation discussed even in the Reichstag.

From 1917 on the army suffered from thousands of desertions; the Navy had very few. Yet the Army benefited by desertion of its subversive elements, whereas the Navy could not get rid of them in the narow confines of shipboard life.

Some of the boredom in the fleet was ameliorated by the dispatch of battleships, with cruiser, torpedo boat, and minesweeper squadrons to the Baltic in the autumn of 1917, to take part in the occupation of the islands of Saaremaa and Hiiumaa and the Riga Gulf area. The *Moltke* (Captain von Levetzow) served as flagship of the commander of these forces, Vice Admiral Erhard Schmidt. The landings here were an excellent example of splendid cooperation between the Army and the Navy. This same splendid teamwork was exhibited the following year, when Finland was freed from Bolshevik forces by German naval units under Rear Admiral Meurer, in cooperation with General Count von der Goltz's troops ashore.

November of 1917 saw the British again take advantage of their success in breaking our radio codes. Our minesweepers had been assigned to clear the "Middle Channel" of mines which the British had laid in this entry into Helgoland Bight. Covering them were the light cruisers and destroyers of our Light Cruiser Group, under Rear Admiral von Reuter, with two battleships in turn, supporting them. Unfortunately the operation orders had to be sent by radio, as some of the units to participate could not be reached by telephone or visual signal.

In the ensuing engagement, the British drove back our light cruisers, but did not dare follow them into our mined area. On the other hand our two battleships did not come up in time to support our light forces. Even so the British succeeded in sinking only one patrol boat and registering a single hit on the cruiser *Königsberg.*

The very next day, Admiral von Hipper received orders to scout the Middle Channel with the battle cruisers of the Battle Cruiser Group to see if any British offensive was developing, but the reconnaissance was without result. It was to be my last sortie with the battle cruisers.

By now I had served five years on the staff of the Commander of the Scouting Forces, in which I had been Chief of Staff since my promotion to junior captain rank the previous April. This new designation in the staff only formalized the position which I had enjoyed since coming to the organization.

Now, if I were to advance in my profession, it was very much to my interest to have actual command of a ship. Admiral von Hipper did not take kindly to my departure and kept postponing it from week to week. However, in the winter of 1917-1918, several new light cruisers were to go into commission, and I finally secured orders to one of them. It was the light cruiser *Köln,* second ship of that name, due to be commissioned on 10 January 1918 at the yard of her builders, Blohm and Voss, in Hamburg. The previous ship of that name had gone down on 28 August 1914 in the first real engagement of the war, taking Rear Admiral Maass with her.

I was still with Admiral von Hipper, however, when the new battle cruiser *Hindenburg* joined the fleet and was made flagship of the Battle Cruiser Group. In a farewell dinner which he gave me aboard, Admiral von Hipper was kind enough to thank me for my services and to express his personal regret at my departure. I was equally sorry to leave the Admiral, for whom I had such great respect and with whom I had worked so very intimately in both peace and war. Yet I looked forward with keen anticipation to joining the splendid new ship of which I was to be the commander. As soon as I could turn over my staff duties to my successor, Commander Prentzel, I hurried to Hamburg.

The atmosphere at the moment was particularly rosy. The Russians had sought peace negotiations, and everyone was full of confidence.

I found upon arrival that the nucleus for my new crew was to come from the light cruiser *Hamburg,* which was just going out of commission. Not only had these men been well tested in the night engagements of Skagerrak, but in addition the *Hamburg* had been for years the flagship of the Commander of the Submarine Forces, and discipline was superb. I could be equally well satisfied with my new officers, for although the pick of the younger ones had been detached to officer the U-boats, those that remained were exceptionally good. The Blohm and Voss Yard had a reputation for efficiency, and the hoisting of the colors on 10 January

1918, went off without a hitch. At this time I formed a personal acquaintance with the younger Blohm, with whom I was to work very closely in later years, when I was Commander in Chief of the Navy.

Being anxious to get into action again, I held all hands to a stepped-up schedule, so that in a few days we were able to drop down the Elbe and proceed through the Kaiser Wilhelm Canal to Kiel.

Thanks to my years as navigation officer, I felt at home on the bridge from the first, and the trial runs went off on schedule. Some of the usual peace time runs for endurance were omitted, as unnecessary damage could result and nothing would be learned that we would not learn in actual operations themselves.

Also these trials interfered materially with the crew's battle training, which I wished to expedite as much as possible. In addition I had always felt that the better educated a man was generally, the more efficient he was professionally. As the material provided for education in the history, traditions, and objectives of the Fatherland was in many ways inappropriate, I arranged a series of lectures to fill the gap. Likewise, when there was no chaplain on board, I usually conducted the Sunday religious services personally.

In March we held a memorial service in commemoration of those who had died in action on the first *Köln,* with the memorial address being given by the veteran chaplain of the Scouting Forces, who had been a friend of mine since the *Seydlitz* days. The families of those lost in battle, as well as the families of our own crew, were present, and the service was most impressive.

All hands were happy when we finally completed our trials at the end of March and were ready to enter the fleet. In the next six weeks of training I specialized in damage control, basing the drills on what we had learned both from peacetime inspections and from actual battle. Brief periods of shore liberty kept the crew from going stale from overwork, and with good news from our Army's spring offensive on the Western front, everyone was highly optimistic.

At the beginning of May the *Köln* was ordered to the North Sea, to join the Light Cruiser Group, under the command of Commodore von Levetzow. The other light cruisers in the group were the flagship *Königsberg,* the *Frankfurt,* the *Karlsruhe,* and the *Nürnberg.* The new *Dresden,* commanded by Commander Prince Adalbert of Prussia, was going through her trial runs, preparatory to joining us in the summer.

Meanwhile, the Fourth Battle Cruiser Group had also been strengthened with the addition of the *Baden* and *Bayern,* our first battleships to be equipped with eight 38-cm. guns.

I found that the main task of our group was to lay counterminefields on the outer edges of the fields which the British had been laying off our shores in the past few years, and our new minefields were planned to sink any enemy ships trying to lay new mines in the gaps. In addition our group commander used these operations for intensive battle training and for stimulating a healthy competition which brought highly beneficial results. The frank and friendly manner in which Commodore von Levetzow conducted the critiques which attended the exercises, and his comradely attitude in the social evening that followed, had much to do with the splendid spirit of teamwork in the group. We were proud to feel that we were doing our part in such a team.

After we had completed our own minelaying, we went back to acting as protective screen for our minesweepers who were keeping our own entry and exit channels clear. In this screen our cruisers, and sometimes a few torpedo boats, too, kept close guard over the minesweepers, while a couple of battleships or battle cruisers formed a second protective line inside, and within visual signal distance. There was no danger of enemy submarines trying to attack through the minefields, so mostly our work was quite monotonous. I found it a great relief to reread Schiller's works in the tedious hours on the bridge.

Each time a group of our U-boats went to sea, it was escorted out to the open waters by a torpedo boat group as well as by escort submarines. When the occasion warranted, a few light cruisers also saw the U-boats safely to sea.

On one of these screening trips, the torpedo boat division that was with the *Köln* ran into an unreported minefield. Although the U-boats we were convoying got through unscathed, several of our torpedo boats were lost. Inasmuch as our torpedo boats were well equipped with boats, life rafts, and life belts, most of the crews were saved, though one boatload of survivors, lost in the darkness, drifted in the North Sea for two weeks before being picked up off the Island of Sylt. Only the cool leadership of the boat officer, Sub-Lieutenant Rollmann, in rationing the limited supply of food and water, saved the lives of his exhausted companions.

Sometimes we in the cruisers also ran into newly laid enemy minefields. On our way back in a heavy fog, after laying mines near Terschelling, the *Köln* ran into such a field, but threaded through it without damage, even though we sighted several mines and sank them.

At the beginning of August, the *Köln* was held up by another cruiser in entering the water gate at Wilhelmshaven, and I seized the opportunity to call on Admiral von Hipper, who was flying his flag on the station ship *Niobe* nearby. Admiral von Hipper was happy over the new changes in the command structure. He himself had been designated Commander in Chief of the Fleet, succeeding Admiral Scheer, who had been made both Chief of the Admiralty Staff and Chief of Supreme Naval War Staff. In this capacity he could direct all naval operations. Admiral von Holtzendorff, who had been Chief of the Admiralty Staff, was retiring because of illness. Commodore von Levetzow was to be Chief of Staff to Admiral von Hipper, and Rear Admiral von Reuter was to be the new Commander of the Scouting Forces. Captain Zenker, who, as captain of the *von der Tann,* had performed so brilliantly at the Battle of Skagerrak, was given the special responsibility for securing the forces and bases against surprise enemy attack.

This reorganization made the Supreme Naval War Staff what it should have been at the beginning, but it came too late. For that very June and July saw the terrific setback of our armies on the western front, and in August General Ludendorff made the startling declaration that a quick armistice was necessary to prevent a total rout for Germany.

I did not realize the full implications of this until, in September, I was ordered to Spa as representative of the fighting naval forces in the commission that was set up to study possible armistice conditions. One reason, perhaps, why I was so delegated was that the *Köln* was in the yard for repairs to a propeller shaft and I could be readily spared.

The Spa conference was headed by General von Gündell, with Rear Admiral Meurer as the chief naval delegate. While waiting between trains at Köln en route, I visited the cathedral, which made a special impression on me in those hours.

At Spa we reported to Admiral Scheer and were billeted with the Supreme Naval War Staff. In addition to Admiral Meurer and myself, the other naval representatives on the armistice commission were Junior Captain Vanselow of the Admiralty Staff, and Commander Kiep. The Supreme Army Command was represented by several officers, and Legation Councillor Baron von Lersner was the representative from the Foreign Office.

The discussions lasted for several days, and we eventually worked out an armistice based on conditions which we thought both sides could honorably accept. However, as is now known, nothing came of the Spa conference, and no armistice materialized until the capitulation at Compiegne, in November of 1918.

It was during the Spa conference that we learned from the Supreme Naval War Staff the true military and political situation. The new Chancellor, Prince Max von Baden, had outlined to the Reichstag the critical state of the country. With the superiority of the Allied armies being increased every day by the arrival of fresh American troops, our armies had been withdrawing under increasingly difficult conditions and with ever increasing losses. The new Foreign Secretary, Rear Admiral von Hintze (retired) had tried unsuccessfully to secure mediation through neutral powers. As to the Supreme Naval War Staff itself, it was determined to continue the U-boat warfare as long as possible in order to use it as a lever in any peace negotiations.

On our very last night in Spa, Admiral Scheer gave a dinner to which Field Marshal von Hindenburg and General Ludendorff were invited. Press of work called General Ludendorff back to his office immediately after dinner, but we had the opportunity to be with Field Marshal von Hindenburg for several hours. It was both surprising and reassuring to see with what steely nerves and resolution the Field Marshal faced Germany's difficult situation.

On returning to my ship I found it, like Wilhelmshaven, and in fact, all of Europe, in the grip of the great influenza epidemic of 1918. Some of our ships had so many men down that they could not go to sea. On the *Köln* we were fortunate enough to weather it in a few days, and go back to our patrol duty again.

One of the proposed changes under the new reorganization was to replace Admiral von Müller, at the head of the Naval Cabinet, with Rear Admiral von Trotha. All through the war Admiral von Müller had had the difficult and, at times, impossible task of carrying out the Kaiser's wishes and also accommodating them to the varying views of officers ranking equally high in the naval command, particularly the Admiralty Staff and the Fleet Command. For example, in the problem of the submarine war, in which the Imperial Chancellor also had a voice, there was this lack of unified opinion in the various commands. In acting for the Kaiser he had to play a role which really was not his as Chief of the Naval Cabinet, and a role which he in no way wanted. As a result, the officers at sea held Admiral von Müller responsible for the vacillating and misunderstood decisions as to the U-boat campaign. Having had little sea duty for a long time, Admiral von Müller also suffered from the disadvantage of being almost unknown to the fleet, and hence was subject to bitter and unjustified criticism.

Admiral von Trotha's appointment to head the Naval Cabinet was received enthusiastically in the fleet, but as long as the Kaiser was at General Headquarters, Admiral von Trotha did not feel that he should leave his present position as Chief of Staff of the Fleet during these critical days. Hence he never took over the Naval Cabinet until after the collapse, and then had the sad duty of deactivating it and incorporating it into the Bureau of Officer Personnel.

In the general changeover I was suddenly surprised to receive orders to turn over the command of the *Köln* to my old classmate, Junior Captain Kaulhausen, and to report to the Naval Directorate as head of the Central Bureau.

While pleased with the honor, I was sad at the thought of leaving my new ship just then, when everything depended upon the morale of the men. I was firm in the belief that in the *Köln,* at least, no subversive elements had made any headway. In my farewell speech on turning over my command, I spoke to the men of my confidence in them, and stressed the point that, in Germany's critical hours, loyalty and obedience from every officer and man were the only things that could help the nation. From the closeness of their attention, I felt that the men agreed with me.

Nor was I deceived. Later, when revolution broke out in Wilhelmshaven, the *Köln* and the *Königsberg* continued resolutely at their patrol stations off the mouth of the Ems. When, during one of their regular patrols, they were alerted to the approach of British Forces, they proceeded immediately to the point threatened. The report proved false, but these two vessels—our last ships with disciplined crews—remained at their stations until ordered by the new government to return to Wilhelmshaven.

When I left the *Köln* at Wilhelmshaven on 11 October 1918 the crew gave the usual three cheers for a departing captain, but I felt that it was not just a routine farewell. I felt a close bond with the whole crew, both officers and men, and was sad that in their greatest trial (which I could even then see approaching) I would not be with them to share it.

On my arrival in Berlin, on Sunday, two days later, I reported first to Captain Seebohm, whom I was succeeding as Chief of the Central Bureau, and then to Rear Admiral von Mann, the Secretary of Naval Directorate. In view of the seriousness of the situation I requested to be allowed to work under Captain Seebohm for a while, and the request was granted. So for the time being I lived in the aide's flat near the main entrance, where I could be close to my office.

Revolution and the Armistice

October was taken up mostly with general routine, revolving primarily around the U-boat construction program which had been inaugurated by Admiral Scheer. He maintained that it should be pressed, as well as the U-boat warfare itself, to the maximum extent in order to use our U-boat power as a lever in any armistice or peace negotiations. The civil government, however, acceded to the enemy viewpoint, which was that no armistice should even be discussed until the U-boat campaign had been discontinued.

News from the war fronts offered no comfort. The Allied offensive in the west, plus the collapse of the Bulgarian front, the defection of Austria-Hungary, and the exchange of diplomatic notes with the Allies all pointed to a near termination of the war. The gloom in the armed forces was increased by the dismissal of General Ludendorff as Quartermaster General of the Army, and his replacement by General Groener.

In the Navy, the Fleet Command had planned an operation at the end of October toward the coast of Flanders and the Hoofden. The primary purpose was to cover the evacuation of the Army and especially, of the Navy corps, from Flanders, and to bombard the naval bases occupied by the British. To protect the fleet in its sortie, an extensive minefield was to be laid, and a picket line of submarines was to be sent out to guard the flank of the fleet and to attack any British forces that approached from the north.

This was a well planned operation which presented small risk, and it was hoped that sending the fleet out on a real offensive operation would improve the morale of the harbor bound crews.

Unfortunately, while the ships were assembling in the Schilling Roads, the rumor was spread by subversive elements that the fleet was being sacrificed in a hopeless operation merely to "save its honor." The much publicized mutinies on several ships then materialized. To be sure, the mutineers were removed, but the operation was called off—and the fleet seemed doomed.

At Kiel, also, there were mutinies. The 1917 disorders had made it evident that this industrial city, with its navy yards and Socialist-minded workers, was a weak spot, but it was unfortunate that just at this time Admiral Bachmann, who had been for several years the Commander of the Baltic Naval District as well as Governor of Kiel, should have been relieved by Admiral Souchon. Admiral Souchon had made an outstanding reputation in command of the Mediterranean Squadron, consisting of the *Goeben* and *Breslau,* but knew nothing of the conditions in Kiel.

The first indications of the coming crisis were the revolutionary disorders among the Kiel workers. However, the intelligent Social Democrat Gustav Noske, a delegate to the Reichstag, forestalled the radical revolutionaries by taking over the governorship of Kiel and establishing working arrangements with Admiral Souchon.

Supreme Headquarters had the plan of sending the well-known and energetic "Lion of Flanders," Admiral von Schröder, to Kiel to take over the naval station, with a detachment of dependable troops from the Army to help him restore the government's authority. However, it was already too late, and furthermore such an action would have violated the agreement already made with the moderator Noske.

Dependable Army units were also to be sent to Wilhelmshaven to suppress the riots instigated by the revolutionists among the personnel of the fleet. I myself was ordered to carry this information personally to the Commander in Chief, Admiral von Hipper, as it could not be entrusted to the telegraph or the telephone.

Leaving Berlin by train on the night of 5 November, I arrived in Wilhelmshaven the next afternoon, just in time to witness most disheartening scenes. When I reported with my message aboard the ship that Admiral von Hipper was using as his headquarters, it was evident that even if dependable troops could be found, they would not be able to handle the situation there. For, on the very day I arrived, a conference of all the commissioned officers of the fleet had been convened aboard the fleet flagship *Baden,* which had been brought into the locks for that purpose. The intent had been to set up a center of resistance around the officers as a nucleus, but the effort was in vain. While their officers were absent, the enlisted personnel of the various ships had been all the easier prey to the propaganda of the Independent Social Democrat Party of Germany, which was advocating peace at any price.

With these unfavorable impressions I started my return to Berlin that same evening. The railroad system had already broken down completely, with the disaffection of the employees, and the train engineer could only run from one signal tower to the next, and on his own responsibility at that. As a rumor had gone ahead that there were mutineers from the Navy on the train, it was stopped repeatedly wherever loyal authorities still had control of cities en route, and on nearing Berlin it was not allowed to enter at all until officers on the train insisted. As it was, I did not reach my office in the Navy Department until the evening of 8 November.

I found the whole Naval Directorate in a state of defense. Captain Pieper, Head of the Ordnance Bureau, had been made commander of the Navy block of buildings between the Landwehr Canal and Bendler Street, and a garrison of Lancers was guarding the main building.

The next day, 9 November, the revolution broke out in Berlin. In an effort to preserve the monarchy, Chancellor Prince Max of Baden had announced that both the Kaiser and the Crown Prince would abdicate and a Regency would be substituted, but the Social Democrats refused the proposal and proclaimed a republic instead. Prince Max thereupon resigned the Chancellorship and handed the conduct of the state over to a provisional government headed by Friedrich Ebert, the Social Democrat leader in the Reichstag. The masses had got out of hand, and in order to prevent bloodshed, General von Linsingen, the Governor of Berlin, had forbidden the troops to use firearms. Our Lancer garrison promptly disappeared, leaving their ammunition. The Kaiser took refuge in Holland.

A Soldiers' Council had been formed among the revolutionaries, and Secretary von Mann now received notice from them that they were taking over control of the Naval Directorate under orders of the new government; meantime Admiral von Mann was to continue work as before. In due time a suspicious looking person appeared, claiming to be from the Soldiers' Council, but his objective was to get possession of the money in the Ministry's safe. He was informed that the officer who had the keys was away and the safe could not be opened, whereupon he disappeared. That same evening he was shot by guards while trying to loot another building.

To what extent the Navy was responsible for the revolution of October and November of 1918 was a subject for debate for many years. I myself can absolve it from any such indictment. For in 1919 Colonel Bauer of the Supreme Army Command published a book stating that as early as July 1918 there were 500,000 mutinous soldiers who would not return to the front after being given leave. In September there were a million and a half soldier stragglers wandering between the frontline and their homes. Even as early as that spring, the commander of a post behind the lines in Belgium had begged for help to defend his station against 10,000 such stragglers. These events showed that the real dissidents were the reserves and draftees of the Army—citizen soldiers—who had swallowed the political propaganda of the Independent Social Democrats and the Communists, and were for peace at any price—even to undermining the war effort against the enemy.

It is true that the fleet had mutinied openly when the plans for the October sortie had become known, and some of the sailors who had deserted their ships appeared in uniform in many inland centers, where they joined up with the Soldiers' Councils, naturally drawing much attention because of their presence so far from the coast. In addition many other persons, frequently criminal elements, donned Navy uniforms in order to gain acceptance to the revolutionary movement. For instance, the so-called "People's Navy Division," which for a while took possession of the royal stables in Berlin, was not recruited from the Navy at all, but from these criminal elements. Unfortunately its name and uniform led the whole country to think that it was the Navy that was the chief instigator and propagator of the revolution, and the Navy was to suffer from this calumny for years.

However, the revolutionary party had established a "Council of 52" for the Navy, and its members shortly appeared at the Naval Directorate "to act in an advisory capacity to the Secretary." They also undertook to check the work of the individual bureaus in the Ministry. Similar councils, with similar purposes, were formed in the Kiel and Wilhelmshaven naval commands, though they consisted of fewer members. In addition the Independent Social Democrat Party assigned Reichstag delegate Vogtherr to the Secretary; this delegate supposedly was to participate in all important conferences and to check all incoming and outgoing correspondence.

Appraising the situation realistically, Secretary von Mann met the Council of 52 with cooperative attitude, and made tactful suggestions as to how they could be of assistance. The preliminary armistice with the Allies having been signed by Reichstag delegate Erzberger on 11 November, Admiral von Mann pointed out that the armistice commission of the Navy would have very important responsibilities, inasmuch as the conditions imposed by the victorious Allies would be much more drastic if the preliminary terms

BATTLE OF JUTLAND

German cruiser SMS *Frankfort* in the thick of the engagement.

SCHARNHORST IS LAUNCHED

At the Naval Dockyard, Wilhelmshaven on October 3, 1936.

SMS *HINDENBURG'S* SHIP'S BELL RETURNED

In 1919, SMS *Hindenburg* was scuttled at Scapa Flow. In 1936, her ship's

were not kept. So the Navy went ahead on its heavy responsibilities, working them out in daily conferences under Vice Admiral Rogge.

The Council of 52 interfered very little, spending most of its time in conventions in the main hall at which they made propaganda speeches and drew up mostly impracticable resolutions.

Apparently recognizing his ignorance of the professional matters under discussion, Delegate Vogtherr attended all the meetings of the armistice commission but took no part in them. His attitude toward the Council of 52 seemed to be one of disassociation, if not of actual opposition.

Some of the Council's members assigned to the various departmental sections tried to study questions "that particularly interested them." In general, the section heads and clerks treated them matter-of-factly, and offered them little interference. The one rather significant thing was that the Council member who was assigned to the Ministry's Central Bureau took great interest in the funds and endowments that were administered from there. Later, when the Council was dissolved, this member requested some support from one of the funds. Fortunately, he had showed little interest in the voluminous and responsible tasks of the Bureau's director, Privy Councillor Giese, through whose hands all important documents were handled.

Rear Admiral Meurer, head of the Navy's armistice commission, had sailed for England on the cruiser *Königsberg*, at the request of the British Admiralty, in order to participate in the armistice discussions as far as they concerned the Navy. Disregarding Admiral Meurer's advice, some radical members of the Soldiers' Council had tried to participate in the negotiations also—under the impression that they could spread the revolution to the British Navy—but Admiral Beatty promptly sent them packing.

The end of the year, after the armistice terms had been settled, found the Navy with plenty to do. Under the armistice terms, there was to be a reorganization of the German Navy, with the Admiralty Staff and the Naval Cabinet dissolved and their duties incorporated into a new Naval Directorate. The fleet itself was to be interned in a neutral port for ultimate disposition.

It was difficult to carry out the armistice terms, but particularly this last one. Only by appealing to the sense of duty of the officers could there be found those who would volunteer to undertake this disagreeable voyage, and experienced seamen who would be willing to obey their officers' orders could be obtained only by paying special bonuses. Britain, however, was obdurate, and threatened to seize Helgoland if a single ship were scuttled on the trip. Eventually Rear Admiral von Reuter, with Junior Captain Oldekop as his Chief of Staff, took the fleet out, but contrary to the armistice terms, it was interned in the British naval base of Scapa Flow instead of in a neutral port.

The Navy was also obligated under the armistice to sweep all minefields it had laid in the North Sea and the Baltic. This requirement permitted us to keep a number of the minesweeper units in operation and to bring their crews back to military discipline. Procuring competent personnel for this, as well as demobilizing superfluous personnel under our new authorized strength, offered difficulties, but it did give us a chance to get rid of untrustworthy men. Consequently, although there were disorders in our naval bases during the winter, just as there were in Berlin and elsewhere, we gradually improved the discipline in the forces afloat.

In this effort we found strong support from the Governor of Kiel, Delegate Noske, when he was called into the new government at Berlin as People's Commissioner for Defense. In December another congress of Worker and Soldier Councils was held in Berlin, where extravagant demands were made for reduction of military authority. Commissioner Noske, however, had a strong appreciation of the necessity for military discipline, without which there can be no dependable forces, and he stoutly supported the military authorities. The entrance of dependable Army troops into the capital, as well as the formation of voluntary disciplined units in the Army and Navy, built the foundation for the gradual restoration of law and order throughout the country.

Of the volunteer units set up in the services, the volunteer naval brigades formed by Commander Ehrhardt and Captain von Loewenfeld were the most notable. Organized in early 1919, they consisted of officers, midshipmen, petty officers, and enlisted men, with the latter being drawn almost entirely from the well disciplined crews of the torpedo boats and the submarines. Their leaders, Ehrhardt and von Loewenfeld, were highly respected officers, tested in action, who knew how to instill both spirit and discipline into their men.

Another naval brigade was made up mostly of warrant officers, who, however chose Army officers as leaders.

In the Imperial Navy, the warrant officers represented a grade that the Army did not have. They were not officers in the strict sense, being merely specially designated petty officers who had served in the Navy for a great many years, and who had a splendid knowledge of their own technical specialties, but without the all-around naval education that a regular officer must have. Many of them had exhibited outstanding loyalty and ability in the fleet, but unfortunately, during the last months of the war and the beginning of the revolution, some did not meet the stern tests of the times. They allowed themselves to be influenced by the politically minded Warrant Officers Association, and, above all, by its chairman, Ahlboldt, who had been retired from active service for years.

In the reorganization of the Navy, plans were made to drop the warrant officer grade and adopt the Army system of petty officer specialists. Noske was in full agreement, and the Navy managed to make the change successfully by releasing the less able warrant officers and setting up a program for eventually promoting the superior ones to regular officer rank. Those who were so promoted more than justified the Navy's confidence in them.

In addition to assisting the Navy in these ways, Commissioner Noske, when the more radical Independent Social Democrats lost their position, replaced their representative, Vogtherr, with the Socialist delegate Giebel, and at the same time reduced the number of the Council of 52, and eventually eliminated it altogether. Again and again I saw him face the Council in bold opposition, despite their accusations of his treason to the cause, and even actual threats of personal injury.

Meantime other, and unexpected, changes had occurred in the Navy's organization. Admiral von Mann, the Secretary, who had gone home to Bavaria before Christmas, now reported himself too ill to return to his duties in Berlin, and requested a relief.

The choice of a new head of the Navy was a difficult one, because the man selected not only had to be acceptable to the government but also must enjoy the full confidence of the Navy.

In the latter respect, Rear Admiral von Trotha was outstanding. After the armistice he had headed the Bureau of Naval Personnel, which derived from the Naval Cabinet, and possessed the respect of all combat officers everywhere.

Another possibility was Vice Admiral Rogge, head of the Ordnance Bureau, who also had headed the Navy's section of the armistice commission. In this latter capacity he had handled the negotiations in exceptional style, sternly resisting any interference from revolutionary elements, and he had substituted for the Secretary during Admiral von Mann's absence. But he had never commanded a combat force at sea during the war, and, outside of his own Ordnance circle, was practically unknown to the Navy. However, he promptly and generously supported Rear Admiral von Trotha just as soon as he learned that the latter was the fleet's choice for Secretary.

Having taken over full supervision of the Central Bureau of the Naval Directorate from Captain Seebohm, who in December had become Chief of Staff of the Baltic Naval District, at Kiel, I was particularly concerned with the question of Admiral von Mann's successor. I had greatly admired Admiral von Mann and had begged him to reconsider his resignation from office, but when he adhered to his decision, I felt that immediate selection of Admiral von Trotha was necessary if calamity was to be avoided.

For it was no secret that radical political circles of the Left had been pressing for choice of one of the three "P's"—von Pustau, Persius, and Paasche—to take over command of the Navy. Of these, von Pustau, who had been retired as a captain in 1908 and whose only naval activity since then had been writing on nautical subjects, would never have been seriously considered by any regular naval officer. But, with the revolution, he had quickly swung to the Left, where he had gained the backing of the radicals. Persius also had left the Navy and devoted himself to writing lurid *exposés* of what he claimed were tyrannical "abuses" of the sailors by his former fellow officers. While lecturing shortly after the outbreak of the revolution, he had been confronted by a number of well informed and quick witted junior officers who completely refuted him in the discussion period that followed the lecture. In time his lectures became discredited, and even his malicious writings made few converts. Lieutenant Commander Paasche, who likewise had been discharged early in his naval career, was an idealist and a visionary. Coming under pure Communist influence, he eventually found his death in a shooting scrape in East Prussia.

With Admiral Rogge's permission, I visited Commissioner Noske to convince him of the necessity of having the Navy commanded by an active officer trusted and respected by the Navy, and gave it as my personal opinion that Admiral von Trotha was just such a person. Noske agreed heartily on Admiral von Trotha's professional reputation, and promised to make himself better acquainted with the admiral's personality. Further, he gave me permission to discuss the matter personally with the head of the government, later President Ebert.

It was characteristic of the times that on the January day when I went to the Chancellery, a supposedly dependable Army division was just marching into Berlin, presumably to restore complete law and order. But just as I arrived, they halted before the north wing of the Chancellery, where they were greeted by speeches by Noske and Ebert from a second story balcony. Without being stopped, I walked right into the room opening onto the balcony, and observed numerous hand grenades and guns laid out on a handy table—evidently for defense of the Commissioners if they were suddenly attacked.

Following Ebert's closing speech, I presented myself and was invited to follow him into his office. There I found that Noske had already passed on my ideas, to which he now listened again with interest. While I realized that the decision would not be made until the National Assembly had met and definitely formed a permanent government, I was assured that a careful study would be made of the problem.

Even as early as my first reporting to duty in Berlin in October of 1918, I had realized that the war would end unfavorably for Germany, and that one of the results would be that she would have a considerably reduced Navy. Under such circumstances, capable and forceful leadership would be a necessity for the Navy if it were to have any permanent position in the new scheme of things. The Navy, like the Army, would undoubtedly be under a political minister, but to return to its original status of dominance by an Army general would deprive it of the necessary financial support to carry out its task. Nevertheless, the earlier organization which had combined both the administrative and operational offices of the Navy under one chief of the Admiralty would, I was sure, be the best solution. The first reorganization under Kaiser Wilhelm II, which had divided the command of the Navy into a Supreme Command separate from the Naval Directorate, had resulted in disrupting friction between two equally ranked activities. Admiral von Tirpitz's type of organization, which permitted numerous independent activities reporting directly to the Kaiser, was no better, resulting in lack of any tight, unified naval leadership in the war. Since in the new State the armed services would undoubtedly have to present their programs to the Reichstag through a political representative, there could be no question of one of the services presenting its needs through a military head, as had been the case when an admiral had been Secretary.

As mentioned before, the Admiralty Staff and Naval Cabinet were to be dissolved, and their duties, along with those of the Naval Directorate to be combined under the Admiralty. The result would be a clear-cut division of the supreme naval authority into a Naval Operations Department, an Administrative Department, and other bureaus, primarily technical, combined together as the General Department. The Central Bureau, of which I was the head, would act in the capacity of a personal staff of the Chief of the Admiralty. Directly under him also would be the Bureau of Officer Personnel, the Bureau of the Budget, the Chief of the Medical Corps, and the Chief Engineer Officer. For some years the Navy's armistice commission, under a special director, was to continue to function, its duties being primarily to handle questions of the League of Nations and of disarmament.

The Naval Operations Department of the Admiralty was concerned with command responsibility in the Navy. The Fleet Division had taken over the tasks of the former Admiralty Staff, while the Organizational Division dealt with problems of organization and enlisted personnel, and the Training Division handled the training, both afloat and ashore.

The first head of the Naval Operations Department was Rear

Admiral Michaelis. The General Department, which included the Yard Division and its administration, the Construction Division, the Armament Division, and the Nautical Division, was headed by Rear Admiral Löhlein.

The Navy leaders deemed it vital to retain at least one naval shipyard, and its preference by far was the Wilhelmshaven yard, with its dependable workers and long experience. For its other needs it would have to depend on private shipyards and the so-called "German plants," with which the Kiel Naval Shipyard was now merged. Only after long debate was the new Socialist Government convinced that in order to develop its equipment according to its special needs, the Navy required its own shipyard. For one thing, this would not only enable it to train its own construction personnel and to progress in ship and engine design, but it would also provide a standard for the work that private shipyards would do for the Navy.

The Construction Division, under Director Presse, labored under the disadvantage of a severe limitation of its funds by the powerful special budget commissioner of economy. These difficulties could be traced to a former naval constructor in the commissioner's office, who, on leaving the Navy, had become a professor at a technical institute. Despite the remonstrances of his former colleagues and even of his own superior, Director Saemisch, he forced the dismissal of many indispensable engineers in the Construction Division.

The Naval Administrative Department, now headed by Director Reuter, still enjoyed the good reputation it had built up during the war under Director Schramm. In addition to general administrative matters, it handled problems of wages, commissary, clothing, and housing. The supervision of this important department remained in the hands of its able civilian directors, Schreiber and Benda, though the corresponding department in the Army was eventually placed in military hands. However, the system in our service had worked most satisfactorily, and I never had reason to wish our system changed.

For a time we debated whether or not a professional technician, instead of a line officer, should be placed at the head of the General Department. But since that department included both the

Armament Division and the Nautical Division, it was decided that a line officer director was absolutely necessary.

The same question arose in connection with the Wilhelmshaven Naval Shipyard, which, although primarily devoted to construction and repair, also constituted a military-technical institute. For a time, after 1919, a compromise solution was adopted at the instigation of of some personalities in the Navy and in the Reichstag. Under this compromise the shipyard was managed by a "Board of Directors," consisting of a line officer as *primus inter pares,* a naval constructor, a mechanical engineer, and an administrative director. But after a few years of unsatisfactory experiment, the yard was returned to its former unified management under a line officer—something, incidentally, which had always been favored by Director Schreiber.

The Construction Division, though at first under the General Department, like the Wilhelmshaven Shipyard, was eventually given full departmental status as the Construction Department, when the growth of the Navy made this change necessary. In it the chief of ship construction and the chief engineer enjoyed director rank, with section chiefs, such, for instance as the manager of submarine construction, subordinate to them.

The cutback resulting from the limitation on the Navy by the armistice and peace conditions made necessary many difficult decisions, which were naturally protested by some of the heads of divisions which were hardest hit.

In my own office I secured, as my chief assistant, Commander Hansen, who had served in the same capacity in the staff of the Battle Cruiser Forces. As second assistant, I had the former able gunnery officer of the *Köln,* Lieutenant Commander von dem Borne, who later on left the Navy after the Kapp *putsch.* My personal aide was Lieutenant Kurt Fricke, who later served almost exclusively with the destroyers and who eventually became Commander of the Destroyer Forces and finally headed the Supreme Naval War Staff.

By the end of the elections for the National Assembly in January of 1919, the more moderate elements had gained control of the government, and Commissioner Noske's cool common sense had done much to restore an orderly atmosphere in the Navy. In company with Vice Admiral Rogge, the acting head of the Navy, I personally attended the opening of the National Assembly[1] in the theater at Weimar. An Army division under Major General Maercker rendered honors to the new Assembly and guaranteed the members' personal safety. Thereafter, during the debates on the new constitution, I frequently visited the Assembly and witnessed the adoption of the constitution and the formation of the new government, with Philipp Scheidemann as Chancellor, Count Brockdorff-Rantzau as Foreign Minister, Noske as Minister of Defense, and Erzberger as Minister of Finance. I saw the election of Ebert as President of the new German Republic, and on 25 March, to my great delight, heard of the appointment of Vice Admiral von Trotha as Head of the Admiralty.

Legislation was passed creating a "Provisional Army," to be headed by Major General Reinhardt, with Major General von Seeckt as Head of the Department of Troops, roughly corresponding to our Naval Operations Department. General von Seeckt had personally appealed to the General Staff Officers of the old Army, calling upon them to remain in the Army after the revolution. Although the Treaty of Versailles later forbade the retention of the German Supreme General Staff, General von Seeckt did his utmost to retain its efficiency in another form in the new Army.

Shortly afterward, on 16 April, the National Assembly created a "Provisional Navy," with an organization such as I have mentioned.

In the reorganization, the Navy was to take over from the Army the coast defense works at Pillau, Swinemünde, and Borkum. With our limited personnel, this was not easy, but the advantage of the additional small bases for our ships was obvious. For one thing, it would aid in tightening discipline through dispersing our personnel from overly expanded centers which were always subject to subversive attempts in times of crisis. Thus it was that Stralsund, which had always been an Army garrison town, became a favorite Navy base and came to play an important part in officer candidate training.

The reorganization period was one of delicate problems, and

[1] The National Assembly was a convention of elected representatives from all over the country meeting to form a new constitution.

the Chief of the Admiralty repeatedly had to issue personal proclamations to convince the fleet of the necessity of certain measures. I remember how Admiral von Trotha went in person to Kiel to address the officers there, who were dubious about taking the oath to uphold the new Weimar Constitution. Also the question of the national flag to be flown by naval forces and stations came up, to be solved by the decision to accept the one which was just being introduced at that time. But when President Ebert decreed that the national anthem was to be *Deutschland, Deutschland, über Alles,* this solved the flag problem and won the President many sympathizers.

One of the Navy's main problems in the new decade was the low morale brought about by the armistice and peace conditions. In the beginning we had counted on being allowed to retain a battleship squadron of the *Nassau* and *Ostfriesland* class, and a cruiser division of the *Regensburg* class. But as a result of sabotage of a number of Navy Zeppelins by their officers and crews, the victorious Allies had made the armistice conditions much more severe, and we learned presently that we were to be left only some old pre-dreadnaughts of the *Braunschweig* class and some light cruisers of the *Nymphe* and *Hamburg* type. As all these ships were already antiquated and there was little chance that we would have money for new construction for a long time, the prospects for a revival of the Navy almost completely disappeared, and with it much of the morale of the officers and men.

Scapa Flow

Perhaps the one inspiring occurrence in that depressing spring of 1919 was the news that came from Scapa Flow. There, as I have mentioned, the German Fleet, under Rear Admiral von Reuter, had been taken after the surrender, despite the strict stipulation in the armistice that the ships were to be interned in a neutral port. With the news from the Peace Conference, being held in Paris, that we would not get a single ship of the High Seas Fleet, it became clear to the Navy that to prevent the ships being divided up among the victors and to save its honor, the ships had to be sunk.

By a strange coincidence this was the very time the British took to require a reduction in the crews aboard the interned ships. As a result Admiral von Reuter was able to send home any unreliable men who might obstruct the scuttling of the fleet.

In his position as Chief of the Admiralty, Admiral von Trotha naturally could not issue a command for the scuttling of the fleet, but it was privately impressed upon Junior Captain Oldekop, Admiral von Reuter's Chief of Staff, that the ships must be scuttled at all costs. This important message was sent through Junior Captain Quaet-Faslem, the commander of the dispatch boat which maintained communications between Admiral von Reuter and Germany.

Admiral von Reuter himself had been giving close attention to the proceedings in Paris, and with the certain prospect of a speedy termination of the armistice, he proceeded to put the concerted measures into effect. Fully aware of his responsibility and the possibility of Allied punitive action against him personally, he gave the command to scuttle the fleet on 21 June 1919. In doing so he not only restored the morale of the Navy, but also laid the foundation for the eventual reconstruction of the German Fleet.

That summer marked the twenty-fifth year since the graduation of our Class of 1894. With what high hopes we 70 naval cadets had donned our new blue uniforms, and with what equal optimism we had celebrated our tenth anniversary in 1904, at a time when the Navy was rapidly expanding under the new naval program. Now we celebrated a quite different anniversary. Those high hopes, it seemed has been extinguished forever by the outcome of the fateful war against the world's strongest seapower.

One of the saddest parts of the little class reunion was the brief memorial ceremony we held for our classmates who had fallen in the war. Among these were von dem Knesebeck and Max Schultz, the gallant torpedo boat captains, and Peter Strasser, the heroic Zeppelin commander.

At that time it was still too soon to foresee that the spirit of the German Navy had not perished with these and with those others —officers and men—who had gone down at Coronel and Falkland and the Skagerrak and numerous other engagements. Ultimately we would be reinspired by the memorable words of the poet, Gorch Fock, who fell at Skagerrak: "Seafaring is a necessity!"

VI

Beginnings of the Postwar Navy

THE RESTRICTIONS imposed by the Treaty of Versailles in June 1919 were so severe that it took a special plea by the Chief of the Admiralty to get the Navy to view them as a challenge rather than a death sentence.

First of all, there was the requirement of the original armistice terms that the Navy's strength was to be reduced to 100,000 total personnel, of whom no more than 1,500 could be officers. Next, in order to prevent a rapid training program and build up of reserves, naval personnel had to sign on for a 12-year enlistment. A complete reorganization was a necessity.

The reduction in strength of the officers corps went off without a hitch, the Bureau of Personnel's selections being accepted without protest. The cutback in enlisted strength permitted the exclusion of undesirables, and the petty officer and seaman ratings were filled largely from the men in the naval brigades and in the so-called "Iron Flotilla" of Commander Lass who had proved so reliable in the critical days of the revolution.

Among things immediately needing to be done was a new program for the training and education of enlisted men, and the reestablishment of strict discipline. A start in the latter field was made by new directives in connection with the court-martial authority of the Navy. Also of first importance was provision for pay and promotion in the new Navy, as well as special systematic education to fit the 12-year enlistees for civilian life and employment on expiration of their enlistments.

In reorganization plans, every effort was made to profit by the experiences of the past, especially as regards qualifications for the various officers corps and their relations with each other and the Navy in general.

One of the inequalities needing adjustment was the position of the Navy's engineer officers. In the early transition days from sail to steam, all that had been needed was a regular crew member with a little extra mechanical aptitude who could learn to run the fairly simple auxiliary steam engines. But with the increased technical development in ship's machinery, the highest type of engineer was needed. This changed situation had never been recognized, however, and engineer officers had not been accorded position and prestige comparable to line officers. Long standing differences in entrance qualifications, rank insignia, uniform, and type of training had not brought closer concord between the engineers and the line, despite initial attempts by Secretary von Tirpitz.

The fusion of the two branches which had been tried, with not too much success, by other navies, did not commend itself to us. For instance, we could not give the chief engineer aboard ship the same disciplinary power enjoyed of necessity by the ship's executive officer, who was in charge of all the departments aboard ship. However, we arrived at a satisfactory solution whereby an engineer officer in charge of naval engineering activities ashore could get disciplinary power over his unit. Some of them could command technical naval schools. Or he could become Inspector of Marine Engines or the Senior Engineer Officer in the Admiralty. These two positions were rear admiral billets. The conditions under which engineer officers were permitted to marry were made the same as for line officers.

This forward step in the Navy's organization owed much to the ability of the Navy's Senior Chief Engineer, Rear Admiral Lemke, of whom I had formed a high opinion when he was staff engineer for the Commander of the Scouting Forces when I was senior staff officer there, and who later had become Fleet Engineer. As the first rear admiral in the Engineer Corps he worked closely with me on the staff until his untimely death in 1925, and he shared with me the satisfaction of seeing a close teamwork develop between the Navy's engineers and line officers.

The Medical Corps was much less of a problem in the reorganization, as by the very nature of the profession it had fewer complicating conflicts with the line. Moreover, the medical officers had always enjoyed a superior place in the Navy's esteem, so that, except for modifications in uniform, very few basic changes had to be made. Heading the new Navy's Medical Corps was the universally respected Navy Surgeon Admiral Professor Uthemann.

The status of the Paymaster Corps, however, required much consideration. Although paymasters had to be high school graduates in order to enter training, and achieved officer status when graduated, they were considered noncombatants on board ship, even though they had regular battle stations in action and were exposed to the same dangers as any seaman. Furthermore, the highest rank they could hope to attain on the average was that of naval staff paymaster—equivalent to a lieutenant commander in rank—although a very few might rise to become chief staff paymasters, equivalent in rank to commander.

Their integrity, devotion to duty, and high standard of work had long been recognized, however, and in the reorganization of 1919 and 1920 we endeavored to create a full recognized Supply Corps, such as had been advocated by the Fleet Command during the war. However, the reorganization change would require the approval of the legislative and executive branches of the government, and the Navy's proposals were blocked during ten years—principally by the Finance Minister.

Thus, for the time being, the only improvement that could be made was a change in entrance and training requirements, and the Supply Corps did not attain full status until years later, when, as Chief of the Supreme Naval Command, I had the pleasure of seeing this long-hoped for development materialize.

Our Naval Ordnance Corps, with its highly trained technicians, was severely crippled by the restrictions of the Versailles Peace Treaty. In order to remain within the total officer allowance of 1,500 for the entire Navy, it was necessary to discharge many highly trained ordnance officers, who could then only be employed in the status of civilian employees—disability that was to continue until the Navy was permitted to expand again. Only then could the Ordnance Corps build up a unified and efficient force of trained officers in the respective fields of gunnery, torpedoes, and mines. Even then there were difficulties, partly owing to the differences in qualifications and training of the older members and those entering under the new conditions. These older ones, nevertheless, had to be retained on duty, thus seriously slowing the flow of promotions of the younger officers in the Corps. Another problem was that the new ordnance officers, entering the Navy with the same educational background as the line and engineer officer candidates, often felt that duty as line officers would give them greater satisfaction than just the technical maintenance and operation of ordnance equipment. During World War II, when there was a great need for officers for the submarines and smaller craft, quite a few ordnance officers transferred over to the line, but this was not possible in normal times.

The morale of the officer ranks of the Navy was badly hurt for a time by the "extradition list" of the Allies—a list of individuals drawn up for proposed extradition and trial as alleged war criminals. On this list, in addition to the Kaiser himself, were such high-ranking naval officers as Admiral von Schröder and Admiral von Hipper, as well as numerous U-boat commanders. I myself was on the list as Admiral von Hipper's former Chief of Staff.

The German people's reaction, however, was immediate and determined. Preparations were made to provide safe sanctuary for the "war criminals," both at home and abroad. When I once asked Admiral von Schröder, the "Lion of Flanders," what he intended to do if they tried to haul him away, his answer was the gruff statement, "I'll put up a fight right here on the front steps!"

Ultimately the Allies gave up the ill-advised measure, but the long period of uncertainty had a considerable adverse effect on the Navy.

One comradely bond that carried over from the Imperial Navy was the Naval Officers' Relief Society, founded in December of 1918 by the able and energetic Captain Baron von Büllow (retired). This organization had as its purpose the aiding of demobilized naval officers in obtaining employment, assistance to the families of officers in need, and, in general, representing the interests of naval officers everywhere. Not only was its philanthropic assistance invaluable, but it helped to maintain a bond between the demobilized and retired officers themselves as well as between them and the active officers in the fleet, practically all of whom came to be members of the Society.

By the beginning of 1920 we could begin to look forward hopefully to a revival of at least a modest Navy. On 31 January of the new year, Admiral von Reuter and his crews who had scuttled their ships at Scapa Flow returned from their subsequent imprisonment in England and were welcomed at Wilhelmshaven by Admiral von Trotha, who greeted them with a most touching speech. Conditions at the two naval district commands of Kiel and Wilhelmshaven were greatly improved, with Vice Admiral Michelsen in command at Wilhelmshaven and Rear Admiral von Levetzow at Kiel, the latter having relieved Rear Admiral Meurer, who had made the blunder of issuing a questionable order of the day at New Year's. Training inspection, torpedo and mine inspection, and gunnery inspection were being efficiently reestablished, with resulting better cooperation between the shore establishment and the operating forces. The few torpedo boats and minesweepers still in commission were being operated under the capable command of the Commanders of the Baltic and North Sea Naval Forces.

Just when things were going smoothly, however, we received an unexpected and serious setback as a result of the Kapp *putsch*. In March 1920 Wolfgang Kapp, a former Reichstag member from the Conservative party who had organized a small reactionary group containing, among others, General Ludendorff and other Army officers, suddenly seized control of the government offices and proclaimed himself "Chancellor of the Reich."

At the time—morning of 13 March—General von Lüttwitz had command of the Army troops in Berlin which were responsible for the security of the government. The first we in the Navy knew of the Kapp *putsch* was when General von Lüttwitz summoned Vice Admiral von Trotha and informed him that the government had fled to South Germany, but that President Ebert had remained in Berlin and would immediately form a new government. General von Lüttwitz stated that he himself had assumed the duties of acting Minister of Defense.

Vice Admiral von Trotha had no reason to doubt these facts,

and a conference of his co-workers called by him unanimously concurred in the decision to place themselves at the disposal of the new government to maintain law and order. The commanding officers of the Navy's main stations were then informed of Admiral von Trotha's decision. The possibility that the Army's leading general had given false information to the Chief of the Admiralty never entered anyone's mind.

Neither had anyone any idea that the volunteer naval brigades, which had performed such notable service in restoring law and order during the revolution, were in any way involved in the Kapp movement. In their security activities they had been placed under the Army command of General von Lüttwitz, and at the beginning of March they were in Döberitz, near Berlin. With stability in the country apparently assured, they were to be disbanded and some of them were to take service again in the Navy. As part of the disbanding ceremonies they were given a final honorary review in Döberitz, which was attended by Admiral von Trotha, Defense Minister Noske and me. The accompanying religious service was very impressive; and at its conclusion the von Loewenfeld Brigade was transferred to Breslau, the Ehrhardt Brigade remaining for its last days of service at Döberitz.

There had been rumors that the Ehrhardt Brigade was disgruntled at the idea of disbandment, but Admiral von Trotha gave no credit to the rumors. His confidence was reaffirmed by a personal conference with General von Oldershausen, the Chief of Staff to General von Lüttwitz. In fact I had so little idea that anything untoward was brewing that I left Berlin for a short visit to Hamburg to settle some personal affairs. An emergency telephone call brought me hurrying back to Berlin, where I arrived on the morning of 13 March, to learn not only that Kapp had seized the government offices, but also that the Ehrhardt Brigade had marched into the city the night before as the initial step in the *putsch*.

Now, Admiral von Trotha and the greater part of the Navy had no thought of anything but complete loyalty to the government and, especially, to Defense Minister Noske, to whom the Navy and all the armed services owed so much. But the orders to the naval stations were considered by leftist circles in Kiel and Wilhelmshaven as countenancing active participation in the *putsch,* the real state of affairs not being known for some time. Disorders completely against Navy policy broke out in the stations. Bullets flew, and there was bloodshed. Captain Mönch was shot to death as he entered the naval arsenal he commanded. Relations between the Navy and the civilian population deteriorated. In Kiel and Wilhelmshaven officers were removed, and sometimes arrested.

In Berlin, the Department of Troops, under Major General von Seeckt, ceased functioning because the proposal of Major General Reinhardt, Chief of the Army High Command, to use troops to prevent the Ehrhardt Brigade from marching on the city, had been rejected in a Cabinet meeting.

Still, the Kapp *putsch* died for lack of any support—especially lack of money. Commander Ehrhardt had been designated by the leaders of the *putsch* to seize the national funds in the government bank, but the bank officials had all denied any knowledge of where the keys to the vaults could be found. The doors, of course, could have been forced, but Commander Ehrhardt said bluntly that while he was willing to fight, he would not under any circumstances be a bank robber!

The Kapp *putsch* died of inanition in four days, Vice Admiral von Trotha and I were present when the leaders of the *putsch*—General District Director Kapp, General von Lüttwitz, General Ludendorff, Colonel Bauer, and Captain Pabst—dissolved the movement and returned the seized buildings to the government.

It was a mystery to me how these men could have had such poor judgment or understanding as to take this criminal step at a moment when Germany's situation was already so difficult.

Minister of Defense Noske, accused of having built up forces not unequivocally devoted to the state, had to resign. Vice Admiral von Trotha had to answer for his credulity in believing General von Lüttwitz's information, and was likewise forced to resign. Although he finally succeeded in establishing his innocence of any participation in the *putsch,* his return to the Naval High Command was manifestly impossible. Thus the Navy lost the distinguished leader who had done most to inculcate in the new Navy an unswerving loyalty to the new state and its constitutional government.

Dr. Gessler, a member of the German Democratic Party and a skillful politician, succeeded Noske as Minister of Defense, while Rear Admiral Michaelis, Chief of the Admiralty, succeeded Vice Admiral von Trotha.

But the heavy blow dealt the Navy by the Kapp *putsch* had lasting effects. The morale of the officers falsely accused of resisting the constitution declined notably. Recently healed wounds were reopened, and so shaken were the Navy's very foundations that hostile circles could openly discuss abolishing the Service entirely. Chiefly because of the indefatigable efforts of Rear Admiral Michaelis and Dr. Gessler, conditions in the shore establishments began gradually to return to normal. The dismissed officers at Kiel and Wilhelmshaven were reinstated and the work of reorganizing the Navy was gradually resumed. One of the most important focuses for rebuilding the fleet was the First Torpedo Boat Squadron, at Kiel, whose commanding officer, Commander Albrecht, had judiciously taken the squadron to Swinemünde during the crisis of the *putsch* and thus prevented its personnel from being in any way involved.

Unfortunately, a great many officers left the Navy because of the unfair treatment they had been given by the public, and their own feeling that the Navy would never regain its former position in the defense picture. The loss of skilled officers was a serious blow, but the whole tragic event brought home to the Navy the fact that, in the armed forces, there must always be absolute loyalty to the State which they serve. Both in the 1918 disorders and in the Kapp *putsch,* parts of the Navy had allowed themselves to be persuaded by outside influences to participate in political action. These two occurrences impressed all responsible naval officers that for them, particularly in times of political upheaval, there was only one straight path—the path of complete abstinence from every type of party politics, and of unconditional loyalty to the State and to the government chosen by its people.

Since I had been one of Vice Admiral Trotha's advisers, I, too, was suspected of unconstitutional behavior. I accordingly turned over my position as Chief of the Central Bureau to my senior assistant, Commander Hansen, pending the action of the Board of Investigation. But the investigation board, whose chairman was Government Commissioner Stock, a Social Democrat, completely exonerated me.

Although I was now free to resume my former office, the strain of the dramatic period made me glad to accept another billet offered to me that spring—the task of assisting in the preparation of the official history of the Navy in the war. The editor in chief of this project was Vice Admiral von Mantey (retired), the Director of the Naval Archives in Berlin, which was publishing the history under the title of *The Naval War, 1914-1918.* Admiral von Mantey had been head of the Naval History Division of the Archives since 1916.

I was to write the two volumes dealing with cruiser warfare in foreign waters. These volumes appeared in 1922 and 1923. Volume 1 concerned itself with over-all cruiser activities, climaxed by the victory of Vice Admiral Count von Spee's cruiser squadron over the British Admiral Sir Christopher Craddock at the Battle of Coronel, off the Chilean coast, and the subsequent destruction of von Spee and his ships by the overwhelming battle cruiser and cruiser force of Admiral Sir Doveton Sturdee, off the Falkland Islands, the following month. Volume II dealt with the widespread commerce-destroying raids of the light cruisers *Emden, Königsberg,* and *Karlsruhe.*

This work I particularly enjoyed. For ten years I had been under almost constant pressure, brought on by the preparations for the war, the war itself, the revolution, and the attempt to reorganize the Navy. Now I could enjoy a quiet and orderly existence, with responsibility only to the Director of the Archives. I had always enjoyed scholarly work. Most of my sea duty had been on cruisers, and I was familiar with all phases of their operations. Lastly, I had been closely acquainted with many of the captains and other officers of the cruisers, going all the way back to my shipboard friendship with Count von Spee on the *Deutschland* in 1897 and 1898. I embarked on the work with a feeling of obligation to these fallen friends, as well as to the Navy.

Relieved from the bustle of straight military duty, I could also devote some thought to my own future. In November 1919, when I had been promoted to captain, I had had twenty-five years of service in the Navy. The future of the Navy was most uncertain, and billets for officers of my rank and service were few. I had every prospect, therefore, of being retired within the not too distant future.

But retiring to a life of inactivity and merely existing on a naval pension had no appeal for me. Consequently, from the summer of 1920 to that of 1922, I took advantage of my spare hours to attend courses at the University of Berlin. There I studied political science under Professor Triepel, administrative law under Professor Bornhack, and political economy and the history of economics under Professor Jastrow. I also took a course in bookkeeping. With a year's credit for my Naval Academy education, I hoped to be able by 1922 to pass the examinations for Doctor of Political Science.

However, my duty in the Naval Archives as well as my studies at the University ended sooner than expected. On 1 July 1922 I was designated Inspector of Naval Education, with the rank of rear admiral. This promotion and assignment predicated a continuing future in the field of the higher naval command.

From my new headquarters at Kiel, as Inspector of Naval Education I would have supervision over all the naval schools: the one at Flensburg-Mürwik for line officers; the one at Kiel-Wik for engineer officers; the training ship *Berlin,* one of our oldest World War light cruisers; and the old four-masted schooner *Niobe* which served as sailing training ship. This ship, which had for a time, been under the command of the famous raider, Lieutenant Commander Count Luckner of World War fame, was now commanded by Commander Krafft.

At this time the future training program for our naval officers had not been definitely established. Officer candidates at first had been inducted along with the seamen volunteers and had received little or no special training. In 1921 the officer candidates had been assigned as regular seamen aboard the old battleship *Hannover,* and, when the ship had gone into the navy yard that winter, had been assigned to the regular working force, which benefited neither their training nor their education. But in February 1922 Lieutenant Commander Warzecha had taken over the prospective officer candidates to prepare them for the officer entrance examinations. As a first step they were to be given shipboard training on the training cruiser *Berlin,* which went into active commission on 2 July 1922.

Basic directives and instructions for officer education had to be made up from scratch. With the help of many suggestions from Lieutenant Commander Warzecha, I could set up initial training regulations for officer candidates, the final directives in finished form being prepared by my excellent staff under Commander Claussen. The commanding officer of the *Berlin,* Captain von Loewenfeld, naturally looked askance at direct contact between his superior, the Inspector, and the ship's training officer, but took a realistic view of the problem and gave his fullest cooperation.

As a basis for our directives, the following points were recognized: (1) Only through firm but friendly discipline can a crew be expected to achieve a high standard of efficiency; (2) The prerequisite for such a state of discipline is a well disciplined corps of officers and petty officers; and (3) A modest but definite feeling of pride and self-respect, commensurate with the officer's rank, must be instilled into the officer corps if it is to fulfill its duties. These fundamentals, first phrased at Kiel, were further developed later at the Baltic Naval District, when I commanded there, and throughout the service when I ultimately became Chief of the Supreme Naval Command. Everywhere, through full cooperation of every one, these fundamentals eventually built up a distinctive *esprit de corps* in officers and petty officers alike, and had much to do with the devotion to service exhibited by them during the critical years following 1933, notably in World War II.

I made it a point to follow in detail the progress of the first postwar class of officer candidates. For instance, not a single officer candidate was dismissed by the Office of Education Inspection until I had personally investigated the entire case. It seemed to me especially important to develop sound character in these young men as a most vital part of their training from the very beginning.

It was a real pleasure to renew contact with youth and its enthusiasm again after a decade devoted almost entirely to staff work. Apart from my few months as commanding officer of the cruiser *Köln,* my official duties had kept me almost exclusively to the company of officers of my age or older. Differently from the happy, companionable atmosphere in a ship's wardroom, which I had enjoyed as a sub-lieutenant as a ship's watch and navigation officer, the wardroom of an admiral's staff, even when it contains as splendid a group of men as did the staff of the Commander of the Battle Cruiser Forces, has always an air of formality and sober responsibility. Thus I immediately felt a serious disadvantage brought on by a certain reserve, a habit of uncommunicativeness, resulting from my years of association, in Berlin, with the variegated strata of both military and political personnel, where even the most casual remarks had to be constantly watched.

To avoid appearing unapproachable, I took every opportunity, while conducting inspections or visiting shore activities or ships, to meet not only the commanding officers and executive officers, but the younger officers right down to the most junior ones present. At the naval schools I was particularly observant of the state of morale, and I was especially pleased whenever my inspections could be concluded with a social evening of fellowship and fun.

Needless to say I had a warm interest in the ensigns of the Naval School at Mürwik, most of whom came from the Ehrhardt and Loewenfeld Naval Brigades, which had now been dissolved. To prepare them for future naval careers in normal times they needed a sound basic education. With special personal interest Captain Werner Tillessen, Superintendent of the Naval School, saw to it that such education was provided.

Shortly after I became Inspector of Naval Education, the Chief of the Admiralty, Admiral Behncke, had inspected the fleet at Kiel along with President Ebert. Now he informed me that he wished me to show him not only the Naval School but also the Torpedo School, which was in the same locality. As the Torpedo School did not come under my command, I knew nothing of the conditions there and was a little hesitant, especially since some phases of the Navy's reorganization were still in the initial stages. However, everything went off without a hitch, and I had the pleasure of getter better acquainted with both President Ebert and the Minister of Defense, Dr. Gesseler. The inspection ended with a simple dinner in the old Flensburg House, in the course of which, at the suggestion of the Government Commissioner for Elections in Schleswig, all joined in a rousing chorus of the old Schleswig-Holstein Song.

The curriculum for the Engineer Officers School at Kiel came in for joint study by me and Commander Heinze of the Engineer Officers Corps, who later became engineer officer on my district staff. We both agreed that the curriculum, as originally planned, went beyond what was needed for practical engineering on board ship. However, any changes recommended had to be approved by the Admiralty.

During the winter months a course of lectures for all the officers of the Baltic District was drawn up by the Bureau of Educational Inspection. The lectures were delivered not only by naval officers, but by university professors and specialists of all kinds. Through the history professor, Dr. Rodenberg, an acquaintance of many years, I was able to form close contact with the University of Kiel. This resulted in our obtaining, for our course, valuable lectures on the Hanseatic League from Dr. Brandt, and on political economy from Dr. Schotte, both specialists in their fields. These course lectures received an enthusiastic reception, and, under my successors, were expanded to the advantage of both officers and civilian officials.

For the winter of 1922-1923, I was assigned another task by the Chief of the Admiralty. This task was to develop a two-week course for executive officers assigned as assistants to commanding officers. About ten officers of the Baltic District took this course, and a similar one was set up at the North Sea District by Rear Admiral Pfeiffer, Commander of Light Forces for the North Sea. The Treaty of Versailles had required that the General Staff, the Army War College, and the Naval War College be abolished. However, the professional training of officers for the Navy could not be accomplished without a Naval War College or Staff School. As a subterfuge, short professional courses were set up which, after 1927, were lengthened to a year and a half's duration. The program was not designated as a War College, however, but was merely called "Courses for Assistants to Commanding Officers."

When I received the directive in 1922 to initiate this program, I had short time to prepare it and no printed books to use as texts. My lecture notes and other material I had used in my 1903-1904 tour of duty at the Naval War College were still in my possession, however, as well as my notes on naval warfare and Admiralty staff duty. The course in naval history I assigned to Captain Claussen, and I undertook the other main courses and the two war games.

While I could utilize my own experience in the development of the officer training program, my staff and I were at a loss to organize the specialist technical program intended to fit petty officers and enlisted personnel for careers in civil life after the expiration of their 12-year enlistments. This was a completely new problem for the Navy. Yet much depended upon it.

We had to recognize that, with enlistments limited to twelve years, the naval careers of petty officers and enlisted men would be but a limited chapter in their lifetimes. These men, in a spirit of devotion, would be giving the best years of their youth to the State, and the State therefore had the obligation to see that they were not penalized thereby when they resumed their civilian lives after their enlistments. From the military view, this was essential if we were to obtain the high grade volunteers we needed. From the political and social viewpoint, it was equally necessary that when they were discharged, they would have the training to fill appropriate positions in civilian life and not left to hang around unemployed on the street corners.

The principal difficulties in establishing such a training program lay in the lack of a trained teaching staff for these specialist schools, and in coordinating the program with the men's regular training and duties aboard ship and in naval units ashore. It was not feasible to devote long periods to this specialist training, so time had to be found for it during the regular naval training year. At the shore establishments, this could easily be accomplished by three-month courses, but in the fleet the only solution was to conduct six-week courses during the winter months, when the ships could be tied up to piers adjacent to the schools ashore. It was not the best solution, but it was the only practicable one for a problem of the first importance to the Navy and naval morale.

On the basis of their previous civilian education as well as their choice of future career, the enlisted men went either to a specialist school for administration and management, under the supervision of School Superintendent Haussmann, or else to a trade school for business or engineering. For the latter type of school, to be supervised by Commander Haarmann (retired), we had the necessary technical facilities in Kiel and Wilhelmshaven. In addition to establishing such a trade school at Swinemünde, we had one at Wilhelmshaven under School Superintendent Dr. Blumenhagen, and one at Kiel under School Superintendent Dr. Franke. Both district commands had specialist school lectures, with Principal Dr. Sieglerschmidt at Wilhelmshaven and Principal Hell at Kiel.

All these specialist schools were organized on a 10-class plan, with Classes One through Four constituting the upper class. The men entered the class appropriate to their previous educational background, with such specialist training beginning after three years in the service. Only about 25 per cent of the noncommissioned personnel qualified for the upper classes, and most of these were petty officers or chief petty officers. But in the last year of his 12-year enlistment every man had the opportunity to attend a specialist school for a full year in order to prepare for his final examination. These examinations were conducted by special examining committees, with the Civil Service represented on each such committee.

In addition to general educational subjects, Civics was given especial attention at each school so that the men would be well prepared to meet the responsibilities of civilian life upon leaving the service.

Teachers for these special schools came from all parts of Germany, and from varied educational backgrounds. Consequently the Board of Education Inspection conducted preliminary indoctrination courses to prepare them for their work, with lectures from outstanding authorities, and discussions in which my staff, the lecturers, and I took active part. Without any red tape, with questions answered immediately and vague points promptly cleared up, we were able to make a good start in fitting these specialist schools in to our regular military framework.

At the beginning there was a natural uneasiness lest these specialist schools rob the Navy of time and effort required for service needs as well as weaken discipline. The outcome was just the opposite. Although some time from regular military activities was unquestionably lost, the men's morale was greatly improved, since they could now look forward to demobilization at about the age of thirty without fear of being unable to find their place in the civil community. This feeling of security actually increased the men's interest in their service duties, and so improved standards of discipline.

My connection with the Navy's educational program ended in the fall of 1924, when I was appointed Commander of the Light Forces in the North Sea.

Only recently the German naval forces had been regrouped; the four battleships were under direct command of Vice Admiral Mommsen, Commander in Chief of the Fleet, and the light forces —the light cruisers and torpedo boats—had been divided into two commands: the Light Forces of the North Sea and the Light Forces of the Baltic. The latter were under the command of Rear Admiral Oldekop, who will be remembered for his part in the scuttling of the fleet at Scapa Flow.

My Light Forces of the North Sea included the old light cruiser *Hamburg* as flagship, the obsolete small cruiser *Arcona,* and the Second Torpedo Boat Squadron at Wilhelmshaven.

It was a joy to get back to sea again, as I had always wanted a sea command, and in my new assignment I enjoyed close relations with both Vice Admiral Mommsen and Rear Admiral Oldekop. I joined my new command during the fall maneuvers and took part in the succeeding winter training cruise of the fleet in the North Sea, during which basic exercises and night torpedo boat attacks were primary elements of the program.

But to my regret I enjoyed my new sea command only a few months, as on 7 January 1925—the very day of the christening of the new light cruiser *Emden* in the Wilhelmshaven naval shipyard —I was assigned to command the Naval District of the Baltic, where Vice Admiral Baron von Gagern had unexpectedly resigned his commission. Although this new command carried with it a promotion to vice admiral, I was sadly disappointed at losing my command afloat, and I offered to remain with the Light Forces of the North Sea and have the Baltic District taken over by a younger flag officer.

However, my offer was disapproved and in the middle of January I took up my duty at Kiel—duty which I was subsequently to look back upon as one of the most rewarding of my entire career.

Not that there were no drawbacks to the new job. For one thing, it had been five years since I, as Chief of the Central Bureau of the Admiralty at Berlin, had worked on plans for the organization of the new Navy, and in the interim notable changes had occurred. From 1920 to 1924 the Admiralty had been headed by Admiral Behncke, who had commanded the Third Squadron at the Battle of Skagerrak and been wounded in the SMS *König,* his flagship, at the head of the battle line. Under Admiral Behncke the organization of the new Navy had got well under way. The warships available —battleships, cruisers, and torpedo boats—had been put back into service and the fleet could put to sea again. The Army-Navy Bill of 1921 had adjusted technical disagreements between the two services, and supplementary directives for the Navy had led toward the substitution of volunteer for drafted personnel. German naval ships were making foreign cruises again. Two training cruisers were in service for training of officer and petty officer candidates, and construction of new ships had already begun, of which the new cruiser *Emden* was the starting point.

The succession of Admiral Zenker as Chief of the Admiralty in late 1924 had again brought to the top command in the Navy an officer who had not only made an enviable reputation at sea while commanding the battle cruiser *von der Tann,* but in addition had held important staff positions in the Navy. He could be counted upon to be in agreement with other naval leaders as to the first importance of battle training and the renovation of the entire fleet, just as he had already developed new forms of tactics.

In organization and importance our Naval Districts of the Baltic and the North Sea ranked with the seven corps of the Army. The Baltic District at this time had under it the three coast defenses divisions in Kiel, Swinemünde, and Pillau. Although, under the terms of the Versailles Treaty, Kiel was unfortified, both Swinemünde and Pillau had coastal batteries and were considered fortresses. The personnel of this whole area came under the administration of the Naval Manning and Recruit Depot of the Baltic, which itself was under the District Command. The recruit depot not only recruited and trained the volunteer recruits for the Navy, but also was responsible for them whether they were attached to shore establishments within the District or on shipboard.

The changeover from drafted personnel to volunteers had

brought its own special problems. In compulsory military service, the petty officer is always a man of more experience and longer service than the draftee; he has greater professional interest and knowledge than the draftee, and therefore has the necessary self-confidence to back up his position of leadership. But in a Navy which is all volunteers, all begin on the same level and do the same work, with the petty officer candidates being selected purely on the superior ability and interest they have shown as compared to their fellows. This promotion over others who were of approximately the same age and grade made for difficulties.

The logical solution, of course, was to take the petty officer candidates out of the general duty groups and put them in a separate and special training program. But some compensation would then have to be made for those volunteers considered not fitted for petty officer. This could be done by establishing a number of grades in the enlisted category, with proportionate pay increases by grades, and by giving them duties in line with their added ages and experience. In this way we could avoid the necessity of having to start all those not selected for petty officer training right back at the beginning again with the newest incoming recruits.

We were fortunate in that we had an oversupply of young men volunteering for the Navy. This imposed upon the recruiting officer of the training and recruit depots in Kiel and Wilhelmshaven the responsibility of selecting only the cream of those volunteering. Lieutenant Commander François, the recruiting officer at Kiel, had been for many years a petty officer in charge of personnel in the First Depot for Seamen Ratings in the old Navy, and his tremendous fund of experience was of incalculate value now. During each summer he traveled extensively throughout Germany, visiting each city and village. Here, in cooperation with an officer of the Navy Medical Corps, he looked into both the physical and mental qualifications of the volunteers, and furthermore questioned teachers, ministers, and priests as to the moral character of the recruits.

In reactivating the petty officer school, we decided to make a change in the system of housing as well as in the professional courses. Although we had to use the antiquated barracks of Friedrichsort, we modernized the rooms, furniture, washrooms, and sanitary facilities to make them as different as possible from the regular housing of the ordinary recruit. This my chief of staff, Captain Albrecht, accomplished, with the aid and cooperation of Burmeister, Head of the Kiel Naval Supply Office, and Chief Government Architect Kelm. Although some old-timers reacted violently to the innovations, they were so successful that they were used as a pattern later in the construction of new ships.

In the matter of officer training, the new officer candidates entered under the same conditions and requirements as the other recruits, and performed the same duties in their initial general training. This was not too bad, but during the closing stages of the war many young officers had had little real, systematic training, and could only perform shipboard duties which they had learned mostly from direct experience. On the other hand there were some who had had duty almost entirely at shore establishments or in the Naval Brigades and hence had had no shipboard training at all. What had to be done in each case was to provide that part of an officer's education which he had not been able to obtain. Further, there was the decline in professional interest and *esprit de corps* as a result of the Kapp *putsch* and its aftermath, requiring a definite program to teach them their duties and obligations in the new State.

Teachers and textbooks alone, of course, could not do it. The example of older officers was a primary tool in building the strength of character necessary in an officer who not only would be responsible for the lives of his subordinates but must, in the last analysis, be ready to give his own life for his country. One of the primary ingredients in such strength of character is firm religious conviction. But, under the Weimar constitution, it was not permitted to order service men to attend church services; attendance could only be on a voluntary basis. Here is where personal example is a first requisite. I made it a point to attend church regularly in company with my wife, and my officers assisted me in establishing this as a custom for all hands. No better way could have been found to influence the men to religious observance.

Wartime inflation and the subsequent distortion of social life had brought in certain customs and manners alien to our German way of life. By talks and discussions I tried to reawaken in my officers an appreciation of the simpler life, not only because of the very modest salaries of the new Navy but also because I hoped they would realize certain values for themselves. Even though I said all that I dared say in regard to the officers' private lives, I sometimes had the disappointing feeling that glamour and fashion often outweighed my words.

The custom of officers donning civilian garb the moment they came off duty was something else of which I disapproved. While I am not one of those who think that a service man should be excessively "blue and gold," I had heard more than a few petty officers complain that they were the only ones above the enlisted grades who would be in uniform and responsible therefore for the discipline of the men in the city's streets. In this, as in the matter of churchgoing, I tried to set a personal example by wearing my uniform to the maximum extent possible.

It would have been a sad state of affairs if my efforts along these lines did not come in for some humorous sallies now and then. Too much seriousness is not healthy in the armed forces, and humor has a distinct place. One of these places is the "gentlemen's evening," which had been a regular custom at Kiel before the war. The younger officers gifted with humor would stage theatricals and satires which poked fun at the naval establishment and its customs and habits, and even at the high-ranking persons in the Navy hierarchy. The Kaiser used to enjoy attending these evenings, at which even the highest officers, such as Admiral von Tirpitz, were not safe from witty attacks.

I now endeavored to revive these social evenings, even though we did not have nearly the scope of talent we had had in the larger Navy of those days. But with my blessing some of the officers at Kiel revived the custom with an annual performance, which found an enthusiastic audience of all officers and officials and invited guests who could manage to attend. Needless to say, I was a prime target for the amateur playwrights. For example, in connection with my known attitude toward wearing civilian clothing, it was maintained that I *did not even own* any civilian clothes. At another time I was depicted on a poster as just starting out on a trip to Guatemala, my only clothing a tropical helmet and a pair of shorts, while in my hand I carried a small suitcase with an admiral's flag painted on it. This my chief of staff, whose duty it was to exercise some sort of censorship in order to prevent things getting completely out of hand, objected to as unorthodox for an admiral, so he required the grumbling artists to paint a white jacket on my naked torso. However, he had not counted on the artists also painting a big red "CENSORED" sign on the poster after he had left. Naturally, when I saw it, I wanted to know the story behind it—which was just what the artists wanted. I was very much amused and pointed out to my chief of staff that censorship does not always attain its objective.

Another activity which I was glad to see revived was the Navy Wives Society. This organization had been formed for the primary purpose of assisting the families of all ranks of the Navy in time of need. Inflation and the curtailment of the Navy had reduced its activities in the postwar years, but with the help of my wife and the invaluable cooperation of Senior Chaplains Dehmel and Kraüter, the Lutheran and Catholic chaplains in the district, I was able to restore it to much of its former status. In cases not entitled to government aid, the society provided practical help in times of illness, and clothes, woolen blankets, and ultra-violet machines were furnished. Layettes were provided for babies, and financial aid given when treatment at sanitariums or rest homes was necessary. The wives of the officers supervised play activities and gymnastic classes for the children, and arranged occasional general "get-togethers," such as Christmas parties, for the children and their parents. The Society did invaluable service in creating a spirit of teamwork throughout the Navy.

Another activity which I took great interest in was the promotion of better relations and understanding between the Navy and the civilian community. Although the effects of the Kapp *putsch* had largely died away, there was still some little tension between the service and the public in Kiel. When I had been Inspector of Education I had tried to promote better relations by arranging numerous lectures by University professors before naval audiences, and an organization—the Skagerrak Club—had been founded for the primary purpose of providing a common meeting place between the naval officers and the civilian circles of Kiel. The sport of sailing also afforded another opportunity for good fellowship along the same lines.

This comradeship among sailing enthusiasts had been splendidly promoted in the days of the old Imperial Yacht Club, and a revival of this activity made a delightful meeting ground between officers of both old and new Navy and other segments of the population. Unhappily, in 1927, upon the occasion of the dedication of a new Yacht Club building, an unfortunate incident occurred. A great many guests had been invited, among them Vice Admiral Mommsen, the Commander in Chief of the Fleet, as well as myself, and retired Admiral of the Fleet Prince Heinrich, who was an inveterate sailor and who resided at his estate of Hemmelmark, not far from Eckernförde. Without anyone having advance notice of his intentions, Prince Heinrich suddenly proposed a toast to Kaiser Wilhelm II, who had founded the Yacht Club and was still carried on its rolls as Commodore. This toast, of course, would have achieved no more than a moment's notice if one of the Kiel newspapers had not taken it upon itself to make a sensation out of it.

Up to this time there had been no objection to naval officers being members of the Imperial Yacht Club, but now the reaction was such that Minister of Defense Groener, who had just recently assumed that post, expressed himself as being strongly opposed to naval officer membership in the old club.

Sailing, however, is a sport particularly appropriate for naval officers, as well as being a professionally valuable accomplishment. Hence we revived the old Naval Regatta Club, which had actually been the predecessor of the Imperial Yacht Club, and staged the official reopening on August 10, 1928.

Most naval officers immediately became affiliated with the Naval Regatta Club, with no objections from anyone. Owing to financial conditions, the Imperial Yacht Club possessed only a few sailboats and lacked the funds to acquire more. As the Naval Regatta Club had a legitimate training function, the Minister of Defense had allocated money to it from the Defense budget to promote sailing in the Navy. Through this means German naval sailing enthusiasts were able to compete again, both at home and abroad.

In the eyes of the Navy, one of the most important benefits of sailing competition was the contacts made with officers and civilians from other nations at the regattas. This was particularly true of the international competitions staged annually in Kiel by the

Naval Regatta Club. On these occasions the German Navy acted as the official host and the officers of the other participating nations were billeted together with the German naval contestants. As the interest in sailing, and the participation of foreign yachtsmen, increased from year to year, it was a pleasure to see the way the friendly relations between the young, suntanned yachtsmen made for better understanding between the respective navies themselves.

Meantime, in the previous October I had taken leave of absence for a couple of months to visit my married daughter and son-in-law in Guatemala. And during my absence, another unfortunate incident occurred in which Prince Heinrich of Prussia again had a leading part.

This retired Admiral of the Fleet, always keenly interested in the Navy, paid a visit to the training cruiser *Berlin* when it anchored in Eckernförde Bay on one of its foreign training cruises. In a short talk to the petty officer and officer candidates aboard, Prince Heinrich pointed out the obligations they had as representatives of the German nation abroad. No one could take exception to what was said, but the fact that a member of the former Imperial family had visited a vessel of the new German republic was made a controversial item in the public press. In fact, one of the Kiel newspapers made it the occasion of a violent personal attack on me, as commanding officer of the district, even though I was away in Guatemala and did not learn of the incident until after it had occurred.

The unfairness of the newspaper's attitude impelled me to take up the matter with the chief burgomaster of Altona, Social Democrat Brauer. He was kind enough to defend me personally, yet the whole affair was to be revived in new attacks later when I became Chief of the Admiralty.

Better teamwork between the Navy and the Army was another of my particular predilections. The First Army had its headquarters at Königsberg, near our naval base of Pillau. We kept a naval liaison officer on constant duty there, and whenever I visited Pillau I made it a point to call upon the Commanding General at Königsberg. We also participated in joint Army-Navy war games in that area. Part of the close relationship between the two services of course grew out of the fact that East Prussia, including its capital,

Königsberg, was separated from the rest of Germany by the Polish Corridor, which the victorious Allies had established after World War I. As a result, the Army in East Prussia, as well as the civilian inhabitants, too, felt that they were living on an island, and that their only connection with the homeland was through the Navy.

In connection with Pillau, an unusual thing occurred. I was accustomed to make numerous inspections of all the activities and bases under my command, and generally tried to stage these inspections so that they came at the end of some definite period of training or exercises. But at Pillau I happened to overhear an officer remark that the only time they ever saw a high ranking officer, such as an Inspector, was in the more pleasant months, and that such officers never visited Pillau during the notoriously bad East Prussian winters. Thereafter I made it a practice to inspect Pillau during the very height of the winter; in fact I had my aide keep in contact with the commander of the Pillau base, and whenever we had word that the winter was at its worst, that was the time we set out for Pillau. I continued this practice later even when I headed the Admiralty.

I also visited the Free City of Danzig, although "unofficially" because of the tense Polish situation. However, I did arrange for the first official visit of German naval vessels to Danzig since the war. The visit was made in July 1927 by the Battleship *Hessen,* escorted by a torpedo boat. The success of the visit was attested by the declaration made by President Sahm of the Senate of the Free City: "Words cannot express the great joy which we in Danzig felt when the news came that the German Government had decided to send a fleet to visit the Free City of Danzig. We owe our most heartfelt thanks to the German Government for this deed."

The anniversary of the Battle of Skagerrak had become one of our most treasured memorials. On 31 May 1926, the tenth anniversary, I received a most unexpected surprise. I had taken the customary anniversary review of the troops at the Kiel barracks and had intended to lunch at the Officers' Club. But while I was sharing a preliminary glass of wine with the troop commander, my aide kept hinting that I was needed at home. I rather resented his interruption, but my chief of staff then came up and said that I should go home immediately, even though he evaded my questions why. Grumblingly, I complied, only to find, at home, an assembly of distinguished professors from Christian Albrecht University in Kiel, headed by Dr. Kossel, the dean of the faculty of philosophy of the University. In a solemn ceremony, Dr. Kossel conferred on me, in the name of the University, the honorary degree of doctor of philosophy for the "scholarly merit" of the two-volume work on the Cruiser War, which I had written in Berlin in 1920-1923.

It was an honor I have always appreciated. I felt that public recognition of the battle record of our cruisers and their crews was proof that the spirit of sacrifice was beginning to be again a thing to be treasured in the Fatherland.

Skagerrak Day seemed destined to have special rewards for me. In May 1927 Field Marshal von Hindenburg visited Kiel to participate personally as President of the German State. He had already visited Wilhelmshaven on 8 May, and now he honored Kiel and the Baltic Sea District. In the course of his visit, he called on my wife and me. He was escorted into the garden between rows of Navy children, and my four-year-old son presented him with a bouquet of flowers. It was the first personal conversation I had had with him since the time of my brief duty on the Armistice Commission at Spa during the distressing days of October 1918. This conversation only confirmed my high opinion of him as a patriot and a leader—an appreciation which was to grow even more when I took up my new duties in Berlin the following year, and which was to continue until his death in 1934. Marshal von Hindenburg never failed to give me his support and backing. The Navy and all other armed forces, as well as the nation as a whole, owe him an immeasurable debt.

The year 1928 was a year of developments of particular interest for the German Navy. On 20 January Dr. Gesler resigned as Minister Defense, and was succeeded by Lieutenant General Wilhelm Groener (retired), the former Minister of Transport.

Dr. Gessler had come to office as successor to Gustav Noske when Noske was forced to resign because of the Kapp *putsch.* During the difficult days of the Navy's reorganization, Dr. Gessler had been a tower of strength, and his able conduct of defense affairs had proved the necessity of having a civilian, able to work closely with the elected government, as head of the armed forces.

In accepting his resignation, President von Hindenburg wrote the following encomium:

"Almost eight years ago, in a period of internal confusion and external oppression, you took over the difficult job of Minister of Defense. Since then you have carried it on with devoted and selfless labor. You have been guided only by your desire to build the armed forces that remained to us into a loyal and efficient instrument of State—an instrument that stands above the strife of political parties."

Though Dr. Gessler's resignation had supposedly been brought about by ill health, it was actually the result of the unfortunate "Lohmann affair." Captain Lohmann, who headed the Naval Transport Section in the Admiralty, had manipulated certain special accounts in war surpluses and funds for the Ruhr district to apply them to various rearmament measures which had been forbidden under the Treaty of Versailles. There was no accusation of personal dishonesty, and Captain Lohmann's accounts were in perfect order. But many of his undertakings were contrary to the basic principles for handling the budget. He had used Navy funds to help the Phoebus Film Company make moving pictures intended to interest the German public in defense and seapower and to build up German prestige abroad. Through the disclosures of a discharged director of the film company the press made public his activities. The Reichstag investigated Lohmann's operations, and Gessler, though innocent, felt that he had been indirectly responsible, as Minister of Defense. He tendered his resignation, which came as a keen blow to me as I had always respected and admired Dr. Gessler; in fact I remained on close terms with him right up to and through the Second World War.

The new Minister of Defense, General Groener, personally attended the launching of the new cruiser *Köln,* at the Wilhelmshaven naval shipyard on 23 May 1928. Also present were various ministers and departmental secretaries, as well as General Heye, Chief of the Army Supreme Command, and, in particular, Stoker Adolf Neumann, the only surviving member of the first *Köln's* crew when she went down in battle on 28 August 1914. The christening address was given by Dr. Konrad Adenauer, the Chief Burgomaster of Cologne. As I had temporarily commanded the second cruiser named *Köln* in the closing days of the First World War, I always followed the new ship with special interest.

With its first new ships since the end of World War I, the German Navy now resumed its practice of visiting foreign countries. Our minesweeping craft were based on foreign ports in their work of sweeping up German-laid minefields as required by the Treaty of Versailles. We began sending torpedo boats, cruisers, and larger ships as they went into commission. It was understandable that one of our first flag-showing visits was to Sweden. This country —and particularly its Navy—had been understandingly sympathetic during the war, and we were correspondingly grateful.

We were pleased at the seamanlike appearance of our ships and the splendid behavior of their crews, and we were warmly welcomed in the countries of northern Europe. Our officers and men renewed long lost contacts and corrected the distorted picture that the enemy's war propaganda had painted of us Germans.

In turn, our ports, especially Kiel, began to receive visits from foreign naval vessels. While I was commander of the Baltic district we had as naval guests Swedes, Argentines, English, Americans, Chileans, Dutch, Spaniards, and Latvians. Our state and city dignitaries participated officially in the welcoming ceremonies, and the civilian populace turned out in great numbers. We tried not only to extend official hospitality, but also to arrange personal recreation for the petty officers and crews of the visiting ships. Games, excursions, sightseeing trips, and other entertainment were carefully planned and conducted by our district sports officer, Lieutenant Commander Hauck, and German crews and shorebased units took care of the details.

Visits of foreign naval vessels were announced well in advance. But on one occasion Alfonso XIII, King of Spain, took us by surprise. The King, on board the newest Spanish cruiser, the *Principe Alfonso,* was on a regular official cruise to Sweden. Finding that his visit took less time than expected, he suddenly decided to use the extra time in a visit to us at Kiel. The first we knew of it was a radiogram announcing his arrival on the morning of 12 September 1928.

I immediately rushed down to the waterfront to receive him. No official program had been prepared. Not even security measures had been taken. I tried to take him for a drive through the outskirts of Kiel, but he insisted on driving right through the heart of the city. We visited the Petty Officer School, in Friedrichsort, where there had been no time to make preparations for an inspection by the head of a foreign state. However, the School Commandant, Commander Witthoeft-Emden,[1] made an admirable presentation, and the regular routine of the school seemed to impress the royal visitor. After a late breakfast on board the flagship *Schleswig-Holstein* as guest of Vice Admiral Oldekop, Commander in Chief of the Fleet, King Alfonso continued on his cruise.

Admiral Oldekop and I were particularly glad to welcome the head of the Spanish nation as a guest of the German Navy. Visits of our naval vessels to Spanish ports had always found hearty welcomes, and the relations between the Spanish and German Navies had been close and cordial at all times.

With the passing of the summer I found developments in the Navy again affecting me personally. For Admiral Zenker, Chief of the Admiralty, innocently accused of being involved in the Lohmann affair, had felt called upon to turn in his resignation. As the next senior admiral I would presumably have been in line of succession. But the campaign which the Kiel newspapers had conducted against me years before now cropped up to plague me again. Apparently even Admiral Zenker, who was personally well disposed toward me, thought I might be tainted with politics. He recommended to Minister of Defense Groener that either Vice Admiral Bauer or Vice Admiral Oldekop be named as his successor.

However, the Defense Minister apparently had formed his own opinions, partly from inspections of the commands of the officers involved, and partly from information apparently given him by senior officers of the Army High Command. At any rate he summoned me to meet him at Bad Kreuth early in September 1928, and there questioned me closely as to my attitude toward political and naval-military matters. The questioning extended through two whole days, during which I was required to put in writing my

[1] Officers attached to the famous cruiser raider *Emden* in the First World War were given the unique honor of being allowed to add the word "Emden" to their names.

concepts of how I would conduct the Admiralty if I were appointed as its head. I placed foremost the requirement of firm, unrestricted command of naval operations by the chief in command. I specified that, if appointed, I should have the right to discuss personally with the Minister of Defense all naval matters that I thought required my attention, even if these discussions were not personally originated by me. I specified further that the Navy was to be completely independent of the Army High Command in everything—matters of command, discipline, maintenance, and, particularly, personnel.

My program received full approval, as I learned when the newspapers on 15 September carried not only the news of Admiral Zenker's resignation, but also of my own designation as his successor as Chief of the Admiralty.

Gratifying as it was to have reached the final goal of any naval officer, I felt almost a regret at leaving the Baltic Naval District. For four happy, challenging years I had been privileged to contribute to the internal consolidation of the Navy. I had had the fullest cooperation of the shore commands, the inspection departments, and the units attached to the fleet command and naval forces everywhere. The various commandants, the corps of officers, the heads of the civilian sections—they had been invaluable teammates, not only through their many helpful suggestions but the cheerfulness with which they had carried out every directive. The new Navy was acquiring *character*.

The improved relations between the Navy and the civilian populace pleased me particularly. One of the happiest farewell messages I received was from Chief of Police Dietrich at Kiel, a Social Democrat. "You have succeeded in getting in close touch with the working people," he wrote. "We are sorry you are leaving."

One other regret I had, in addition to leaving the Baltic District: I regretted that I was achieving my promotion through the forced resignation of Admiral Zenker. From our first associations in the Battle Cruiser Forces, I had known him as a brave and able officer, an honest, unselfish individual. As the first Commander of the Naval Forces in the postwar period he had laid the foundation for sound fleet training and tactics suitable for our meager strength. Further, he had awakened the government to the value of naval forces in its international relations.

However, Admiral Zenker's misfortune confirmed me more than ever in my determination to travel the road of unquestionable correctness, in an absolutely loyal and well defined relationship to the State and its government. Nor would I permit any deviation by any other member of the Navy.

My fitness to occupy my new position was not universally accepted. In an apparent attempt to block my appointment at the last minute, the old press attacks on me in the early Kiel days were dug up again, with gratuitous comments not designed to increase Defense Minister Groener's confidence in me. To meet the criticisms, the Defense Minister had Colonel von Schleicher, head of his political department, call a conference of all the press representatives, where my defense against those attacks was presented for their information. Later I was privately told that even Minister Groener at the time doubted that I could last out the campaign very long.

VII

Head of the Navy

I TOOK OVER the Admiralty in Berlin on 1 October 1928. The Navy had incurred a bad reputation as a result of the Lohmann affair. Although, as I have said, there was no question of personal dishonesty on Captain Lohmann's part, some of the unauthorized projects on which he had embarked without sufficient expert counsel had resulted in financial losses. One of the other armed services had lost much more at this same time; this fact was soft-pedalled at the expense of the Navy.

When I made my first official calls in my new capacity I found an attitude of open distrust. The officials on whom I called were Chancellor Hermann Müller, Finance Minister Rudolf Hilferding, Minister of the Interior Carl Severing, Minister of Transport von Guérard, and Minister of Economics Julius Curtius. Foreign Minister Gustav Stresemann was ill, so Minister of Economics Curtius accepted my call in his stead. For the first time in my life I was shocked to find my veracity questioned. I met distrust with frankness. Two years later I was told confidentially by a Finance Ministry official in charge of the Navy budget that my bluntness had restored that Ministry's full confidence in the Admiralty.

My new position in the framework of the armed services was not rendered any easier by the attitude of Defense Minister Groener. The former Minister, Gessler, the last Quartermaster General before the Armistice, had repaid the Navy's wholehearted cooperation by cordial confidence. Minister Groener, a retired Army general, made no secret of the fact that he had no love for the Navy. During his first few years in office, on occasions when he was presenting naval matters to the Reichstag, he repeatedly emphasized that he was "no fleet enthusiast." Such a public expression was exceedingly damaging to the Navy. Whether or not a Navy is needed should not be a matter of emotional reaction but of sober consideration and judgment. But since the defense of the State is a fundamental obligation in all national constitutions, including that of the Weimar Republic, the defense of the nation's coasts is a first duty under that obligation.

The Office of the Defense Minister was in process of expansion, largely due to the efforts of Colonel Kurt von Schleicher. On the Defense level, a new Legal Division was established, and the Military-Political Intelligence Division was enlarged. In the discussions concerning this reorganization I found it useful to fall back on the written program I had drawn up when I was being considered for office. We succeeded in getting our own Legal Administrative Office set up in the Admiralty. Such an office was vitally necessary, since under the Versailles Treaty the Navy had court-martial authority on board its ships. We also got a billet for a naval liaison officer in the Military-Political Division, which had to do with domestic matters within the Minister's office.

The question of rearmament for the Army and Navy was something which General Groener put entirely in the hands of the Reichstag, since any such plans would be contrary to the terms of the Versailles Treaty. Previous governments under the Weimar Republic had refused to take any action, but now Chancellor Müller showed great understanding of the matter, as did the Minister of the Interior. Minister Severing could always be counted on to take an interest in military matters. Economics Minister Curtius took a neutral attitude, probably at the direction of Foreign Minister Stresemann, but Minister von Guérard, a member of the Roman Catholic Party, was openly opposed.

The Navy needed first the legalization of measures initiated by Captain Lohmann. A son of a former director of the North German Lloyd Steamship Company, Captain Lohmann had a keen comprehension of naval and nautical matters in general. As head of the Sea Transport Division, he had participated in the negotiations of the Armistice Commission, during which he had secured needed modifications in the strangling restrictions placed upon

German shipping. He had organized the repatriation of German prisoners of war from foreign internment camps. But his main activities had been the effort to evade the disarmament provisions of the Versailles Treaty.

The conditions of this treaty were exceptionally hard on the Navy. Opposition to carrying out some of the terms of the compulsory disarmament was widespread. Statesmen and military leaders were trying to obtain every possible modification by negotiation. Others—bureau chiefs, supervisory officers, etc.—were secretly trying to evade the requirements for the surrender of weapons, munitions, and other material, even at extreme personal risk to themselves. Through cunning subterfuges, 119 guns ranging from 8.8-cm. to 28-cm. were withheld from the victors and hidden away for national use. Constant arguments with the Allied Control Commissions arose from things like this, but fortunately quite a few members of these commissions sympathized with the German point of view and were consequently liberal in their interpretations.

One of the secret undertakings that Captain Lohmann had set in motion, was the further development of small motor torpedo boats and minesweepers. Another was a program for designing and constructing submarines abroad. These things, of course, were especially prohibited by the Versailles Treaty.

In the case of submarines, a false front, a Dutch firm established at The Hague, more or less in actuality a combination of several German shipyards, was used. It employed a number of former German submarine designers and engineers. Thus these valuable technical experts were kept together, and through construction work for foreign navies they were kept constantly up-to-date in their professions. As a subsidiary development Commander Bartenbach (Retired) became a consulting naval architect in Finland where he supervised the construction, in Finnish shipyards, of several submarines built on plans provided by the Dutch firm.

In Spain, Commander Canaris, through his personal acquaintance with King Alfonso and Prime Minister de Rivera, arranged for construction of a German-type submarine of 750 tons at a Cadiz shipyard. Upon completion of its trials the submarine was to be commissioned into the Spanish Navy, but the Spanish Revolution terminated that arrangement, and the boat was finally sold to the Turkish Navy.

Incidentally, this latter boat became the prototype for the later German submarines *U-25* and *U-26,* just as the Finnish submarines were the models for the later U-boats in the series from *U-1* to *U-24.*

I had had no connection whatever with the Lohmann enterprises until I took up my duties in Berlin in 1928, but then I immediately had to determine which of the projects should be continued if the government legalized them. It is to the credit of Defense Minister Groener, and the government as a whole, that they found ways to liquidate those projects no longer deemed vital, and to sponsor and finance those with real military value, even if for a time these projects had to be carried on under cover.

The Reichstag demanded a controlling voice in such activities to prevent assemblage of a politically dangerous "secret fund." To supervise secret expenditures by the Defense Ministry, a Committee was formed of the Chiefs of the Army and Navy Supreme Commands, Dr. Popitz of the Finance Ministry, and Dr. Saemisch of the Accounting Division. The Committee members or their deputies had to pass on all secret expenditures, which, since they were illegal under the Treaty terms, could not be carried officially in the regular budget. A sort of legality, however, was provided by carrying them in a secret budget which in every other way complied with regular government budget regulations.

Many government offices, such as the Treasury, were involved, and those members of the Reichstag who were on the budget committee were always completely informed of all the details. For sharing of the heavy responsibility—a risk cheerfully accepted, regardless of political party—they cannot be given too much credit.

I always enjoyed the closest relations with the Chief of the Army Supreme Command, General of the Infantry Wilhelm Heye, who had a sound understanding of the special characteristics and duties of the Navy. There were others in the Army, however, especially in the Department of Troops, who maintained that a Navy was unnecessary for the country's defense and that the money could be better allocated to the Army. That very winter of 1928 a group working on the Army budget managed to get 20 million marks of Navy funds transferred to the Army budget. General Groener laid the blame on what he claimed was stupidity on the part of the officials who worked out the Navy budget.

In the Army, differently from the Navy, the chiefs of department habitually took up matters directly with the Minister of Defense, instead of going through the Army Chief of Staff. General Groener, consequently, had a tendency to bypass me in matters concerning my own department chiefs, and I had to remind him at times that this had been strictly ruled out in the written program upon which my appointment to office had been based. It is true that, prior to the war, the administration and command of the Navy had not been too well unified, as the Admiralty Staff, the Naval Directorate, and the Fleet Command, had direct access to the Kaiser without having to go through any central naval command. I absolutely rejected any type of general staff organization which would permit such faulty command structure.

It was not that I wished to set up a dictatorial type of leadership or to suppress divergent views; on the contrary, when the annual changes in the Admiralty occurred each fall I convened a meeting of all officers, civil officials, and others in the organization and demanded of each one a frank presentation of his personal views. I made it equally clear, however, that once the Chief of the Admiralty had made his decision on any question, each subordinate would be expected to implement it loyally. I also told them that the manner in which the subject had been debated, as well as any previous differences of opinion, should be kept completely confidential. I invited free and forthright expressions of opinion from ship commanders and flag officers of the fleet, and made frequent visits to all the Navy's activities, and participated in maneuvers, exercises, and inspections, as every ranking officer should do.

The Navy being rather small at this stage, I knew all of the older officers from close personal acquaintance, but I now endeavored to get to know as many of the younger officers as possible, so that I could evaluate their capabilities personally. Here, too, I invited all officers, regardless of rank, to feel free to communicate their views and opinions to me, through regular channels, even if these communications might be critical, and I did my utmost to avoid disappointing the frank confidence they demonstrated in their communications to me.

Invariably I returned from these trips with a long list of notes and with numerous questions to be thrashed out with the various bureaus and divisions of the Admiralty. Some questions and requests from the operating forces turned out to be insufficiently thought out in advance, or otherwise impractical. But they were answered completely and tactfully. For only by a healthy exchange of opinion between the central authority and the operating forces can real efficiency be attained and the Admiralty avoid becoming a cold and distant agency.

The regular rotation of officer personnel every two or three years served to bring fresh and stimulating influences to the various bureaus and divisions, and at the same time gave more naval officers a better idea of the responsibilities and limitations of the central authority. To a smaller degree, there was also a regular turnover in the civilian staff as well.

In concentrating on a firm, unified leadership in the Navy, it was not my purpose to effect greater centralization; on the contrary, I strove for decentralization whenever possible. Because of the small postwar Navy and its limited budget, it had only been natural that many officers in the Admiralty had come to make many decisions themselves without reference elsewhere, and even to allocate small sums from the naval budget. This was not good organization practice, as the officials in question had more important things to do than to engage in such trivial matters. I had to insist on their turning over such details, as well as the allocation of funds, to the lower echelons, whose primary duty it was to attend to such matters. Not until the Navy grew by leaps and bounds in later years did some of these older officials recognize the need for greater decentralization.

Discipline and Comradeship

While trying to establish a unified command structure in the Navy, I nevertheless tried to make it a rule that the central authority's every decision, whether it related to training, construction, or organization, should take into consideration the possible resulting effect on discipline. The principle which we had adopted in the

Education and Training Division had been, "Discipline and comradeship are the basis for every military success." This I tried to instill into all the activities of the Navy. In the difficult earlier years Admiral Behncke had laid a firm foundation for dependable discipline. However, during the last few years everyone, it seemed to me, had been working at a tense, stepped-up tempo that was unnecessary, since we could not possibly fight a war anyway, and the frantic pace did not leave time to promote real discipline. Every year there was a great turnover in personnel aboard ship, with the result that battle training had to begin all over again, in the course of which division training—the place where each man received his primary training in military discipline—was given short shrift.

In 1929, with the concurrence of all the ranking flag officers, I introduced a two-year training system in the fleet—one year of training and one year of maneuvers. Few personnel changes were made at the end of the first year, so that battle training was stretched out over a two-year period instead of being confined to one year. Thus, though a man took two years to reach his maximum fighting efficiency, he had more time under training in his ship's division. The tasks of the naval detachments on shore were reduced as well as the time the artillery battalions were absent from their garrisons. Inspections were reduced in number, and some training courses were shortened. We were motivated by the same considerations as had influenced us during the buildup stages just before the war, though it had not been possible at that time to reach any definite results.

However, those had been the unique days of the old Imperial Navy—a Navy which, like the country itself, had been built up on a system of class distinctions. That period had gone, and the armed forces could not ignore the basic changes that had occurred in the State itself. There could not be a different code in the armed services from that established by the people whom they served. The new Navy could not blindly follow the pattern of the old.

It was gratifying to me to see how wholeheartedly the entire Navy supported me in my policy of sound discipline and morale. Every superior officer in the Navy silently swore that there should never again be a *November 1918* in the Navy, just as each one realized that with the transition of a nation of classes to a democratic State, the position of the enlisted man within the community had likewise changed. I never missed an opportunity to point out this fact to the officers of all ranks. And I insisted, above everything else, on humane and intelligent treatment of all subordinates, and a respect for the dignity of the individual. While reprimands and punishments for infractions of military rules are necessary for discipline, they should never be administered in a form to produce humiliation, and whenever offenders were treated in a non-regulation way I took prompt action against the superior concerned. Even when extenuating circumstances existed, I always called the officer involved sharply to account, and in the worst cases even saw to his dismissal or forced resignation from the Navy.

Another thing I tried to point out was that instilling decent convictions, dependability, and a sense of duty in an enlisted man was more important basically than even intensive technical training. And education in turn depends upon the character of the educator —that is, the superior officer—and the personal example set by him. Primary factors in the impression he makes are his bearing and his known capabilities. As a text for the use of the officers I had had especially written a rather sizeable pamphlet on the subject of "Educational Problems in the German Navy."

Additional ideas and concepts were presented in an excellent book by Commander Siegfried Sorge. Entitled *The Naval Officer as Leader and Educator,* this book was available in all service libraries, and many officers owned copies.

In 1944, the High Command of the Armed Services banned this book because it "was based on classical principles!"

Only the verdict of history will say whether or not our program was correct. But I personally am convinced that, as military organizations, the armed services as we developed them in the days of the Weimar Republic were unequalled. Theft and brutal treatment were unheard of. Morale of officers, petty officers, and men was high. So well trained and indoctrinated were our chief petty officers and officers that without difficulty they could advance to fill the gaps in the commissioned ranks caused later by the enormous expansion of the Navy and the Second World War. The toil, sacrifice, and enthusiasm that naval men of all ranks had put into building up the Navy bore rich fruit.

My fondest wish was fulfilled when people, in speaking of the bearing and accomplishments of the service and of service personnel, began to use the term, "Navy style." That very expression was the recognition of our success in the fields of morale and discipline.

Such recognition was a constant reminder of our own obligations to the nation and the people. They had not only entrusted us with costly ships and property, but something far more valuable still—the youth of the nation. For a shorter or longer period the Navy would be entrusted with their education and care. Our responsibility was not only to make them useful to the service, but also capable and worthy citizens when their service terms expired.

In addition to promoting a close fellowship among the officers, petty officers, and enlisted men in the Navy, I endeavored to further the spirit of cooperation and mutual understanding with the Army. Every ship was assigned to some particular Army regiment as a sort of foster brother. Officers and men of all the Army regiments were invited to make cruises as guests of their host ships, and in the same way the ships' officers and crews became guests of their respective Army regiments ashore.

We tried to establish the same close relations between the Navy and the civilian public. The Navy kept up close contact with former servicemen, whether officer or enlisted, and with former civilian employees. What I particularly wanted to avoid was any segregation of the Navy from the general public. Our goal was to form one large "Navy family" throughout Germany. We maintained close relations with naval societies and similar organizations wherever they existed.

The christening of new vessels always provided us with the opportunity to establish relations with the cities for which the vessels were named. When the ship was named after a person, we always invited members of the family, as well as other prominent people associated with the person, to attend the launching. In the case of cruisers, named after cities, we invited the chief burgomaster to make one of the addresses. Later, the cities were invited to send representatives to visit their nameships, and even to make cruises aboard. The cities generally reciprocated with invitations to the officers and men of the ships. Thus, when the *Emden* was launched, in 1925, the honored guests included Dr. Mützelburg, Chief Burgomaster of the city, and also former Minister of Defense Noske in his new capacity of President of the Province of Hannover. Similarly when the cruisers *Königsberg, Karlsruhe, Köln,* and *Leipzig,* were launched, Chief Burgomasters Lohmeyer, Finter, Adenauer, and Rothe made the christening speeches. Later on, most of these gentlemen were aboard for a training cruise.

We gave the members of the Reichstag, Reich Council, and others the opportunity to become intimately acquainted with our Navy, and especially with its seagoing activities. The officers and crews of the ships went out of their way to cement the cordial relations thus established. The resulting friendly understanding proved invaluable to the Navy later when the naval budget or other important questions concerning naval affairs came up for discussion in the Reichstag.

These Reichstag visits gave us the opportunity to point out to the government the urgent need of new vessels to replace those already badly obsolete.

One of the main objectives of the Versailles Treaty had been to limit Germany's naval potential so that any resurgence of German seapower to a point where it would influence power politics would be impossible. Under the Treaty construction of submarines and airplanes was forbidden. Germany's Navy was limited to a strength of six battleships, plus two in reserve; six cruisers, plus two in reserve; and twelve destroyers and as many torpedo boats, with four of each class in reserve. The battleships that could be retained were all of 1902-1906 vintage, the cruisers of 1899-1903 vintage, and the destroyers and torpedo boats of 1906-1913. All the newer ships of the High Seas Fleet had had to be scrapped.

The Treaty stipulated that capital ships could be replaced by new construction when they were twenty years old, and the destroyers and torpedo boats at fifteen. New construction was limited in size: battleships to 10,000 tons, cruisers 6,000 tons, destroyers 800 tons, and torpedo boats 200 tons.

Even when the Treaty was signed, most of the ships Germany had been allowed to retain were already so old that they could have been replaced at that very time under the conditions of the

Versailles Treaty. The strength of the Navy was far below what our former enemies had allowed us. No self-respecting Navy could tolerate such a condition. The problem the Navy faced was how many new ships the country, in its limited financial condition, could afford, and how this new construction was to be allocated to get the maximum fighting power from the tonnage that the Versailles Treaty allowed. Everybody in the Admiralty, everybody in the Navy, had been convinced that the reconstruction of the fleet should be undertaken as soon as possible. The obsolete ships were worthless for defense purposes. All that they could do would be to serve as training ships to give the crews some familiarity with the sea.

In considering which class of ships should be first replaced, the cruiser class had been chosen as being less handcuffed by the Treaty restrictions. Therefore a light cruiser, the *Emden,* began the new construction program in 1921. It was completed under extreme difficulty. The personnel of the design division had been reduced almost to the vanishing point, so it had not been possible to prepare a completely new design for the *Emden.* She had been built, therefore, from the plans of the last cruisers built during the war. Nevertheless, with the launching, in 1925, the Navy had the cheering sense that some headway was being made, and that the Reichstag recognized in principle that the obsolete ships must be replaced by new construction.

After 1925 other light cruisers were authorized. The Navy built these from new designs and by the most modern methods. The new process of welding was used instead of the old system of riveting, with a resulting decrease in weight of hull which could be used for increasing the gun calibers and the ship's speed. The building of torpedo boats began in 1926.

Encouraging as the reconstruction of even a few cruisers and torpedo boats was to the Navy, the decisive factor was when the construction of new battleships would begin—and what form they would take. Since the tonnage had to be kept within the 10,000 ton limit, the choice was between two alternatives—a stoutly armored and hence consequently rather slow ship, of the monitor or coast defense type, or a fast ship with medium guns and armor, but with greater versatility of action. In actual tables of specifications, three types were discussed: a ship with 30.5-cm. guns, 200-mm. armor, and 21 knots speed; a ship also with 30.5-cm. guns, but with heavier armor of 280-mm. and, consequently, only 18 knots speed; and, a ship more like a battle cruiser, with gun caliber of only 28-cm. and armor of only 100-mm., but capable of making 26 knots speed.

In 1927, when the discussions first became spirited, opinions were divided. At that time I favored the more heavily armored but slower ship as being best fitted for the Baltic, where her services would most probably be needed—a view in which Admiral Zenker, then Chief of the Admiralty, concurred. Later, after long deliberation, we had both veered to the C-type of ship, and finally the choice had settled on such a cruiser-like ship with an armament of six 28-cm. guns in the main battery, eight 15-cm. guns in the secondary battery, 100-mm. of armor, and a speed of 26 knots. In firepower and armor protection this ship would be superior to 10,000-ton cruisers of foreign navies, though not quite as fast. On the other hand, it could escape much larger, stronger enemy battleships through its ability to out-speed them. In propulsion also it represented a distinctly new type of cruiser; its eight engines were diesel driven instead of steam propelled, and hence its operating range was greatly increased. The man mostly responsible for this development was Technical Adviser Laudahn of the design section of the Admiralty, with the assistance of the Machine Plant Augsburg-Nürnberg (M.A.N.).

With the approval of the design there began the battle for Reichstag approval and appropriations for Pocket Battleship "A," as the new ship was designated in Navy files, though it was intended that the actual ship would be named the *Preussen* when completed.

The first appropriation toward construction was approved by the Reichstag in 1927; however, the Reichsrat, influenced by strong opposition from the Prussian Government, decided that the authorization for the ship would have to be approved also by the new Reichstag, which would be elected on 20 May 1928. Actually Pocket Battleship "A" was not voted on until the middle of November, and then only after a long and acrimonious vote involving party politics. The phrase, "Pocket battleship—or food for children?" was used in the debate, with little consideration to the fact that the building of the ship would give work and bread not only to the shipyard workers, but also to workers in many plants throughout the country. The proposition barely carried, with 255 delegates voting in favor, and 203 opposed.

Upon taking over the Admiralty I found some groups, even in the Reichsrat, who had no understanding of the Navy's requirements. In 1929 we asked for appropriations to replace the old gunnery tender *Drache*. We wanted to construct a type that could be used as a destroyer, if necessary, as well as a gunnery tender. I was swamped with innumerable questions as to why the replacement ship had to be so much larger than the old one. Some Reichsrat members obviously had no appreciation of the fact that in some cases full explanations could not be given for reasons of military security.

These varied experiences convinced me that the prevailing system, whereby appropriations for naval expenditures had to be approved annually for each item, was unsatisfactory for the Navy. All too often the approval or rejection depended upon party politics and private political bargains, generally at the expense of the Navy. Some better way had to be found if the buildup of the Navy was ever to be put on a systematic, economical basis.

The construction of a capital ship requires several years. Appropriations made annually must be so dovetailed that all the most modern improvements can be incorporated as the work progresses. Moreover, considering the useful life of a capital ship as twenty years, if you have a fleet of only eight ships, a new replacement must be begun every two or three years if a systematic program is to be developed, a uniform workload established, and replacements join the fleet at the time intended. To effect this, the naval budget must have regular appropriations for new construction which are not subject to change because of the political expendiency of the moment.

Accordingly we tried to get approval of a "ship construction replacement plan." This was to guarantee a systematic construction program geared both to the requirements of the Navy and the actual financial condition of the country. Such a long-range plan, if accepted, would eliminate the annual controversies in the Reichstag, the Navy could do better planning, and the over-all results would be far more satisfactory than could ever materialize from the usual short-range, annual plan.

Obviously the Reichstag and the government could not be bound to any rigid long-range plan, and the constitutional requirement for approval by the Reichstag of the annual national budget—including the naval budget—could not be disputed. But if such a long-range plan could be initiated in its general aspects, it would provide a formula, then, for agreement in principle on the annual appropriations. It took more than two years, however, to get the Navy's idea for a ship replacement plan accepted.

As a result of our lack of success with our 1928 budget, I assigned to head the budget division an officer of unquestioned loyalty, honesty, and competence in public relations, Captain Bastian. As Chief of the Naval Budget Division, this officer established most favorable relations with the Reichstag and its budget committee, as well as with the Reichsrat, the administration, and, above all, with the Finance Minister and his budget commissioner of economy. Supported by the Admiralty, he had the bureau and division chiefs make personal presentations before the government and Reichstag offices involved. The frank answers and full information thus supplied as to the Navy's needs and intentions were largely responsible for overcoming the initial distrust of some persons toward the Navy and bringing about a complete and friendly understanding.

By the very next summer we could already see results. In May 1929 a kind of maiden speech I delivered before the Budget Committee of the Reichstag was well received both by the Reichstag members and Defense Minister Groener. However, there was no hope of obtaining approval for a second pocket battleship in the budget for 1929, and little chance in 1930. Meantime, Dr. Heinrich Brüning, from the Center Party, had become Chancellor on 30 March 1930, and Baron von Gayl, the Reichsrat member for East Prussia, had proposed a motion for a second pocket battleship on the basis that the sea route from Germany to East Prussia needed stronger protection against Poland, which, by the Treaty of Versailles and subsequent developments, had been put in a position to isolate East Prussia from the rest of Germany. Accordingly, Captain Bastian and I contacted the individual members of the Reichsrat and tried to show the need for the ship. Amazingly enough, the representatives from the old Hanseatic ports of Hamburg and Lübeck opposed the ship, though Bremen was in favor of it. Although the motion carried in the Reichsrat, the government felt that for political reasons, which the Defense Minister explained to us, the appropriations for a second pocket battleship could not be included in the 1930 budget. Thereupon a motion for construction of such a ship was again put before the Reichsrat, which again approved it, with Bremen this time voting against it. Nevertheless, the government and Reichstag continued to reject the replacement construction plan.

But we had succeeded in one thing: the government promised to include an appropriation for another pocket battleship in the 1931 budget, and also to consider the Navy's proposed long-range ship construction replacement plan. And in 1931 this plan was actually approved, with a long-range program for the construction of four battleships, though the approval carried the provision that each ship had to be individually approved in the budget for the year. Pocket battleship "B," for which we had so assiduously campaigned, was approved by the same Reichstag.

The political atmosphere toward the Navy had completely changed since I had taken up my duties in Berlin. This legislation had been victoriously pressed by the Brüning Cabinet with Chancellor Brüning and Defense Minister Groener stoutly supporting the Navy. In the Reichsrat, Dr. Tischbein, representative from Mecklenburg, and Dr. Hamacher, from the Rhineland, had both fought for the Navy's interest. Delegate Schöpflin of the Social Democrat Party and Delegate Klöckner of the Center Party were very sympathetic, and prelate Dr. Schreiber of the Center Party was also a staunch advocate. The Socialist delegate Stücklen, whose duty it was to report on the Navy budget, did so very objectively, as did also his assistant, Delegate Ersing of the Center Party.

This legislation brought me into close touch with Delegate Schöpflin, for whom I formed a very high opinion, and with whom I carried on a regular correspondence thereafter right up to his eightieth birthday in 1943.

The international situation was behind the Navy's repeated requests for new ships to replace its obsolete fleet. Within a very short time after its independence was established by the war, Poland had build up a strong army, superior both in numbers and equipment to our limited army of 100,000 men. Danzig, which had been denied Poland by the Peace Treaty, was an open, defenseless city, which Poland was seeking by every possible means to dominate. It was not beyond the bounds of possibility that Poland might some day seize the city by force, and ultimately do the same with East Prussia, which was cut off from the mother country by the sixty-mile wide Polish Corridor. The armed seizure of Memel by Lithuanian volunteers and of Vilna by Polish volunteers in 1920, neither of which any other powers had contested, made it seem quite possible that the same fate could overtake Danzig and East Prussia unless Germany was in position to offer immediate and energetic resistance. And since Poland had a close alliance with France, Germany would have to reckon on meeting French forces as well as Polish, if Poland staged a surprise attack on Danzig or East Prussia.

In the twenties three separate studies had been devoted to planning defense against such attacks:

(a) "Study East" provided for German armed forces to strike a counterblow in case Poland invaded East Prussia. This counterblow was to strike at Gdynia, Poland's largest seaport and naval base, located on the Baltic about 10 miles west of Danzig. The Navy would have to carry the entire operation, inasmuch as the Army could give no support here. In addition to bombarding the incompleted Polish costal fortifications with the heavy guns of the old battleships, the Navy would block the entrance to Gdynia with minefields. If executed successfully, such an operation should do much to check the Polish aggression.

(b) "Study Baltic Sea Defense" provided for the defense of the Baltic—especially its entrances—against Polish naval forces or Polish forces aided by French naval forces. The French-Polish military alliance of 1926 stipulated that the French Government would provide a squadron of two battleships, four cruisers, four destroyers, three submarines, and one minelayer for the defense of Poland's Baltic coast and the seaport where French troops were to debark. Naturally, the most effective counter to such operations would be the rapid execution of "Study East," so that German minefields and light naval forces at the entrance of the Baltic would prevent entry of the French warships, transports, and expeditionary forces into the Baltic.

(c) "Study Protection of German Commerce at Sea" provided for maximum protection of Germany's seaborne commerce in case France joined Poland in the war. As Germany required a daily importation of 60,000 tons of goods through her seaports, the Navy could not hope to give much protection for the time being, and no improvement could be expected until the fleet had been increased by at least three pocket battleships. Germany's only hope would be to gain some other sea power as an ally. Britain remaining neutral was a *conditio sine qua non.*

In every case only defensive warfare after an attack was envisioned. On 26 April 1929 the government had issued a directive for "Defense of the Nation and Its Boundaries," but the Prussian Government had prevented its implementation until 1930. Under these circumstances nothing would have been less welcome to the leaders of the German armed forces than to have to resist a Franco-Polish invasion with the inadequate resources at their command. As for an aggressive attack against Poland, it would have been considered utter madness. It never came under discussion.

The Navy plans to meet the three problems were prepared principally by the Naval Operations Department, headed by Rear Admiral Dr. Groos, aided by Captain Assmann, Chief of the Fleet Division of the Department, and Captain Boehm. Individual details were tested in war games and smaller exercises. As limited as the objective was, and our resources to achieve it, the very studies themselves aided greatly in advancing the Navy's tactical and operational understanding.

Vice Admiral Zenker had already worked toward the same end in his years as Commander-in-Chief. He had aimed at devising tactics suited to the means at hand. Torpedo boats had specialized in training for surprise night attacks, and special attention had been given to joint operations of capital ships and torpedo boats, as night actions had to be counted on to compensate for the numerical inferiority of German ships as compared to the enemy. The battleships' mission was to break through the enemy's screen and give the torpedo boats a chance to strike home. Additional training concentrated on gunnery and fire control.

With our woefully obsolete and inadequate forces, naturally it was impossible to expect any great improvement in battle efficiency. The exercises stimulated the officers' interest in tactical problems, and resulted in a splendidly trained group of commanding officers for ships and torpedo boat squadrons.

These tactical studies also stimulated fresh thinking when the plans for pocket battleship "A" were made known. Compared to the old ponderous and sluggish battleship, the new type offered tremendous new tactical possibilities through its speed and maneuverability. Meantime, our new, faster light cruisers were coming into service, as well as replacements for our old torpedo boat squadrons.

The war games and other studies made it evident that the day of mass formations of fleets and squadrons was over, a victim of the need for mobility. The development of air forces in all countries would force this tactical change in the navies. Thus, the development of "task forces" was originated and tested by the Fleet Command under Admiral Gladisch and his Chief of Staff, Captain Boehm. The "task force" idea was simply that of assembling in a single combat unit all those ships and their accompanying craft that would be required for a specific combat purpose. For example, such a task force might consist of a pocket battleship grouped with several cruisers and a corresponding number of destroyers—a tactical unit that would be exceptionally maneuverable and, under a broad directive from the Commander in Chief, could operate independently. Our own officers and men were enthusiastic about the new tactical form when it was tried out.

To a great extent our plans and maneuvers were centered around the tasks and possibilities of the Baltic, and were especially concerned with the control of the Baltic entrances. In 1930 we staged our first expanded North Sea maneuvers in the area between the English Channel and Norway. Nothing was more evident than that the proposed modernization of the fleet through introduction of the new pocket battleships had breathed new life into the whole Navy. Later, the extension of the problem to the Atlantic was studied. But in no case did the assumed enemies include other than the French and Polish navies. Any idea of a war with England, even after we had our pocket battleships, would have been considered as complete insanity by any one of us.

Development of a Naval Air Force

One thing we did recognize, however, was the need for a naval air force to work closely with the fleet and underwater craft, and whose personnel would be completely familiar with the use of naval forces and the characteristics of naval warfare. As long as we were bound by the Versailles Treaty, nothing could be done about acquiring either planes or aviation personnel. In October 1928 Defense Minister Groener had obtained the government's consent for the Navy to acquire a few planes—but for experimental purposes only, not for building an air fleet. Fortunately the Navy could lay its hands on a number of seaplanes as well as the necessary trained personnel. The Versailles Treaty allowed the Navy the right to possess some antiaircraft guns. The Navy interpreted it as also conveying the right to conduct antiaircraft firing at air targets towed by planes. Accordingly, an undercover organization operating under the camouflaging name of "Air Service, Incorporated" was formed. It was highly instrumental in the development of the Navy's future air force. Naturally, the greatest secrecy had to be maintained, especially in mounting and testing the aircraft guns, and activity carried out at only the most remote locations. No outsiders were permitted to witness any joint exercises of the Navy's surface ships and its air forces.

Under Captain Zander, a nucleus of naval aviators of World War I was assembled. These were augmented by a selected group of potential cadets given a year's advance training in flying before being sworn into the Navy. There was no *open* violation of the Versailles Treaty. However, this whole promising program was killed after 1933, when Marshal Hermann Göring became chief of the German Air Force and monopolized practically everything aerial for his Luftwaffe, to the grave disadvantage of the Navy and its mission.

VIII

The Early Thirties

THE YEAR 1931, which saw government and Reichstag approval for the Navy's pocket battleship "B," was also the tenth anniversary of the new armed forces of the republic. On New Year's Day Defense Minister Groener in a nationwide broadcast emphasized the Navy's need to replace obsolete ships with new construction if it was to fulfill its obligation to protect the country. He pointed out that Germany was spending only six and a half per cent of its total budget on its armed forces, whereas its neighbors, Poland and France, were expending one-third of their entire budget on their armed services. He also made the following public pronouncement:

"Germany's military policy has only two choices: either to renounce armed forces altogether and depend forever afterward solely on the good will of other nations for the safety of the nation or resolutely to take advantage of the limited possibilities allowed us. A people that no longer is willing to defend itself surrenders its sovereignty irretrievably. . . . The armed forces know no course to the right, nor to the left. In Germany, just as in other lands, the whole population must stand behind the defense of the country. Whoever opposes or derides the nation's will to defend itself shakes the very foundations of the State. . . . The constitutional right of freedom of opinion must not be prostituted to treasonous and subversive practices."

19 May 1931, the day of the launching of pocket battleship "A," now known as the *Deutschland,* at the German Shipyard in Kiel, was a red-letter day for the Navy. Chancellor Brüning, in his chris-

tening address, said, "In this ceremony witnessed by the world, the German people are demonstrating that even under the shackles imposed upon them and all their economic problems, they have the strength to guard their peaceful existence and to defend their honor. . . . We conscientiously disarmed and are waiting for equal action from other nations if treaties are to hold out any hope for humanity. . . . But peace can not be achieved by establishing two codes of justice and two kinds of security in the community of nations. We can forget our long period of suffering if other nations will grant us the same national pride and the same love of our country which they claim for themselves."

President von Hindenburg in person christened the *Deutschland,* and, after the launching, went to sea aboard the cruiser *Königsberg* to observe its gunnery and torpedo exercises. The fellowing day, the fleet staged a war game, after which there was a grand review at Kiel of all the ships of the fleet, including torpedo boats, minesweepers, and auxiliary craft. At the officers' mess in Kiel I had the opportunity to thank the aged President, in the name of the Navy, for his visit. In his response he reminded the officers, in his concise and impressive military manner, of their duty to the country. It was the last time President von Hindenburg was to visit the Navy.

In the same year I attended the seventy-fifth anniversary celebration of the Wilhelmshaven Naval Shipyard, now under the command of Rear Admiral Eichel. This shipyard had become an indispensable adjunct to the Navy, with its availability to perform emergency repairs as well as extensive unscheduled maintenance work without the usual delaying negotiations necessary in the case of private shipyards. The yard's main function was repair work, but enough new construction was undertaken to keep skilled workmen employed at all times. Workers could always be taken off new construction at any time to do emergency repairs, whereas in a private shipyard the straight terms of the construction contracts had to be observed if the yard was to be run on a profitable basis.

Furthermore, only a naval shipyard can maintain equipment and technical engineers to install and maintain such primarily naval gear as ship's guns, torpedoes, and fire control and communication and navigation systems. In addition naval shipyards necessarily maintain close liaison with the nation's harbor and river engineers. Lastly, constant exchange of personnel between the yard and the fleet and the central naval authority is necessary if a Navy, in equipment and performance, is to keep abreast of today's rapid technical progress. The Wilhelmshaven Naval Shipyard, in fact, was a combination of purely naval and purely engineering organizations.

A loyal and contented corps of workmen was essential to the success of the shipyard, and a considerable sum of welfare money was provided by the Navy for this purpose. In addition to good housing and a hospital, shipyard workers were provided with kindergartens and other social services. For protection in wartime, every worker had a bombproof shelter both at his work location and at his home; as a result, during World War II very little loss of life occurred at Wilhelmshaven Naval Shipyard despite the more than one hundred bombing raids. The largest industry in the Wilhelmshaven area, the yard not only was the center of community activity but also drew skilled workmen from as far off as the Frisian coast. It never failed to meet the demands put upon it, and was an indispensable factor in the accomplishments of the Navy during the war.

In October 1931 Defense Minister Groener also became Minister of the Interior in the Brüning Cabinet, the idea being that in this way the armed forces could favorably influence the country's domestic policy. This amalgamation of military and domestic policy, however, proved disastrous, as it almost invariably does. After struggling for ten years to avoid being embroiled, the armed forces were now dragged bodily into party politics.

Fortunately the Navy, with its principal activities at sea and on the coast, was farther removed from domestic entanglements than was the Army, with its numerous smaller garrisons scattered throughout the country. In addition, the Navy had been thoroughly trained and indoctrinated to abstain from all party politics.

On the whole, 1931 was a most favorable one for the Navy. The *Deutschland* was launched, pocket battleship "B" was approved, and the Navy's long-range ship construction replacement program was accepted in principle. The public distrust of the Navy which I had encountered on first assuming office had largely evaporated, and Chancellor Brüning demonstrated increasing understanding of the needs of the Navy and the other military services. His objectiveness and unimpeachable character had won him universal respect and confidence, and I had no reluctance in affirming this in my various speeches here and there. Altogether I looked forward to the New Year with great expectations.

Contrary to my hopes, 1932 brought both personal and official troubles to me. In April and May I lost both my parents within a few weeks of each other, and on 25 May my admired former commander, Admiral von Hipper, died. In close daily relations with him through the fateful war years, both in combat and in training, I had had a tremendous respect and affection for him.

On 18 August Admiral Zenker, another comrade whom I admired and who had been my predecessor in the Admiralty, died. His funeral coincided with a national memorial service for the dead of the schoolship *Niobe.* This training ship, while under sail off Fehmarn Island on 26 July, had suddenly capsized in a rare and unpredictable line squall. With it went down 69 officers and men, the greater part of her crew. At this one stroke the Navy lost almost all of the year's new class of candidates for line officer, medical officer, engineer officer, and petty officer.

All Germany went into mourning, a grief in which I shared deeply. Although seamen, by their profession, must always be prepared to pay the toll exacted by the stern forces of nature, the suddenness of the calamity was shocking. In order to clear up even the most minute detail of the tragedy in order to draw any possible future lessons from it, the Commander of the Battle Cruiser Forces was ordered to convene a full Board of Inquiry.

The list of witnesses called before the Board included two experts in handling ships under sail—Rear Admiral von Karpf (Ret.) and Captain Petersen, of the Laeisz shipping firm, who had sailed the five-masted *Preussen* for years. Another witness was Prof. Defant, the famous meteorologist and oceanographer of the University of Berlin, who testified as to a similar line squall that he had encountered personally on the *Oderhaff.* Dr. Schütte, an expert naval architect and president of the Society of Naval Architects, testified as to the ship design of the *Niobe,* and Commander Mewis, a former commander of the *Niobe,* testified as to the sail-

THREE GERMAN ADMIRALS

Grand Admiral Raeder is greeted by General Admiral Albrecht and General Admiral Carls at the Baltic Naval Station at Kiel.

WILHELMSHAVEN
The Great Port of the Naval Dockyard in April 1939.

SCHARNHORST
On a training cruise in the Baltic before the war.

ing qualities of the ship. In every possible respect the investigation delved into the causes of the tragedy, and at its conclusion found that there had been no culpable neglect or inefficiency in weather observation, shiphandling, or precautions during storm, and that the catastrophe was purely and simply an act of God. If fully acquitted Lieutenant Commander Ruhfus, commanding officer of the *Niobe,* of blame for the loss of the ship and its officers and men.

I had more than an ordinary interest in the investigation, as upon its results would depend whether or not we should continue our postwar system of training in sailing ships. This was a question which had been debated in all the navies of the world. After careful consideration, I concurred in the opinion of the Navy's expert advisers, that we should continue this form of training. In my opinion, training in sailing ships is an invaluable factor in building character, courage, and resourcefulness.

My decision was also influenced by the designs of the Blohm and Voss Shipyard for a new sailing schoolship. These contained all imaginable safety measures, and, after quick approval by the Reichstag committees, was included in the next year's budget, with the contract being awarded to Blohm and Voss. Eventually named the *Gorch Fock,* it established a pattern for similar training ships put into service by almost all the navies of the world. In fact even Palestine was interested in our designs for sailing schoolships.

Domestic Unrest

If the Navy was beginning to find greater stability, however, the same was not true of the country at large. The National Socialist German Workers Party, founded by Adolf Hitler, was gaining ever-increasing strength and successfully challenged, first the Brüning Government, and then the interim governments of Franz von Papen and General Kurt von Schleicher. The political atmosphere became one of open physical conflict akin almost to civil war.

One of the main contributing factors to the unrest was the SA (Sturm Abteilung), a semi-military organization of adherents of the National Socialist Workers Party. In the spring of 1932 General Groener, as Minister of the Interior, seriously considered banning the SA entirely. When I was summoned, along with General von Schleicher and General Baron von Hammerstein, head of the

Army, to confer with Minister Groener on the matter, I gave it as my opinion that if one such semi-military unit was banned, the same ban should be extended to all other party units of semi-military nature.

Nevertheless, on 9 April, against my advice and over the strong protest of General von Schleicher, Minister Groener obtained the consent of Chancellor Brüning, and the SA ban was signed by President von Hindenburg and duly proclaimed on 12 April.

The reaction in the Army was immediate. General von Schleicher reported to the Chief of the Military Political Division that all the military district commanders disapproved of the ban, and that it would have a devastating effect on the Army. He informed Minister Groener that he was a "dead duck," and that the ban would bring about the fall of the Cabinet. Although the chiefs of staff of the military districts were informed that the Ministerial Office disavowed the ban, I, as Chief of the Admiralty, refused to make any such declaration to the operating forces. I considered it as rank disloyalty as well as a military paradox for the Defense Minister's own subordinates to repudiate him by any such actions.

On 20 May, Minister Groener was violently attacked on the Reichstag floor by National Socialist Hermann Göring, and in replying he suffered a serious parliamentary defeat. General von Schleicher then asked me to tell President von Hindenburg that Minister Groener's dismissal was necessary in the interests of the armed forces. Again I refused, convinced that while such a procedure might be correct in a political office, it was certainly not for the Chief of the Admiralty. President von Hindenburg had repeatedly expressed himself on the subject of involvement by the military in the political sphere, and I knew how he would answer any such unwarranted assumption on my part. However, the chief of the Army Supreme Command, at General von Schleicher's instigation, did make the suggestion to the President, whose reaction was just as I had expected.

Nevertheless, on 12 May General Groener resigned as Minister of Defense.

Now I became involved in the maneuvering, but as no desire of my own. On 13 May, in Kiel, where I had gone for a short leave period, I picked up a newspaper with banner headlines: "Admiral Raeder To Succeed Minister of Defense Groener!"

I had not even heard of any such proposal; in fact I knew that General von Schleicher had confidently expected to be the next Minister of Defense. Obviously I was being made a catspaw by someone who would like to see me take General Groener's place then, and so sink along with the Brüning Cabinet when it inevitably fell within a few weeks time. I immediately got in touch with Captain Carls, my Chief of Staff in Berlin, and had him publish a strong denial, in my name, in that very evening's newspapers. During my entire career I had steered a strictly military course and had done everything possible to keep the Navy and myself out of politics.

Next the name of General Hasse appeared in the press as a likely successor to Minister Groener. By now I had received confidential information from most reliable sources that General von Schleicher had taken personal exception to me because I had refused to go at his suggestion to President von Hindenburg and press for General Groener's dismissal, and that it was General von Schleicher who had dropped my name at the Chancellery as a successor to Groener. Almost simultaneously Rear Admiral von Levetzow (Retired), an old friend now associated with the Hitler movement, came purposely to inform me that General von Schleicher had told National Socialist Delegate Göring that I was not suitable for the post of Minister of Defense because I was "too far to the left." Apparently in confirmation, articles appeared in some very left wing newspapers pointing me out as "quite acceptable" for the post of Minister of Defense. Again, this news originated in the Ministerial Office as I found out through its press chief.

I was all the more determined to maintain my policy of abstaining from any political activity whatsoever. Consequently when, as a result of General von Schleicher's maneuvers, the Brüning Government fell and Herr von Papen was invited to form a new Cabinet, my name no longer appeared in the newspapers. As I expected, General von Schleicher was named as the new Minister of Defense. However, I continued to hold the confidence of President von Hindenburg and was left unmolested during the short period of the von Papen Cabinet and through the next one, which was headed by General von Schleicher.

When the von Papen Government came into power, it felt that smaller circumventions of the Versailles Treaty disarmament conditions were entirely permissible in light of the international situation. So, in November 1932, even when the international naval disarmament conference at Geneva was getting nowhere, the new Minister of Defense approved the conversion replacement plan I had proposed for the Navy. Under this plan during the three periods of 1932-1933, 1934-1937, and 1938 and thereafter, new ships would have joined the fleet in the following classes and numbers: six battleships or pocket battleships; six cruisers; six squadrons of torpedo boats or destroyers; three squadrons of minesweepers; three squadrons of motor torpedo boats; three squadrons of submarines (16 U-boats in all); one sailing schoolship; and one minefield guard ship, along with the necessary tenders, gunnery schoolships, and experimental and auxiliary ships. There was an urgent need to set up nine naval aviation squadrons as the nucleus of a naval air force, and also a skeleton organization for the submarine arm, plus material for building submarines in 1933. The letting of the actual contracts for U-boat construction had to wait on the foreign situation, especially the results of the Disarmament Conference at Geneva. Meantime personnel plans for the first part of 1933 were approved, with an increase of 1,450 petty officers and men definitely set for 1 July 1933.

The Navy was prepared to expand to any degree that might be necessary. Even in the middle 1920's, from 30,000 to 40,000 volunteers were reporting to the Kiel Naval Depot alone, of whom barely 1,000 could be accepted. Now volunteers were streaming into the Navy from all parts of Germany and from all classes of the people. In 1932 we had 618 applicants for admission to the line officer career, with only 45 vacancies available. For the 14 vacancies in the engineer officers' branch, we received 522 applications, and the naval medical corps was equally swamped with 121 requests to fill only 6 vacancies.

This gave us opportunity to be extremely selective in accepting candidates for both officer and enlisted ranks. A trained psychologist assisted in the selection, and the volunteers were processed individually by the Bureau of Personnel, which, in cooperation with the discipline officers, supervised all special training, technical school courses, and selection for petty officer candidates.

Under the Versailles Treaty, with its rigid limitations on personnel, many billets, such as inshore installations, formerly filled by military personnel, were assigned to civilians, who did not come under the Versailles Treaty. This freed regular naval personnel for strictly military assignments, especially aboard ship. Furthermore we could use these civilian billets to give employment to service men whose 12-year permitted term of enlistment had expired—a particularly valuable alternative during the depression years of 1929 and thereafter.

One of the main responsibilities of the Naval Manning Depot had been to have available competent trained personnel to fully man each new ship as it went into commission. Since many specialists are needed in a modern naval vessel, the plans for a ship's complement had to be made a long time in advance.

It was not just a question of throwing together a crew of so many persons of this and that rank or grade and special training; new ships, in making their trial runs, had to have a competent crew already well disciplined, since during trials there was no time for drill or instruction in military discipline. The system we adopted was to take a nucleus of well-trained officers and men from a ship that was going out of commission for overhaul or other reasons, and to assign them to the new ship, with additional personnel fitted around this nucleus to bring the complement up to standard. New recruits were ordered to their ships long enough in advance to learn their duties and responsibilities under their new officers before the ship was commissioned. This was particularly true of the ship's engine-room personnel, who learned their duties under the close "constructional training command" of the chief engineer and his assistants, and fitted into the watch, quarter, and station bills while the construction of the ship was still going on.

I placed special emphasis on not rushing ships into commission to meet any arbitrary date. I was more than willing to accept an unavoidable delay in battle readiness.

During the recent years, all of our schools, technical courses, and general training had been geared to a definite and intensified program. While we tried to keep up with foreign developments as much as possible with our limited resources and obsolete vessels, we also tried to develop new ideas of our own. New tactics were originated and tested through war games and exercises, and it was my conviction that our very absorption in these professional challenges saved us from involvement in the political and social unrest ashore.

Our training cruisers were also sent abroad on regular annual training cruises. When, in 1931, the *Emden* visited East Asia and Africa, it received a warm reception everywhere. The German Lutheran pastor, Schrader, in East London, South Africa, wrote: "the ship showed that German order and discipline still exist in postwar Germany. The English population, especially, was impressed in this respect, and its tributes heightened the feeling of national pride in our German communities. The ship's visit brought distant Germany nearer, and revitalized the spirit of the German Evangelical Lutheran Church in South Africa."

The cruiser *Karlsruhe* also made a similar cruise in 1932 to the West Indies, Panama, Honolulu, and both coasts of North America. It was the first time that a German naval ship had visited New York since World War I, and its reception was most cordial there, as it was in all other former enemy ports.

Regular units of our fleet also visited numerous foreign ports, beginning with Norwegian ports, Danzig, and the Canary Islands in 1932. These frequent contacts with foreign countries aided considerably in giving our officers and men a broad view on foreign affairs, as well as in awaking in them a pride in the contributions of German culture everywhere. At the same time it impressed upon them the fact that the regard which is given to every nation by other countries is largely dependent on the impression its armed forces make in the matter of strength, equipment, efficiency, courtesy, and discipline. Without exception, our ships and their crews upheld the prestige of Germany. The years of training and the indoctrination of our men with the principles of discipline and teamwork fully justified themselves.

The social and political unrest that swept Germany in 1932 and 1933 provided the acid test for the Navy. I repeatedly declared that we could put complete trust in the integrity and political acumen of our Supreme Commander in Chief, President von Hindenburg, and managed to cool off some firebands as well as stiffen the backbone of those who seemed susceptible to the intensive political propaganda with which they were assailed. Throughout all crises the Navy remained staunchly loyal, and the President's appointment of Hitler to the Chancellorship and the corresponding appearance of a new Cabinet caused neither upheaval nor friction in the sea service.

Proof of the Navy's complete dissociation from politics was provided by the cruise of the *Köln,* which left Wilhelmshaven on 8 December 1932 for a year's training cruise to the Orient and Australia. Everywhere the ship, commanded by the able Captain Schniewind, was received in the ports of both friends and former enemies with respect and hospitality, and not a man of the ship's complement was involved in the slightest incident of a political or disciplinary nature.

I made my first acquaintance with Adolf Hitler, the new Chancellor, at the home of General Baron von Hammerstein, Chief of the Army Supreme Command, on 2 February 1933. The occasion was the sixtieth birthday of the Foreign Minister, Baron von Neurath, who had held his office through both preceding Cabinets. After dinner Hitler, in his first speech to the admirals and generals present, introduced himself and his policy to the armed forces. After a brief summary of his former career and his general objectives, he emphasized that he was taking over the leadership of both domestic and foreign policy, and that in the future the armed services would never be used for purposes of domestic policy; that, instead, they were to give their entire attention to military development and training and to the defense of the country against external enemies.

Hitler's Views on the Navy

A short time later I made my first official report to the new Chancellor in the presence of General von Blomberg, the new Minister of Defense. My report dealt entirely with the condition of the Navy, its degree of preparedness, and its tasks. On this occasion Hitler gave me his concept of Germany's future naval policy, and ended with the statement that it was his firm resolve to live in peace with England, Italy, and Japan under all circumstances. "I never want to have war with England, Italy, or Japan," he said. "The German Fleet's role lies within the framework of its responsibilities toward European continental policy."

Names of countries that might possibly become opponents he never mentioned. However, since the Russian naval forces were as yet of little significance, the only European power left against which the strength of the German Fleet had to be measured was France.

At this period, the French Navy had for a long time been steadily increasing in ships and personnel under the veteran Navy Minister, Georges Leygues—a development that would be continued under Navy Minister Piétri and Admirals Durand-Viel and Darlan. Significant of the expansion had been the construction of the French battle cruisers of the *Dunkerque* class. However, neither at this time nor later was there any actual talk of preparation for, or even possibility of, war against either France or Russia.

Shortly after this, Hitler told me that he had no intention of disputing Britain's claim to a sea supremacy commensurate with her world interests; that, in fact, he would like to confirm this by an Anglo-German agreement fixing British and German relative naval strengths in order that Britain would know beyond any doubt that a conflict between the two fleets was entirely out of the question as far as he, Hitler, was concerned. He stated that he was thinking of a ratio of one to three as a reasonable preponderance of British seapower. In this conversation Hitler showed himself well informed on previous thinking along these lines; Admiral von Tirpitz's proposal for a ratio of ten to sixteen in 1912, for instance.

The idea for making such an agreement with Britain was entirely Hitler's, but I was in complete accord. However, for practical reasons, I suggested a thirty-five per cent ratio for the German Fleet instead of the thirty-three and one-third per cent—a suggestion which he promptly accepted.

It was immediately apparent what far-reaching consequences such an agreement, if effected, would have on the German Navy. For one thing, it would eliminate all debates over the position of the Navy in Germany's foreign policy. By tying the German Navy ratio to Britain's, Germany could not be accused, in future disarmament or fleet conferences, of starting an armament race. At the same time the ratio would provide a pattern for future naval development as far as the Reichstag and the government were concerned, thus insuring a steady and continuing construction program.

It was equally apparent that the proposed 35 to 100 ratio would be a tremendous benefit to the British also. Since German naval rearmament in some degree was inevitable, a fixed ratio such as this would relieve the British from constant uncertainty and anxiety in regard to their own naval program. This limitation on our own naval power would mark a radical shift to an entirely continental policy—a limitation which no other nation had ever voluntarily set upon herself.

Naturally such a concession would not be made without asking some political compensation in return. England's acceptance of such an agreement would automatically annul the disarmament decrees of the Versailles Treaty, which, as far as the German Navy was concerned, would thus be replaced by a voluntary agreement. A momentous decision was at stake.

Hitler's intention of reaching a sane and friendly agreement with Great Britain was completely in accord with my own ideas. It was regrettable that such an agreement on relative naval strength had not been reached before World War I, for we in the German Navy well realized that it was British and American seapower that had brought us to our knees despite the great victories of German arms on land and the Russian breakdown. Such a situation should never be allowed to recur.

Any idea of a future armed conflict with the United States would have been regarded by us as sheer lunacy, for we could not possibly imagine how any German continental policy could ever drag us into war with the United States. Hence, if a naval agreement with Great Britain could eliminate the possibility of war with that power, we would avoid the difficulties and dangers which had resulted from our foreign policy before World War I. I for one was convinced that Germany had thoroughly learned that lesson from the defeats of the past.

Meanwhile, though, until such a naval agreement could be reached, it behooved us to avoid the appearance of anything that might be considered a violation of the disarmament conditions—i.e. a "rearmament"—to which we were still bound. While Hitler, in December 1933, had given his approval for another pocket battleship for the 1934 budget, even as late as June 1934 he would not give definite approval for increasing the firepower of the two pocket battleships already authorized under the 1934 budget by adding a third 28-cm. triple turret to the armament already planned, and all that he would allow was preliminary plans for the mounts. However, the 1934 battleships were given greater tonnage in order to increase their defensive armor. While it would have been militarily desirable to step up the main battery caliber to 38-cm., this would have been an error politically. Furthermore, in order to mount 38-cm. guns in the 1934-budget battleships, later named *Scharnhorst* and *Gneisenau,* their whole design would have had to be changed, which would have greatly delayed their construction. But there would be no violation of the Versailles Treaty in the laying of the keel of the new *Nürnberg,* of the *Leipzig* class, nor of the four reserve destroyers already contracted for. From the designs of these last ships our first 1,850-ton destroyers eventually were developed.

But there was not enough money in the Navy budget to construct all the ships which would have materialized from our "conversion construction plan." The 186,000,000-mark naval budget of 1933 was little more than the preceding budgets. This money was doled out according to plan. In February 1933 the Navy received 14,000,000-marks additional, to which was added another 21,700,000-marks in April, largely from a "make work" plan. At the end of April the Navy received 80,000,000 more marks, with the prospect of receiving the same amount every year.

If the Navy hoped to gain a larger budget, it would have to show that the money was being used to the best possible advantage. Having learned its lesson in the Tirpitz period, the Navy had its budget division directly under the Chief of the Admiralty.

To insure that the money was spent exactly as the Reichstag had intended, the budget division had to be able to account for the expenditure of even the smallest amount. This our budget division did with such efficiency that I could pass on any proposed expenditure without delay, and without a single overdraft ever occurring or a single other violation of budget regulations. Knowing the sad aftermath of the Lohmann affair, I maintained closest touch with the Minister of Finance and kept him informed at all times, particularly with regard to new billets of civil servants and employees. To avoid any possible accusation of personal favoritism or carelessness, personnel selected for such positions were always discussed with the Ministry of Finance, and the selection made in strict compliance with the government's directives in such matters. At the same time we gradually reduced the percentage of civilian personnel to naval personnel in these offices, to prevent any possible buildup of an office bureaucracy.

Every year I informed all subordinate offices of the military needs of the service, and made them understand that the emphasis lay on the construction of new ships and training the necessary personnel for them. No delay could ever be tolerated in these particulars. And I repeatedly reminded them that their responsibility increased in proportion to the increase in the large sums now being allotted to them.

By the middle of 1934 I had outlined a general plan for the Navy's development, along with an estimate of the funds that would be needed. This formed the basis for the report that I, like the heads of the other armed forces, had to make personally to Hitler at Berchtesgaden in August 1934. With the concrete figures I was able to provide, my report received general approval, especially from Hjalmar Schacht, the president of the Reichsbank. He considered the Navy's demands as moderate, and not Utopian. This understanding made our further planning much easier.

The year 1934 also brought two important events, which, while primarily political in nature, could have had marked effects on the German Navy. The first of these occurred on 30 June while our third pocket battleship was being launched at the Wilhelmshaven Naval Shipyard. This ship was to be named the *Admiral Graf Spee,* in honor of Vice Admiral Count Spee, with whom I had served in the Far East in the old *Deutschland* and whose exploits at Coronel and the Falkland Islands I had described in my volumes on the cruiser warfare in the *History of German Naval Operations.* I felt honored at being invited to give the christening address. In the presence of numerous naval representatives, a large crowd of spectators, and a pitifully small group of survivors from the Falklands battle, in which Admiral von Spee had gone down with his two sons, I memorialized the old cruiser squadron, its brave crews, and its unforgettable commander. As the *Graf Spee* slid down the ways, Huberta, the admiral's daughter, christened her.

At this very moment, elsewhere in the country, dramatic events were taking place. An alleged revolt under the Chief of Staff of the SA, Ernest Röhm, had been suppressed by force under the personal direction of Hitler. As first reported, the revolt constituted a grave menace to the State, and immediate and severe countermeasures by the government had been officially sanctioned by the Minister of Justice, Dr. Gürtner, who was not a member of Hitler's party.

The day following, General von Blomberg, the Minister of Defense, had issued a proclamation in which he emphasized that the armed forces, as defenders of the entire nation, had no part in internal political battles. Certainly the Navy had taken no part whatsoever in them.

Gradually, however, other information and details leaked out which made it apparent that during the government's police action, many measures not only morally unjustifiable but highly illegal, had been taken. This convinced me more than ever that the Navy, like all the other armed services, had to stay completely clear of all political squabbles and oppose an impassable barrier to all influences attempting to persuade them otherwise.

The second nationally important occurrence was the death, on 2 August 1934, of Field Marshal von Hindenburg, President of the German Republic. He was one of the great men of our age, and I was proud to have served under him through five Cabinet changes. His clear conception of the separate spheres of the soldier and the politician, and his unswerving faithfulness to the Constitution, had been a guiding light to me.

When, in succession to von Hindenburg as President, Hitler also became Commander in Chief of all the armed forces, I naturally took my oath of allegiance to him, as did General von Blomberg, General of the Artillery Baron von Fritsch, and General of the Air Force Göring. None of us had any hesitation in doing this as, in addition to being von Hindenburg's legal successor by universal interpretation and by von Hindenburg's own preference, his appointment as Chancellor had been unquestioned and the German people had repeatedly voiced their unanimous confidence in him. In fact, at this time the public confidence in Hitler's abilities was such that no one would have suggested any other person as better fitted for the Presidency.

As soon as we had all taken our oaths, in writing, Hitler assured us spontaneously that he would not make any basic changes in the structure of the armed forces. Certainly none of us in the armed services could at that moment have foreseen the developments of the future.

At the moment the Navy's thoughts were concentrated mostly on construction and personnel. The 15,000 officers and men allowed Germany under the Versailles Treaty would not even be enough to man the ships actually allowed under that treaty, much less the increase we anticipated in 1933 and 1934. Our worst shortage was in young officers, as it took three and a half years to educate one for even the lowest commissioned rank.

One measure we took to cope with the situation was to increase the number of officer candidates, and to put two, instead of one, training cruisers into commission for officer and petty officer candidates. As another measure we took into the Navy a large number of young merchant marine officers for training for commissions. Having already had excellent sea training, they needed only special, short-time training in ordnance. The German shipping firms generously released all who applied for entrance into the Navy. These men from the merchant marine all proved excellent officer material, and many eventually distinguished themselves in World War II: Lieutenant Commanders Prien, Endrass, and Bleichrodt as U-boat captains, and Kohlauf and Feldt as commander of torpedo boat and motor torpedo boat squadrons, respectively.

The screening of officer candidates rested in the hands of the Education Inspection, in Kiel, and the officers of this activity were distinguished by their understanding of youth, their concept of naval responsibility, and their ability to indoctrinate their young charges in corresponding manner. It was not just through chance that the commanders of the sailing schoolships performed notably, later, as commanders of auxiliary cruisers and regular fleet units.

Once an officer had finished his early training, his future career, both as to promotion and assignment to duty, rested in the hands of the Bureau of Naval Officer Personnel in the Admiralty. This Bureau, directly under my command, I kept under the immediate supervision of one of my most dependable subordinates, who recognized the heavy responsibility he assumed in accepting the command. When it came to the selection and assignment of captains and flag officers, I personally made the ultimate decisions.

One of the most critical duties in the Navy is the assignment of officers to the particular duties for which their personal and professional qualifications best fit them. Not every officer is qualified for duties to which his age and previous training would normally entitle him; the responsibilities of the positions he has held, as well as his performance in those positions, must be carefully analyzed. Considering the differences in character, intelligence, zeal, and health of any half dozen officers, and the impossibility of knowing them all equally well personally, it is inevitable that errors of judgment in selection and assignment of officers will occur at times.

Nor do I hold myself blameless of errors in decisions I myself have made at times relative to assignment of officers or their fitness for promotion. Despite the most careful analysis, in which my chiefs of personnel and other advisers cooperated, I realize instances where my judgment was wrong. I can truthfully say, however, that my decisions, bitterly disappointing as they sometimes probably were for the officer concerned, were never held against me; the bond of comradeship that united us in the Navy was too strong for that. Equally loyal were those few officers in high positions of responsibility whom, for reasons of basic disagreement, I felt necessary to remove, or who requested reassignment themselves. For my part, I never let them feel that I had in any way lost confidence in them because of these disagreements.

But just as I realize instances in which my judgment of an officer was wrong, there was one decision which I know without shadow of doubt was right. That was my selection, in 1935, of Junior Captain Karl Dönitz, just relieved as commander of the training cruiser *Emden,* to be the head of our new submarine force. His passionate devotion to duty, his energy and his leadership of the submarine force through the years to come earned both my respect and admiration. And his frankness and sincerity in all his dealings with me, both then and when, later, he became my successor, equally earned my gratitude.

This frankness of expression is one thing which always delighted me in the officers and civilians under my command, and especially the more senior ones. They were no "yes men," but men of character, never afraid to give their views even when they disagreed with me. I was only too happy to encourage their frankness.

The year 1934 saw an increase in the exchange of visits between German naval ships and foreign vessels. The British cruiser *Achilles* visited Kiel, and HMS *Leander,* flagship of the British Second Cruiser Squardon, with Rear Admiral Noble embarked, spent several days at Stettin. Also five ships of their Second Destroyer Flotilla visited Swinemünde. In return, Rear Admiral Kolbe, Commander of our Scouting Forces, visited Portsmouth with his flagship *Königsberg* and the cruiser *Leipzig.* It was the first time a German man-of-war had visited an English port since World War I, and both the British Navy and British public in general gave our visiting ships a warm welcome.

This was of particular significance, because it seemed to indicate a favorable atmosphere for the naval agreement discussions which were to begin in Germany or England early the following year.

This was the agreement that Hitler had told me he hoped to achieve shortly after he had become Chancellor. After preliminary approaches, the British and French Governments had notified the German Government, early in February 1935, that they were ready to discuss the question of armaments in general, with the aim of substituting new disarmament provisions for the original ones of the Versailles Treaty. The German Government answered favorably, and a British delegation was expected to arrive in Berlin in the near future.

But on 16 March 1935 Hitler denounced the armament limitations of the Versailles Treaty and proclaimed the resumption of compulsory military training. Two days later the British Government registered a stern protest against this unilateral action of Germany, and called an inter-allied conference of France, England, and Italy, to be held in Stresa, at which Britain's two allies joined her in rejecting Germany's action.

Yet, oddly enough, at the very time Britain protested Germany's rearmament pronouncement in March, she also asked whether the German Government still was ready to receive British representatives in Berlin to discuss the naval situation. Upon Germany's affirmative reply, British Foreign Secretary Sir John Simon and Lord Privy Seal Anthony Eden arrived in Berlin on 25 March for their well-known meeting with Hitler.

Hitler promptly informed them of his desire to arrive at an agreement with Britain on the relative strengths of the two fleets, and stated that he would be content with a fleet only 35 per cent as strong as Great Britain's. The British delegation took note of the proposal, without any expression of opinion, and arrangements were made for a preliminary discussion by naval experts from both countries in the near future.

To understand British willingness to enter into such discussions, a review of the naval armament situation since 1919 would be in order.

Before World War I Britain had claimed for herself a traditional superiority in fleet strength over the combined fleets of the two next strongest sea powers. But the United States determined to build up an American Fleet inferior to none. Faced with this prospect, the British in 1921 had agreed to the American proposal for a conference of the five leading naval powers—England, the United States, Japan, France, and Italy—to discuss national armaments. The conference, held in Washington in 1921 and 1922, achieved no agreement in over-all armaments, but did result in a limitation of capital-ship tonnages on a proportionate basis, as well as limits as to displacement and gun sizes on the individual ships of certain classes. Great Britain, with numerous bases all over the world, had wanted a strict limitation on the sizes and gun calibers of cruisers, but the United States, with few bases, had held out for the same allowed tonnage in fewer cruisers, but larger and more heavily armed and with longer range. France and Italy had refused to consider any limitation on submarines or auxiliary ships. The net result was that while there was a naval holiday in capital ship construction, there began a race in the construction of light forces.

Further disarmament conferences, in Rome in 1924 and in

Geneva in 1927, brought no results except to increase the disagreement between the British and the Americans over the cruiser question.

At the Washington conference, all further capital ship construction had been banned for ten years. At the London Conference in 1930 among the same five powers, Great Britain and the United States proposed the prohibition on capital ship construction be extended for another five years, but France and Italy objected on the grounds that Germany had begun construction of a pocket battleship. Britain then endeavored to persuade Germany to drop the pocket battleship, but Chancellor Brüning refused.

The next Disarmament Conference between the five powers was scheduled for 1935. Meantime a preliminary conference was held at Geneva in 1933. At this conference Great Britain had presented the so-called "MacDonald Plan," under which the great sea powers could continue arming within the framework of their special treaties, but the smaller naval powers were to be kept to their level at the time. Germany for the first time had been invited to confer on disarmament, and an effort was made to persuade her to postpone until 1937 her battleship replacement construction program. The net result was that the MacDonald Plan was rejected by practically everyone.

Then in December 1934 Japan announced that she was withdrawing from the joint agreement as of 31 December 1936, which was the two years' notice required by the London Agreement of 1930.

Thus, Great Britain's attempt to form a system of naval disarmament controlled and influenced by herself had broken down almost completely. It is no wonder that she now welcomed support from any side. This support was offered her by Germany's proposal voluntarily to limit her Navy to only 35 per cent the strength of Britain's. As a *quid pro quo* Germany asked only that the disarmament clauses of the Versailles Treaty be abrogated in favor of the new agreement.

Naturally any such agreement would be primarily a political rather than a naval one, and hence would be a matter for action by the government itself. Hitler, after the visit of the two British delegates, bided his time; in fact he did not even react upon inquiries by the British naval attaché until the British Government itself instituted regular diplomatic negotiations.

Evidently at this stage the British did not want to offend their partners in the Versailles Treaty by rush negotiations. Hence their delegates proposed that naval experts from the two countries meet for preliminary study.

To study the matter from the German Navy's side, I appointed a small special commission under Rear Admiral Guse, Chief of the Naval Operations Department, to work up our own proposals and viewpoint. This preparatory work was especially important, as Special Envoy Joachim von Ribbentrop, who was to head the German diplomatic delegation, had no knowledge and no understanding of naval affairs at all. Hence I had Commander Bürkner of my personal staff brief von Ribbentrop on our problems, as well as to maintain continuous contact with Captain Muirhead-Gould, the British naval attaché in Berlin, during the preparatory stages. Rear Admiral Schuster and Commander Kiderlen were to be the German Navy's representatives in the actual delegation to London.

Hitler had assured me that in the negotiations whereby we voluntarily limited our naval strength to 35 per cent of Britain's, no vital German naval interests would be sacrificed. In the preliminary "expert discussions," we would give away no information about our construction then underway or our future plans until von Ribbentrop had succeeded in obtaining a definite political success by an exchange of diplomatic notes between Ribbentrop and British Foreign Secretary Simon.

To make certain that von Ribbentrop would understand this and make no concessions in London at the Navy's expense, a private conference was held in Hitler's home in Munich on 31 May 1935. I spoke privately with Hitler first, and then we were joined by Foreign Minister von Neurath, Defense Minister von Blomberg, Department Secretary Lammers, Special Envoy von Ribbentrop, and Rear Admiral Schuster. After an hour and a half's discussion, the Navy's proposals were unanimously accepted. Thereupon I put the proposals in writing. Hitler approved them, and they were given to von Ribbentrop. Hitler impressed upon the delegation that rather than making any concessions beyond those stipulated, the delegation was to break off negotiations and return home.

The German delegation was received most hospitably in London, and on 3 June, only a day or two later, they participated in the parade celebrating the King's birthday. Negotiations began on the next day, and the German embassy succeeded in securing the presence of the British Foreign Secretary at the opening session. This was in direct accord with the German conviction that the objective was even more political than military.

But the British were of another opinion; they thought the discussion by the naval and military experts should begin before any political questions were considered, and the British Foreign Secretary left the conference. However, after two days the British Cabinet declared itself in agreement with the German political standpoint, and the discussions between the naval experts began. The German views had been prepared most capably by Captain Wassner, the German naval attaché in London, and the discussions proceeded rapidly and favorably.

Then at the very last moment, the British Foreign office took a different tack. They had previously declared that the legal adviser of the British delegation would have to "check" on any texts arrived at, and now this adviser, without any instructions, inserted a preamble which, in its political effect, would have bound the whole agreement to the Versailles Treaty again. However, the British Admiral Little, who represented the Admiralty in the discussions, and the British Under Secretary of State, Sir Robert Craigie, intervened in time to prevent serious discord.

The Anglo-German Naval Agreement was concluded on 18 June 1935, and was confirmed by an exchange of notes between British Foreign Secretary Sir Samuel Hoare, and German Ambassador von Ribbentrop. By a coincidence the agreement was concluded on the hundred and twentieth anniversary of the Battle of Waterloo, where Napoleon had been defeated by the combined British and Prussian armies.

The agreement included the following principal points: the German Navy's strength was to be 35 per cent of the British Navy's strength, including the naval forces of the entire British Commonwealth as well; the size and fighting power of ships were to be measured according to the standards set in previous British agreements with other nations; Germany was granted parity with Britain in submarine strength. However, Germany agreed that the 35 per cent limitation applied not only to total strength, but also to the individual categories of ship classes—something very important to Britain, since she differed materially from France on this question. Germany also declared that she did not plan to build beyond 45 per cent of Britain's submarine force, and that if she ever felt that outside considerations forced her to build beyond that percentage, she would discuss the matter amicably with Britain before additional building.

The significance of this Anglo-German naval agreement probably was not realized by many in Germany at the time, partly because the British delegation had asked that the agreement be given minimum publicity in the newspapers. The British suspected that their former allies—particularly the French—would not give unreserved approval to Britain's procedure in concluding an independent agreement with Germany.

This naval agreement was a political success for Germany in that Britain's willingness to substitute a voluntary agreement in place of the rigid Versailles Treaty conditions not only broke up the so-called "Stresa front" but also sanctioned Germany's right thereafter to re-arm. Now, at last, Germany could no longer be justly accused of violating the disarmament conditions of the Treaty of Versailles.

But the British Government also gained a great deal. Till now it had been forced to play a lone hand in negotiating with other nations in the areas of naval armament, and hence could negotiate only limited separate treaties with each individual power. Now she could count on German support in the international conference which would shortly meet to discuss general naval armaments.

It seemed only fitting that at last these two naval powers should have reached a rapproachement. In its early days the Imperial Navy had patterned itself after the older British Navy in innumerable ways. At first, most of its ships were constructed in British shipyards, and up to the end of the century they spent much time in visits to British ports. Its ceremonial and shipboard customs were adopted from the British Navy, just as the regulations for the German Navy—*Service On Board*—drew from the British *King's Regulations*. Technical developments had often been parallel, and up to the First World War the political disagreements between the two governments had created no unbridgeable gap between the two navies. Each service had respect and understanding for the other. In World War I, the German and British Fleets had faced each other as stout opponents, not as relentless enemies. And after Germany's defeat, the British Navy, while loyally carrying out the policy of its government, rarely did anything deliberately to aggravate the humiliation and bitterness of defeat suffered by the German Navy.

On one occasion, it is true, there was every opportunity for such a spirit to materialize: at the time of the surrender of the German High Seas Fleet. But Rear Admiral von Reuter's scuttling of that fleet in Scapa Flow eliminated those ships as bones both of future contention and of personal animosities. Von Reuter's proud statement to the British admiral there—"I have done nothing that any British admiral would not have done in my place."—was something which the equally proud British could well understand. Now the Anglo-German naval agreement of 1935 bid fair to lay forever the ghosts of those scuttled ships at Scapa Flow.

I think a great deal of the British Navy's sympathy and understanding can be credited to Admiral John Jellicoe, that able seaman whom his country had honored by putting him in command of its Grand Fleet through the Battle of Skagerrak, and, later, by creating him First Sea Lord. In his later high positions he had always worked toward a closer agreement between England and Germany. He was the first Britisher after the end of the First World War to resume associations with the German Navy. It was at his suggestion that the British Legion, the British veterans' association, invited Vice Admiral von Trotha, Admiral Scheer's Chief of Staff, to attend its 1927 meeting. The following year Admiral Jellicoe wrote Admiral Scheer, his opponent at the Battle of Skagerrak, suggesting that they meet, as he tactfully and sociably expressed it, "to discuss some questions which history writers on both sides have left open." Unfortunately Admiral Scheer's death shortly afterward prevented any such meeting of the two great admirals of World War I.

I had endeavored in every way possible to meet this spirit of goodwill halfway. In addition to promoting exchange of visits of naval vessels between the two countries, I reconstituted the old "Kiel Week" on a new basis by instituting a series of "Naval Cup Sailing Races" open to participants from all navies. The British took a special interest in these races, and each year saw closer relationships between the officers of the two navies.

In this year of decision, and within five months of the signing of the Anglo-German naval agreement, Admiral of the Fleet Lord Jellicoe died on 20 November. The British Government arranged for his interment in St. Paul's Cathedral, in London, where England's greatest naval hero, Lord Nelson, also rests. I had known and respected Admiral Jellicoe from my youthful service in the Far East in 1898, when he commanded the British cruiser *Centurion* there. Now I tried to show not only our Navy's great respect for the dead admiral, but also our desire for future cordial relations between the two Navies. I therefore published a memorial eulogy of our honored opponent, and inasmuch as official duties prevented my leaving Berlin, I appointed Vice Admiral Foerster, Commander in Chief of the German Fleet, to represent the German Navy at the the state funeral.

The British Navy understood my intentions and assigned Vice Admiral Foerster a place among the twelve honorary pallbearers selected from the most prominent military and naval leaders. After the ceremony the Prince of Wales, substituting for the ill King George V, thanked Admiral Foerster in the name of his father and the English people, and assured him of his friendship for Germany.

By my further orders, at the very moment that the mortal remains of the commander of the Grand Fleet in World War I, Admiral of the Fleet John Rushworth Jellicoe, Viscount of Scapa, and Earl Brocas of Southampton, were lowered into the grave, the flags of all German warships, at home or abroad, were lowered to half-mast in a final honor to a great and gallant former opponent.

As I look back now, this was a peak in our progress and in my own hopes. The naval agreement with Great Britain, I believed, would offer a basis for peace for Germany and the rest of Europe far into the future. And with peaceful foreign relations and freedom from the bitter aftermath of the Versailles Treaty, I thought our domestic turmoil would calm down. Within the decade and a half since the end of World War I, the German Navy, by restricting itself to its own tasks, had avoided the political and social unrest of the times and had made substantial progress in its role of defender of the sea frontiers of the nation. I thought I had good reason to look to the future with confidence—especially as the Chief of the German Government, Hitler, had declared emphatically time and again that an assault upon Britain was henceforth unthinkable.

It was the tragedy of my life that our future took a completely different path.

IX

The Harvest of Versailles

ONLY A German who lived through those critical years can understand the deadly effect of the terms of the Versailles Treaty. That treaty had marked the end of a war which had broken out after forty years of peace—a war for which the German people themselves did not feel responsible. This was one reason why the treaty was detested by every German, for one of its main points was the demand that Germany acknowledge its guilt for the war. In addition there were other provisions which, imposed by force, were incomprehensible to the Germans. For instance, some of Germany's oldest national territory was confiscated, German land to the west of the Rhine was to be forever demilitarized and was to be occupied by foreign troops for long years; the city of Danzig was made a separate political entity; and all of Germany's colonies were taken from her. The award to Poland of German territory, particularly that part known as the "Polish Corridor," was something which impressed even the French Marshal Foch to the point of declaring, "There lie the seeds of a future war."

Futhermore, Germany's most important coal and iron district, the Saar, was to be removed from German sovereignty for fifteen years, and perhaps forever. The union of Austria with Germany—*anschluss,* which was wished by the people of both countries and which had been provided for in the German and Austrian constitutions—was prohibited. Rigid restrictions were placed on any German national armament or defense forces in order to keep Germany in a permanently dependent position, and Germany was ringed by a system of foreign military alliances and forces designed to keep the nation continually under military pressure.

Finally, practically all of Germany's merchant marine fleet was taken from her, and she was burdened with additional reparations of material and currency beyond all reason.

In light of the even greater tragedy that has since befallen Germany, it is difficult to visualize today the problems which the country faced after its defeat in World War I. All the German governments of that period—and especially the government in which General Groener was Minister of Defense—lived in continual fear of attack by Poland. Germany was so completely defenseless that even when French troops moved in and occupied the Ruhr district in 1923, Germany had nothing to oppose it except passive resistance. This occupation lasted over two years, and the occupation of the German Rhineland by foreign troops was to be more or less maintained until 1930.

The statesmen and politicians of the victorious Allies who had created the Treaty of Versailles were completely unrealistic in believing that they could keep the German people shackled forever. Such subjugation, including confiscation of national territory, occupation and military control, disregard for a people's sovereignty, and corresponding humiliation of its government, can lead only to inevitable currents of revolt.

One of the early results in Germany was a split among the German people themselves, with innumerable political parties. Enforced isolation and impossible economic situations brought on a wave of uncontrolled inflation which bankrupted many and reduced the whole nation to a state of poverty. Unemployment grew by leaps and bounds, and with it the menace of Communism. And the uniformed soldier and sailor, representing the only reliable protection for the government, were subject not only to vilification but to personal attacks by the Communists. Nor were they immune from similar attacks by political leaders in Reichstag debates and elsewhere, although they always had firm defenders in Presidents Ebert and von Hindenburg and leaders of the caliber of Noske, Gessler, Severing, Heinig, Bruning, Groener, Schopflin, and Ersing.

It is a sad commentary on the Allied leaders that although they refused any discussion with the Weimar Republic tending toward readjustment of the Versailles Treaty's inequities, they unhesitatingly entered into such discussion with the National Socialist State of Hitler, and granted it everything they had refused the Weimar statesmen.

But equally worth noting, though for a different reason, is the unquestioned support that the German armed services gave to the various governments of Germany, regardless of their composition, so long as these governments represented the will of the German people.

Certainly it was a position which the Navy had always maintained, except for minor dereliction by some individuals in the Kapp *putsch* days, and one which I emphasized from my first day as Chief of the Admiralty. To me, the German Navy and its personnel were an integral part of the nation and the people, and could not be separated, like a foreign body of mercenaries. The Navy's firmness, its loyalty, were all a part of the discipline and training it had received, beginning even with the early days of the Weimar Republic. There were those later in the National Socialist Party who tried to claim that this discipline and professional achievements were due solely to the influence of the leadership of the National Socialist State. Doubtless the increased aid and support the service received from the State did play some part, but without the foundations laid under the Weimar Republic, the Navy could never have achieved its later record.

The officers and men in the Navy, being but a cross-section of the whole German people, had writhed under the bitter penalties of the Versailles Treaty. They could not have done otherwise—it was simply a manifestation of the longing for freedom that is present in every vigorous people and in every reasonable individual.

Later, during the Nürnberg trials after the end of World War II, the Allies had good reason to forbid any discussion or even mention of the Versailles Treaty and its consequences. For the political circumstances which led to National Socialism and the call for a "strong man," a *Führer,* to lead Germany out of its difficulties, were merely direct consequences of the situation created by the victorious enemy powers in 1918. National Socialism, conceivable only against such a background, harped upon the shackling treaty, and, with the goals its party program offered, struck a chord which resounded in the heart of every disappointed German of the day.

As long as National Socialism was still on the upgrade the

German Navy in unshaken discipline proceeded to give the same loyalty it had given to all the previous governments under the Weimar state. There were no incidents. Had there been, I would have suppressed them with immediate severity. The accession of the new government was in any case an accomplished fact, and directly in accord with the constitution since Hitler's party was the strongest single party in the electorate. To have attempted to prevent its accession, President von Hindenburg would have had to break his oath, as President and Commander in Chief of the Armed Forces, to uphold the Weimar Constitution. The legal transmission of the government from Schleicher to Hitler in January 1933 spared the armed forces civil war.

When the Hitler Cabinet took over the government, it did not affect the armed forces, which continued, as always, under the President as head of the State. And in its composition the new government did not seem to offer any radically new departure, as few of the new Ministers came from the National Socialist German Workers' (Nazi) Party. However, the various polls and elections showed that the new government had the solid support of all segments of the population. On 24 March 1933 all the parties in the Reichstag, except the Social Democrats, voted in favor of legislation giving emergency powers to the new administration. The concordat signed in July between Germany and the Vatican also gained public approval. The work relief projects which were started on a grand scale did much to relieve the unemployment situation, and a general improvement in many fields brought satisfaction, hope, and warm approval from the people. It is true that national conditions generally were more favorable, and that many projects of the Weimar regime which had been started without success now achieved excellent results. Hitler gained credit in the public eye for impressive successes which previous administrations had failed to attain, and, after the squabbles of the Weimar Government, he received the German people's acclaim and confidence.

The armed services were quick to note everywhere a growing understanding of the responsibilities of the services, and increasing approval by the civilian public. In the Navy this was particularly noticeable in the shipyards, where Navy men and civilian workers came into close contact. This does not mean that everything was smooth sailing and that friction did not sometimes arise between naval personnel and members of the Nazi Party. Frequently commanding officers had to defend themselves against biased charges and to settle touchy problems. Inside the Navy, though, such quarrels were insignificant and generally settled without my having to intervene.

Naturally the views and personalities of the individuals had a great deal to do with this relationship toward the Nazi Party. There was quite an air of skepticism among the older officers, especially, but they were perfectly free to express their doubts or criticisms without fear of retaliation. I knew a number of officers who did not agree with the system of the National Socialist State and the Nazi Party, and who did not hesitate to speak their minds. As long as these officers did their duty—and they did it right to the end of the war—they lost nothing in anyone's estimation and suffered no adverse action. Whatever the person's views—enthusiastic approval, cautious reserve, or open rejection—the important thing was that the Navy, in its entirety, gave to the new government the same dependable loyalty that it had given to previous administrations in the days of the Weimar Republic.

I saw no reason to depart from my concepts and principles as to the responsibility of the armed services toward the duly elected government. My duty lay in the field of cooperation and loyal obedience—an attitude common to the Navy and the German people everywhere. Had I not felt I could conscientiously do this, I would have immediately resigned, as without being loyal to the State I could not demand that the Navy be loyal to me.

And my duties, as I saw them, consisted in developing, training, and educating the Navy's personnel and in maintaining and improving its material so that it could contribute its just share toward the security of the nation. In those days no one could have foreseen the future into which that course would lead, but for my part in leading the Navy along that course I take full responsibility before the bar of history.

The naval agreement which the new administration had achieved with Great Britain made necessary immediately a whole new analysis of the Navy's role and the developments essential to fulfillment of that role.

In the matter of personnel we were fortunate in having made a head start. Although the Versailles Treaty had limited the entire Navy to only 1,500 new recruits per year, by deft selection and training we had built up a nucleus of disciplined, well trained officers and men. So high had been the standard of the petty officers and enlisted men that we were able to promote an unusual number to higher ranks and grades and greater responsibilities with the expanding Navy.

One tremendously encouraging thing was the attitude of the British toward Germany's new position under the naval agreement. This was made public in a speech delivered on 26 June 1935 before the British House of Lords by Admiral of the Fleet Earl Beatty, who, as commander of the British battle cruisers, and later as Commander in Chief of the British Fleet, had faced the German Navy in the most important naval battles of the First World War. "I am of the opinion," he said of the naval agreement, "that we owe thanks to the Germans. They came to us with outstretched hands and voluntarily proposed to accept a 35 to 100 ratio in fleet strength. If they had made different proposals, we would not have been able to stop them. That we do not have an armament race with one nation in the world at least is something for which we must be thankful."

This was no overstatement. The sacrifice that Germany had made in voluntarily accepting a 35 to 100 inferiority in naval strength compared to the British was indeed great. We had made this sacrifice because through it we hoped to eliminate any possibility of England ever again being an enemy—and we hoped, circumstances permitting, eventually to secure her alliance. In a conversation Baron von Neurath and I had with British Ambassador Sir Neville Henderson at one of Hitler's receptions in the winter of 1938-1939, we were discussing the naval agreement, and I observed that Great Britain seemed to be taking it all just as a matter of course. This was definitely not the case, replied the Ambassador emphatically, and the British attitude would be evident when the settlement of the colonial question was taken up. This was the first

I had ever heard of any intended settlement of the colonial problem.

The new naval agreement would give us plenty to do to build up the German Fleet to the strength required for the new German continental policy which Hitler had outlined to me in my first official discussion with him. As the naval holiday set up in the Washington Disarmament Treaty of 1922, and renewed with changes, would expire in 1936, with almost no chance of being extended, Great Britain would undoubtedly move sooner or later to increase her fleet strength, which would automatically raise the proportionate allowed strength of the German Navy.

At the moment—early 1935—Great Britain's naval strength consisted of: 12 battleships, 3 battle cruisers, 8 aircraft carriers, 19 heavy cruisers, 35 light cruisers, 19 flotilla leaders, 150 destroyers, and 54 submarines. On the 35 per cent basis, this would permit Germany, in terms of equivalent tonnage, 184,000 tons of battleships, 47,000 tons of aircraft carriers, 51,000 tons of heavy cruisers, and 119,000 tons of light cruisers and destroyers combined. Since our permitted ratio in submarines was 45 and not 35 per cent, this would permit us immediately to build up to a strength of 23,700 tons of submarines. But that particular moment the German Navy had, in modern, postwar ships, only 3 pocket battleships of the *Deutschland* class, totaling about 35,000 tons, plus 6 light cruisers totaling 40,000 tons, and 12 destroyers totaling only about 11,000 tons—and no submarines.

Before any public announcement of our existing construction plans and future intentions, however, it was determined to complete and commission the first postwar German submarines. This U-boat construction program had been planned with greatest care, with designs already completed for three different types of submarines—250-ton, 500-ton, and 750-ton classes. In addition, work was already underway for prefabricating the parts of the smaller 250-ton class, so that the assembly could be completed and the boats launched and commissioned within a very short time. In fact, by 27 September 1935 the first submarine squadron was operational, with six boats joining the fleet and another six going for training activities at the submarine school. This first U-boat squadron was appropriately named the Weddigen Squadron, after the famous U-boat commander of the First World War. This squadron was at first commanded by Captain Dönitz, but I soon made him commander of the entire Submarine Force with the responsible task of developing the new German submarine arm.

Special attention was given to the selection of officers for the Submarine Force. Thus, at Dönitz's request, Commander Thedsen (Eng.) was designated Squadron Engineer, and, later, Force Engineer. An officer with a distinguished record in submarines in World War I, he rose to the rank of Rear Admiral (Eng.) as Chief Engineer Officer in the Submarine Force in World War II. From the newly trained submarine commanders Lieutenant Commander Godt was selected to be Chief of Staff of the Commander of the Submarine Force, which position he held throughout World War II. Naval constructors who had a prominent part in building up the Submarine Force included Schürer, Bröking, Aschmoneit, Diestelmeyer, Sperling, and Friese.

On 9 July 1935, we announced for the first time the commissioning of the new submarines, as well as our fleet construction program for the future:

> To expand the Navy to the level of 35 per cent of British displacement, as set down in the naval agreement with England, the following new construction has been laid down, or will be laid down during 1935.
> 1. Two battleships of 26,000 tons each, armed with 28-cm. guns.
> 2. Two cruisers of 10,000 tons each, armed with 20-cm. guns.
> 3. Sixteen destroyers of 1,625 tons each, with 12.7-cm. guns (most of these have already been laid down in 1934 and 1935).
> 4. (a) Twenty submarines of 250 tons each (one of these is already in commission and two others have been launched).
>   (b) Six submarines of 500 tons each.
>   (c) Two submarines of 750 tons each.

Plans were being made for the construction of the first German aircraft carrier, as well as for additional battleships which would be laid down in 1936 and in subsequent years in accordance with the ratio provided in the agreement.

At this time the French Navy already was building two battleships of the *Dunkerque* class. With a displacement of 26,500 tons each, an armament of eight 33-cm. guns, and a speed of 30 knots, these had been proclaimed the answer to the German pocket battleships with their 10,000 tons displacement, six 28-cm. guns, and 26 knots speed. In addition France had provided for a 35,000-ton battleship, construction on which was to start in November 1935.

In total strength the French Fleet was about 60 per cent of the British Fleet. But in submarines, the French, with 96 submarines in commission and another 15 building, far outnumbered the British submarine arm of 54 submarines in commission and another 6 building. If the French Fleet did nothing but replace obsolete ships, it would nevertheless be almost double the strength of the German Fleet even if we built to the maximum allowed under the Anglo-German naval agreement. Hence there was no cause for French uneasiness over the agreement, as to either number or size of ships allowed Germany.

On its part, the British public might have taken exception only to that part of the agreement which permitted Germany immediately a submarine strength of 45 per cent of Britain's, with provision to build right up to parity after friendly discussions between the two powers. But Sir Bolton Eyres-Monsell, British First Sea Lord, calmed any such fears by announcing in the House of Commons that Germany had declared her willingness to subscribe to the international agreements relative to submarine warfare, one provision of which prohibited the sinking of merchant ships without warning. And on 23 September 1936 Germany proved her good faith by officially signing these agreements, known as the London Submarine Protocol.

This Protocol limiting submarine warfare was a direct outgrowth of the unrestricted submarine warfare of World War I, and it signified something new not only in the military sense but in international law as well. Opinions on the conduct of submarine warfare had been widely divergent among the naval leaders, politicians, and international lawyers of the various countries, especially in connection with the much debated point of armed merchant vessels. Among the agreements discussed at the Washington Naval Conference of 1921-1922 had been one which would have required submarines to observe the same general rules of warfare as surface ships. England, France, Italy, Japan, and the United States had signed such an agreement, but the French Government had refused to ratify it, whereupon in 1934 Japan rescinded her concurrence.

At the 1930 London Conference, the submarine question had

ADMINISTRATION BUILDING, BALTIC NAVAL STATION, KIEL

LECTURE HALL, BALTIC NAVAL STATION
Grand Admiral Raeder addresses a distinguished group.

ADMIRAL'S INSPECTION

again been discussed, with several changes suggested. For one thing, France objected to the provision which would have made submarine commanders who violated the agreement subject to the same treatment as pirates. It was the French viewpoint that if the submarine commander acted under military orders, under international law it was the government that should be tried, and not the submarine commander. It is notable that in the later international trials against German military commanders after World War II, this earlier standpoint of the French Government was completely ignored.

In any event, neither France nor Italy would ratify the London Naval Treaty of 1930. Accordingly, in 1936 the same five great naval powers again assembled to discuss the problem of submarine warfare. The agreement eventually arrived at was in the form of a separate treaty dealing with submarine warfare alone, and it was this London Submarine Protocol that Germany signed. The provisions of this important agreement were made a part of the Prize Regulations of the German Navy, and they formed the basis of the directives under which German U-boats operated at the beginning of World War II.

This London Conference of 1935-1936 was important to the German Navy in other respects also. The Washington Naval Treaty of 1921-1922 and the London Naval Treaty of 1930 would expire at the end of 1936 unless renewed before then. Hence the representatives of the five powers convened at the end of 1935, well in advance.

Since Germany, owing to her resurgence and to the naval agreement she had signed with Britain, was clearly marked as a future naval power, it was proposed that she be invited to participate in the conference, and Germany declared that she would accept such an invitation if extended. However, France objected on the ground that such recognition would be tantamount to acknowledging the demise of the Versailles Treaty. The difficulty was settled by agreement that, in addition to the regular treaty to be signed by the five convening powers, the provisions of such an agreement would be embodied in a separate treaty which England would sign with Germany. Russia was to be brought into the picture by a similar bilateral treaty between England and the Soviet Union.

In the London Naval Treaty of 1936, as finally formulated, the old ratio of relative naval strengths was dropped completely. About the only restrictions continued were limits on the size of ships and the caliber of guns they could carry, and also the holiday in building of heavy cruisers and battleships over 10,000 tons. Otherwise, each power could now build any naval ships it thought it own position and responsibilities demanded.

Japan did not even join the conference, and Italy refused to sign the final agreement because England and France had applied sanctions against her during the Ethiopian War. As for Germany, she was restricted to a percentage of British naval strength by the conditions of the Anglo-German naval agreement which she had voluntarily accepted.

Germany, however, was particularly hit by the five-year extension of the naval holiday as to construction of heavy cruisers and battleships of less than 17,000 tons. All the other leading navies already had plenty of such ships in commission, whereas Germany couldn't even continue building ships like the *Deutschland* or *Graf Spee*. Furthermore, Russia was demanding the right to build seven ships in the prohibited class.

Accordingly, a compromise was worked out in a special agreement with England whereby Germany could build two more heavy cruisers in addition to the pocket battleships already laid down, but she would build these additional two only under press of exceptional circumstances, as Germany in her own words, "did not want to do anything that might revive a general armament race."

These various agreements established in broad outlines the total composition of the new German Fleet and the various types of ships. However, before actual construction was planned, a number of important points had to be considered, not only from the naval and technical angles, but from the foreign policy aspect as well.

The first decision was whether the German Fleet was to be built for a definite, limited purpose or for meeting any situation that might arise anywhere. The size and nature of any nation's Navy is determined primarily by the enemies she would be likely to face in case of war. A Navy whose most probable opponent is a land power would place primary emphasis on construction of ships that would be used along a coast—destroyers, minesweepers, small submarines, and high speed motor boats. If she anticipates war with a country which is essentially a sea power, she would build ships capable of conducting operations at sea—such ships as aircraft carriers, surface ships of wide range and high speed, medium and large sized submarines, and supply ships. But rarely can any nation predict her future enemies so accurately as to be able to concentrate her entire naval program on these enemies alone. Generally, all that a nation can do is to build a Navy that will meet the maximum number of situations.

Our own construction program was based on what Hitler had told me at the time of my first official conference with him—that he "never wanted to go to war with England, Italy, and Japan, and therefore the expansion of the German Fleet was to be in conformity with the requirements of German continental policy."

This statement of policy naturally excluded the above mentioned States as eventual opponents, and, as a natural corollary, the exclusion would extend to the United States also. Within the limits of a European continental policy only the Soviet Union and the French—and probably the Polish Navy, with French support—could be regarded as possible opponents whose strength and composition should be considered in our expansion. Of these powers, Russia was predominantly a land power, while France was both a sea power and a land power. But I must reiterate that neither then nor for many years thereafter was there any talk by the leaders of the German State of preparation for, or even the possibility of, war against one of these nations.

In addition Hitler repeatedly reaffirmed his first statement to me that his strong desire was to live in peace with England, and I was convinced at that time that this was truly a basic policy with him. Considering the relative military strengths and geographical positions of the two countries, a naval war against England would have been nonsensical and I would have raised objections at once. Whenever possible I pointed out how hopeless it would be.

On the basis of naval thinking in those days prior to the great development of aviation, we based our construction plans on the theory that in a fleet the component ship types should be both complementary and interdependent. This was particularly true for Germany, with her few harbors and shallow coastal waters. Our submarines could not leave their harbors unless the channels were kept swept clear by minesweepers. Minesweepers in their turn require light, and sometimes heavy, forces to screen them against raiding enemy destroyers and cruisers. Destroyers and escort sloops also are necessary to screen heavy forces, to cover ships entering and leaving port, and to lay mines and perform countless other general tasks. For us the natural, and strategically correct, thing was to build a fleet whose component ships would form a properly proportioned whole.

Thus we planned for an all-round force, rather than one projected for any particular enemy. Although during the war of 1939 to 1945, with England our unexpected opponent, we found a major need for submarines, in our original plans submarines had occupied but a minor position, since, under the international agreements we had signed, the submarine's effectiveness as a weapon had been greatly limited. In addition, at the beginning of our expansion, we ourselves were not decided as to which type of submarine we should develop. Many officers in the Supreme Naval Command[1] held that in any future war, as in World War I, the submarine would operate alone and far afield, and therefore would have to be large. On the other hand Captain Dönitz, Commander of the Submarine Force, felt that our need was for a maneuverable submarine of medium size, which we could build in large numbers and still remain within the tonnage limitations of the Naval Agreement. He could then stage attacks with whole groups of submarines on enemy convoys, since even under the international rules convoyed merchant ships were subject to attack without any warning or search. Furthermore Captain Dönitz proposed to direct his submarines either at sea or from a central operations headquarters ashore. His views were accepted, and the subsequent tactical use of submarines in groups, or "wolf packs," was one of the outstanding advances in World War II, and was largely responsible for the remarkable successes achieved.

Captain Dönitz plunged wholeheartedly into his work of building up the submarine arm. Yet he was never narrow-minded or

[1] When the Germany Navy was increased, the old term "Admiralty" was changed to "Oberkommando der Kriegsmarine," or Supreme Naval Command, and the Chief of the Admiralty now became Commander in Chief of the Navy.

opinionated, either then or later when he was commander-in-chief of the Navy. Even so, mine was the over-all responsibility for the systematic development of the Navy as a whole, as well as for its integration into the political picture and, the industrial economy of the whole country. I had to take into consideration the capacity of the shipyards, the productivity of industry, and the development of harbors and locks, as well as the procurement and training of the necessary personnel for the ships. One of my heaviest responsibilities was to push the Navy's program with the government—generally against competing demands of the Army and Air Force, to which Hitler had to give equal attention.

Within the Supreme Naval Command, final decision on the construction program was made only after much discussion and debate, in which all members were invited to express their views. I owed much to Admiral Witzell, Chief of the Naval Ordnance Bureau; the Chief of the Construction Office, Director Schulz; clerks Burkhardt and Brandes; Admiral Guse, the Chief of the Command Bureau; and Admiral Densch, my chief of staff.

On 9 July we had publicly announced the laying down of two battleships, to be designated the *Scharnhorst* and the *Gneisenau*. Further construction of the *Deutschland* class of pocket battleships, of which we had laid down three, was given up, as France had begun construction of the battle cruisers *Dunkerque* and *Strasbourg*, whose superior size, higher speed, and heavier guns would outclass our smaller pocket battleships. The whole trend in foreign navies was to heavily armed and thickly armored high-speed battleships.

Hence we had to redesign the *Scharnhorst* and *Gneisenau* to provide them with much larger power plants and considerably higher speed than the three pocket battleships, and at the same time provide for heavier armor. To do this it would be necessary to increase their size to 30,000 tons each. Under the treaty classification of battleships, the *Scharnhorst* and *Gneisenau* should equal the *Dunkerque* and *Strasbourg* in sturdiness, and have somewhat higher speed. On the other hand the two French ships, with their eight 33-cm. guns mounted forward in two quadruple turrets, would presumably outclass the nine 28-cm. guns mounted in three triple turrets in our ships. After careful target tests we believed that our 28-cm. gun, with its specially designed high-explosive, armor-piercing shell, would be fully effective against the armor of the French ships. In addition our triple-turret guns could be fired more rapidly than the French quadruple turrets. Lastly, our ordnance specialists doubted that the French could fire full salvos from their quadruple turrets without suffering serious structural damage.

Naturally we thought about increasing the size of our main battery guns—perhaps shifting to six 38-cm. guns instead of the nine 28-cm. guns—but this would have slowed down construction of the ships seriously. Also, it could have had political repercussions. In planning our next two battleships, the *Tirpitz* and the *Bismarck,* our preliminary designs were for 35,000-ton ships carrying a main battery of 38-cm. guns. Attention was given to developing a gun especially for them that would penetrate the armor of any battleship built under the treaty limitations of the day.

Perhaps our most important problem was the type of power plant to install in the *Scharnhorst* and *Gneisenau.* We had spent a great deal of time developing a diesel power plant which, after initial difficulties, proved eminently successful in the pocket battleships. The diesel motor was so economical in fuel consumption that it gave the ships an exceptionally wide cruising range, making them particularly well adapted to operations far distant from any base. Much of the success of the diesel engines was due to the devoted efforts of our engineering officers, the engineroom force, and, especially, the work of the designer Laudahn, of the Supreme Naval Command, in cooperation with the MAN works (Engine Plant Augsburg-Nürnberg).

Lately there had been a new development—the introduction of high-temperature, high-pressure steam installations for industrial plants ashore. There was wide divergence of opinion both as to the relative advantages and disadvantages of the two types of engine as well as the risk connected with the use of the terrifically hot, high-pressure steam.

The normal thing, of course, would have been to install the two competing systems in experimental ships and conduct rigorous comparative tests. We had done just this when steam turbines were introduced before World War I, and had conducted similar tests before adopting the diesels for our pocket battleships. Unfortunately it was not possible now to go through such systematic, time-consuming tests.

For, although continuing development of the high-temperature, high-pressure steam power plant was a high priority project at the MAN plant, the new engines had not yet proved up to the high speed and high performance requirements for the new battleships. Waiting to develop them further would have caused unacceptable delay in the completion of our new battleships, cruisers, and destroyers. I had to decide at once. My decision was to take the risk and to go straight to the turbine engine with the new high-temperature, high-pressure steam.

We had made a start by hooking up the new type boilers to standard auxiliary engines in test plants in our shipyards, where topnotch experts, such as Professor Bauer of Bremen, gave them exhaustive tests under shore conditions. The engineer officers who were to run the power plants on our future ships participated in the tests and were favorably impressed.

As a beginning, we installed the new plants on the fast minesweepers, escort sloops, new destroyers, and the tender *Grille*. Defects promptly revealed themselves, mostly in connection with the increased weight and space requirements of the new installations. Close supervision by highly trained personnel was necessary for successful operation. Our designers and engineering experts argued, however, that these were only necessary "growing pains" and that the defects would soon be overcome.

Special effort was devoted to systematic training of engineroom personnel, exhaustive tests were made, and anything learned was immediately made available to everyone else. However, consistent high performance had not been attained by the time war broke out; only with the experience gained in wartime operations were the defects finally overcome.

Too much credit can not be given to the chief engineers and their men who kept the ships running during the war, despite all the strenuous, high-speed operations required during their activities. In those first months of the war only the devotion and herculean effort of all hands brought and kept the power plants up to a high degree of performance.

Even before then, however, the power plant on the heavy cruiser

Prinz Eugen showed marked improvement over those on the earlier built *Blücher* and *Admiral Hipper.* It was clear from the very beginning, though, that despite advantages in higher speed, less weight, and smaller space requirements, the new power plants would never give the long cruising radius of the older diesel with its low rate of fuel consumption. I considered the first high-temperature, high-pressure steam plants as but an intermediate step in the development of an engine that would satisfy all our naval and technical requirements. The decision had to be made, however. It seemed that only by going to such a steam power plant could we build the *Scharnhorst* and the *Gneisenau* without unacceptable delay.

X

Expanding the Navy

THE London Naval Agreement eased international tension, particularly between England and Germany. Beginning in 1936, every branch of the German Navy felt an upsurge of optimism. Because of the need for more officers and petty officers, three schoolships were always at sea on training cruises. Everywhere they were received in a most hospitable and friendly manner. Our captains brought back excellent reports of the cordial relations with the British Navy, and the same was true of the French and American navies. When our pocket battleship *Admiral Scheer* visited Stockholm in June of 1936, King Gustav V of Sweden came on board, received her commander and some of the officers at a special audience. In October, Czar Boris of Bulgaria visited the cruiser *Emden* when it was at the Black Sea port of Varna.

Similarly, foreign naval ships visited German ports. In the summer of 1937, the French training ship *Jeanne d'Arc* visited Kiel, the first French warship to enter a German port since the end of the First World War. That summer an American squadron of three battleships spent a week at Kiel, and Argentine battleships visited Hamburg and Wilhelmshaven. Kiel also received, for the first time in thirty years, a Japanese naval visitor, the cruiser *Ashigara,* whose crew also made an excursion to Berlin. Swedish cruisers, destroyers, and submarines were regular visitors at German Baltic ports.

The staging of the eleventh Olympic Games in Berlin in 1936 also made for friendly relations with foreign navies, as the German Navy was responsible for the sailing races, which were held at Kiel in August of that year. Commander Rogge, one of our best yachtsmen, was a member of the international committee of judges.

Shortly afterward, Kiel received visits from two Swedish naval training ships, as well as the Italian cruiser *Gorizia* and the British cruiser *Neptune.* Captain Bedford, of the *Neptune,* had an unusual commission to execute. Two years earlier, Germany had returned to the British general, Sir Ian Hamilton, the drums of the Gordon Highlanders which had been captured during the First World War. Now, as a return of courtesies, the British Admiralty had sent Captain Bedford to return the ship's bell of the battle cruiser *Hindenburg,* which had been salvaged from the scuttled ship at Scapa Flow and since then had been used on the British battle cruiser *Revenge.*

I made it a point to accept the ship's bell personally at Kiel, in order to express not only my appreciation but also my desire for a friendly understanding between the two nations and their navies. Our newest pocket battleship, the *Admiral Graf Spee,* participated in the international naval review at Spithead on the occasion of the coronation of King George VI in 1937. At the coronation in Westminster Abbey, all the German armed forces were represented by Field Marshal von Blomberg, while Admiral Otto Schultze, one of our U-boat aces in the First World War, was the Navy's special representative.

In those two years after the signing of the naval agreement, our Navy expanded notably. In October 1936 Field Marshal von Blomberg christened the new *Scharnhorst.* Two months later the *Gneisenau* came down the ways and was christened by the Commander in Chief of the Army, General Baron von Fritsch.

But when the *Admiral Hipper,* the first of our new heavy cruisers, was launched at the Blohm and Voss Shipyard in Hamburg on 6 February 1937, I spoke in honor of this great cruiser commander, and my wife christened the ship. For me, as for the Navy generally, it was self-evident that our first new heavy cruiser must bear the name of that great seaman whose character combined so ideally both personal gallantry and the offensive spirit. Never have I revered any of my superiors as I did the simple, frank, and fearless admiral whose self-confidence never left him, even in the most desperate situations, and whose inner spirit enabled him so fully to accept responsibility. As his chief of staff, for almost five years, both amid daily routine and in deadly combat, I had known him intimately. But I never lost sight of the fact that in the last analysis, regardless of what advice or suggestions are offered, when the chips are down it is the leader himself who has to take the responsibility of making decisions and making them stick. Admiral von Hipper had never shirked that responsibility.

Even in our rapid expansion, however, there was never any need in the Navy to depart from the training and educational concepts with which we had begun our postwar revival. First and foremost were discipline and morale, and with them the determination that our expansion should take the form of new ships and increased battle readiness. Everything else would be secondary.

This was the principle under which we divided the Navy budget. The Naval Operations Department and the Budget Division, with the help of the technical bureaus and the Administrative Department drew up the preliminary table of tasks and priorities, and I then made the final decision, endeavoring always to get maximum naval benefit out of minimum funds.

All our decisions had to take into consideration a number of factors. In the choice of the type of ship, for instance, purely operational requirements were the first consideration: the tasks for which the ship was intended, and the qualities needed to carry out those tasks. The foreign policy situation and the relative strengths of other navies also were important factors. All these things having been established, it was up to the technicians to decide how many of the demands could be considered, and to what extent they could be met. From this team of naval officers and technicians came the solutions—almost invariably compromises for the objective of a resultant ship that would best suit our needs in light of the naval capabilities of any probable opponents. The final decision could be made only by the person responsible for the whole service and for deploying its forces in time of war.

But a Navy does not consist of ships alone. It requires men to operate it, and munitions, food, fuel, and other supplies to service and maintain it. Fuel, in fact, may be a decisive factor in the field of tactics and strategy. When it comes to personnel, the care and housing of the men and the welfare of their families are of major importance.

In munitions, an important field was mine warfare. All the warring nations in the First World War had used mines. The enemy tried to block our waterways and exit channels with mines, which we then did our best to sweep up. We laid mines both in enemy waters and on our own coasts as defense barriers.

The British Navy had given a decided impetus to mine warfare by the new type of mine it laid off the Flanders coast in summer 1918. Prior to then, the usual mine was anchored to ride just under the surface of the water, where it would be detonated by the enemy ship's striking it. But the new British mine was designed to lie on the ocean or river bottom, and became activated only by the magnetic field of the ship passing over or near it. Such magnetic influence was effective only at limited distances; these mines could be used only in fairly shallow water—a condition ideally fulfilled by our North Sea and Baltic coasts.

After the war we recognized that we had not given mine warfare the attention it deserved. Accordingly as early as 1920 our Navy set up a specific mine warfare research and development command. I gave the mine warfare command a free hand in its work, contenting myself merely with laying down general goals.

Considerable progress had been made in perfecting our own magnetic mine. Its detonating apparatus was effective, but other problems such as satisfactory equipment for sweeping up magnetic mines were still to be solved. We had been experimenting with the laying of mines by airplane since 1931. Now we set aside a larger share of our limited budget for developing and testing. We took into consideration the capabilities and moral effects of mines in our strategical and tactical studies, including war games and fleet exercises. All our cruisers, destroyers, and torpedo boats were equipped to lay mines, and they all carried out regular minelaying exercises.

For minesweeping craft we used principally "M-boats" of 500 to 600 tons, whose design was based on the well-tested lines of our World War I sweepers. In 1929 we had developed a large motorboat minesweeper of 100 to 150 tons—the so-called "R-boats"

—which proved so successful, both for minesweeping and general purposes, that we eventually built about 400 of this class. The proposed "escort sloop" type of fast minesweeper of 700 tons was given up because of its failure to meet the requirements.

In 1933 a second minesweeping squadron had been set up under a Commander of Minesweepers who had charge of all minesweeping activities. We made it a practice to select our minesweeper commanders and squadron chiefs from officers who had already had long service on minesweepers, thus making use of their practical experience as well as starting a "minesweeper tradition." With the revival of compulsory military service, reserve officers and short-term crews were also assigned for training, so that in case of war there would be an ample reserve of trained personnel to man the additional auxiliary sweepers that would be taken into service —such as fishing trawlers and luggers.

Every year we staged a large minelaying and minesweeping exercise, conducted as much as possible under war conditions. I personally attended the one held in Helgoland Bay in June of 1939, and visited each boat in order to observe the exercise and to give the crews the feeling that the High Command considered their work important. For high morale is essential in an activity which ordinarily is tedious routine but which in time of war is absolutely necessary and, in fact, indispensable.

The minesweeper squadrons gave an excellent performance, due in no small part to the splendid leadership of Commodore Ruge, Commander of Minesweepers.

Probably the German Navy did more intensive work in the field of mine warfare than did other nations. Its naval forces were weak. Its shallow, restricted coastal waters lent themselves ideally to mining by the enemy. As a result of the Navy's keen interest, we eventually possessed a whole arsenal of mines of various types: the magnetic mine; the acoustic mine, set off by the propeller noises of a ship passing above it; the pressure mine, detonated by the change in pressure caused by the ship passing overhead; and finally, the ingenious new "delayed action" or "ship count" device which could be attached to any type of mine and which, when appropriately set, would detonate the mine after a definite, pre-set period or after a certain number of ships had passed over it. By varying the combinations of devices and mine types, we could lay a minefield that would be a nightmare for enemy minesweepers.

We spent a great deal of time in mine detection apparatus and methods of sweeping any type of mine we should meet. As a result of teamwork between our naval, technical, and scientific specialists we had the upper hand later, in the war, in both offensive and defensive mine warfare.

In electronics—especially radio communications and direction and range locating—we did not fare so well.

Even in the First World War wireless telegraphy had played a considerable part in operations, but the science had not been developed in proportion to its importance. In that war, the standard procedure was to keep the volume of the signal as low as possible with the hope that the enemy could not hear it. The coding system intended to prevent the enemy's deciphering any wireless signals he might pick up was primitive. But before the end of 1914 the British got possession of a copy of the German secret code book, and not until we changed our whole coding procedure in 1917 could we transmit wireless signals the enemy could not read. Our own naval intelligence had considerable success in interpreting the enemy's signals.

While recognizing the importance of the whole field of wireless communications, we had neither personnel nor funds to do much about it for some time after the war. All that we had to work with was makeshift equipment and the cooperation of amateur and civilian personnel. For instance, the short-wave transmitter and receiver which our cruiser *Hamburg* carried on a world cruise in 1924 were of amateur construction. Interested amateurs and civilians, however, did carry on extensive work in the short-wave field, with the radio officers of both German naval ships and merchant ships cooperating. In 1926 the Navy's first short-wave transmitter, built by the Telefunken Company, went into operation at Kiel.

Private industry also made an important contribution in 1928 in the form of a coding machine. This machine not only speeded up the transmission of coded dispatches but was also so immune from outside codebreaking that, as far as I know, not once did the enemy succeed in breaking the German code during the whole of World War II. Documents seized in the French Navy Department after France's defeat in 1940 proved that up until then, at any rate, neither the British nor the French had any success in breaking the German codes.

In 1929 our Navy also assigned an officer to head up an intelligence department whose mission was to intercept and analyze enemy radio communication—an activity that performed valuable services in evaluating the enemy's radio communications for our own operations in World War II. The need for well trained specialists was recognized throughout the service, and exercises for communication officers and personnel became a standard part of all fleet training and war games.

In equipment, also, progress was made through the cooperation of private industry. In the early thirties, the Telefunken Company developed a compact, highly efficient radio for the motor torpedo boats, minesweepers, and other smaller craft which were joining the fleet. It was an instrument that could be manufactured in quantity, and was so good that the Air Force, too, adopted it in 1935.

From 1932 on, the Navy sent radio messages to cooperative merchant ships which in turn relayed them to other ships. This not only aided in estimating possible ranges but also insured that the merchant ships kept in close communication with the homeland. Thus, in cases of international tension, orders could be sent out promptly to all merchant ships. The Spanish Revolution of 1936 was an excellent proof of the value of this program.

Of one thing we were all convinced—that in future wars the naval forces, wherever they were, would be directed operationally by orders and instructions transmitted by radio from headquarters ashore. With us, these headquarters would be our Naval Group Commands. The result of our study and developments was that in World War II we could communicate almost instantly with our surface ships and submarines in any part of the world, so that our naval operations were conducted along considerably different lines from those of World War I.

In the early thirties our naval experimental laboratory for communications had begun work on an electromagnetic range and direction finding device—the instrument which the Allies developed under the name of radar. At the outbreak of the war, progress had been such that good equipment was ready for use on ships, ashore, and by the Air Force. Unfortunately the exigencies of the war prevented our keeping up with the enemy, who after intensive and systematic research, had come upon a wave length much more suitable than ours. Thus England's new radar devices, not perfected until after the war began, soon outclassed ours in efficiency; and they could be fitted into airplanes.

It is a moot question whether by broader scientific research, and by allocation of more funds to the project, we could have maintained our earlier advantage in the field of radar. The responsibility for that would have rested with the Naval Command, and hence with me. Certainly the development of radar by the Allies, and its inclusion in a wide reconnaissance system, especially by means of aircraft, had a decisive influence on the naval war in the Atlantic.

But during the two decades we had to work upon electronics devices we were sadly limited in funds and personnel. What success we had we owed to the zealous younger officers and petty officers, technicians and civilian scientists, and to the cooperation of civilian industry—a huge undertaking of countless individuals, all imbued with the same imagination, devotion, and love of country.

Food, clothing, and other supplies were provided by civilian industry generally under government contract and supervision, but fuel was something with which the Navy was more directly concerned.

With our small Navy, in the decade following World War I we had no difficulty in obtaining the fuel necessary to keep our ships in commission. The industrial plants which processed oil from the brown lignite deposits of Central Germany furnished us with all the fuel the fleet needed. Additional diesel oil, as well as fuel for ships on foreign cruises, could be obtained by ordinary purchase.

But after 1934 it became evident that the requirement for diesel and fuel oil for our expanding fleet would increase many fold.

This requirement ran head on into the recently adopted restriction on purchases with foreign currency, so that, from 1934 on, the Treasury no longer granted the Navy foreign currency with which to purchase petroleum abroad.

The lifeblood of a Navy is oil. In time of peace, fuel is necessary for training; in time of war, operations can not be conducted without it. An immobilized fleet is ineffective in peacetime and utterly useless in war, for the Navy's weapons—mines, guns, torpedoes—must be carried to the field of action against the enemy. Hence the stockpiling of diesel oil and petroleum, and provision for a continuing supply of fuel, were problems of major importance in the expansion of our Navy.

Such problems plagued me time and again. Regardless of the nature of the conflict, we had to reckon with the fact that during a war we could import no oil from abroad—or if we did, could do so only under extreme difficulties. The only solution for us was to promote the production of petroleum at home, and to try to get for the Navy a fair share of that production. We also needed to procure oil from abroad through neutral ports or by routes that, in wartime, would remain open, and to stockpile as much fuel as possible in advance.

The official in the Supreme Naval Command who took care of all our oil procurement was Dr. Fetzer, an experienced man with an intimate knowledge of oilfields everywhere, and a man with influential connections both at home and abroad. He did an excellent job for the Navy, and the only disagreement I ever had with him was once when he wanted to go on a mountain climbing expedition to the Himalayas—mountain climbing being his hobby. That idea I had to veto firmly; he was indispensable to the Navy.

Part of our fuel we could obtain from the lignite mines of central Germany, with which we entered into a long-term purchasing agreement which not only insured us a definite share of their production but also enabled the plants to expand their processing equipment. However, good diesel oil could not be processed from brown coal, so we procured oil through a double exchange. The pit coal of our Ruhr could be processed into an oil which was not fit for Navy purposes but which was readily salable for coal tar industries. Accordingly we acquired it from the Ruhr plants and sold it to coal tar industries in the United States. With the proceeds we bought diesel oil abroad, being able to get about four tons of diesel oil for every ton of coal tar oil. During the war we later obtained foreign currency from neutral countries through this same system of barter-purchase.

Shortly before the war broke out, a new process was developed which could produce suitable Navy fuel oil from the pit coal. Through contracts with the Verkaufsvereinigung für Teererzeugnisse (Merchandising Association for Tar Products) of Essen and the coal refining plants of the Schaffgottschen Werke in Gleiwitz, the Navy secured continuous delivery of this fuel.

We in the Navy were not the only ones who needed oil. With German rearmament, the Army and Aid Force also became major consumers, and at the same time private industry, expanding with the improvement in the domestic economy, was advancing its needs. All these considerations, plus the deteriorating position of German currency abroad brought about the measures known as the "Four Year Plan." This plan provided for vast expansions of all the domestic sources from which fuel could be obtained. New processing plants were set up especially to produce fuel for the Army and the Air Force, though the Navy was still restricted to the sources with whom we already had contracts. But it soon became evident that Germany's total domestic oil industry would not be sufficient, in the foreseeable future, to fill all the military and civilian needs.

The Navy was thus faced with the necessity of obtaining from abroad much of the oil necessary for the fleet's growing needs. Our solution was to import into Germany great quantities of crude oil from abroad, and to store it in underground tanks from which it could be drawn out and refined for use later.

As a first step in this direction, the Navy signed a long-term contract with the Estonian Petroleum Company in Kiviöli. This contract, arranged through the Mendelsohn Bank in Berlin, with the technical assistance of Professor Drawe, guaranteed the Navy a large and steady supply of shale oil. Of good quality and considerably cheaper than German-produced oil, this petroleum could be loaded into Navy tankers directly from the company's port installations in Estonia and thence brought straight to our own storage tanks in Germany.

In 1936, also, the Navy managed to acquire a sizable interest in the British Oil Development Company, which had the exclusive concession to drill for oil in Iraq, west of the Tigris. These shares were actually purchased by the Dresden Bank in Berlin, but at the instigation of the Supreme Naval Command. Again it was a system of barter-purchase. The Navy would pay the German companies for the exported goods in German marks. It was presupposed that the German Finance Ministry would guarantee the German exporting firms the value of the exported goods and would make good any loss suffered by them in the transaction. However, the Finance Ministry rejected this proposal on the grounds that German interest in oilfields abroad was superfluous, since all Germany's petroleum needs would be supplied when the home industry got going under the Four Year Plan.

The Navy met with the same difficulty when we proposed to acquire a concession in the Poza Rica oilfields in Mexico. The value of these fields had been certified by the authoritative German geologist, Professor Bentz, and, again with the cooperation of the Dresden Bank, a tentative agreement had been worked out with the Mexican Government. Under this agreement we would pay for crude oil from the Poza Rica fields with German products—principally from the Siemens-Schukert-Werke—and would then compensate the German manufacturers in German marks. Again the project fell through, the Finance Ministry and administrators of the Four Year Plan proving utterly devoid of any understanding of the Navy's vital needs.

Such blindness was amazing. The Four Year Plan was simply an emergency measure, not an end in itself. The critical need for oil was clear to every one in the Navy. It seemed to us that this hole in our defenses should be plugged. When, at an Allied victory banquet on 23 November 1918, the British Foreign Secretary, Lord Curzon, had said, "We swam to victory on a sea of oil," his words should have made any government official appreciate the need for acquiring sure sources of oil for future needs. But the administrators of the Four Year Plan remained completely deaf to the Navy's remonstrances.

Having failed in all these attempts to acquire interests in oil-fields abroad, the Navy was forced to contract for diesel oil and petroleum requirements from foreign firms who would be willing to accept payment in German currency or in German products. In this manner we were able to secure some of our supplies from the United States, Russia, and Rumania, and, to a larger extent, from Mexico. In particular, we could thus refuel our cruisers in foreign ports without having to pay for the fuel from our dwindling amount of foreign currency.

Oil purchased overseas was largely transported to Germany in German tankers such as those of the Essberger Shipping Company of Hamburg. J. T. Essberger, the founder of this tanker company, was among the first to realize the economic importance of an independent tanker fleet sailing under the German flag.

By the end of 1939 the Navy had acquired a reserve supply of some 650,000 tons of diesel oil and 350,000 tons of fuel oil, mostly stored in underground tanks. In our stockpiles, diesel oil was given preference over ordinary fuel oil, because, in case Germany was blockaded, fuel oil could be produced locally from domestic coal, but this was not true of diesel oil.

According to our estimates, our stockpile of petroleum, augmented by steady additions of fuel produced from domestic coal, would be sufficient to supply all the Navy's needs even for several years of major warfare. But by the beginning of the war Germany's vital industries were already suffering for lack of diesel oil. In addition, despite my violent objections, the Navy had to turn over to the Army some 300,000 tons of the Navy's diesel oil just before the Army's 1940 offensive in the west, and a further 30,000 tons to the farmers for their spring plowing. Then, after Italy entered the war as an ally, we had to provide her navy with fuel from 1941 on.

Even after the war began we could still obtain some fuel abroad, mostly purchased with foreign currencies we had banked in neutral countries. The Canary Islands and Mexico were important links in this fuel traffic. But after the enemy's blockade, strengthened by his system of navicert,[1] and especially after the United States entered the war, we were almost completely blocked from importing oil from abroad or from supplying our ships through neutral ports. Because our communication lines with Estonia could not be cut, however, we continued to import Estonian shale oil throughout the war. We likewise obtained limited amounts of fuel oil from Austria and the Rumanian oilfields, but the expected supplies of crude oil from Russia never became a reality for the Navy, even after our armies had gained control of a good part of Russian territory.

In addition to building storage tanks and utilizing German commercial tankers, we also built a number of naval tankers for bringing in oil by sea. In this field our Design Division produced plans for a combination oiler and supply ship (*Trossschiff*), which we began putting into service in 1937 and which was to prove invaluable in the war. With a capacity of 12,000 tons, mostly oil, but with holds equipped for carrying other types of stores as well, these ships had a speed of 21 knots and could cover a considerable range.

In this critical business of securing oil for the fleet, we had the unlimited cooperation of civilian officials and technicians. With these, and our own engineering officers and engine room personnel, we managed to maintain an unimpeded, continuous flow of oil to our naval forces on all battlefronts practically until the end of the war.

Without suitable harbor and base facilities, any naval force, however large, is ineffective. Our World War I facilities were utterly inadequate. Our first concern, then, was where to locate the main bases for our new fleet, and how to render them useful for a long time to come. The two battleships we were constructing —the *Scharnhorst* and the *Gneisenau*—were larger than any ships we had had in the old Imperial Navy, and our next ships—the *Bismarck* and *Tirpitz*—would be larger still. Furthermore, to keep up with other navies, we had to anticipate even larger battleships and, above all, aircraft carriers.

[1] A system of cargo inspection established by Great Britain in World War II. Inspections were conducted either at the port of loading or at certain designated contraband control stations, and an inspection certificate, called a "navicert," issued to oceangoing ships of neutral nations.

For these future combat ships the Baltic—including Kiel—had to be rejected immediately as a base, because the Kaiser Wilhelm Canal, the necessary communication to the North Sea, would never take them. Widening the canal would have cost entirely too much even if it could have been accomplished in an acceptable time. The Great Belt, the only other exit from the Baltic practicable for large ships, offered too many navigational difficulties, and in addition lay in foreign territorial waters. The only possibilities left were the mouths of the German rivers emptying into the North Sea. And the only one of these that filled requirements was the River Jade.

Even in its natural state, the Jade had advantages over the Elbe, Weser, and Ems, as far as depth, width, and tides were concerned. As far back as 1908, the Navy had begun improving its natural features by construction supervised by the very able harbor engineer, Krüger. But a satisfactorily deep channel had not been attained between the inner and outer Jade harbors even by the time of World War I. The inability of large ships to exit from Wilhelmshaven Roads into the outer channel and open sea had been one of the causes of the naval disaster of 28 August 1914. After the war improvements had continued, despite the handicaps of the Versailles Treaty, and new facilities had been added under Eckhardt, the director of river works. By 1929 a broad channel, 10 meters deep at low water, linked the Jade to the North Sea.

The tidal locks connecting with inner Wilhelmshaven harbor had not been improved correspondingly. The *Scharnhorst* and *Gneisenau* would be able to pass through the third, and largest, lock only with difficulty. And for the *Tirpitz* and *Bismarck* to attempt the passage would have meant serious danger to both ships and locks.

The only solution was to build a completely new lock, wide and deep enough to take all future ships. Profiting from bitter experience, the Navy decided to lay out the new locks along the line of the river, and to provide them with an outer tidal basin large enough to pass the largest units in and out with a minimum of delay.

The planning and implementing of this vast project was put in the hands of Director Eckhardt, who had now been promoted to head the Harbor Construction Division in the Supreme Naval Command. He proved to be one of those pleasant and able administrators with whom I delighted to work. His genius produced a plan which, although almost startling in its magnitude, completely eliminated all the difficulties of the old harbor.

Eckhardt personally explained the lock construction plan to Hitler in my presence. It was typical of Hitler's thinking that, after listening attentively, his inquiry was not as to costs but, "Will the locks now really be large enough?"

We could set his mind at rest on this point, and work began in the spring of 1936 with the construction of a seawall to block off the new construction ditch. Cement pouring began the next year. Some idea of the magnitude of the locks can be gained from the fact that each of the six steel sliding lock gates weighed 2,200 tons, and on top of that had a protective cement shield four and a half meters thick.

Construction of this fourth exit presented great difficulties. Before construction began, the water table for the entire area had to be lowered by more than 23 meters—which meant that all of the neighboring sections of the city would be affected. But by hard labor, enthusiastic teamwork, and the genius of the engineers, the work was successfully completed within only six and a half years—a remarkable achievement for a construction containing over a million cubic meters of concrete and steel-reinforced concrete, and costing a total of 250,000,000 marks.

The new Wilhelmshaven lock chambers far surpassed the sea lock at Ijmuiden, Netherlands, which up until then had been the world's largest. Each of the lock chambers was 60 meters wide, 350 meters long, and had a depth of 16.75 meters over the sill. We estimated that any warship then existent or that would be built in the foreseeable future would be able to pass through the lock without difficulty under any conditions of tide or current, and on the average such passage could be made within 15 minutes.

The lock was dedicated by the transit of the cruiser Emden on 7 November 1942, and I had the pleasure of opening it personally. I took the opportunity to express the Navy's thanks to the construction firms, technicians, engineers, and workmen, both naval and civilian, who had contributed to the success of the great undertaking. Particular acknowledgments were made to Chief Naval Architect Franz Bock, to Chief Construction Supervisor Beck, and to Professor Agatz of the chair of hydraulic engineering at the Technical Institute of Berlin-Charlottenburg.

In the matter of naval personnel, we already had an excellent foundation going back to the Weimar days. However, nothing contributes so much to naval morale as an efficient medical corps and ample medical facilities to care for both the men themselves and their families. I felt this so deeply that I took especial interest in the Navy's Medical Department.

Ever since 1934 this department had been administered by the Surgeon General of the Navy, who was not only the chief medical officer in the Navy but was also the Chief of Bureau of Medicine in the Supreme Naval Command. Holding this position when I took office in 1928 had been the nationally known Dr. Moosauer. I enjoyed the closest relations with him for eleven years, and for other years afterward with his successor, Dr. Fikentscher. Following in the path of their eminent predecessors, Dr. Uthemann and Dr. Brachmann, they combined the high personal and professional qualities of both doctor, and naval officer, and strove to develop the same superior combination in their subordinates.

Up until 1935 the Navy's personnel limit made it possible to accept only one out of every 12 applications for Medical Corps officer candidates, but by 1938 our expansion made it necessary to admit 30 candidates out of the 130 to 150 who applied. After brief military indoctrination with the line officer candidates, the Medical Corps candidates were sent to medical colleges to complete their studies. They spent each summer vacation afloat on naval ships, and were required to pass the regular state medical examinations before becoming full-fledged naval medical officers. From 1934 to 1940 they received their medical schooling at the Military Medical Academy in Berlin, but after 1940 they were given their professional training at the newly established Naval Medical Academy.

The duties of a naval medical officer were many and varied; he had duty on regular naval ships and at shore hospitals, where he attended the dependents of naval personnel as well; he was medical supervisor of sports, and he served on fishery protection vessels. He also had duty at naval shipyards, and in general was responsible for naval hygiene on both ships and shore stations.

After several years of general service, most naval medical officers were ordered to postgraduate study at university clinics, leading civilian hospitals, or the Tropical Hygiene Institute in Hamburg, with which latter institute the Navy maintained close connections. Besides working under almost all the leading German medical authorities, our naval medical officers also had the opportunity to study abroad. For instance, when World War II broke out, one of our naval medical officers was serving with the Dutch Colonial Administration in the Dutch East Indies, where he was specializing in tropical medicine.

Medical equipment at sea and in shore hospitals matched the high degree of training of the medical officers. In addition to enlarging and modernizing existing hospitals, our Navy had built many new ones, and specialist treatment could meet the demands everywhere. Even the smaller vessels were provided with medical attendants and facilities, and all of the larger ships had complete operating rooms with the most modern X-ray machines. Great emphasis was placed on preventive medicine and general and specific shipboard hygiene, with regular lectures and instruction on pertinent medical matters. As a result, health conditions in the Navy were exceptionally good.

At the beginning of the war the Navy was able to call to active duty a great many reserve naval medical officers, so that it was possible for all naval activities everywhere to have expert medical attention. Under the direction of a special division in the Navy Medical Bureau, these reserve officers performed outstanding service everywhere.

In both World Wars the German naval medical officers proved equal to any in the world. Equal reputation was gained by their dependable helpers, the medical corpsmen and naval nurses.

Fully as important in the field of morale, but in a different way, was the Naval Law Bureau, staffed by those officers concerned with enforcing the Navy's rules and regulations and maintaining discipline. In the tightly knit military services, even more than in the civilian community, there is a constant need for the enforcement of law and order and the dispensation of justice. Discipline and teamwork, the indispensable foundations of any military service, die the moment any decent soldier or sailor begins to believe that no reward is given to the conscientious man and little or no punishment to the idler or wrongdoer. Hence not only must those in the legal branches of the Navy know their law thoroughly, but they must have an innate love of justice and pride in the service. Only thus can they win and hold the respect and loyalty of the Navy's personnel.

With a history as far back as 300 years, the legal branches of the German armed services had won a deserved reputation for probity. However, with the collapse at the end of World War I, the "Council of People's Commissars" had dissolved the lower courts of military jurisdiction, and in August of 1920 the legal branches of the armed services were done away with altogether except in the Navy, which was still allowed to exercise necessary disciplinary measures in connection with its personnel aboard ship. Even those political parties not well-disposed toward the armed forces recognized that civilian courts, especially if women participated as judges or jurymen, were not capable of passing judgment on conditions aboard ships of the Navy.

Hence, in contrast to the Army and, later, of the Air Force, the Navy still possessed a small but experienced nucleus of legal officers when full military jurisdiction was reintroduced in 1934. Recognition had to be given, however, to the change in social and political conditions ashore, and the Navy's new courts were made to correspond with equivalent civil courts ashore. The Court-Martial Board, established in 1936 to be the court of highest jurisdiction in the armed services, was headed by one of the Navy's most noted legal officers, Senate President Sellmer.

As Commander in Chief of the Navy, I exercised in peacetime only general supervision over naval courts, with a special privilege of extending clemency in some measure. But I did not have—and did not want—any authority over the actions of the actual courts themselves. My main interest was to keep myself continually informed of the incidence of a specific type of offense—the sort that was apt to have a strong effect on the morale and discipline of the men. This I did by inquiry and discussion with the higher ranking commanders and their legal officers. I was particularly concerned with any mistreatment of subordinates by their superiors, and gave instructions that such cases should be pressed to the fullest, without consideration for either rank or person, and in any proven case of such mistreatment I refused to show any clemency whatever.

I could always count on the sound professional advice of the Naval Law Division, headed by Chief Naval Court-Martial Councillor (and later Naval Staff Judge) Rudolphi, an outstanding jurist with an innate sense of justice. When the Department of Enlisted Personnel and Discipline was created in 1937, the coordination of all divisions concerned with judicial and disciplinary matters was unexcelled. The two early department chiefs, Schniewind and Warzecha, each of whom later became a General Admiral, developed a tradition of cooperation and probity which stood up to even the most difficult conditions during the war.

The new courts of the Navy were able to conduct their affairs without outside political pressure until 1938, when, the Blomberg-Fritsch crises and the establishment of the new Oberkommando der Wehrmacht, or Supreme Commander of Armed Forces, such pressure began to develop. Numerous Nazi officials and organizations began to object against what they alleged to be too strict standards of discipline enforced against old Party members or too mild treatment of naval personnel who were either unsympathetic toward the Nazi Party or else where actually opposed to it. I made it a point to investigate every such complaint, and in not a single instance did I find the naval courts at fault. As a result of these experiences the Chief of the Supreme Command of Armed Forces, on my suggestion, reached an agreement with the deputy of the Führer that any complaints from the Party offices be made to the Commanders in Chief of the respective services only through the deputy himself. This acted to prevent any direct and illegal attempts by subordinate Party officials to influence the military courts, and resulted in uniform handling of all such problems—even though it brought an extra load of work to the already overworked Department of Enlisted Personnel and Discipline and to the Naval Law Division.

But after 1938 the Führer tried personally to influence promotions among the judge advocates and high legal officers of the Defense Ministry. The Supreme Commander of Armed Forces was forced to give him the right to be consulted before officer selections, but right to the end of the war we succeeded in defeating the attempts of the Party to control all promotions. This was no easy matter, as the central organizations of the Nazi Party and their units tried constantly to secure overriding positions in the court-martial field, and long and tedious investigations had to be made—none of which ever brought to light any justification of the claims made by Party officials.

After the war broke out, however, attempts to interfere with the Navy's judiciary processes began to materialize at even the highest Party levels. For instance, in the summer of 1942 a naval court-martial had freed several Norwegians who had returned to their homeport after a vain attempt to flee in a tug. Even before the court's decision was published, the German administrator of occupied Norway, Terboven, interfered in what he chose to designate as a "political" affair, and he phoned Hitler personally, as a result of which the naval court-martial's action was summarily disapproved. In addition Hitler demanded that the Supreme Naval Command give him the names of the three court-martial judges so that they could be punished. This, at my direction, was not done, inasmuch as the judges had only been doing their duty—and Hitler never again mentioned the matter.

In another case, in 1942, a naval court-martial acquited a naval chaplain whose only accuser was another chaplain, with no verifying witnesses. Too, this second chaplain, upon investigation, was found to be an instrument of the Gestapo, the secret state police. I felt that the circumstances not only justified the acquittal of the first chaplain, but also the dismissal of the accusing chaplain from the service. Martin Bormann, one of the highest officials of the Nazi Party, disagreed sharply, and made a peremptory demand in writing for the dismissal of the acquitted naval chaplain and the reinstatement of the Gestapo man and the discharge of the presiding judge. These unheard of demands were ignored then, and later.

Naturally my responsibilities in the naval law field increased tremendously with the opening of hostilities, as the courts of appeal and review ceased operation in favor of direct confirmation or disapproval by the convening commanders or higher authorities. The experienced and impartial decisions of these higher ranking officers, with the concurrence of the able jurists on their staffs, was never to be questioned.

However, I reserved for myself the final decision of all important cases involving serious naval disciplinary matters or civil crimes in which naval personnel were concerned except cases reserved to the Supreme Commander of the Armed Forces. In addition I wanted the lower naval authorities to have all the facts so that they would have this as a basis in future decisions. Consequently, even though there was no regulation requiring it, I circulated all such cases to all bureaus of the Supreme Naval Command who were concerned, and called for advice and information that would enable me to make the fairest possible decision in the case. The final action, with reasons, was then circulated in the form of "Court-Martial Orders" to all commands in the Navy.

As compensation for the many difficult punitive decisions, I had wide powers of clemency during the war, and it was a great delight to me when, without impairment to discipline and morale, I could "temper justice with mercy." A further compensation came through the recognition, documented time and time again, that throughout the war the Navy's judicial system, operating under extreme difficulties and often without opportunity to consult other authorities, established a record that was no whit behind the record of the operating forces themselves.

XI

The German Navy During the Spanish Civil War

IN THE SUMMER OF 1936 the Navy was assigned a task which kept it busily occupied for the next two years. Extremely unpleasant internal dissensions had developed in Spain. One could not help recognizing an increasing Bolshevist influence behind these disorders. This Bolshevistic influence showed itself, among other things, in anti-clerical legislation which suppressed Church schools and expropriated Church property as well. The Socialist Spanish Government changed face every little while as one or other faction gained power. In many cities there were bloody riots and uprisings. In Asturias province a Communist government was proclaimed; in Catalonia there was a separatist Catalan current along with a Communist one. Finally the situation developed into open civil war when a military revolt broke out in Spanish Morocco under the leadership of General Franco, who proclaimed an insurrection against the so-called "Popular Front Government" in Madrid, and followed his proclamation by an invasion of the Spanish homeland itself.

The effects of this civil war, now breaking out in all its bitterness, spread far beyond the borders of Spain itself and became for years a cardinal point of European policies. Soviet Russia, which had long been carrying on the subversion of Spain, saw in this civil war a test of strength and a decisive struggle for an important European bastion on its way to world revolution; therefore it supported the Popular Front Government. Germany and Italy, on the other hand, owing to their anti-Communist attitude, sided with General Franco, while England and France adopted a policy of "non-interference." At the same time, the sympathies of these two countries were unequivocally on the side of Red Spain.

As a result of the riots, revolts, and general terror, conditions in Spain had gradually become unbearable for foreigners living there. As far as democratic government was concerned, the "Popular Front" served only as a false front. In most communities, Communists, syndicalists, and anarchists had seized power. Unimaginable atrocities were committed during this time, as our naval commanders, who had an opportunity to investigate conditions in port cities, later reported. The European powers who were concerned about the welfare of their nationals found themselves compelled to take measures to protect them. Owing to the uncertainty of conditions and the untrustworthiness of the various Red governments in the individual provinces and cities of Spain, they could take protective measures only with their own forces.

Spain's geographical position made any such action a question primarily of naval forces. As numerous cries for help came from the Germans living in Spain and from the consulates, the German Government—like England, France, Italy, the United States, and several smaller naval powers—decided to send naval units into Spanish waters. At the same time the German Government took over the protection of the nationals of other lands, such as Austria and Switzerland, which had requested us to do so. I was in agreement with Foreign Minister Baron von Neurath's estimate of the situation and the measures to be undertaken by the Navy. It was a foregone conclusion that fleet units would be used for the protection of Germans in Spain. Surprisingly enough, it had not been easy to obtain Hitler's agreement to the use of naval forces. He was at this time attending the festival plays in Bayreuth and I had his naval aide, Commander von Puttkamer, speak with him. Hitler was very worried lest some international incident occur. Later, too, the thought that German warships entered Red Spanish harbors in their necessary activity worried Hitler again and again. To carry out this naval task, the kind and extent of which could not yet be seen in detail, I ordered the commander of the pocket battleships, Vice Admiral Carls, on the afternoon of 23 July 1936, to put to sea immediately with the pocket battleships *Deutschland* and *Admiral Scheer*. The ships broke off their maneuvers in the North Sea, fitted out overnight in Wilhelmshaven, and put to sea the next morning. A few days later the cruiser *Köln* and four torpedo boats followed. Our ships were peaceably received in the Nationalist Spanish ports as well as in the Loyalist Spanish ones, and were able to insure the safety of German nationals and also of other foreigners. In the first few months alone, about 15,000 Germans and other refugees of widely scattered nationalities were evacuated from Red Spain under the protection of German warships. In addition, asylum was offered many persecuted Spaniards, and thus the lives of these were also saved. One of these refugees was the aged Archbishop of Cartagena, Miguel de los Santos.

When the struggle had spread over the whole unfortunate land, almost all Germans were evacuated from Spain, and with them usually the Spanish members of their families. German merchant ships aided the warships in this task in an exemplary way. These ships, by radio request of the naval commander, were ordered to those Loyalist or National Spanish ports, where German warships had taken over the task of evacuation and the necessary diplomatic negotiations with the Spanish officials. To do this the merchant ships interrupted their voyages to their Levant or East Asian destinations, took on board the Germans and their families who were streaming out of the entire country, and landed them safely again in Nationalist Spanish, Italian or French ports. The keen sense of responsibility of the German steamer captains must be given high credit for this, since these captains often had no contact with their shipping lines and had to act on their own initiative. The size of the task of evacuation can be seen, for example, in the fact that in only a few days about 2,000 refugees were evacuated from the Loyalist Spanish Mediterranean port of Almeria alone.

As a result of the timely intervention of our warships and merchant ships, there was little loss of life among the Germans in Spain during the civil war. The calm and resolute behavior of the German naval commanders and merchant skippers made possible the rescue of German families and the protection of their property even in Communist-ruled ports. Because of the presence or intervention of our naval forces, the German merchant ships, with one exception, could be protected from interference by Loyalist Spanish naval forces.

The latter made themselves very noticeable, especially in the opening period of the war, since the greater part of the Spanish Fleet had remained on the Loyalist Spanish side. By planned infiltration and subversion of the crews, and through murder of most of the officers, the Loyalists made impossible any defection of naval personnel to Franco. The superior Loyalist Spanish naval forces prevented the ferrying of the Franco troops in Morocco across to the Spanish mainland by sea. Therefore these troops had to be transferred by air, which was time consuming because of the limited number of planes available. Only gradually did Franco succeed in strengthening his own forces by putting new ships into service and opening the sea routes to the Nationalist Spanish ports. In the long run, the Loyalist components of the fleet could not maintain their superiority, especially since, having murdered so many of their officers, they lacked trained and experienced direction.

On 30 September 1936, General Franco had been proclaimed "Head of the National Spanish Government and the Spanish State." His troops had begun the attack on Madrid, and the Loyalist Spanish Government had moved to Valencia. Shortly after that, in November 1936, Germany and Italy recognized the government of Franco, thereby documenting their intention of preventing the spread of Communism to southwestern Europe. England and France did not announce their recognition until February 1939, shortly before Franco's final victory. The United States followed on 1 April 1939, a few days after the end of the civil war.

However, in accordance with its political principles, Soviet Russia supported the Loyalist Spanish Government in every way from the very beginning. The heavy influx of Communist volunteers from various European countries, as well as the extensive supply of war material and foodstuffs, contributed to halting Franco's original victory procession outside the very gates of Madrid. This support for the Loyalist Spanish forces was provided principally through Russian and French steamers voyaging from the Black Sea ports.

When in turn the German Government decided, for its part, to aid Franco, the military supplies intended for him and the German volunteers for the "Condor Legion" were transported by sea. From our naval supplies we sold to the Nationalist Spanish Government first and foremost some coastal batteries, then anti-aircraft artillery, mine detection gear, and mines. Deliveries went smoothly and without incident. The direct aid to Franco, which I too considered necessary, in sending the "Condor Legion" and providing war matériel, resulted from the foreign policy of Germany, whose determination was to prevent the rise of a Communist state in Spain. Even though the German aid to Spain was camouflaged, and everything that happened on land or in the air was officially covered by the Spanish flag, the actual state of affairs was pretty universally known. For one thing, the moral effect of the presence of the German warships could not be overlooked. The many vessels running supplies and volunteers for both belligerent parties into Spain, the declarations of blockade by both the Nationalist Spanish and the Loyalist side, the presence of warships of various nations, and the general interest of foreign powers all offered numerous possibilities for friction and international conflict. Incidents therefore became more and more likely as the war progressed.

The activity of the German naval forces naturally could not be directed in all details from Berlin. To be sure, the radio channel of communication, which we had improved carefully and systematically as a result of our experience in the First World War, proved good. However, in the last analysis, the success or failure of the naval forces depended primarily on the independent judgment of the naval commanders, and their understanding of the political situation, as well as their willingness to make decisions. It was particularly Admirals Carls, Boehm, von Fischel, and Marschall, with their squadron leaders and commanders of individual ships, who showed themselves equal to the constantly changing situations and unexpected trend of events. Aside from a general briefing on the policies of the German Government and the High Command of the Navy, and the necessary arrangements for relief and supplies, I did not need to interfere in any way with the measures taken by our naval command on the spot. Not only the older commanders and skippers with their greater experience, but also the younger torpedo boat and submarine skippers showed in many individual cases an intelligent initiative and a well-planned line of action. In particular, heavy demands were placed on the officers and personnel of the engineering group to keep the ships ready and running, and these demands were fully met. Throughout the war period, the individual training of the German naval crews was not neglected despite the unusual requirements of the duty in Spanish waters, though to be sure, it was not possible to conduct the usual ship exercises. However, with the help of the Italian Navy, which obligingly placed its facilities at our disposal, our ships could carry out part of the required artillery, anti-aircraft, and torpedo practice in the Mediterranean; and also do routine overhaul work in the Italian naval shipyard in Naples. The Nationalist Spanish Navy also kept the shipyard facilities in Cadiz and El Ferrol ready for our ships.

Without prejudice to the diversified policies which the individual powers pursued in the Spanish question, the naval forces assembled in Spanish waters were on surprisingly good terms: English, Americans, French, Italians, and Germans were all genuinely concerned for the safety and property of their nationals, and they aided each other in this humanitarian task. This cooperation extended far and wide. In Barcelona, for example, where the anarchists had the power in their hands, the warships of these five nations made common cause under the leadership of the senior officer present, the French Vice Admiral Gensoul, and set up a joint precautionary plan of operations in case a blood bath should break out on land. Our own officers could see that many of the British naval officers made no secret of their sympathy for Franco, although the British commander, Vice Admiral Cunningham, naturally represented the official course of his government. It was futher gratifying to see, at the frequent meetings with French naval forces, how the French naval officer corps extended the warm welcome of the fraternity of the sea to our officers. For instance, when our third torpedo boat squadron was proceeding to Spain in November 1936, the rudder of the torpedo boat *Wolf* broke in a heavy storm, so that the squadron was compelled to enter the French naval harbor of Brest. It was received there with great politeness and friendliness, far above what was otherwise usual, and without any political differences coming to the fore. The French naval shipyard, under the chief director, Rear Admiral Petit, did all in its power to finish the extensive repairs quickly, and the German officers and crews received numerous official and private invitations from French naval ships and shore stations. A very friendly attitude toward the Germans was expressed everywhere. In connection with the whole Spanish question, too, the foreign aid coming to both sides in the civil war finally led to the setting up of a "Non-Intervention Committee," in which the European powers all joined. Naval supervision of all outside support for either warring faction was decided upon, and this went into effect on 12 March 1937. This supervision was exercised jointly by the naval forces of England, France, Italy, and Germany. However, it was never very effective, since the supervising forces themselves were partisan and were primarily interested in aiding one side or the other. Furthermore, the supervision activity of the German and Italian forces in their theater of operations off the Spanish east coast, assigned them by the Non-Intervention Committee, was taken by the Loyalist Spanish party as an excuse for causing incidents by planned aggressive actions.

After the first months of the supervisory patrol had passed without unpleasant events, there suddenly came on 29 May 1937, a surprise bombing attack by a Loyalist Spanish plane on the pocket battleship *Deutschland,* lying at anchor in a protected bay of the Balearic Island of Ibiza. Coming out of the direction of the low afternoon sun, the plane could not be seen in time; furthermore, because of its masquerading insignia as a Nationalist Spanish plane, it would not be suspected of hostile action anyway. Consequently, it was able to drop its bombs before the anti-aircraft batteries of the *Deutschland* could get into action. Two bombs struck the vessel. The effects on the ship itself were slight; far greater was the destruction in personnel. Thirty-one crew members were killed, and seventy-eight wounded.

An immediate retaliatory blow necessarily had to follow this unprecedented attack, otherwise further unprovoked attacks might occur.

Hitler, who had just left Berlin by plane, returned immediately upon news of the attack. It was decided in Government Council to bombard the Loyalist Spanish port of Almeria as a retaliatory measure. On 31 May 1937, the pocket battleship *Admiral Scheer* bombarded the fortified Loyalist Spanish port of Almeria with a number of 28-cm. shells. Loyalist Spanish batteries returned the fire unsuccessfully. Before the report of the German commander concerning the accomplishment of the bombardment had reached Berlin, however, unfriendly foreign press dispatches had already appeared, in which the Germans were accused of the bombardment of the "open" city of Almeria.

General von Blomberg and I were immediately summoned to the Chancellery, where Hitler was in an agitated mood because of the news accounts. And of all days, just on this one particular day the ordinarily good radio communication with the forces in Spain was poor because of unusual atmospheric conditions, so that the official report of the German naval commander there took an extremely long time for transmission. Hitler did not calm down again until the impatiently awaited report finally arrived. This report stated that the batteries of Almeria had returned the fire. Hence the press accusations of the bombardment of an "open" city were completely false.

A statement by the Caliph of Tetuan, Mulay Hassan, on the occasion of an official visit of the *Deutschland* in Ceuta in the summer of 1938, throws light on the effect this surprise bombing attack had in Spain and on the troops in Spanish Morocco: "I stand here on holy ground, which is drenched with the blood of so many fallen and wounded, and am proud to be able to aid Spain in its battle against those who believe in no God. Victory will surely be ours."

On the occasion of the bombing of the *Deutschland,* the English also showed a respectful sympathy, although their official Spanish policy was opposed to that of the Germans. This sympathy was expressed by the exceptionally solemn burial of the dead of the pocket battleship in Gibraltar, as well as by the friendly admission of the wounded to the British hospital there and their excellent care by the nurses who were brought over by plane from England just to do this. Out of consideration for the families of the fallen, Hitler ordered that the dead be returned for burial in the homeland, and that the bodies be transported aboard the pocket battleship *Deutschland* to Wilhelmshaven for this purpose. The chief of the British Gibraltar station, Admiral Evans, responded with prompt courtesy to the German desire, and had the bodies exhumed.

When, as a result of the attack on the *Deutschland,* the German Government demanded in the Non-Intervention Committee that further violence against the naval forces in the services of international supervision be answered by joint countermeasures of all the participating powers, the proposal was rejected. Therefore we, along with Italy, withdrew from the joint supervisory naval patrol. From then on, the naval forces of the foreign powers limited themselves again to a general routine of observing and being present, as well as the protection of their country's own special interests.

By this time, however, Franco's forces—the Nationalist Spanish—had won military superiority in Spain. After Franco had captured Barcelona and Catalonia, and thus forced the retreat of the Loyalist Spanish forces to internment in southern France, the civil war came to an end: on 28 March 1939, the Nationalist Spanish troops entered the capital, Madrid. The German naval forces in Spanish waters had already been reduced before that, and at the end of the year 1938 they were completely withdrawn.

During the two years of the Spanish problem, the German Navy always had combat units attached to the Fleet Command in the sea area around Spain's coast. By the continual relief of these ships, a great part of the German Navy had had the opportunity to participate in this program. Because of this, naturally it had not been possible during this time to carry on the regular training program of the fleet. In particular, training of the individual ships in fleet operations had been impossible during this time. But neither the Commander in Chief nor I had regretted this. The deficiencies we had to make up in tactical and unit training were more than compensated by what the fleet had gained in general comprehension and judgment, political understanding, and self confidence. The special employment of the ships had strongly stimulated the initiative of the skippers and commanders as well as that of their officers, in the training of the crews. These officers were more than satisfied that every member of the crew now through his own experience knew how varied are the tasks of the Navy, even in peacetime. Out of the narrow bounds of the North and Baltic Seas, German naval forces had been thrust into a broad foreign policy framework for a task which each could recognize as necessary and important. Dealing with other navies and appearing in foreign ports had become normal events to them, and handling many new types of problems had brought new knowledge and experience. During long stretches of sea duty, far removed from their home bases, the crews had to keep their ships at the peak of readiness, both for cruising and fighting. The common task and the dependence of one on the other had furthered discipline and the bonds of fellowship. Lastly, the Navy had become clearly conscious of its significance and its possibilities. Its own responsibilities and its future had now become recognized.

From their patrol duties, furthermore, our sailors brought back to their homeland one other gain which cannot be valued highly enough: the sympathy and gratitude of broad circles of the Spanish people. The German Navy has always had good relations with the Spanish nation. In the frequent visits of our warships in Spanish ports after the First World War, the hospitable reception there had always given us a feeling of pleasant obligation. Now the Navy was happy that it had had the opportunity, in its two years of operations in Spanish waters, to repay its obligation with deeds.

XII

The Battle for a Naval Air Force

EVEN IN THE DAYS of the First World War, the German Navy had a naval aviation component, though its early emphasis was on the use of airships for reconnaissance and air attacks. Naval airplanes were also being developed, and during the course of the war over 2,500 were built and used as scouting, combat, and torpedo planes. Special attention was given to reconnaissance work. By the end of the war the Navy had built and was testing a four-motor, long-range reconnaissance plane. In general, German naval planes were the equal of any of those flown by the enemy.

The Versailles Treaty ended all that. All German planes had to be surrendered to the Allies. Germany was forbidden ever again to have any type of air force. Planes for civilian use could be built only in limited numbers and under many restrictions which made it impossible for Germany to keep up with the rapid progress of aviation abroad, or to compete commercially with foreign-built planes. The leading airplane builders and designers in Germany emigrated elsewhere, where they could develop and build planes without hindrance. Among these emigrating firms were those which had specialized in seaplane construction during the war.

For example, the Dornier firm set up an aircraft plant in Pisa, Italy, in 1921 and there developed the Do-Wal plane, so successfully used by Amundsen in his polar flight in 1925, by Balbo in his trans-Atlantic flight to South America in 1926, and by the German naval pilot, Lieutenant Commander von Gronau (retired) in his transoceanic flights. The firm further progressed through the four-motor Super-Wal to the Do-X, a flying boat that had twelve engines and that weighed 50 tons.

In similar fashion, Dr. Rohrbach moved his firm to Copenhagen, and Ernst Heinckel founded his own firm for building commercial craft at Warnemünde in 1923. His first large order was a contract from the German firm of Hugo Stinnes for "ten planes for South America." Actually this was a camouflage order for the German Navy, parts of the planes being manufactured at Warnemünde, shipped to Sweden for assembly, then flown into German disassembled and packed away in crates for future use.

By 1926 some of the restrictions had been lifted from German civilian aviation, though the Versailles Treaty still prohibited any sort of German air force, either military or naval.

However, the Navy was keenly interested in the development of the seaplane, and, from 1924 on, assigned Captain Lahs and Captain Lohmann, the latter the head of the Naval Transport Division, to look after its interests in the aviation world. By using money from his Naval Transport office budget, and other devices, Captain Lohmann aided the German firms that were doing seaplane construction. Captain Lahs, by equal subterfuge as a private customer, bought seaplanes really intended for naval use. Simultaneously a group was formed inside the Admiralty for the purpose of developing, ultimately, a naval air force. Among the brilliant naval officers and civilians in this group were Captain Lahs and Captain (later Air Marshal) Zander.

The Versailles Treaty did, however, permit the Navy to have anti-aircraft guns. To practice anti-aircraft fire, you have to have planes to tow the targets. Accordingly, a special company, the "Severa," was formed and equipped with civilian planes for this activity. In 1928 a "Seaplane Testing Station for the United German Aviation Companies" was established at Travemünde—but it was headed by Lieutenant Commander Moll (retired) of the Navy, who, oddly enough, later became a Lieutenant General in the Air Force. The seaplanes tested here between 1927 and 1930 were manufactured by German firms or were foreign-built planes, all purchased through the Ministry of Transport, but at the instigation of the Admiralty.

When the Lohmann undertakings were liquidated in 1928, as described earlier, there was danger that the Navy's part in promoting these camouflaged operations would be doomed. I gained the approval of Chancellor Müller, Defense Minister Groener, and others in authority to continue.

Thus the technical basis for a regular naval air force was ready at the beginning of the thirties, merely awaiting political clearance to come out into the open. About the same time the Communications Experiment Institute perfected a radio for planes that was so successful that it was standard equipment for the Navy throughout World War II.

By 1932 we had completely designed, and had in model form, a multiple-purpose plane for dropping bombs, mines, and torpedoes, as well as a pursuit fighter plane. Also the Navy had developed a promising dive bomber design which was being tested for its intended use later on airplane carriers. The Deutsche Werke in Kiel had built an effective catapult for shipboard use, and the Navy had under development and in the testing stage an airplane torpedo at the Eckernförds Torpedo Experimental Institute and a 2-cm. naval gun at the Oerlikon Company in Switzerland.

Altogether the development of the Navy's future air arm was mainly the work of former naval aviators who had dedicated themselves to the task, and who received warm support from the German aviation industry.

We did not, however, limit ourselves to the technical and piloting aspects of aviation, for both the Admiralty and the Fleet Command endeavored to familiarize all active officers with the new problems that would result from the introduction of a naval air arm. The tactical as well as the strategic effects of aviation were studied in war games and maneuvers in which planes were actually used, some of these planes being from the "Severa" company. The work went ahead untiringly, despite every handicap, and the moment the Versailles Treaty restrictions were lifted, we had the "know-how" and the trained personnel to proceed immediately with the formation of a naval air arm that could be a powerful striking force.

The creation, in 1933, of a separate German Air Force, however, had brought up the question whether the Army and the Navy should have their own distinctive air arms, or whether the aviation tasks of these two services should be taken over by the new third service, the Air Force.

This was a problem the Navy had been studying for years, using not only its own experiences but those of foreign powers as well. In Japan and the United States there had been a clear separation into Naval Air Force and an Army Air Force, and from all evidence this arrangement had been completely successful. In France they had come to a similar solution, which, as the French Commander in Chief, Admiral Darlan, later told me, was also successful there. Only in Great Britain had the Navy, in spite of its traditional position as the senior service, had to fight a hard bitter battle to retain sufficient airpower for the conduct of naval warfare. The decisive point in its argument for a fleet air arm was the necessity for aircraft carriers and special planes and pilots to man them.

It has been consistently held by all the larger navies that naval components, whether surface ships, submarines, or air forces, must be controlled by a single commander in chief, and for this reason naval air forces must be an integral part of the Navy. In Germany, Air Force General Göring and his circle had made the repeated assertion that "Everything that flies belongs to us!" Such a concentration could have advantages in engine development, general flight training, and industrial expansion, but the proponents of the Göring thesis apparently could not realize that the employment of planes and air forces in land warfare is totally different from their employment in naval warfare. On land, the attack and defense will be predicated on the principles of *land* warfare, and hence the pilot must be a master of the methods and tactics of land warfare. Naval warfare requires men, machines, and tactics especially fitted to the techniques of *sea* combat—only here the requirements are more difficult to fill, since the element of water is so utterly different from the element of earth. The resulting tactics and methods are so different that only flyers trained in the tactics of naval warfare and trained in the ways and idioms of the sea can be really useful in naval operations.

One of the distinguishing features of naval forces is their great mobility and vast range of operations, so that they can exert force in the most unexpected places in the minimum of time. Far-ranging reconnaissance is a necessity. A single observer's report often changes the whole position of his commander in chief. A prime essential in such a reconnaissance report, therefore, is its accuracy, so that whether the report emanates from a cruiser, a destroyer, a submarine, or an airplane, the commander can depend upon it. Such reports are the result of extensive training and long experience. Furthermore, since a plane can scout at greater distances and greater speed, can cover far larger areas than any other type of craft, and can make aerial photographs, such air reconnaissance can provide far speedier and more valuable information than reconnaissance by submarine or surface vessel. But reports are good only when the observer knows what to look for and how to assess it. Accordingly, up to 1933 our naval flyers had been trained with these things especially in mind, and had become familiar with naval doctrine by living constantly in and with the Navy.

This viewpoint on aviation was common throughout the Navy, and all staff members and unit and force commanders shared my opinion that the plane was as important an element of naval warfare as the surface ship or submarine, and would become even more significant in the future. Even in World War I, when reconnaissance had been done principally by airships, the dependence of naval operations on air forces was recognized. We in the German Navy shared the conviction of all the leading foreign navies, that close support of air forces would not only be important in the use of naval units, but would often be decisive. But no plane and pilot can be effective if on one day the plane must attack targets deep in enemy territory, the next day fight in close tactical support of ground troops, and the third day operate as an effective part of a naval force joined in all-out combat with the enemy.

For effective support of naval units, a plane unit or squadron must have an intimate knowledge not only in the characteristics of its own and the enemy's naval craft, and the principles of naval operations and tactics, but also of the signal system and the phraseology of command of the Navy.

With the rapid development of plane and aviation equipment, the plane had begun to take over many of the functions that had formerly been the exclusive province of floating units. In scouting, it is indispensable; in screening ships and boats against enemy air and submarine attacks, and against mines, the airplane is as effective in its way as a destroyer or convoy escort. For mining enemy waters, the plane is a full teammate of the submarine and the surface ship. In battle between opposing naval forces, the combat will be waged in the air as well as on and beneath the sea. For such teamwork and close support, the air forces concerned must be under the same direct command that is responsible for the whole operation at sea. Inescapably, scouting, fighter, and pursuit planes for naval support, whether they are ship-based or shore-based must be an integral and inalienable part of the naval force they support, and under the same command authority. If such air units are not a direct part of the Navy's own air arm, then they must be assigned that their training and employment will be under the sole jurisdiction of the naval commander.

While these concepts were self-evident to every Navy man, Göring and his associates, all either former Army fliers or ground officers, contended for the necessity for an all-inclusive, independent Air Force, with both Army and Navy aviation units as parts of it. They held that flying in itself was the important thing, and that special training for Army or Navy purposes was only secondary.

But successful integration of an Army flier into the Navy or a naval aviator into the Army could never be attained in this way, and brief training in another service, with limited duty with it, could never provide the fundamental indoctrination necessary. The pilot would only wind up eventually feeling not completely at home in either service.

Ordinarily even the most difficult problem can be solved by some sort of compromise which is fair and beneficial to all parties concerned. But, unfortunately, the Air Force had practically no knowledge whatsoever of the essential requirements of naval warfare, and hence had no common ground which could be used to begin discussions. In fact, the issue was often decided from the standpoint of prestige alone, the Commander in Chief of the Air Force often seeming to think this was the all important factor.

With the decision against it, the Navy had to make request of the Commander in Chief of the Air Force for the establishment of the aviation units who were to serve with the Navy. The original 1935 plan was for 25 squadrons of about 300 planes total, but this force proved all too small. The following year the Navy included an increase to 62 squadrons in its plans, and so notified Göring. Göring's reply was that he would be glad to set up a special Air Force organization—Air Force Command (Sea)—and put it under the tactical command of the Navy's Commander in Chief and the Commander in Chief of the Fleet. This restriction to the tactical field alone was completely unsatisfactory to the Navy, since the naval aviation units would be components of the Air Force in all other respects. Nevertheless the Navy's contention that it should have the say in the selection, training and indoctrination, and assignment of its flyers was not acceptable to the Air Force, and Göring did not even give consideration to the Navy's desires as to the particular types of planes to be assigned.

However, even an imperfect organization can be made to work if all parties will give their full and cheerful cooperation. Accordingly the Navy released to the Air Force all its officers with flying experience and background, and I hoped that through them we could develop in the Air Force a better attitude toward the Navy's interests. I wrote a personal letter to each of the senior naval flyers we were transferring, explaining that his transfer was in the best interests of the Navy, and requesting that he keep this in mind in his future duties. Unfortunately, not all the naval personnel thus transferred were assigned by the Air Force to naval aviation; some were given duties not in any way connected with the Navy.

Some sections of the Air Force did work unmistakably for the Navy's interests in aviation. The science of naval warfare was treated in a regular course both at the Air Force Academy and other Air Force schools. The lecturer at the Academy was Admiral Gladisch of the Navy, and another naval officer was assigned as liaison officer on the staff of the Chief of Communications in the Air Force, where he received such cooperation that the communications sections of both services profited greatly.

But while some compromises were made from time to time, no basic change was ever made by the Air Force in its attitude toward the Navy. Thus, despite my best efforts, our Navy never secured its own air arm as other navies did, nor was any real consideration ever given inside the Air Force as a whole toward the necessities of naval warfare. Meeting after meeting, conference after conference, was held, with no other result than friction, extra work, and constant delay.

We held to our contention of 62 air squadrons for naval purposes until 1938, when we finally secured an agreement from Göring that these would be provided in two steps, the last to be completed by 1942. However, even in making his promise in 1938, Göring stated that the Air Force felt it had the complete responsibility for all air forces operating over the sea or in combination with the Navy at sea, and that the Air Force had set up its program accordingly. Hence, he said, the Navy's request for its own air units for combat and reconnaissance could not be granted. And, he added, he was sure that the Air Force's 13 squadrons designated for naval purposes would far better fill the needs than the reconnaissance and combat squadrons of the proposed naval air units.

The Navy could not agree to this view, and the quarrel widened. My deputies and I contested this unrealistic viewpoint of the Commander in Chief of the Air Force in every way possible, but with small success. I could get no support from the Army, which had nothing at stake to similar degree. I even included the matter in several personal reports to Hitler, hoping to get a more favorable decision for the Navy, but apparently Göring had already reached Hitler's ear privately and sold him an enticing picture of the all-powerful air force he was going to build up. Ordinarily Hitler was receptive to the Navy's expansion program, and not only listened to my own suggestions, but often contributed ideas of his own. But in the matter of naval aviation, he was on the opposite side, and I could never get any decision unfavorable to Göring. Also, it seemed to be Hitler's regular policy to play off two contending parties against each other in the belief that the resulting battle would produce better results than an amicable agreement. A typical example was the competition of the three services for workers and raw materials—which, incidentally, did not bring results in accord with Hitler's theory.

From the Navy's point of view, it was a tragic situation, since the Air Force was the sole arbiter of requests in the field of naval aviation. As a last resort, and in order to salvage at least something, I was willing to enter into a written agreement with the Commander in Chief of the Air Force, which we both signed on 27 January 1939. Under this agreement there were to be 41 squadrons designated for naval air purposes, and provision was also made as to the manner and areas of their employment. But the Air Force still retained complete control of all air combat operations over the sea, including aerial mining and attacks on surface ships, submarines, enemy naval bases, and shore installations. What few units were assigned to the Navy's jurisdiction were to be purely for reconnaissance purposes and for close tactical air cover for fleet units. The Navy's original naval air arm was completely wrecked.

Presumably to help the Air Force handle the job, an Air Force general was assigned as liaison officer on my staff, and Major General Geissler of the Air Force, who had been a former naval flier and longtime naval officer, was assigned to similar duty on the staff of the Commander in Chief of the Air Force. But nothing could alter the fact that the situation was completely unfavorable for the over-all conduct of war. All that we could do was to hope for changes for the better in the future—especially when the aircraft carrier we were constructing joined the fleet. We hoped that, as in the British Navy, this carrier's requirements for air squadrons would point up the absolute need for the Navy for its own air arm.

The whole matter seemed to me so adverse to the Navy's—and the country's— best interests that I thought seriously of staking my own career by forcing a decision at the highest government levels. However, Hitler had already refused to interfere in the dispute, and his decision might be against the Navy—which would strengthen Göring's position still further and make the position of my successor, whoever he might be, still weaker. And even in the faint contingency of my winning, I knew that Göring would never accept a solution contrary to his wishes and his ambition.

XIII

The Navy, Hitler, and the Nazi Party

MY FIRST ACTUAL MEETING with Hitler was, as I have mentioned, at a private dinner at the house of General von Hammerstein, Commander in Chief of the Army. It was 2 February 1933, and except for Hitler and Foreign Minister von Neurath, the only persons present were the heads of the various armed services. After dinner Hitler had given us a detailed statement of what his policies would be as the new Chancellor of Germany.

Briefly, after a striking tribute to President von Hindenburg, he declared that his main objectives would be to break the shackles of the Versailles Treaty, build up a strong sovereign nation for all the German people, and abolish unemployment, then widespread. He himself would conduct the country's foreign and domestic policies, and the armed forces would not be used as police to settle internal matters, but would devote their entire energies to the defense of the fatherland against external enemies. The armed services were to be the only organizations permitted to bear arms in the country.

With these policies I could be in thorough accord, especially in the matter of keeping the armed forces out of politics.

Hitler as a Person

In his earlier days Hitler apparently had no special liking for the Navy. His book, *Mein Kampf,* had been extremely critical of the Imperial Navy and of Admiral von Tirpitz's fleet program. This disparaging material, we later learned, actually was suggested by a military collaborator who, though a military man, by no means was a naval expert. However, Rear Admiral von Levetzow (retired) a brilliant naval officer whom I had known intimately in the Battle Cruiser Forces during World War I, had become an early member of the Nazi Party, and saw to it that Hitler gained a better understanding of the Navy. He had pointed out that the well-disciplined Navy had abstained from all party politics, and was a reliable instrument of the legitimate state.

Even before 1933, Hitler had applied himself to a zealous study of the Navy and its affairs, and had already indicated that he would personally support the revival of the fleet.

About this time the British Admiral Harper had published his study of the Battle of Skagerrak, *The Riddle of Jutland,* Hitler had had it translated by Rudolf Hess, and had read the complete translation at one sitting, between noon of one day and daybreak the following morning. He kept constantly at hand the British book *Jane's Fighting Ships,* and its German counterpart, *Weyer's Handbook of Naval Fleets.* Through constant reading and an excellent memory he had acquired a wide knowledge which gave him an exceptionally fine basis for making judgments. In some respects he was even superior to supposed experts. He was always receptive to the suggestions and reports I made to him in those early years, and would listen attentively to everything I had to say. Very often I found it easier to reach an agreement with him than with Minister of Defense von Blomberg, who often could see military problems only through the eyes of his own service, the Army.

Of one thing I was quickly convinced: that Hitler disagreed with many of the political policies of previous decades and had drawn from them the same lesson that we in the Navy had.

One of the basic points in his policies, as he more than once emphasized, was that we should never again enter into an armament race with England, and that we should make every effort to establish close and friendly relations with her. Hence he moved with extreme caution, not only before the conclusion of the naval agreement with Britain, but even afterward, in his anxiety not to suffer any setback in foreign policy over naval matters. Hence I had to moderate some of my own suggestions and programs now and then to a greater extent than I liked. Especially true was this in the case of the design of the ships we wanted to build as successors to our pocket battleships. The next two in our construction program were the battleships *Scharnhorst* and *Gneisenau,* and only after long argument would Hitler consent to their having three main battery turrets instead of two. And he completely rejected our proposal to increase the caliber of the guns from 28.5-cm. to 38-cm. This latter decision was a disheartening one for me, charged as I was with responsibility for the fighting ability of the Navy. Equally discouraging was the clause in the naval agreement restricting us forever to a strength only one-third that of the British Fleet.

However, Hitler's decision to limit our fleet in relation to England's strengthened my confidence that we would pursue a moderate and cautious foreign policy that would be a judicious reflection of the world state of affairs.

In my actual command responsibilities, Hitler gave me a completely free hand. Though keenly interested in types of ships, armament, and other technical details, he rarely interfered in any way in the basic structure of the Navy. This applied to the training, education, and performance of both officers and men, and to the judicial system also. Never once did he attempt, in those earlier days, to exercise any influence on the selection or assignment of personnel, or even any intimation of personal preferences. Had he done so, I would have been adamant in refusal, for the Commander in Chief of one of the armed services has a responsibility that he can share with no one.

The personal impression that Hitler made on me during that period was the same that he made on every one—that he was an extraordinary man who was born to lead. His knowledge, acquired through intensive study, was vast and varied. Not only had he stored this knowledge up in his memory, but he had also digested it, and his ability to get immediately to the heart of a problem and reduce even the most complicated matter to a common denominator was amazing. He could put his thoughts into clear and intelligible language, in words best suited to the individual listener. No wonder the German people accepted him not only with hope but with the firm conviction that he would lead them from the depression and distress brought on by the Versailles Treaty and would be willing to grant him almost any authority necessary for the purpose. I could only concur in this view.

In both personal and official meetings, Hitler at all times treated me with the courtesy due my position and my greater age. He listened attentively even when the views I presented did not agree with his own—and from the very beginning I made it a point to address him frankly and openly, concealing nothing. I never avoided controversial subjects, and fought stoutly for what I believed were the best interests of the Navy.

The same was true of any other naval officer who had occasion to report to Hitler. When, in my presence, Junior Captain von Harsdorf of the cruiser *Karlsruhe* described to Hitler the friendly reception generally accorded his ship abroad, he also complained strongly of the ill being created by some foreign branches of the Nazi Party. Hitler not only listened, but promised to take remedial action.

It was my impression that such frankness paid better dividends than sidestepping of issues. Hitler, being himself of a distrustful nature, was quick to sense equivocation or evasion in anyone else. So, while not too fond at time of gratuitous information or advice, he was at least willing to listen. I believe that my open approach helped me to gain his confidence. This was an absolute requisite if the Navy was to attain any of its ends and to win any support in its differences with the other services.

Even in my battles with Göring over the naval air arm I sometimes had the feeling that Hitler privately agreed with me more than he did with Göring.

In the beginning, I tried to arrange regular conferences with Hitler, to keep him informed of the Navy's needs as well as its progress. Occasionally I would even ask to dine with him because this gave me opportunity for intimate discussions before the meal in which I could bring naval matters directly to his attention instead of having to present them indirectly through the Minister of Defense. But gradually I began to feel that too close personal association with Hitler had its perils. For one thing, Hitler had an almost fatal charm, an amazing ability to influence people in his favor. I often saw him win over even the skeptical individuals—not only

Germans of all classes and professions, but foreigners as well. Even foreign diplomats were not immune.

Hitler had an almost incredible sixth sense in determining how far he could go in his relations with others. On one occasion, in later years, when there were often serious differences between us, I had to make a report to him which was directly opposite to his desires. I was resolved to be sharp in my opposition, but he received me with such cordiality and readiness to listen that I felt the rug had been pulled right out from under my feet. This remarkable personal charm, I believe, had much to do with his success.

Although my resistance to this atmosphere of charm was at first instinctive, I came within the course of time to shun it with firm resolution. For my spiritual independence was important to me; without it I could not do my duty. Hence I began to limit my personal reports and visits, especially after the war began, to those occasions only which required my personal presence. And when I did go, I went with a definite agenda on which I could demand a definite decision.

Hitler usually kept to the subject under discussion, asking questions that showed his keen interest and often enlarging upon details personally. Rarely would he open the discussion to subjects other than those in the department of the man who was reporting. Only after some time did I realize that this was not so much a personal characteristic as a system. His objective was to keep his various subordinates sharply separated from each other so that they could never present a united front. And, correspondingly, each department had to get his decision individually. In this way no one could bring up questions involving someone else's field of operations. If anyone tried—and I did, on several occasions—Hitler, with his superior sources of information, had so many effective replies right at the tip of his tongue that one could not easily dispute him.

Also, I began to realize that while he demanded complete information himself, he was very reticent personally, and frequently withheld information on matters which I needed to know about. Even when both the Commander in Chief of the Army and I were raised to Cabinet rank later, neither of us was ever invited to attend any Cabinet meetings—if, in fact, any ever took place. I was never called in to discuss either foreign or domestic policy except where these specifically concerned the Navy, and after disagreement with England arose in 1939, even these discussions ceased.

Thus it was difficult to get any dependable picture of Hitler's own ideas and intentions whenever these lay at all outside one's own department, or to get a really accurate understanding of the man himself. He was a master of dialectic and bluff, and he interspersed so many clever evasions and bits of double talk in his discussions that it was impossible to discover what his real intentions and aims were. I eventually gave up trying to solve the enigma, but I did come to the conclusion that although he never let this aspect show on the outside, his natural inclination was always to the more radical of any solutions under study.

Hitler's reticence in official matters was only equalled, if not exceeded, by his disconcerting frankness, amounting almost to criminal carelessness on some social occasions. At large luncheons or dinners he would frequently express the most uninhibited criticisms or personal comments on leading personalities at home or abroad —even in a numerous and mixed company. During the war I came to be extremely wary of reporting on plans before the time of execution, in order to make sure that military secrecy was not violated.

On the whole, however, I would say that in the early years it was generally possible to deal with Hilter objectively, and to gain a favorable decision from him when the matter merited it.

Relations with the Nazi Party

So far as the Nazi Party was concerned, I tried to keep the Navy strictly aloof. And in those days, whenever news came of some unsavory act of the Party or the secret police—some incomprehensible government statement, for instance, or some attack on the Church, or some brutality of the Gestapo—I was convinced from Hitler's bearing and words that such acts were not ordered by him, but had been done on the sole responsibility of some Party functionary or other, and without Hitler's authorization.

Certainly, when it came to Navy matters, I made my own decisions as to the promotions and assignments of officers, without any consideration of their relation to the Party or their attitude toward the National Socialist State. I appointed Captain Patzig, predecessor to Admiral Canaris in the Intelligence Division of the Supreme Commander Armed Forces, to command the newest pocket battleship even though he had had violent disagreements with the Gestapo, the SS (Hitler's own bodyguard), and Party functionaries. When he had completed this assignment I made him my Chief of Personnel, a position he retained until well into the war. At another time I dismissed Hitler's personal naval aide because that officer acted in a manner unbecoming an officer and a gentleman. In none of these cases did I suffer any retaliation.

Other cases of friction between the Navy and the Party came up, but a sensible presentation of the Navy's side generally smoothed things over. In this connection the Navy was in a much more favorable position than the Army. The Navy was concentrated in a few large bases where they constituted the major part of the population; the Army, however, was divided into numerous activities scattered over a wide area, where it was outnumbered by the civilian population, so that there were many more possibilities for disagreement with the local Party members. In addition, the Navy offered no competition to the Party's military activities, whereas the Army encountered rivalry from both the SA (the Nazi "Storm Troopers" militia or "Brownshirts") and the SS (or "Blackshirts"), a personal bodyguard for Hitler organized by Heinrich Himmler, chief of the Gestapo.

Whenever disagreements arose between lower echelons of the Navy and local Nazi leaders, I was generally able to settle the difficulty by direct negotiations between the Supreme Naval Command and the higher officials of the Party. Perhaps one reason for our success was that I stood up for the Navy boldly; another reason was that the Navy's tradition for patriotism and disinterested service to the State was so good that even the Nazis did not dare attack it. In fact it was not considered very good form in the Party to quarrel with the Navy.

The two Party officials with whom I had the greatest trouble were Reinhard Heydrich, Deputy Chief of the Gestapo and head of the SS Security Service, and Marshal Göring, Commander in Chief of the Air Force. I felt that I had to be on guard constantly against both of them. Heydrich had been a naval officer himself, entering in 1922, but had been dismissed in 1931, while a lieutenant, because of disgraceful conduct in connection with a young girl. He had never forgiven me for this, and probably influenced his superior, Himmler, to the same way of thinking.

Heydrich lost no opportunity to complain about me to Nazi headquarters and even to Hitler himself, a typical instance being his attack on me for my defense of Parson Niemöller. Since his charges were always unfounded or downright false, I combatted them easily with unequivocal letters directly to Himmler, to the considerable discomfiture of the accuser. Heydrich broke off ties with all other old comrades in the Navy, and, when the war broke out, performed his military service in the Air Force and not in the Navy.

Of all the men close to Hitler, however, Göring was the one with whom I had my most violent battles. We were perfect opposites, both personally and ideologically. While he might have been a brave and capable flier in World War I, he lacked all the requisites for command of one of the armed services. He possessed a colossal vanity which, while amusing to some, and pardonable if it had been associated with other more significant qualities, was dangerous because it was combined with a limitless ambition. His penchant for show, and the exaggerated luxury in which he lived, set a bad example for the Air Force, whose attention should have been devoted exclusively to its task of swiftly building up this branch of the armed services.

At first Göring adopted a superficial attitude of friendliness toward the Navy, but his envy of it was evident in the way in which he set out to copy its best features for the Air Force. At the same time, as was soon discovered, he privately criticized the Navy and maligned both it and me to Hitler. I was convinced that Hitler saw through his malice, but it suited him to use Göring for his own purposes. My belief was that Hitler deliberately loaded Göring down with tasks outside his service command in order to prevent the ambitious marshal from becoming a dangerous political opponent. The natural result was that Göring had so many assignments that he could perform none of them properly.

On his part, Göring pretended the utmost devotion to Hitler, but did not hesitate to make slighting remarks about his leader. These Hitler always overlooked—whether because of old comradeship or not, I do not know. In any case it was impossible to obtain anything from Hitler that might be at the cost of Göring.

As a result of Göring's ruthless energy and his influence on Hitler, I had to fight continuously against his efforts to build up the Air Force at the Navy's expense. My relations with Göring are probably best characterized by my warning words to Hitler when eventually I resigned as the Navy's Commander in Chief: "Please protect the Navy and my successor from Göring!"

The year 1938 was the first time I began to revise my early opinions of Hitler. The occasion that first shook my faith in Hitler's sincerity was the von Blomberg case and its aftermath.

Field Marshal von Blomberg, the highest ranking Army officer and Minister of War in Hitler's Cabinet at the time, had made a very questionable marriage. Hitler and Göring had been witnesses at the wedding, as was natural considering the high position of the groom. Upon learning more about the bride, Hitler expressed severe disapproval.

I was unable to understand, under the circumstances, how Marshal von Blomberg could have expected to remain as Commander in Chief of the Armed Services after such a violation of all officer traditions; he should have resigned and married as a private individual. Even less could I understand his inviting Hitler to be a witness at the wedding.

I became embroiled when, upon request from Hitler to recommend a suitable successor as War Minister, I named General Baron von Fritsch, at that time Commander in Chief of the Army.

I had known and respected General von Fritsch for a long time, and had been delighted when President von Hindenburg had designated him to succeed General von Hammerstein as head of the Army in 1934. In fact, upon being asked for my opinion by Major General von Hindenburg, the President's son, I had expressed a preference for either General von Rundstedt or General von Fritsch as von Hammerstein's successor. I knew that I could work harmoniously with General von Fritsch, for we thought alike on many points: our attitude toward the Church, for instance and our endeavor to keep our branches of the armed services completely out of politics. Like me, too, von Fritsch had no high opinion of Göring.

I had never had any cause to alter my original estimate of the keen-witted and able General von Fritsch. When, in 1935, Hitler had offered to promote me to the rank of Admiral of the Fleet, I had turned it down as I did not wish to have a rank superior to that of von Fritsch, who headed the Army with the four-star rank of Colonel General. As the Navy had no comparable rank, I suggested introducing the rank of General Admiral in the Navy, and accepted that promotion from Hitler in 1936. And it had given me great pleasure to invite General von Fritsch to make the christening speech at the launching of the battleship *Gneisenau* on 8 December 1936. It was typical of this highminded, selfless officer that he should begin his speech by quoting from an ode by Field Marshall Gneisenau: "First let mankind be concerned for its duties, and only then for its rights!"

I was therefore astounded when, in reply to my recommendation of von Fritsch as von Blomberg's successor, Hitler told me curtly that it was out of the question, as von Fritsch himself was under accusation on a morals charge.

Reviewing the case of von Blomberg's marriage, Hitler undoubtedly could believe anything. He went on to say that for some years he had known of accusations of moral turpitude against General von Fritsch—accusations which he had always disregarded, but now, in light of the von Blomberg case and of new accusations against General von Fritsch, he was ordering an investigation. He concluded by stating that General von Brauchitsch was to replace von Fritsch as Commander in Chief of the Army.

I had always known that Hitler did not especially care for von Fritsch because of that general's somewhat reserved nature, but this new development was a shock to me—especially as I was to be one of the members of the investigating court. The other two members were Göring, who presided, and General von Brauchitsch, the new Commander in Chief of the Army.

Later I learned that Dr. Gürtner, the Minister of Justice, had demanded the court primarily to clear up the clandestine accusations against von Fritsch.

Early in the investigation it became apparent that the accusations were founded only on the false testimony of an unprincipled scoundrel closely connected to the Gestapo. All other witnesses, whether from the Army or the Hitler Youth Organization, testified in favor of General von Fritsch. Even Göring joined in clearing the general, his deft probing of the accuser doing much to bring out the fact that General von Fritsch's only connection with the affair was his having the same name as another officer who was not so guiltless.

Immediately after our unanimous vote for acquittal, I went over to General von Fritsch, shook hands with him, and congratulated him on his complete exoneration. I assured him that now nothing stood in the way of his remaining in the service, and that he could not be spared by the Army. I also told him that I was ready to take any measures he considered necessary to clear his reputation. He would not let me take any steps at all, however, in his personal affairs, and persisted in handing in his resignation, which was accepted.

On 13 June of that year Hitler again called together the admirals and generals who had been present at the 4 February meeting, and stated that the court of investigation had fully proved General von Fritsch's innocence, and that his character was stainless. He declared that he had deeply regretted having to call the investigation, but that it had been necessary through force of circumstances. The perjuring witness had been shot for his crime, and everything would be done to repair the injury done to General von Fritsch. However, he concluded, he did not believe it advisable to restore the general to his former position because he did not think von Fritsch could now give him the same confidence he had formerly given.

I was convinced that Hitler spoke the truth, but I realized that General von Fritsch could never expect complete vindication in this matter. No statement of exoneration was ever issued to the officer corps in general, inasmuch as the whole matter had supposedly been kept confidential in the small circle of topmost service people. The only official recognition of his innocence was the naming of General von Fritsch as "Honorary Chief" of one of Germany's distinguished regiments.

Determined that the Navy should express its confidence in General von Fritsch, I invited him to take part in the June 1939 fleet exercises as a guest on board the *Gneisenau,* the battleship which he had helped to christen. Baron von Fritsch and his aide spent a week on board, in full uniform, and at his departure he was given full military honors by Admiral Boehm, though he was no longer on active duty. At a farewell breakfast attended by all the senior officers of the fleet, Admiral Boehm eulogized the general, and topped the ceremonies by honoring von Fritsch with a 17-gun salute.

Looking back on all the peculiar circumstances connected with the von Blomberg and von Fritsch affairs, I came to suspect that Göring was not entirely innocent of some hidden connection. By this ill-advised marriage, von Blomberg had removed himself from the office of Commander in Chief of all the Armed Services—a position which the ambitious Göring would have loved to have. The disposal of von Fritsch had removed the rival who would have been the most likely successor. However, if Göring was implicated, he failed in his plot, because Hitler knew him too well to place this ambitious self-seeker in a position of such power. Hitler simply abolished the special post of Commander in Chief of the Armed Services and took command personally—a solution that Field Marshal von Blomberg himself had suggested to him at the time of his resignation.

The more I thought about it, the more pleased I was that I had turned down a suggestion Hitler had once made that I become Commander in Chief of the Armed Services. For one thing, I had not the necessary military background to make proper decisions in Army and Air Force affairs. For another thing, I was already turning over the idea of retiring. Indeed, circulatory troubles from which, fortunately, I had recovered, had almost forced my retirement years earlier, in 1934.

Hitler's role in the Blomberg and von Fritsch affair was something I could never quite get clear in my own mind. While Hitler's anger at being deceived into taking part in von Blomberg's wedding was understandable, his method of getting rid of von Fritsch was not. Von Fritsch's throat trouble, as a result of which he had had to spend the winter of 1937-1938 on sick leave in Egypt, would have been a good enough excuse for retiring him. I could not see how Hitler could possibly have avoided seeing the plot that had been woven around von Fritsch.

As for that sturdy general, he went to the front, when the war came, at the head of the regiment whose honorary chief he had been made. During the Polish campaign, he sought and found a soldier's death in the front lines.

Up to this time, it had been part of my job to make proposals and suggestions to Hitler, some of which he did not approve; in return he sometimes made demands to which I could not agree. While these discussions were often lively, they generally had resulted in a sensible agreement. But from now on I began to have violent clashes with Hitler. For instance, at the end of November 1938 I reported to Hitler on the ship construction program we were planning, and showed him designs of the new ships. General Keitel, chief of the Joint Armed Forces Staff, was also present. For some inexplicable reason, Hitler became very insulting, criticizing everything about the plans of the two battleships *Bismarck* and *Tirpitz.* He objected to their guns as too weak, their speed as too slow. Yet it was this same *Bismarck* whose power and speed and, above all, whose unsinkability convinced the British and Americans in its final battles that we had discovered some special new secrets in ship construction.

I was later to discover that such attacks by Hitler usually were the result of some biased person having given him false information in private, beforehand. I did not know this then, however, and the vilification was so unbridled that I rose and asked to be relieved of my command, since Hitler so obviously condemned the results of my decisions. And with that I walked out.

Hitler immediately followed me to the door, caught my sleeve, and asked me to come back in. He sought to retract some of his words and begged me not to think of resigning. But I replied that not only had I already held my position for ten years, but that I was now 62 years old; it would be better if I were replaced by a younger man.

Hitler then brought in my chief of staff, Junior Captain Schulte Mönting, and asked him to try to persuade me to remain. Schulte

Mönting had been my aide, and later became my chief of staff. He always had my complete confidence. He now stoutly sustained my viewpoint and finally secured from Hitler a promise that I would have complete freedom of action in my program for the fleet's expansion. Hitler insisted on putting down in writing his personal notes on our difference of opinion—to justify himself before history, he said—but was still solicitous that I should continue in my position. In the following weeks, typically, he tried to be especially friendly. I have an idea that it was at this time that he conceived the thought of promoting me to the rank of Admiral of the Fleet.

In May of 1939, however, I had another violent brush with Hitler. The officer who had recently been appointed his naval aide requested official permission to marry, in accordance with the usual procedure. I naturally granted it. Shortly afterward, though, a civilian official reported that the marriage had transpired under circumstances which would invalidate it. Investigation proved this report to be correct, with the alternative that either the marriage should be invalidated or the officer should leave his assignment. Hitler's decision, however, was that the marriage should be approved and also that the officer should remain his naval aide.

I held the diametrically opposite view, and dismissed the officer from the Navy. When Hitler objected to my decision, I wrote him a personal letter in which I stated that in my opinion the officer could no longer be permitted to wear the naval uniform, and that if it was Hitler's decision that he stay in the Navy, then I myself requested permission to resign. To insure against delay, I sent the letter by an officer of my staff, with the request that he be given the answer to bring back directly.

After two days Hitler answered with the promise that he would not require that the officer be retained in the Navy, but that he would make him one of his personal aides inside the Party organization. This was satisfactory to me, but it was characteristic that Hitler would not allow any other naval aide to be ordered to his staff right up to the beginning of the war.

The recurring experiences through 1938 and 1939 made me more and more consider the thought of retiring from active duty. I did not care at all for the honors and ceremony that went with the position of Chief of the Supreme Naval Command. The exaggerated importance which this ostentation and display was given by the National Socialist State and its functionaries still further disinclined me for introducing them into the Navy. I refused the suggestions of well-wishers that I thrust myself more into the limelight. Several times during 1938-39 I had proposed to Hitler that I be allowed to retire in October of 1939. Hitler's reaction was to name me to the rank of Admiral of the Fleet upon the occasion of the launching of the battleship *Tirpitz* at Wilhelmshaven on 1 April 1939.

The additional honor did not impress me, but it did give me cause to consider the matter of retirement from all angles. For one thing, as long as I could secure for the Navy the good will of Hitler, and still maintain my independence, I might be able to obtain both the material and personnel that the Navy needed for its growth. I was in a position to interfere directly when the Navy's basic principles were threatened from any direction. Also, to resign without achieving anything other than a change of command would not benefit the Navy at all. I remembered that General von Blomberg's resignation had resulted in the elimination of the newly created position of Commander in Chief of the Armed Forces, and that General von Fritsch's resignation likewise had been to no profit. In both cases, successors were immediately available—and I knew only too well how anxiously the Nazi Party circles were waiting just to fill the vacancies with individuals more subservient to Party dominance. The Air Force, with Göring as Commander in Chief, was a prime example, and the State Police, with Himmler as its head, was another.

I therefore felt that it was an obligation upon me to remain in my position as long as I could bear the burden of the office. All the Navy's senior officers, from whom I sought frank advice, were of the same conviction.

Among the factors influencing this decision was that in the decade I had been in office I had succeeded in winning the respect of the National Socialist State as well as that of Hitler. Through my part in connection with the naval agreement with England, I had aided Germany to a success in its foreign policy, and as long as I held office and could influence Hitler, I could perhaps contribute toward friendly relations with Great Britain. I also felt that as a result of my long and careful nursing of relations with England I had won some confidence abroad, particularly as Baron von Neurath no longer headed the Foreign Ministry.

Naturally I made every effort to prevent any knowledge of my disagreements with Hitler from leaking out to the Navy or the public; the Navy's unity was too much at stake. But any thought I had of resigning went by the board with the outbreak of war in 1939. As Commander in Chief I could not desert the Navy at such a time of crisis.

However, there were two other fields of conflict with Hitler and the Nazi Party that concerned my personal beliefs so deeply that I knew there could be no compromising them. Sooner or later, I felt, there must be a parting of the ways. Those two things were the Nazi's attacks on the Christian Churches, and their treatment of the Jews.

GRAND ADMIRAL ERICH RAEDER

GERMAN NAVAL SHIPYARD AT WILHELMSHAVEN

A BRITISH CASUALTY

Aircraft carrier HMS *Glorious* sinking on June 8, 1940.

XIV

The Navy and the Religious Question

FROM MY EARLIEST DAYS I had acquired in my parents' home a firm and abiding faith in Christ and the Christian Church. My parents took us to religious services regularly and discussed religious matters with us at home, but most of all they taught us Christianity through personal example. To them I shall ever be grateful for the Christian foundation which gave me strength to bear the responsibilities which came to me in my career and which, above all, gave me the inner courage to endure the difficult days of the Nürnberg trials and my ten-year confinement in Spandau prison.

The significance of faith and the Christian Church, and its power to bind together nations and peoples, regardless of state boundaries and political disagreements, I had learned early. No historical event, no war, no world conquest, no intellectual current has ever moved the world so deeply as has Christianity. Unknown to the individual, perhaps, the effects of Christian teachings reach into his innermost life, and alone are responsible for the moral conscience and social culture under which we live. They form the basis of all Western society.

A nation like ours, I was convinced, must consciously rest on a Christian foundation. It must support and promote the churches, and, through them, the religious understanding of its people. And this was no less true in its armed forces.

In the old Imperial Navy, as I knew from experience, religious observance had been a matter of official regulations, these being publicly issued in 1903 in the form of *Regulations for Lutheran and Catholic Naval Churches.* The requirement for attendance at religious services gave each man the opportunity to think on the subject. And the close connection between the Church and the military services provided a strengthening bond in a common Christian belief.

In the old Navy we had had both Lutheran and Catholic chaplains, serving on board in ever-increasing numbers as the Navy expanded. Lutheran and Catholic chaplains worked together in close harmony, the very interdependence of shipboard life being a guarantee against any schism growing out of differences in creed. Shipboard services were conducted for both denominations, and if no regular chaplain was available, the senior officers of the ship conducted services themselves. As captain of the cruiser *Köln* I had often led the Lutheran services. We had a regular corps of naval chaplains who, through long service in the Navy, were fully familiar with the naval life and earned the high esteem of the service men. In the First World War they had more than justified this esteem, standing at their posts under fire and earning war decorations. Chaplain Ronneberger (later chief naval chaplain) served aboard the squadron at Scapa Flow throughout the entire internment.

With the Weimar Republic, after the war, there had come an entirely new concept: religion would be the private affair of the individual. No longer could the armed forces order officers and men to attend church or Bible classes. The one way left to influence the Navy's personnel to a religious way of life was by personal example.

Our Navy was still allowed six naval chaplains under the Versailles Treaty, however—four Lutheran and two Catholic—and this quota we always kept filled. The old "Church Regulations" of 1903 were reissued in 1929 in modified form under the title *Regulations for Lutheran and Catholic Military Churches.* While it was forbidden to order service men to church any longer, it was entirely within the scope of the regulations to permit them "free hours" to attend if they wished. Furthermore, so-called "barracks hours" were established which gave further time for personnel to seek the chaplain's advice on religious and moral problems.

With the Navy's replacement construction program in 1929, and the ensuing increase in chaplain strength, naval chaplains were stationed on all ships, especially schoolships, making long, foreign cruises. In foreign ports our naval chaplains frequently conducted religious services for German nationals residing there. They performed marriages and baptized children, and in some cases, were even in port long enough to hold confirmation classes.

They were admirably fitted to do so: Before qualifying for the Navy, our chaplains had to have practical experience as pastors in civilian parishes ashore.

Chaplains, afloat or ashore, performed the same sort of ministrations as civilian pastors did for their congregations. Where no regular naval chaplain was available, our men either attended services at the civilian churches ashore or were ministered to by pastors from ashore on a regularly scheduled basis.

To some extent my keen interest in the spiritual welfare of the Navy's personnel was due, perhaps, to the inspiration of Chief Naval Chaplain Fenger. He had conducted himself gallantly in the Battle of Skagerrak, and, despite his wounds, had served continuously for long years in the Navy. I had always held that the essential quality in every military leader is character, and that a firm and dependable character cannot exist without a religious foundation. Those clergymen whom my wife and I were privileged to know preached a practical and universally intelligible Christianity with which I was in full accord.

The year 1933, which marked the advent of Hitler and the Nazi Party and the National Socialist State, brought no apparent change in the religious practices of the Navy or in any other of the armed services. The Nazi Party had declared for "positive Christianity" as part of its program. Service chaplains would continue to work unrestricted, as before.

When Hitler visited Kiel in May 1933 I asked him bluntly why he had chosen Military District Chaplain Müller as his special adviser. Müller had at one time been active in the Navy, and had shifted from there to the post of military district chaplain in East

Prussia, but in my opinion did not quite measure up to the stature of a real religious leader. Hitler's reply was that he knew very few other service chaplains, and that he had become acquainted with Müller in Königsberg and considered him an energetic Lutheran chaplain. At the same time Hitler informed me that he planned to bring the Lutheran Church back to an even position with the Catholic Church, to which it had lost ground during the Weimar Republic. How far this remark was influenced by the approaching concordat between the new government and the Pope, I could not say. In any case I received the impression that Hitler fully meant what he said at the time.

Others in the Nazi movement, however, had no such respect for the Church. Their ringleader was Dr. Joseph Goebbels, Minister of Propaganda and National Enlightenment, who labeled me the Party's *bête noire* because of my intercession for the Church. He and others of his kind were behind the formation of the new so-called "German Religious Movement," whose tenets seemed more closely akin to the super-race myth of the Nordic gods than to any aspect of the gentle Christ.

Conflicts soon began to break out between the Nazis and the Church. In these conflicts the Lutheran Church, internally split and lacking a tight organization and leadership, was in a more difficult position than was the Catholic Church under its single head and with powerful congregations all over the world. Furthermore the concordat signed between the German Government and the Papal authorities on 22 July 1933 gave certain guarantees to the Catholic Church in Germany.

With the Lutheran Church thus endangered in the armed forces, I felt it obligatory that I lend all the authority of my person and my position to defend the Navy's chaplains, and its religious freedom, against attacks. I tried to encourage closer communion between the officers and the Church. At officer assemblies I spoke emphatically against deserting the real Christian faith for the political inducements of the German Religious Movement. I invariably concluded with the statement that I was a Christian by conviction and would remain one.

On 17 August 1934 Hitler, speaking at Hamburg, said, "The National Socialist Party stands for a positive Christianity. It will be my honest endeavor to protect both great religions in their rights, to safeguard their doctrines from attacks, and to bring harmony between them and the present-day State." I seized the opportunity to issue my views to the whole Navy: "In view of this [Hitler's statement] I give no consideration to the conflicting statements of other officials of the Party. The religious regulations now observed in the armed services are official regulations. I cannot tolerate a renunciation of them, such as leaving the Church purely in order to make an impression outside. Such matters are not open to question by outsiders—either by the Führer or by representatives of the German Religious Movement. Specifically, I forbid participation in the 'German Religious Movement'."

In my efforts to safeguard the religious practices of the armed forces against outside interference, I had able support both from General Baron von Fritsch, Commander of the Army, and his successor, Field Marshal von Brauchitsch. A stout joint front by the heads of both Army and Navy was necessary. A strong chaplain system was completely lacking in the third service, the Air Force; and the Lutheran Field Bishop of the combined armed forces was not equal to the responsibilities involved.

In the Navy, I designated, as chief chaplains, Chaplain Ronneberger of the Lutheran Church and Chaplain Estevant of the Catholic Church, both of them religious leaders of reputation and ability. Their superiors in the religious field were the field bishops of the Lutheran and Catholic Churches, respectively. However, I maintained personal supervision over their official naval activities, and kept as much freedom as possible from the religious authorities of the Supreme Command of Armed Forces, with whom I disagreed widely in their attitude and action in religious matters.

Much of my counsel in this respect I secured from my old and trusted friend, Chaplain Ronneberger of Wilhelmshaven, whom I frequently called to Berlin for conferences. I had known him from the World War I days when he had come abroad the battle cruiser *Von der Tann* as staff chaplain of the Battle Cruiser Forces. I also had cordial relations with Chief Catholic Chaplain Estevant, and with the Catholic station chaplain, Breuer, in Wilhelmshaven when matters came up that concerned the Catholic Church alone or which concerned both religions jointly.

In addition I had contact now and then with Dr. Kerrl, the Minister for Church Affairs. He was fully cognizant of the difficulties facing the Lutheran Church and our naval chaplains, and confidentially showed me a memorandum he had given Hitler in which he had made recommendations for the settlement of the Church problem that I thought were highly promising. However, as he wryly commented, he rarely got a chance to see Hitler personally, and thus never received an acknowledgment of his proposals right up to his death.

In selecting our naval chaplains, the only things considered were their fitness for the job; outside influence counted not a whit. Thus, in 1938 I named Pastor Poetzsch as station chaplain at Cuxhaven, although he had been removed from his parish in Saxony because of his resistance to outside interference by Nazi functionaries. Three other naval chaplains had been given their commissions despite the fact that they were all opposed by the Party, and two of them had even been arrested for their opposition.

I repeatedly impressed upon our chaplains that they should hold themselves aloof from any political activities whatsoever, and aloof even from disputes with the Lutheran Church itself. When a new chaplain was given his appointment, I received him for a personal conference in which I pointed out to him both his duties and his responsibilities. A typical case was the directive I gave to Chaplain Hölzer when he entered the Navy in December of 1937: "It will not be your duty to wage a religious-political battle in the Navy, or to go expressly into an analysis of the intellectual currents which National Socialism has aroused. As chaplain, you are to *preach Christ* earnestly and without compromise. Never cease to do that!"

Despite Hitler's early assurances, I gradually became aware of a change in his attitude toward the Church. In part, perhaps, this was due to his personal quarrel with Parson Niemöller.

Martin Niemöller had entered the regular line officer corps of the Navy in 1910, and had shown himself to be an officer of exceptional capability; in fact his last wartime assignment had been as commander of a U-boat. Following the war he had entered the Church, and by 1931 he had became pastor of the Berlin-Dahlem Lutheran church. Though he had at first been a member of the

Nazi Party, he had broken with it over the Party's attempt to institute totalitarian control over the Church, and had headed the Pastors' Emergency League for the defense of the Lutheran Church.

During the ensuing persecution of Niemöller, I interceded for him with Hitler, apparently with success. Then Niemöller's telephone had been tapped, damaging statements had been placed before Hitler, and Niemöller had been sent to a concentration camp in 1937. Hitler's explanation to me was that Niemöller had injured the interests of the Lutheran Church, and that he himself had no further confidence in Niemöller's honesty.

Nevertheless, I did not abandon my efforts to obtain Niemöller's release. I obtained permission from Himmler and Heydrich, heads of the State Police, for Admiral von Lans, an old and trusted friend of mine, to visit Niemöller in the Oranienburg concentration camp. As one of the oldest living officers of the old Imperial Navy, Admiral von Lans enjoyed the personal esteem of everyone. It was my hope that Admiral von Lans would be able to persuade Niemöller to give a written promise that he would engage in no more political activity from the pulpit, which promise would almost certainly secure his release. However, Niemöller refused to commit himself to any such declaration, and despite my further efforts, Admiral von Lans was not even allowed to visit Niemöller again.

It became evident that the Nazi Party's attacks on the Navy's religious activities would only increase. These attacks extended to the most petty measures. The supply of hymn books, ordinarily issued free to every individual, became exhausted. Chief Naval Chaplain Ronneberger was assigned to prepare the new edition of the *Lutheran Naval Hymnal,* and Chief Chaplain Estevant to do the same for the *Catholic Naval Hymn and Prayer Book.* But when the Lutheran Hymnal was ready, Dr. Goebbels, the Minister of Propaganda, refused permission for its printing. We went ahead and produced it ourselves, doing the printing outside of the country in printing plants in The Hague, Reval, and Oslo, with the press officers of the Army at those places assisting us to get paper and printing services. Again, when war came, Nazi Party officials considered it their prerogative to inform the relatives of men who fell, and to take care of dependent survivors.

On the other hand we considered it the duty of our Naval Chaplain Corps to maintain contact with the widows and other dependents. Accordingly my wife and the Navy Wives Organization compiled and maintained a list of these dependents and their addresses, so that the Navy could keep up its relationship with its people. To each one of the bereaved we sent a copy of the *Consolation Book for All Who Mourn for the Fallen,* written by Chief Chaplain Ronneberger. And at Christmas and on special memorial days, other communication was made in what we considered as a self-evident obligation.

In 1942 other manifestations of the Nazi Party's persecution were evident. Chaplain Hölzer was accused of making derogatory remarks about leading political functionaries. His denouncer was another chaplain who had entered the Navy from the Bavarian Church, and the accusation led to court-martial proceedings. The Gestapo attempted to have the case transferred for trial before its own court, but I rejected this, since the chaplain was entitled to trial by naval court-martial. The accusing witness was found to be not only untruthful, but also a secret stool pigeon of the Gestapo. Upon the court-martial's acquittal, I not only approved the verdict but dismissed the accusing chaplain for his false witness.

During the war we held a number of chaplains' conferences in Dresden as well as elsewhere in Germany and France. Lutheran and Catholic conferences were addressed and counseled by eminent religious leaders. Although adhering to the special directives of their own faiths, the naval chaplains of both churches gave each other mutual support and made a united stand against outside interference. Admirals Schniewind and Warzecha, and, in fact, all the officers of the Navy, cooperated with the Supreme Naval Command, not only under me but under my successor as well. At my express order, directives from the Supreme Command of Armed Forces which sought to restrict the religious work of our service chaplains were completely disregarded. It was a great satisfaction to me, a Lutheran, to receive the support of His Excellency, Catholic Field Bishop Rarkowski, who informed me that in their religious freedom all the armed forces owed everything to this firmness of the Navy.

I believe that my success in holding the line in the Navy was in no small part due to the firm stand I had taken with Hitler from the very beginning. In 1942, Göring said of me, "Raeder's Navy is O.K.—*but he goes to Church!*" I took the occasion to reiterate to Hitler my dedicated belief in religion and the Church. Whether this attitude made Hitler cautious, or whether for other reasons he had decided against suppression of religious freedom in the armed forces, I do not know, but the fact remains that the Navy's church organization not only remained active but expanded as the Navy increased in size during the war. From the four Lutheran chaplains allowed by the Versailles Treaty, our chaplain strength increased to ten in 1939, and to seventy-four before the war was over. The same proportionate increase took place among our Catholic chaplains.

These chaplains served wherever the Navy operated—at home, in occupied territories, at the front, and on board ships everywhere. Out of their total number, five Lutheran and three Catholic naval chaplains gave their lives in battle.

The other question on which we battled the Party—the Jewish question—concerned not the Navy alone but the whole German people.

As far as Jews in the Navy were concerned, I took their part personally and was almost completely successful. Two Jewish officers in the Navy were forced out of the service on the basis of the Nürnberg Anti-Semitic Laws; we saw to it that they obtained good positions in civil life. When the war broke out, they were immediately recalled with their full naval rank, and justified our action by performing excellent and wholehearted service. In another case I managed to persuade Hitler and Hess to permit the excellent officer concerned to stay in the service.

It is an indication of the high state of unity and morale in the Navy that in every case where an officer's position was endangered because of his non-Aryan descent, his superiors took up the fight personally for him, seeing to it that he received the same treatment and promotion, even to top positions, as other officers. Few people knew in which cases the question of ancestry had ever come up. And without exception every naval officer of Jewish blood performed capable and devoted service during the war.

I was even able to intercede for Jews outside of the Navy,

though of course in such cases my actions were entirely personal, and not official. I realized only too well that no action or words of mine would have changed the laws or directives, and any such effort on my part would only have embroiled the Navy in political and civilian matters—something which I would never have permitted. By intervening personally with Hitler and other high Party functionaries, I was successful in securing freedom from molestation for a number of Jewish people known to me, and even of obtaining the release of some of them from the concentration camps.

On one occasion I even had the opportunity of advocating a change in one of the government's major policies. The occasion was the wrecking of Jewish business establishments and the burning of synagogues, which occurred in November of 1938. These excesses had created general indignation in the Navy, and a great number of officers intervened with me, among whom were the Chief of Personnel, Rear Admiral Patzig, and my own chief of staff, Junior Captain Schulte Mönting. Admiral Foerster, Commander in Chief of the Fleet, reported to me that Captain Lütjens and Captain Dönitz had also made the same protest to him. Other officers of my staff pointed out the damaging effect of these anti-Jewish outrages on public opinion abroad.

I personally and emphatically presented these facts to Hitler, pointing out not only the criminality of these outrages but also the resulting damage to German prestige.

Hitler assured me emphatically that his plans and policies as well as his personal beliefs had been violated by the lawless outbreaks, and that these represented only a popular retaliation for the death of a member of the German embassy in Paris, who had been murdered by a Jew. He also said that the party authorities had lost control of the situation, and that not only had he not authorized the mob actions, but had no knowledge of them until after the event. He concluded by saying that he realized the damage to Germany's good name, and would act accordingly. I was by no means satisfied with these explanations, but in light of Hitler's emphatic disclaimer, confirmed by Göring, there was no further action that I could take.

As to other brutalities and crimes such as went on in the concentration camps, I had not the slightest information. Hitler, at our first meeting, had promised that he would keep the armed services completely out of any internal affairs, and in this case he certainly succeeded. Had anyone in the Navy even suspected what was going on in the concentration camps, I would certainly have learned it, for to keep me informed on such matters was the specific duty of the Intelligence Division under Admiral Canaris. Not until the actual crimes were proved during the Nürnberg trials was I aware of those terrible outrages, and even then I could scarcely believe that Germans could have acted in such a bestial manner against a helpless minority. There was no justification whatsoever for these crimes, and I, like every decent German, was utterly ashamed of them.

XV

The Critical Years—1938-1939

From the time of its acceptance, the Anglo-German Naval Agreement of 1935 had formed the basis for all our strategic thinking. War with England was unthinkable; I had given strict orders that an assumed war with England should not even be made the basis for any war games or exercises.

It was Field Marshal von Blomberg's report to Hitler about the coronation ceremonies in England, and Hitler's reaction, that first caused me to have vague doubts. Marshal von Blomberg had been the official German representative at the coronation of King George VI, and in his opinion the British attitude toward Germany had been distinctly favorable. Queen Mary, the widow of King George V, had shaken hands cordially with him and had asked him to do all he could that a war situation like that of 1914 would never occur again between the two nations. I was present when von Blomberg made his report, and it seemed to me that Hitler's attitude was distinctly skeptical.

Of course certain circles in England were opposed to an understanding with Germany. It was therefore important that we establish contacts with those English who were favorable to us, make them familiar with our problems, and strengthen their hand in every way possible. Unfortunately we in the Navy all felt that Ribbentrop, our ambassador to England, was not the man to do this.

It is true that, as special plenipotentiary for the Reich, he had signed the Anglo-German Naval Agreement in 1935, but the negotiations had already been set up by the Navy and Foreign Office before he came into the picture. In fact I had made sure that Ribbentrop had received such clear directives that he would have no opportunity to disturb the agreement. Ribbentrop had been successful in London because the British themselves already wanted an understanding—though whether Hitler, on account of Ribbentrop's success in London, gave him credit for exceptional diplomatic acumen, I do not know.

My uneasiness was awakened again in 1937, when Hitler discussed the situation at a conference on 5 November. The only persons present were Field Marshal von Blomberg, General Baron von Fritsch, Foreign Minister von Neurath, Field Marshal Göring, Colonel Hossbach, and I. The Sudeten question as well as possible union with Austria were then problems of international interest. Hitler stated his firm intention to settle the question of Austria's Anschluss and the elimination of Czechoslovakia as a possible opponent between 1943 and 1945 at the latest. Although his speech was phrased in a somewhat pungent style, it left me with the impression that he had no intention of changing from his former policy of peaceful negotiations to one of warlike threat. Furthermore, he made no mention at all of increasing the Navy.

At the conclusion of the speech, both Marshal von Blomberg and General von Fritsch told Hitler that any conflict with England and France was out of question, since our armed forces would be utterly inadequate to wage such a war. However, General von Fritsch, who was about to go on leave, offered immediately to stay on duty to draw up any necessary advance military plans of a precautionary nature. Hitler replied that there was no need of such haste, and that von Fritsch could go on leave as planned. Hitler further added that he was sure that England would not inject herself into the situation, and that consequently France would not either.

Just before the conference Göring had told me that the real object of the speech Hitler was going to make was to spur the Army to greater speed in rearming, and after the speech I was convinced that this was so. And on the way out of the room von Blomberg assured me once more that the whole thing was not meant seriously. Anyway, I did not feel at all that our foreign policy was to be changed.

However, with the seriousness of the international situations that were coming up, preliminary plans had to be made. Regardless of how improbable a conflict with England or France might seem, it now lay within the bounds of possibility. In every country it is the responsibility of the armed forces to study and plan for any and every possible involvement in war, and to be as well prepared materially as possible, irrespective of probabilities.

Ribbentrop's replacement of Baron von Neurath as Foreign Minister on 4 February 1938 by Ribbentrop was a bit of a shock. Von Neurath had entered Hitler's Cabinet at the express wish of President von Hindenburg. He united experience and moral courage to a degree that fitted him admirably for diplomacy. I am convinced that had von Neurath remained in office he would have had a far different policy in relation to England than Ribbentrop exhibited, and would have found means to carry it out.

In May 1938 Hitler for the first time intimated in a discussion with me that in our military thinking we must begin to consider the possibility of England and France as opponents in case the situation deteriorated. He demanded that battleships "F" and "G" (later the *Bismarck* and *Tirpitz*) be rushed to completion in time for commissioning by the fall of 1940. In addition, six building ways for large ships must be made ready so that a later expansion of the fleet would not be held up for lack of construction ways. At the same time the shipyards should be organized so that, when the order was given, construction could be started to bring our submarine strength up to parity with England.

Parity with England in submarines had been provided for in the Anglo-German Naval Agreement of 1935. The speeding up of battleship construction and the expansion of shipyards were also compatible with the terms of the Agreement, so that, regardless of Hitler's sometimes fiery political speeches, I had no cause to believe that he had any intention of abandoning his prudent policy of good relations with England. The success of his conference with British Prime Minister Chamberlain at Munich in September 1938, ending in an Anglo-German nonaggression declaration, and a similar pact with France on 6 December, seemed to confirm my belief. And the successful solution of both the Sudeten and Austrian problems seemed further proof that Hitler had merely achieved another of his amazing political successes through diplomacy alone.

Despite my own personal feeling that the German moves in the Czechoslovakian dispute had damaged our relations with England, Hitler did not consider them materially hurt. Still, he felt that now was the time to exploit every possibility that the Naval Agreement gave us.

First step in this direction was a construction program for the U-boat force which would give us 129 submarines by the winter of 1943—the same parity with Britain which was permitted under the Agreement after friendly discussions with the British Government. Accordingly Admiral Andrew Cunningham and Captain Tom Phillips of the Royal Navy were invited to come to Berlin in December 1938 to discuss the new agreements with us. On our side the principal negotiator was Admiral Schniewind, Chief of the Naval Operations Department. Agreement was reached without difficulty, not only on submarine parity but also on the building of two additional heavy cruisers by Germany to match the Russian building program. At the end of the discussions, I invited Admiral Cunningham and his colleagues, and we found them most sociable and friendly.

But in addition to the buildup of the submarine force and the cruiser and battleship construction program, Hitler had privately impressed upon me one additional requirement—that, class for class, every one of our new ships must be a stronger fighting unit than her opposite number in the British Navy.

I took the opportunity to remind Hitler in all of these conversations, however, that our fleet was only in the initial stages of buildup, and that even by working our shipyards 'round the clock we could not think of contesting the British Navy before 1945 or even 1946.

In the studies we had begun making I had already set up a committee in September 1938 to prepare plans for expansion of the fleet to meet a possible threat from the British Navy. These plans, though, were based on the supposition that we would have long years of peace to put our program through. The idea that we could within a year or two create a German Navy that could contest the British Navy effectively was completely unrealistic. And Hitler himself had repeatedly reassured me that the fleet would not be needed before 1944 at the earliest, and that he counted on a peaceful atmosphere until then. Nevertheless I thought it my duty to survey any approach that might bring the fleet to a reasonably effective strength earlier.

That winter I reported to Hitler that there were two possible courses we could take. If we stuck to building nothing but submarines and medium battleships, we could within the shortest time create a fleet that would be a serious threat to England's oceanborne commerce, the very lifeblood of the island kingdom. Such a fleet would have restricted use, however, as it could not offer battle with the stronger British fighting forces. To build a Navy that could boldly contest the British Fleet at sea, however, would take a much longer time. Such a Navy would have to possess the most powerful types of ships so that it could not only war on British seaborne commerce but also meet major British naval forces with some prospect of success. A Navy like that would undoubtedly carry greater weight, both politically and militarily, but I emphasized to Hitler that during the time we were building such a powerful fleet, we would have only a weaker and unbalanced force to take the sea if war broke out in the next years.

Hitler again assured me emphatically that for his political purposes he would not need the fleet before 1946, and even said that political developments were in the making which would give us ample time for an unhurried, peaceful naval expansion. Therefore, he stated, he preferred the more powerful fleet even if it took longer to build, and gave me directions to plan on that basis.

Thus Hitler assumed the responsibility of making no political moves that would endanger the peace then existing. Although I had begun to realize that Hitler's assurances could be misleading and that he had a genius for keeping his real intentions hidden, I could not believe that he would have given me these assurances and directives if he had adopted a policy that might bring on war with England. If he had such a policy, then he should have vigorously demanded the construction of U-boat forces and other craft to make war on the enemy's oceanborne commerce. That he did not do this was for me an even greater guarantee than his words that he had not deviated from his policy of friendly agreements with England. I still remembered the enthusiasm with which he had told me in 1935, just after conclusion of the Anglo-German Naval

Agreement: "Today is the happiest day of my life. First, the doctor has just told me that my throat trouble is not of a malignant nature, and just now I have been informed of the completition of the Naval Agreement with England!"

Right up to the outbreak of the war, Hitler had repeatedly emphasized to me that the goal of his policy was an understanding with England. An Anglo-German alliance would mean a crowning success. Never did he so much as intimate otherwise. He did explain his desire for a strong German Navy by saying that it would influence England not to join the other side in case of any political difficulties arising between us and any other nation.

Building a fleet for political purposes demonstrated Hitler's naval thinking. He was concerned with warships—particularly battleships—purely as symbols of power, and he showed little interest in their deployment and use in actual operations. He had little understanding of the indirect potency of seapower and the continual pressure it can exert on the enemy from a favorable geographical position. As far back as the beginning of February 1937, I had endeavored to give him and von Neurath, von Blomberg, Hess, and other Nazi Party leaders a detailed explanation of the principles of naval warfare, and to point out the bitter lessons we had learned in the last war.

Unfortunately Hitler, with his pronounced predilection for the technical, insisted on comparing the speed, size, armor, and firepower of German warships with the corresponding characteristics in vessels of other nations, and drawing conclusions therefrom that were often purely theoretical. He never was really conscious of the fact that many other factors—like the possession and location of naval bases, the dependence on sea imports for the national economy, and the support of allies overseas—play a decisive role in the value of a fleet. Hitler never sufficiently appreciated England's full superiority over us as a seapower, by virtue not only of her naval strength but also of her superlative geographical location. I tried continually to warn him against any policy that could bring this superior power into the scale against us.

In the Nürnberg trials later, I was to be accused of preparing for aggressive war—an accusation which, I am sure, no one credits any more. All that I did was what any responsible officer is required to do. When the German Government, as represented by Hitler, considered that national policy required a fleet that no opponent could ignore, it was the task of the Navy to plan the type of fleet that would best implement that policy. Though such planning would have to take into consideration the possibility that the British Fleet might figure in the list of potential opponents, this did not imply that peaceful relations with Britain were in danger. All that the entry of the British Navy into the picture did was to broaden for us the field of study. Wars are not brought on by the studies and precautionary preparations of the military, but by the intentions, actions, omissions, and errors of politicians and statesmen.

The careful studies we made soon convinced us that in the event of war with England, major emphasis should be placed on operations against her commerce, using all the means at our disposal—submarines, surface ships, and naval aircraft. England's economy required an annual import of 50,000,000 tons of goods and materials, and she was absolutely dependent on getting these cargoes through. To operate against this lifeline of commerce, in case war came, should be the primary objective of the German Fleet. For such operations, a fleet needed not only have considerable fighting strength but also the ability to operate over the full expanse of the Atlantic. Because of Germany's lack of naval bases and her unfavorable position, hemmed in as she was by the barrier of the British Isles, these ships must have great cruising range, plus speed to prevent their being caught by stronger enemy forces.

The naval construction plan which we evolved, and to which we gave the name of "Z Plan," had as a nucleus six battleships of a type new in many respects. They were to be of about 50,000 tons displacement, propelled by diesel motors, and carry a main battery of 40-cm. guns. To raid the enemy's supply lines, there were to be three battle cruisers, also of a new type, displacing about 30,000 tons each, with a speed of 34 knots, and with turbine drive, using high-pressure, high-temperature steam, as well as diesel motors. With this 34-knot speed and with the proposed main batteries of 38-cm. guns, these battle cruisers should outclass the battle cruisers of any foreign navy. For operations in the Atlantic, light cruisers would be constructed with high-speed turbine drive and considerable cruising range. These were to be supplemented by additional new destroyers, torpedo boats, and other craft. And, lastly, the U-boat force was to be built up to a strength of 249 boats. Before embarking on this ambitious construction plan, immediate political negotiations with Great Britain would be required to modify the Anglo-German Naval Agreement of 1935.

The naval strategy behind the Z Plan was this:

Britain's overseas trade would be attacked by groups of battle and light cruisers as well as by U-boats and auxiliary raiders. To guard their convoys against the more powerful ships, the British Navy would have to send out units much stronger than the usual light naval forces which would have been sufficient protection against the U-boats and auxiliary cruisers. To get this heavy striking power, the British would have to split up their heavy naval forces and scatter some of these out over all the high seas, thus weakening and wearing down their main fleet. But these lumbering British battleships would not be able to catch the German battle cruisers and fast light cruisers, while the German battle cruisers would be able to fight off any lighter British forces that attacked. The powerful German super-battleships, however, with their speed and wide range of action, could support the pocket battleships and regular cruisers against attack even by enemy battleships, and could even overwhelm the enemy battleships that might be acting as guard for the enemy convoys. The heavy German units developed under this construction plan, therefore, would present the British with an entirely new strategical problem.

I presented this Z Plan to Hitler in the middle of January 1939, and told him the whole program could be completed by about 1948. He replied, however, that while he approved the plan, it had to be completed within six years, and that to achieve this, he would give the Navy's program priority over the programs of all the other services.

To make for orderly planning and development, I thereupon ordered that construction should begin first with the battleships and the submarines. The battleships, which were to form the nucleus of our fleet but which took longer to build, would thus have the advantage of an early start. And the speedup of submarine construction would provide us in the least possible time with the only force which we could use effectively at sea as long as we were weak. Under this speedup, the long-range U-boats and submarine minelayers were to be completed by 1943.

However, as it turned out, most of this extensive program was never carried out, and only a small part was actually begun and completed. For one thing, this heavy naval expansion required careful political preparations in advance, and for another thing it would tie up the nation's total shipbuilding industry and most of its armament plants for a long, long time. Worse still, a shift to a short-term naval construction program, was proved necessary with the earlier outbreak of war, was extremely difficult. And I had been careful to point out to Hitler that during the long construction period of the long-range plan, the only ships we could send to sea would form a very weak fighting force, and therefore no political demands, such as were constantly arising, should be permitted to provoke an armed conflict. Hitler could make fiery and threatening speeches, and could keep other nations guessing as to his real purposes, but the fact that for the next six to eight years a naval war against Britain was entirely out of the question and that Hitler knew it, carried much greater weight with me when judging Hitler's true intentions. This point I emphasized to Hitler time and again, and right up to the outbreak of war he always agreed with me on this. Not once in this time did he direct that we drop our long-range plan and take up the quicker short-term construction plan instead. I, and all the rest of the Navy, had to take it for granted, then, that Hitler's knowledge of our inferior naval position compared to England's for years to come, would induce him to talk very cautiously when dealing with that country.

Naturally if our new plan for naval expansion was to have any effect other than merely starting another general armament race, the ships had to be rushed to completion and their speed, armament, fire-power, and other characteristics kept a dead secret until the last possible moment. That was the way the British had tried to get the jump on the other navies of the world by their sudden unveiling of their new *Dreadnought* design back before World War I. Hitler agreed to this view, with the statement that presenting the British with an unexpected accomplished fact by the completion of the Z Plan would incline them to a favorable understanding, especially if we met them halfway in other fields of dispute in the meantime.

To avoid all delay and argument, it was necessary to give one individual the complete responsibility for putting the program through, and the necessary authority to go with it. I found such a person in the extremely capable Admiral Fuchs. In the same way, construction of the six battleships was put entirely into the hands of the Blohm and Voss Company. The first ship was laid down at their Hamburg yard on 15 July 1939; the second was laid down at the Deschimag in Bremen on 15 August. The third was to be built at the Deutsche Werke in Kiel, but before her keel was laid the war broke out. This put a stop to the work on the first two ships also, as the material had to be used for other more urgent purposes.

In the spring of 1939, though, with the Z Plan and its time schedule already decided upon, I tried to find out how Hitler regarded the situation brought about by the marching of our troops into Czechoslovakia, and the Anglo-French guarantee of the safety of Poland. Then at the ceremonies attending the launching of the *Tirpitz* at Wilhelmshaven on 1 April 1939 Hitler, in a speech at the public square, threatened to terminate the Anglo-German Naval Agreement. But when I asked him about precautionary measures for a possible war with England, he gave me explicit directions not to prepare for such a war. Consequently I was stunned when, without the slightest hint to me in advance, Hitler, speaking before the Reichstag on 28 April, announced his decision to abrogate the Naval Agreement.

In contradiction to this, however, on 23 May Hitler made remarkably inconsistent remarks on the Polish question to a small circle of intimate associates. He declared that the ship construction program was to continue just as scheduled, and that the other phases of rearmament for the three services were to be completed by 1943 or 1944. Nowhere did he refer to any change from his original concept of friendly relations with England, and the only clear thing I could get out of his remarks was that Hitler intended to set up a small special group outside the normal staff organization to study the Polish question.

Immediately thereafter I sought out Hitler alone and told him it seemed to me completely contradictory to believe war against

Poland possible on one hand and aiming at a peaceful settlement on the other. But he told me I could set my mind at rest: he had the political situation well in hand, and England would never go to war just because of the demands he was making for the return of the Polish Corridor.

So explicit was his reassurance that without misgivings I sent the new battleship *Gneisenau* on a several weeks' trial trip into the Atlantic in June. As one of the main purposes of the cruise was to hold target practice, she carried for the most part practice ammunition, and practically no battle ammunition.

In any but the most peaceful times, no warship ever leaves home waters without full war-readiness magazines, and had I had any apprehensions of war I would never have permitted her to sail unprepared. Neither the Commander of the Battleships Division nor the Commander in Chief of the Fleet expressed to me any concern over the matter.

In June, too, there was a big mine warfare exercise in the Bay of Helgoland and I told Captain Ruge, the Commander of the Minesweepers, he might go on leave—something he had been deprived of, the year before, by the Sudeten crisis. I told him that he could go on leave without any worries this time.

Then, in July, came the annual Kiel Naval Cup Regatta, and the representation from foreign navies was unusually large. Officers from the British, Italian, Swedish, Spanish, Dutch, Danish, Rumanian, and Estonian navies participated amid a general atmosphere of goodwill, with the President von Hindenburg Challenge Cup being won by the English crew. As was my regular custom, I attended the regatta and personally acted as host to the foreign naval officers.

While most of my advisers agreed with me that summer that no real war cloud was in sight, despite the previous year's crises and the Anglo-French guarantee of Poland, there were some who did not regard the political situation nearly so optimistically. Captain Dönitz, Commander of the Submarine Forces, for instance, had often expressed his fears of an approaching war, and he now told me that his officers generally shared his concern; and that, in case of an early war, his U-boat force, with its small number of submarines, would not be prepared. I reported this to Hitler at the very next opportunity, but he told me the submarine officers could rest easy, for there would be no war.

In the middle of June I inspected the Submarine Forces during war exercises, and found their level of training excellent and the tactics of attack developed by Captain Dönitz highly effective. In the following month I had an opportunity to congratulate Captain Dönitz and his officers and men for their splendid performance, and to tell them that I would increase the number of submarines in the Navy's next construction program. I also told the officers that their fears of an outbreak of war had been reported to me, and that I could assure them in Hitler's name that there would be no war with Britain—a war which could only mean the end of Germany. Immediately thereafter Captain Dönitz went to a vacation resort for the several weeks' vacation that he had planned.

On 22 August, however, Hitler called a conference, on the Obersalzberg, of almost all the very top military leaders. Later, at the Nürnberg trials, the prosecution presented two documents which were claimed to be a record of Hitler's speech at this meeting. However, neither document had either a signature or a date, and the prosecution was not able to establish any clear proof as to who was the source of the documents. As a matter of fact, they were both proved to be false by the notes made personally by Admiral Boehm, Commander in Chief of the Fleet, who had been present throughout the conference. There was no doubt in my mind that Admiral Boehm's notes, which he submitted to the court at Nürnberg, were an accurate record not only of the form and content of Hitler's speech, but also of the impression those present gained from it. To me it seemed that Hitler's desire was to defend before the nation's military leaders the correctness of his policy, now that there was a possibility of war. He emphasized that Poland's attitude was responsible for the crisis. He tried to convince us that England and France would not risk war over Poland, and hence that Poland would not carry things too far, but would be ready to settle by negotiation. In any case, Hitler asserted, the path for a negotiated settlement was not closed.

Hitler's speech impressed us all that we stood close to the brink of war, but we were promptly reassured when on that very same day Foreign Minister Ribbentrop left for Moscow to sign, as Hitler told us, the no aggression pact which had been successfully negotiated with the Soviets. We felt that once more one of Hitler's clever political chess moves was coming up, and that he would win peacefully again, just as he always had done before.

Nevertheless, I went up to Admiral Schniewind, Chief of Staff of the Naval War Staff, the moment Hitler had finished speaking, and found that he shared my doubts as to the correctness of Hitler's estimates of the British Government and its readiness to yield rather than to go to war over Poland. I then went to Hitler to warn him, but he assured me again that he had the situation well in hand and that it would be solved by negotiation and not by war.

The various moves of foreign policy which occurred in the next few days seemed to confirm this. Just as he had done during the crisis of 1938, Hitler conducted all the negotiations personally. With the expectation that any conflict that arose would be localized, we did not even mobilize the Navy completely when the other armed services were mobilized. Hitler's orders on 26 August holding up the advance of our troops (which had already begun) seemed another proof of the shrewdness of his estimates.

Consequently the third of September came like a bomb shell. When that day, in the Chancellery, Hitler told me that England and France, in accordance with their promise to Poland, had declared war on Germany, it manifestly was a most unpleasant task for him. He was embarrassed over his faulty judgment when he had to admit to me, "I have not been able to avoid war with England."

Naturally I have often asked myself since then how I could have failed to see things sooner. When Hitler's determination to extirpate the territorial relocations of the Versailles Treaty, the possibility of some armed conflict or other could not be ignored. Knowing intimately how impossible it would be for our small Navy to contest England on the seas, I had used every means to influence Hitler against allowing any such conflict ever to come. It had been my duty to determine the way in which the Navy should expand, bearing in mind the relative advantages and disadvantages of short-term programs as compared to long-term plans. The nation's military forces and their armaments must always be in accord with the nation's foreign policy. I had thought that through my influence on Hitler I had attained this necessary coordination of political policy and naval armament. In fact, I am convinced that Hitler personally never wanted war with England; nevertheless, in spite of his repeated assurance to me, the policy that he followed inevitably contributed to the outbreak of war.

This self-deception of Hitler, and his resulting policy, had tragic results for the Navy. His decision for a long-time building program did not correspond at all to the actual political situation. Whether a radical change in the Navy's expansion was feasible cannot be determined until all documentary evidence is in. As long as Hitler kept to the agreements of the treaties, we had some elbow room, because the framework of these agreements set the scope of our expansion. On Hitler's assurances, the Navy had developed a long-time construction program, and the whole capacity of our shipyards and armament industry had been set up for a balanced fleet of heavy and light surface ships and submarines.

If Hitler had ever conceived of an early war against England, the Z Plan should never have been adopted, and the entire program should have been given over to building the greatest possible number of submarines in the least possible time. This would have implied, politically, a provoking violation of the Anglo-German Naval Agreement. The course taken by Hitler's foreign policy, however, was completely contrary to all the assurances he had given me and in defiance of all the warnings I could give him. The consequences for the Navy and for all Germany were doomed to be fateful in the extreme.

Not until Hitler's conference of 22 August 1938 had the Navy ever had any real concern over having to meet England as a definite opponent. Even the studies which were made as a result of Hitler's directives then were centered around a war with Poland, and were given the code name "White Case." The inclusion of England in these studies, as well as the development of the Z Plan, had been purely a subsidiary issue evolving out of the Polish situation. And in these subsidiary studies, everyone—Admiral Boehm, Commander in Chief of the Fleet, and Commodore Dönitz, Commander of the Submarine Forces, as well as I—agreed that the German Navy could not expect much success in an open, ship-for-ship and fleet-for-fleet war with the mighty British Navy. All we could hope to do was to make war against the British supply lines. I told both my advisers that it had been my constant effort to remind Hitler that in any war with England, the German Navy could do little more than go down fighting.

On 1 September Commodore Dönitz had given me a memorandum confirming that the only effective means of damaging England was by carrying the war to her sea lanes in the Atlantic, and that since we did not have enough surface ships for the job, it would have to be done largely by the submarines. For that matter, even if we had had a sizable surface fleet, the most effective weapons against Britain's seaborne commerce would still be submarines. However, we did not have enough submarines available, either. For any worthwhile success at least 90 U-boats would have to be operating against the Atlantic lanes themselves, and that meant that we needed 300 submarines actually available for operations. Dönitz had arrived at this proportion as a result of war games in the winter of 1938-1939. For instance, of the 57 U-boats we actually had on hand on 1 September 1939 we could assign only 26 for actual operations against the Atlantic lanes, the rest either being unfit for such distant patrols or needed elsewhere for defense purposes in the Channel and North Sea. Of the 26 boats assigned to the Battle of the Atlantic, only eight or nine would actually be attacking the enemy shipping, since the remaining 17 or 18 would be on the long trip out or returning home or undergoing repairs and taking on stores. Dönitz therefore demanded realistically that every priority should be given to building more submarines, even at the cost of cutting down or stopping all other construction.

My own estimate of the situation was such that on 3 September, the day France and England entered the war, I recorded for the official files my own personal views on the possibilities for the German Navy in a war with England.

After calling attention to the fact that Hilter had assured us that there would be no war before 1944, and that he believed until the last moment that he could avoid war even if he had to postpone settlement of the Polish question, I stated that earliest date we could have expected to fight the British Navy on acceptable terms would have been at the completion of the Z Plan in 1945. In the meantime, we were in no way equal to a war with England. Granting that in the short period since 1935 we had built up a well organized and excellently trained submarine arm, it was still too weak to have any decisive effect. And our surface fleet was so inferior in strength and numbers to the British Fleet that it could do little more than show that it knew how to die valiantly.

This grim analysis did not by any means signify that the Navy was resigned to the inevitable, or unwilling to accept the challenge; that would have been contrary to its spirit. During the war years that followed, its courage and efficiency were to prove a real threat to the enemy despite continuing scarcity of materials and the overwhelming advantage of the enemy in numbers. After my 45 years in the Navy I had thought that I knew it thoroughly, yet in its devotion and accomplishments it exceeded anything I could have thought possible.

The situation confronting the German Navy at the beginning of hostilities can be clearly shown by contrasting the numerical strengths of the opposing surface navies. There were 22 British and French battleships against our 2 battleships and 3 pocket battleships. The enemy had over 7 aircraft carriers; we had not one, as the construction of our *Graf Zeppelin,* though nearing completion was stopped because the Air Force had not even developed suitable carrier planes. The allied enemy had 22 heavy cruisers to our 2, and 61 light cruisers to our 6. In destroyers and torpedo boats the British and French, combined, could throw 255 against our 34.

Nor were we in much better position geographically than in World War I. We could, it is true, use part of our forces for a short period against the enemy commerce lanes beyond the Channel and North Sea, especially if we could improve our organization of supply ships, oil tankers, and other auxiliaries to resupply our surface raiders and U-boats without their having to come all the way back home after each attack on the enemy. To offset this, however, the development of long-range aviation had given the enemy a far better weapon against our surface ships attempting to break out of the North Sea into the Atlantic.

With the ten-to-one numerical superiority of the enemy forces, augmented still more by his numerous, well-located bases, our only hope of hurting him was by concentrating all our efforts against his oversea supply lines. Seaborne imports were England's one vulnerable spot, and that was where we had to strike. Submarines, cruisers, pocket battleships, and battleships, as well as auxiliary cruisers, destroyers, and motor torpedo boats had to be employed in a well-planned, coordinated assault. And while direct successes against the enemy were, of course, our first goal, also to be considered were the indirect results against the enemy's war effort from our attacks on his commerce in the Atlantic and from raids by our individual surface raiders on enemy shipping everywhere on the globe. We had to seize the initiative, and, by rapid movement and unexpected strikes against the enemy in as many different places as possible, force him to break up his consolidated efforts against our submarines and pocket battleships.

Stout and intelligent cooperation by the Air Force would have been a great help to the Navy in this matter. The Supreme Command of Armed Forces, in planning the national war strategy had, on 31 August, issued their Directive No. 1 for the Conduct of the War. Under it the Navy was to "carry on war against enemy commerce, with priority given to British commerce." On the other hand, the Air Force was to have as its principal task the duty of "preventing operations of the enemy air forces against the Army and German territory." As additional missions it was to "destroy the English armament industry, British sea commerce, and troop transports operating to France, as well as attacking, when opportunity offered, massed English Fleet units, especially battleships and aircraft carriers."

According to this directive of the Supreme Command of Armed Forces attacks against English maritime supply lines were to be only a secondary goal for the Air Force, and, as it soon turned out, the Commander in Chief of the Air Force did not sufficiently appreciate the importance of such attacks. As a result the Navy, in attacking English seaborne commerce, got little support from a sister service which, differently from the Navy, could equal or even surpass the enemy in numerical and material strength. Consequently the Navy was limited almost completely to its own forces in the war at sea against England. In such combat the Naval War Staff[1] agreed

[1] The Naval War Staff was made up of a combination of the Planning and Operations Departments, including the Intelligence Division. The Head of the Operations Department, Admiral Schniewind, was in the same capacity Chief of Staff of the Naval War Staff.

unanimously that submarines must be the main weapon used, and all other naval forces must be used to augment the U-boat war.

With our naval forces so overmatched, it was inevitable that sooner or later they would either vanish through attrition or else would be out of action for long periods while undergoing repairs. Construction of new ships to replace lost or damaged ships was a matter of first importance. This meant a radical end to the Z Plan, with its long-term program, and the substitution of a program that would produce the most effective ships in the greatest numbers in the least time. Such ships were, essentially, submarines. Therefore all further work was immediately stopped on all large ships except the battleships *Bismarck* and *Tirpitz* and the cruiser *Prinz Eugen,* all of which were already well along toward completion. This freed the capacity of the nation's shipyards for the predominant construction of submarines.

This, however, was not enough; the scarcity of materials and skilled workers, and the heavy demands on industry by the Army and the Air Force, made it essential that the government itself back the Navy in giving priority to submarine construction, even at cost of slowing down the buildup of these other services.

This Hitler was not willing to do, and despite constant personal reports, recommendations, and other reminders of the first importance of U-boat construction, the Navy had to fight a continuous battle to obtain materials and workers and industrial plants to carry on its war construction program.

Hitler, it was true, had his own reason for his attitude, though it was a reason I did not consider valid; namely, his hope of yet avoiding an all-out war with the West. He was convinced that the quick successes he was sure he would obtain in land warfare would so strengthen his position that we would be able to negotiate anew a settlement with the Western Powers.

This view of Hitler's was a terrific handicap to the Navy in its initial operations. For instance, when the Polish Corridor question became hot in the latter part of August, I had, with Hitler's approval, sent the pocket battleships *Admiral Graf Spee* and *Deutschland* to sea along with a supply ship, on the 21st and 24th. Then if war actually did break out, they would already be in position for immediate operations against the enemy. This was merely a general precautionary measure, just as both England and France had mobilized naval forces during the tense Czechoslovakian crisis the previous fall, and it in no way altered my view that a war with England and France would be avoided if a sensible policy was adopted by our government, after the conclusion of the Russo-German nonaggression pact.

It was Hitler's opinion that inflicting naval losses on the enemy —losses that would hurt England's pride and prestige as a sea power—would spoil the chances for favorable negotiations with the West. Accordingly, by Hitler's specific instruction, the pocket battleships were directed at the outbreak of the war not to appear in their area of operations without special orders. The U-boats were likewise hedged with severe restrictions.

Undoubtedly this cautiousness on Hitler's part cost the Navy many opportunities for quick successes, as the enemy merchant shipping, scattered all over the world, was some time in changing to war conditions, such as wartime convoys and anti-submarine reconnaissance.

Even though I did not share Hitler's optimism as to agreements with the West, the Navy had to carry out the government's policy, and I therefore drew up the necessary implementing orders. For some time, I even allowed myself to believe that extra care not to strike seriously at French shipping and naval forces would pay worthwhile dividends in the end. But when all these hopes proved vain in short order, I did my utmost to persuade Hitler to lift the shackling restrictions, but he gave in only little by little. Meantime our naval commanders, particularly the U-boat captains, were faced with constantly shifting orders and, consequently, awkward situations.

The restricting of naval warfare in order to win a political battle was perhaps justified for a short period. But even so, we should have been preparing in every way for a long, hard struggle, which in all probability would come. And speeded-up U-boat construction was our best preparation. But Hitler could not see that, and it was to be a bitter lesson to him later.

It was a remarkable phenomenon that Hitler, imaginative as he was, never appreciated England's attitude toward us despite everything I told him. He witnessed a rapid and favorable development in the Polish campaign, yet at the same time knew that France could attack from the west while the war in Poland was going on in the east. Furthermore he must have thought about what he intended to do toward France after the Polish campaign was over. But he obviously had never given any thought to the force that England, as a sea power, could bring against us. He never took sufficiently into account the influence that the British Fleet, along with England's strategic position geographically, would exert in both the military and political field, and least of all reckoned on the support that England could count on, in one way or another, from the American president Roosevelt.

As long as the Polish campaign was going on and we had to face war on both the eastern and western fronts, it is understandable that fear of a French attack on Germany was Hitler's principal anxiety. But after the quick successes in Poland, which showed the superiority of our generals as well as the better training and equipment of our troops, the threat of an attack from England, which our Navy could poorly oppose, should have been clear. We should have been taking all possible measures to overcome some of the vast superiority of British seapower, but Hitler, although apparently agreeing with me in our many conversations, never would take the appropriate action. I can only conclude that his dangerous procrastination was the result of a warped, land-minded outlook shared by many of his advisers.

Whatever hopes he might have had of peaceful settlement with the Western Powers at the end of the Polish campaign, their prompt rejection of his peace offer then should have brought him back to the realities and the necessity of giving first consideration to combating British seapower. It was my constant and thankless task to warn him that now, and in the long run, England was our most dangerous adversary.

England's strength rested on two foundations. First, the British Isles lay squarely across the exit from the German ports and the North Sea into the open seas beyond, and the British Fleet, aided by the British Air Force, could seal off that exit most effectively, even if not 100 per cent hermetically. Secondly, that same British Fleet could operate everywhere at sea. Without even firing a single shot it had cut us off almost completely from all communications overseas.

In the minimum of time German seaborne trade was practically at a standstill. Even so, a great number of our merchant ships, caught at sea by the sudden outbreak of hostilities, managed to evade the British net by devious and difficult routes and eventually come slipping into German home ports. In this feat the skippers and crews of our merchant ships exhibited skill, ingenuity, and seamanship of the highest order. Back in port this same merchant marine combined with the German fishing fleets in giving sensational support to the Navy in its own operations. Spirited, tough, and dedicated, these merchant seamen worked with the Navy side by side, and took their sacrifices and losses in their stride.

With our own overseas trade wiped out almost automatically, we had to do our utmost to equalize things by hitting at British seaborne commerce. Outnumbered as we were, there was no question of trying to meet the great British Navy in open combat; it was our business to avoid such encounters, and, by scattering our forces all over the globe, try to strike at holes in the enemy's defenses at sea. There we might hope to hit damaging surprise blows before the enemy would bring up superior forces to meet us.

This type of warfare demands great resourcefulness both in the naval leadership ashore and in the forces at sea. Certain factors were evident in advance. The submarines, for instance, owing to their ability to dive, could operate successfully even in areas under surface control by the enemy. The pocket battleships with their economical diesel motors, had a wide cruising range and could operate far from home. The battleships *Scharnhorst* and *Gneisenau,* and the destroyers, all with high-temperature, high-pressure steam propulsion systems, had high emergency speed for battle as well as high speed for operations of considerable duration. Although all these forces were weak by comparison with the enemy, the support by well-camouflaged auxiliary cruisers, and an extensive organization for resupplying submarines and surface ships at sea, would give good prospects of successful warfare against the enemy's commerce at sea.

Just what the results would be, no one could predict. But the better the planning, and the more skillful the deployment, the greater would be the effect on the enemy. The fact that eventually the surface ships and submarines would be lost or used up should

IN A NORWEGIAN FJORD
German destroyer *Z-33* at anchor.

SCHARNHORST IN ARCTIC WATERS

CAMOUFLAGE

never be allowed to delay the undertaking. As the weaker side, we could not afford to wait and attack only at lucky and favorable times; this would let the initiative pass over to the enemy. From the very beginning it was my intention—and one approved by the entire Navy—to use all possible means to damage and disrupt the enemy to the maximum extent. And I was ready to risk much in order to do this.

By this decision the Naval War Staff placed great responsibility on the individual squadron and U-boat commanders. They were to obtain all possible successes, yet at the same time they were to keep their ships at sea and fighting fit as long as possible. Their operation orders were to avoid battle with superior enemy forces, and, as a rule, even with a weaker opponent. In addition, the ship commanders had to keep in mind their limited fuel and ammunition supplies, and to weigh the prospects of success against the risk involved in a fight. With his numerical superiority and his numerous bases, the enemy could take risks, knowing that his damaged ships could probably reach some port where they could be repaired. But with us, each damaged ship, even would probably mean a ship lost—and every lost ship would be practically irreplaceable.

Lastly, we had to consider the neutrals, both as to their shipping and their sympathies, and avoid any possible unfortunate incidents with them. All this mounted up to an almost razor-thin pathway which our commanders at sea had to negotiate through decisions made on the spot.

In naval warfare, success and failure are only a hairline apart. A wrong decision or one a minute late, the wrong interpretation of a message, a bad change in the weather, an unfortunate hit—any of these can change victory into defeat in a twinkling. In the same way an apparently hopeless battle may turn into a victory through errors of the enemy. With a landsman psychology, Hitler could never understand these factors in war at sea. On the one hand, he always worried whenever our capital ships were at sea; on the other, he believed that the main mission of warships was to fight enemy warships, not attack its shipping. Any unfavorable issue he analyzed as reluctance for real battle.

As I have mentioned, although our pocket battleships *Deutsch-*

land and *Admiral Graf Spee* had been sent into the Atlantic several days before the outbreak of war, Hitler's political policy prohibited their engaging in operations until the end of September. When they did, the effect on English shipping was immediate, calling for intense countermeasures.

The *Deutschland* put back into home port at the end of November, after a not too successful cruise in the North Atlantic. But the *Admiral Graf Spee,* under the command of the extremely able Captain Langsdorff, left a trail of sunken ships behind her from the South Atlantic to the Indian Ocean as she skillfully shifted her area of operations. Her captain planned to return home shortly after the end of the year for urgent repairs, but decided first to strike a blow at the dense enemy shipping lanes off the east coast of South America.

Unfortunately, on 13 December 1939, off the mouth of the Rio La Plata, he encountered a British search force consisting of the British heavy cruiser *Exeter* and the light cruisers *Ajax* and *Achilles,* under the comand of Commodore H. Harwood. The initial fire of the *Graf Spee* was so accurate that the *Exeter* was driven out of action, listing heavily and with only one turret left in fighting condition. The *Ajax* had both of her turrets put out of action and, in addition, lost her topmast. However, the *Graf Spee* had also been hit heavily, suffering much damage and many casualties, and when the enemy withdrew from action to the east, Captain Langsdorff, himself wounded, took his damaged ship into nearby Montevideo for repairs.

The repairs were necessary to make her seaworthy enough to withstand the winter storms of the North Atlantic on the way home. Captain Langsdorff had every hope of obtaining the needed repairs in the neutral port of Montevideo, and so radioed the Naval War Staff in Germany. However, the Uruguayan Government, under strong pressure from Britain, refused to allow a repair period longer than 72 hours, far too short for any effective repairs to be made.

This was a heavy blow to Captain Langsdorff after having driven the enemy force out of the battle area. The latter, however had turned to follow at a safe distance and had noted that the *Graf Spee* was heading for the mouth of the La Flata. The pocket battleship's captain reported in his message to the Naval War Staff that a strong enemy force was lying off the river mouth waiting for him to come out—misinformation cleverly leaked out by skillful British intelligence agents, whereas the supposed British carrier, battle cruiser, and other ships presumably waiting were actually a long way off.

Neither Captain Langsdorff nor the Naval War Staff knew this, however. By running into Montevideo, Captain Langsdorff had gotten the *Graf Spee* into a position where he could only escape by fighting his way through the supposed powerful cordon of enemy ships off the estuary.

When Captain Langsdorff had decided to enter Montevideo, the Naval War Staff had not interfered, feeling that neither the situation nor the condition of the ship could be as well known in Berlin as it would be to the captain right there on the spot. Now Captain Langsdorff reported his intention to try to fight his way out, but asked for a decision as to whether he should intern the ship or blow it up in shallow water in case he could not win clear. I took the matter up with Hitler personally.

Hitler agreed to my suggestion that Captain Langsdorff's decision to try to escape be approved, but he would not hear of the ship being interned. If the *Graf Spee* could not escape, she might at least be able to sink an enemy ship before going down herself.

In the last analysis, what the *Graf Spee's* captain should do had, of course, to be left to him alone to decide, since he alone knew all the factors in the case.

As it was, Captain Langsdorff decided that with his battle damage and his short supply of ammunition it would be hopeless to try to fight a way through the strong forces supposedly waiting outside. In the relatively shallow waters where the fight would occur, the whole crew might be sacrificed with the ship, or, worse still, the ship might be disabled and fall into the enemy's hands because she could not be sunk by her crew. Therefore the captain decided to sink the ship himself where he could be sure of utterly destroying her and also of saving the lives of every man of his crew.

This he did on 17 December, steaming out into the shallow estuary just beyond territorial waters, and blowing up the ship's magazines. Every man of the crew was taken back safely to Buenos

Aires on tugs and other craft especially chartered for the purpose. Then, having fulfilled his last bitter responsibility as a commander, Captain Langsdorff took his own life.

Though I had discussed the ship's situation and whole problem in detail with Hitler, he was dissatisfied and indignant at Captain Langsdorff's decision, and, especially at the Naval War Staff for the general operating orders it had given Langsdorff. He sharply disapproved the directives for ships to avoid battle in order to perform their more important task of destroying enemy commerce and cutting the enemy's supply lines. With no appreciation of indirect effects, he held that the warships—especially the large ships—should be used primarily in combat with the enemy's fleet. While he approved of using submarines, auxiliary cruisers, and other light forces in war on the supply lines, he considered employment of cruisers and pocket battleships for this purpose as barely justified, and of battleships not at all. Convinced that some few submarines could accomplish more at less expense, he little realized how the very threat of the large ships could tie up the enemy's forces, spread his defenses thin, disrupt his supply system by forcing him to do convoying, and in general keep him uncertain and worried. What Hitler wanted was victories the whole world could see.

Hitler further felt that once a captain joined battle with the enemy he should fight it out to the end, damaging the enemy as much as possible even at cost of losing his own ship. Such a view can be justified to a degree, but rarely are the circumstances that simple. With no repair bases anywhere on the wide seas, and with no help to call on in need, any of our ships that sustained even moderately severe damage in action was done for—and with her, any threat by her to the enemy's supply lines. Hence, at every contact with the enemy, the captain of one of our ships had a difficult decision to make.

My feeling was that in the case of the *Admiral Graf Spee,* the captain's real error lay in ever letting himself be enticed into battle with the enemy. By merely being at large in the oceans, our few surface raiders were keeping eight separate enemy search forces at seat to a total of 22 ships, ranging from cruisers to battle cruisers and aircraft carriers.

Unfortunately Captain Langsdorff, on sighting Commodore

Harwood's force, had mistaken them for two destroyers and a cruiser, and in the belief that they were the escorts for a convoy, had given battle immediately in hope of crushing them and then getting at the convoy. This decision was an excellent proof of Captain Langsdorff's fighting spirit, but it was directly contrary to the general directive the Naval War Staff had given him. Furthermore, as it turned out, as soon as the *Graf Spee* was done for, the numerous British ships searching for her—not less than five combat groups—were promptly assigned to other pressing duties.

Hitler, however, thought that in both the operational orders and in Captain Langsdorff's last actions, there was indication of a lack of fighting spirit. Furthermore, he held the unjust suspicion that the Navy's senior officers, differently from the daring young destroyer and submarine skippers, were moved too much by strategic considerations and paid too little attention to the immediate job of fighting. I believe that this difference between my concept of the basic principles of naval warfare and Hitler's idea of them was one of the causes of our quarrel later.

Apart from the war on enemy commerce, the Navy took a great many other measures at the beginning of the war. The first step was to safeguard our routes into and out of the Bay of Helgoland. On 3 September, the day war broke out, Admiral Saalwächter, Commander in Chief of Navy Group Command West, got orders to lay a series of defensive minefields immediately in the North Sea—the so-called "West Wall." This wall stretched in a wide arc from Terschelling, well to the south, off Holland, to Horn Reefs, far to the north, off Denmark. It was a marked difference from the short stretch of mines just off Helgoland in the First World War. The new minefields protected a great stretch of coast against invasion by enemy forces, and were particularly set to bar his minelayers. In addition to regular mines for surface ships, additional mines were laid well below the surface at strategic points to destroy enemy submarines running submerged. Swept exit channels through the West Wall were maintained both to the west and the north. At the same time a mine-free channel for neutral shipping was set up outside the minefields, and was marked at first by lightships, and public announcement was made of the location of the dangerous areas.

These defense minefields were laid during the first nights of the war through the terrific efforts of the cruisers, destroyers, and the fleet tender *Grille,* of Vice Admiral Densch, Commander of the Scouting Forces. To our surprise, the British offered no opposition, and the initial guarded area in the west was soon extended farther and farther north, providing splendid protection for our forces entering and leaving Helgoland Bay. Our swept channels remained secure from enemy interference throughout the war.

Once these defensive fields were laid, we began using destroyers and submarines to lay offensive mines off the English coast. Taking advantage of their high speed and the early fall and winter darkness, these destroyers made nightly trips to the English coast without loss from the enemy, but unfortunately one of our Luftwaffe planes, not being properly briefed, mistook two of our destroyers for enemy ships and sank them both. Here was bitter proof of the fallacy of having part of the striking forces in a naval operation under a command separate and distinct from the Navy.

Minelaying by the planes of the Luftwaffe off the English coast was also a definite part of the minelaying program, and this immediately led to a difference of opinion between Marshal Göring of the Air Force and me as to when the minelaying should begin. The Navy's mines were ready, and I considered it vitally important to begin laying them as soon as possible, while the nights were long enough to permit our minelaying destroyers to make the cross-North Sea trip and back in the dark, and before the British had a chance to lay their own defensive minefields to shut us out. But the Air Force wanted to wait until the mass production of airplane mines had risen. Finally it did begin to cooperate in the mining, but unfortunately one of the planes dropped one of our newest mines by error onto a sandbank instead of in the water, and the British immediately salvaged it and disassembled it for study. In short order they developed the necessary countermeasures, and our mine warfare lost a lot of its effectiveness as a result.

As I mentioned, Hitler laid heavy restrictions on our submarine warfare campaign in order to avoid incidents with neutrals. By his orders our U-boats had to operate strictly in accord with the Prize Regulations, which were based on the international rules and agreements concerning submarine warfare. Despite all our precautions, however, a very damaging incident occurred only a few hours after the declaration of hostilities. In violation of its orders, a German submarine sank the British passenger liner *Athenia* with the loss of many lives, including a number of Americans. The U-boat had come upon the liner outside the usual steamer lanes; furthermore the *Athenia* was zig-zagging and running without lights. The U-boat's captain assumed that he was dealing with a British auxiliary cruiser, and, to avoid being radio-located by British antisubmarine forces, maintained radio silence after the sinking. Consequently the only reports received by the Naval War Staff came from foreign sources, and, knowing the directives the U-boats had, the Navy believed that the sinking had not been the work of a German submarine, and accordingly issued a declaration to that effect. Not until the U-boat returned to a home port was the real story known. For political reasons, however, Hitler insisted that the real facts should not be made public, either for German or for foreign information. His reason was that he wanted to avoid complications with the United States of America over an incident that, no matter how regrettable, could not now be reversed. All that the Navy could do was to comply with his direction to keep the matter secret.

It was a complete surprise to me, then, when, only a short time later, Dr. Goebbels' Minstry of Propaganda spread the news that the *Athenia* had actually been sunk on orders from Churchill, the First Lord of the British Admiralty, in order to embroil Germany with the United States. This childish propaganda measure, taken without either the knowledge or the advice of the Navy, had exactly the opposite effect to what was hoped for.

The sinking of the *Athenia,* despite all our efforts to guard against it, was directly damaging to the Navy, and the awkward mishandling by the Ministry of Propaganda only made matters worse. All that we could do in the Navy was to tighten our existing directives still further, and we even issued orders that enemy passenger ships were not to be attacked, even when they were under convoy of enemy warships. We kept this directive in force until August of 1940, though there was no legal obligation under international law for such exceptional treatment.

Every U-boat that went to sea operated under naval orders based strictly on the London Submarine Protocol of 1930, to which we had subscribed in 1936. Under this agreement, submarines had to carry on the same stop-and-search procedure of merchant ships that surface warships had to observe. Sinking without previous search could be done only in the case of ships positively identified as enemy troop transports, or merchant ships under convoy of enemy warships or planes, or merchant ships which participated in hostile action or which were used to transmit information to the enemy. Thus only those merchant ships which took active part in hostile action by the enemy could be sunk by submarines without warning. Even armed enemy merchant ships were to be considered as peaceful merchantmen so long as they used their armaments for defense only, and not for attack. These conditions, along with other international agreements, were included in our official Prize Regulations, and had been carefully worked out by our Navy in cooperation with representatives of the Foreign Office, the Ministry of Justice, and the Institute of International and Foreign Public Law.

These were not the only restrictions imposed by us on our submarines, however. For political reasons, for instance, our U-boats were forbidden to attack any French ship. On the other hand, the British Admiralty issued directives which brought English merchant ships more and more into actual hostile operations, compelling us to take equivalent countermeasures. Almost at the beginning of hostilities, British merchant ships were ordered to report by radio any German submarine they sighted. As this action made them directly a part of the British intelligence service, we ourselves had to order our submarines to take hostile action against any enemy merchant ship that used its radio when stopped for search by a U-boat. When the British ordered their merchant ships to run without lights at night, we were compelled to order our submarines to attack any such darkened vessels, since at night it could not be distinguished from an enemy auxiliary cruiser. When, on 26 September 1939, the British Admiralty announced that it was arming its merchantmen, and when on 1 October it ordered its merchantmen to attack and ram any U-boat they encountered, we were compelled to allow our submarines, in self-defense, to attack any merchant ship that was seen to be armed; in fact, this order had to be extended to include *any* enemy merchant ship, since very often hidden guns were installed on such ships which could be deadly to any U-boat that surfaced on order to investigate it. However, even under these circumstances, enemy passenger ships were still sacred from our attacks, and in the case of ships which our U-boats sank, our men were to make every possible effort to rescue the enemy crews.

The necessity for our countermeasures was apparent almost from the start. Within the first three months of the war, guns and other weapons were placed on 1,000 British merchant ships, and a German submarine was shot at by a British steamer within a few days after the declaration of war. And in almost all cases, enemy ships reported by radio every submarine sighted, as well as its position, with the result that enemy antisubmarine forces rushed to the scene within the minimum of time. The fact that the action of our submarines against enemy shipping was absolutely correct and in accordance with international law was demonstrated when all attempts by the prosecution in the Nürnberg trials to prove the contrary failed. The International Military Tribunal there found both Admiral of the Fleet Dönitz and me innocent of any violation of the international rules of submarine warfare.

Despite the stiff restrictions placed upon them, however, our submarines obtained initial successes far beyond all expectations. In September 1939 they sank 40 ships for a total of 153,000 gross registered tons. In addition the enemy lost 9 more ships for a further 31,000 gross tons from mines laid by our submarines off English ports.

Right after the end of the Polish campaign, I induced Hitler to visit the submarine base at Wilhelmshaven. It was my intention to interest him, through conversations with the commander in chief and crews of the submarines, in more active support of the U-boat arm in its battle against the enemy's sea communications. Several U-boats had just returned from their first war cruises, and the crews lined up just as they were, unshaved and rugged looking. On 17 September, just a few days before, the U-29 had sunk the British aircraft carrier *Courageous* in the western approaches to the British Isles, and her commander, Lieutenant Commander Schuhart, was among those who personally described their cruises to Hitler.

Hitler was greatly impressed. The impression was deepened when Lieutenant Commander Gunther Prien, of the *U-47,* who, on 19 October, had sunk the British battleship *Royal Oak* right inside the British naval base of Scapa Flow itself, reported to Hitler in Berlin and with his crew received a public ovation from the citizens.

This amazing penetration into the very heart of strongly defended Scapa Flow had been planned personally by Rear Admiral Dönitz after he and his staff had discovered through painstaking study that it could be done. However, in the opening months of the war Dönitz's plan of "wolf pack" attacks could not be put into effect because we as yet had so few submarines that they had to be sent out individually. Right from the beginning it was evident that the skill, the aggressiveness, and the leadership of our U-boat commanders were things we could count on. Admiral Dönitz issued his general directional orders to the U-boats by radio, wherever they might be operating at sea.

We kept in ready communication with our surface ships in all seas by the same means. Thus the Naval War Staff could, if it desired, send a ship commander direct instructions for any combat, but it tried always to avoid any such interference with the freedom of decision of the commander at sea. Things look different on the open ocean from the way they do on the map at home, and the commander on the spot should always have a better insight into the correct tactics to use. These personal observations and analyses he cannot pass on to the Naval War Staff at home, however, because unless he is already in actual combat with the enemy he cannot send a radio message without betraying his own position. On the other hand he can make splendid use of information which the Naval War Staff can give him from its many sources.

Like all other senior officers, I believed in giving our commanders at sea the benefit of all possible information we could pass on to them, without ever making their decisions more difficult by issuing specific orders. Only in exceptionally urgent cases did I permit higher commands to interfere by giving specific directives, and in all such cases I required the one issuing such orders to take the full responsibility for the resulting operation.

In the German Navy's organizational set-up, the Naval War Staff exercised direct supervision only over the forces which were carrying on the war against the enemy's supply lines; this supervision extended also to the oil tankers and supply ships by which these commerce destroying forces were supplied. All submarines were under direct control of the Commander of the Submarine Forces—in accordance with the general directives of the Naval War Staff, of course. The surface ships and craft operating in the North Sea and the Baltic came under direct command of Naval Group Command West and Naval Group Command East, respectively.

A development out of the studies we had made in peacetime, these two Group Commands were charged with the preparation and employment of the forces assigned to them. When these forces were at sea, it was the responsibility of the Group Commands to keep them fully advised of all the information funneling into the Group Commands through air reconnaissance, intercepted enemy radio signals, and all other means. It was the Group Commands' responsibility also to safeguard the coastal waters and the passage of all convoys through proper employment of subchasers, minesweepers, patrol boats, and other security units—the Naval War Staff being thus relieved of these onerous details.

Putting control of the forces at sea under appropriate commands ashore provided for transmitting all possible information to the units at sea, as well as all directives and orders, without these units having to ask. These forces would have the confident feeling that they were getting their commands from an authority which, through continuous, close association, was thoroughly familiar with their problems—a confidence which was increased by the feeling that they were being left to make decisions from their own on-the-spot observations and at their own discretion.

Naval Group Command East had been set up in October 1938 under Admiral Albrecht, primarily with the Polish situation in mind, and had proved itself during the short naval campaign of the Polish War. Naval Group Command West, for the North Sea, had only been set up with the beginning of the war, and both the

Fleet Command and the Command of the North Sea District were operatively under it.

Up until now the Commander in Chief of the Fleet, with the Fleet Command, had traditionally been at the head of the naval forces, and, when the situation warranted it, the Commander in Chief of the Fleet had personally gone to sea with it. In any case the direction of operations had been entirely in his hands. Under the new set-up, though, with operational command now being transferred to the Group Commander, and with the Fleet Command now subordinate to the Group Command in the preparation and carrying out of orders, there were inevitably questions as to where the proper authority lay, and what were its limitations as to giving orders.

Only a fairly long trial could show what advantages could evolve from this separation of operative command, and from the insertion of the Group Command between the Naval War Staff and the Commander in Chief of the Fleet.

Looking back, it was unfortunate that this new organization was not introduced until the transition from peace to war conditions had actually begun. This period already had enough complications, what with new ships being commissioned, the development of patrol and security services, and breaking in the whole machinery of command. Serious breakdowns in the war effort were avoided by the wholehearted cooperation of all concerned, but still there were tensions, growing mostly out of the different viewpoints of the Fleet Command and the Group Command as to the use of destroyers to lay minefields off the English coast. The Group Command wanted to use the destroyers, during the dark fall and winter nights of 1939, without having them directly supported by major units of the fleet. On the other hand Admiral Boehm, Commander in Chief of the Fleet, held out for taking the heavy forces under his command out to meet the destroyers and give them protection on their trip home. He wanted to be on hand, with powerful support, in case a destroyer broke down and had to be shepherded in—and destroyer breakdowns were easily possible with the terrific strain put on their machinery by these high-speed operations.

The Naval War Staff agreed with the views of the Group rather than the Fleet Command on this point, as well as on the question of status and command methods, and this unfortunately led to a personal disagreement between Admiral Boehm and myself. When Admiral Boehm, as a result, asked to be relieved of his post, it presented me with a very difficult decision, because Admiral Boehm was one of the most experienced admirals in the Navy, with a splendid reputation as a seaman and a fighter which went all the way back to World War I. Though I saw no other answer to the problem than to grant Admiral Boehm's request, my personal confidence in him remained unchanged, and I earmarked him for future responsible positions in the Navy—which came up even sooner than I was expecting.

XVI

"Operation Weser"—The Norway Undertaking

THOUGH British seapower had completely destroyed our oversea trade, Germany was not completely blockaded. Two important trade routes still remained open: The trade route along the Norwegian coast up to Narvik, and the trade route through the Baltic to Sweden and other nations bordering that sea.

Through these channels we received vitally necessary materials, especially the ten million tons annually of Swedish ore for the steel that was the heart of our war economy and without which our armament industries would have died overnight. This ore came down from the mines of northern Sweden via the "Lapland railroad" to the Swedish port of Lulea on the Baltic and the Norwegian port of Narvik on the North Sea. There it was loaded aboard ships for Germany. The port of Narvik is ice free the whole year, but the port of Lulea at the extreme northern part of the Baltic is frozen up from December to May. Therefore, about one-third of the ore—from two to four million tons annually—was shipped via Narvik, where it was put aboard ore ships which ran down the Norwegian coast, inside Norwegian territorial waters. Within those waters they were protected from enemy attack so long as the Allies respected Norway's neutrality. At the foot of Norway the ore carriers entered waters controlled by Germany.

This trade was going so well that we took it for granted.

Never having studied seriously a war with England until that war practically broke out, we had not seriously questioned how far

Norway could guarantee her neutrality and the security of the Narvik route in case of war between England and Germany. Even the political leaders, including Hitler, had given little thought to this matter, as I soon found out. Right at the start of the war we had formally notified the Norwegian Government that Germany intended to respect Norway's neutrality fully. In the same note we had expressed our confidence that Norway, on its part, would maintain its neutrality and tolerate no infractions of it. This note was actually handed to the Norwegian Government on 2 September 1939, the day before England's declaration of war. The Naval War Staff had nothing to do with drawing up this note, and nobody in the Navy, and probably almost nobody else in Germany, gave the Norwegian problem a second thought during the first month of the war.

The impulse that caused reconsideration came from the outside, at the end of September, in a note to me from Admiral Canaris, Chief of Intelligence of the Defense Department. Admiral Canaris informed me that certain ominous signs pointed to Britain's intention to land forces in Norway. This report from our Intelligence Service carried greater weight with me because Admiral Canaris handed me the note in person, something he never did except in the most exceptional cases. Almost at the same time I received similar reports in a letter from Admiral Carls, Commander of Naval Group Command East. Carls expressed great anxiety about the consequences that could arise from an English move into Norway, and suggested that the Naval War Staff study whether the danger could be met by moving German bases of operation into the Norwegian area, circumstances permitting. I ordered that this question be looked into.

The resulting study soon brought in fundamentally unequivocal facts.

(1) The present situation was most favorable to us in every respect, for as long as Norway was neutral and her neutrality was not violated by the Allies, we would continue to have unrestricted access to Swedish ore. Our shipping could continue to move undisturbed through Norwegian territorial waters almost under the noses of the British Fleet. Furthermore, the Baltic was safe from enemy air attacks, since, except for the narrow Schleswig-Holstein

area, these enemy planes would have to approach over neutral territory. Thus the neutrality of the Scandinavian nations protected us in the north, and it was to our every interest to maintain that neutrality.

(2) The situation would be completely different, however, if the British disregarded Norwegian neutrality and set up naval and air bases in Norway. The northern part of the North Sea would then be flanked on both sides by the British Fleet and Air Force, which could definitely deny it to our use except for submarines. Our surface ships would no longer have any chance of reaching the Atlantic, and with enemy mine barriers set like those in World War I, the exit even for submarines would be extremely hazardous.

The effect on the ore situation could be even more critical. With the coastal route from Narvik blocked, Germany could import the absolutely essential Swedish ore only through the port of Lulea, and then only during the warmer six or seven months of the year.

Furthermore, any occupation of Norway by England would put tremendous pressure on Sweden—and Britain could be trusted to leave no stone unturned to stop the delivery of Swedish ore to Germany. Once British bases were established in Norway, the extension of them into Sweden would not be too distant a step. A new enemy front up there would not only bring the whole Baltic effectively under enemy control but would also bring enemy air bases into deadly proximity to our Baltic provinces. With all these added menaces in the north and northeast, we would have to weaken our war effort in the west to defend against them. Such a chain of events might well mean the loss of the war for us.

Every incoming bit of intelligence confirmed such British intentions. To defeat them there was but one way: to beat the British to the punch by setting up strategic bases ourselves in Norway before the enemy could get there.

How we were to get these bases was not immediately clear. By diplomatic negotiations the Russo-German nonaggression pact had given us the use of Murmansk Bay. But it was very dubious that diplomacy would work with Norway.

Regardless of how such bases were obtained, they would have to be protected by armed forces. Under constant assault by the English Fleet and Air Force, the bases alone could not insure us a safe sea route through Norwegian territorial waters. We would have to expend an inordinate part of our strength in just fighting off attacks, and while a scattering of bases would help us materially in our naval operations and still more in our aerial reconnaissance, the cost would far outweigh the gain. Therefore the acquisition of bases in Norway would never justify a military campaign. Our later occupation of Norway was in no way motivated by a desire to gain bases there.

In short, the present status was to the very best advantage of Germany. A sure and safe neutrality on Norway's part fulfilled our every requirement. So long as this neutrality was maintained, we wanted no change.

If this neutrality, however, could be disregarded at any time by the enemy, as suited his purposes, or if he established bases himself in Norway, then our whole northern front would be exposed to deadly peril. The crucial question was whether, and how far, the Allies would respect the neutrality of a small country whose own interests and, to a great extend, sympathies, were with the British.

Regardless of our analyses and conclusions, Hitler had to be kept informed of the problem so that he could make his own decision as to its solution. For it was immediately evident to us in the Naval War Staff that the Norwegian problem was essentially a political one and therefore was one for the civilian government to handle.

Accordingly I requested an audience with Hitler, and on 10 October 1939 I reported to him on the whole nexus of problems. I gave him the latest intelligence that had come in on British intentions, and pointed out that if England established bases in Norway, the consequences could be fatal to Germany's hope of winning the war. For even if we could get bases along the Norwegian coast, continuous naval conflict with Britain could be the certain result. In the long run we had not the fleet strength to wage such a war on acceptable terms. Thus the very best thing for us would be if Norway's neutrality could be absolutely assured.

I had not expected any decision at this meeting, and there was none. What I had wanted to do was to make Hitler aware of the danger and to point out to him that under certain circumstances we might have to act in self-defense. Believing the whole matter to be primarily one for political assessment, I made no suggestions nor advocated the establishment of German bases in Norway. In fact I emphasized then, and reiterated many times later, that we could lose our entire fleet in operations for the establishment of such bases, and that I would consider ourselves very lucky if we could hold the losses to as little as a third.

Hitler's comments in the 10 October conference revealed that he had given no thought to the Norwegian problem. It was out of his normal perspective, he said, since he was not very familiar with the conditions of naval warfare. He promised to give it thought, and told me to leave my notes with him so that he could study them further. Meantime I was to wait for further instructions.

Weeks passed without my hearing anything more from him.

Meantime, intelligence that many people in Norway were counting on English landings mounted. At first these landings were indicated as probably planned for southern and central Norway, but now Narvik was increasingly emphasized. Part of these intelligence reports came from Commander Schreiber, our naval attaché in Oslo, who had made friendly contacts with quite a few Norwegians and had become well acquainted with conditions in Norway. His reports, clear and concise, showed excellent powers of observation and judgment.

Then, on 30 November 1939, the Russians, then our allies, invaded Finland. Intelligence from numerous sources warned of Allied intent to intervene in aid of Finland by troops dispatched through Norway and Sweden. To us the conclusion was inescapable that the dispatch of troops through these two neutral countries would end in some of them being left there, and air bases being set up, and a whole new front built up there against Germany. By the beginning of January news of this imminent Allied aid for Finland was even being printed in foreign newspapers.

A new stage in the crisis had already been reached in early December upon the arrival in Berlin of Vidkun Quisling, former Norwegian Minister of Defense, who had now established his own political party. On 11 December the chief ideologist of the party, Alfred Rosenberg, asked me to see Quisling.

My only contact with Rosenberg had been an occasional glimpse of him, and I had never met Quisling. But almost simultaneously my Chief of Staff reported to me that a Mr. Hagelin had brought a request from Quisling that I give him an appointment, as he wished to discuss conditions in Norway with me.

Since such information might be valuable to us, I readily gave the appointment.

Quisling's visit was but a short one, concerned entirely with the situation in Norway. According to him, not only was the attitude of the Norwegian Government distinctly biased toward England, but the British had definite plans for a landing in Norway. He stated that his main motive for thus warning Germany was his fear of Bolshevism, with which he had become well acquainted in many years of residence in Russia. He believed that Germany was the only real bulwark against this menace from the East, and if an Allied occupation of Norway led to the crushing of Germany, it would be the beginning of the end for Western culture.

My answer to him was that this was a political matter which lay outside my province, but that I would relay his message to Hitler.

The following day, therefore, I reported the discussion in full to Hitler, and suggested that he receive Quisling personally so that he could form his own opinion of the Norwegian. I added casually that a politican like Quisling might have his own private axe to grind, and it might be well to be cautious. I repeated my warning that a German attempt to occupy Norway would carry great risk and might be very disadvantageous in the long run. Hitler had personal discussions with both Quisling and Hagelin on 16 and 18 December. I was not present on either occasion.

While the Operations Staff of the Armed Forces Supreme Command was engaged in "Study North" and in drawing up preliminary plans, we in the Naval War Staff were of varying opinions as to whether England would actually move to occupy Norway within the near future. Rear Admiral Fricke, the Chief of the Naval War Staff, and several of his staff felt that such a move by England would bring on a violent political protest by Russia as well as German countermoves in the Danish and Swedish spheres, and that the British move, to say the least, was questionable. I could not subscribe to this view. We were receiving too many reports which pointed to direct action by the Allies in the very near future. We had information that Allied general staff officers were appearing in Norway, where they were showing especial interest in harbor facilities, airfields, railroads, and highways. English naval officers at the various British consulates were also very active. At the same time the British press had begun a heavy propaganda campaign, as if laying the groundwork for something.

Then, on 20 January 1940, Winston Churchill, First Lord of the British Admiralty, invited the northern neutrals to join the Allies. All the northern neutrals rejected this request. Yet it was obvious that the basis on which "Study North" had been developed was no longer applicable to this new and threatening situation. Accordingly, on 27 January Hitler order a staff to be set up within the Supreme Command of Armed Forces especially to work out a plan of operations in case it became necessary to occupy Norway. This staff was to be made up of one very senior officer from each branch of the armed forces.

The violations of Norwegian neutrality by the British reached a climax on 16 February, when the British destroyer *Cossack* flagrantly attacked the German supply ship *Altmark* in Jössing Fjord. The *Altmark,* an unarmed cargo ship, had been provisioning and fueling the pocket battleship *Admiral Graf Spee* in the South Atlantic, and was now on her way home through Norwegian territorial waters with some 300 prisoners on board whom she had taken off the *Graf Spee.* Although the *Altmark* was even under escort of Norwegian torpedo boats, the British destroyer boarded her in the dark and forcibly removed the 300 prisoners. Seven German sailors were killed by British bullets during the boarding; none of the Norwegian torpedo boats interfered to defend Norwegian neutrality. A protest from the captain of the Norwegian torpedo boat *Kjell* was rejected by Captain Philip L. Vian of the *Cossack,* who stated that he had strict orders from the British Admiralty to take the prisoners out of the *Altmark* even against the opposition of the Norwegian Government.

This incident proved without a doubt that Norway was completely helpless to maintain its neutrality even if the Norwegian Government wished to do so, which obviously not all authorities did. It further showed that the British Government had no hesitancy in violating Norwegian neutrality when the liberation of prisoners was at stake. Now it seemed almost sure that the English would not hesitate to occupy bases ashore in Norway if they could do so without a fight, since such bases might give them the decisive advantage to win the war.

Now at last the necessity of moving into Norway to forestall the enemy had to be strongly considered. Accordingly, on 21 February, General of the Infantry Nikolaus von Falkenhorst was ordered to prepare an operation against Norway. This campaign was given the code name "Operation Weser."

On 23 February, only a week after the attack on the *Altmark;* I once more stated to Hitler my conviction that a neutral Norway would be the most advantageous solution for Germany, but that a Norway occupied by England would be intolerable for us. We would not be able to end it once it was in being, and its pressure on Sweden might not only cut off all imports of Swedish ore but might also extend the war to Sweden and our Baltic backdoor.

On 1 March, Hitler approved the basic plan for Operation Weser. Each branch of the armed services was to prepare for its own part in the undertaking. No definite order was given to implement the plans, nor was any time set for the operation to begin. These critical decisions depended upon the day-to-day situation in Scandinavia.

A sudden tremendous increase in British movements in Norwegian waters developed, and British radio messages which we deciphered revealed that an allied operation was actually underway—its objective apparently a landing in Norway.

Then on 12 March Finland suddenly made peace with Russia, ending the Russo-Finnish War, which had given the Allies an excuse for landing in Scandinavia on the pretext of aiding Finland in her defense against the Russian invaders. Both Norway and Sweden rejected the Allied demands for their troops to march through those countries to the relief of Finland. Yet intelligence from Norway made it obvious that England still had aggressive intentions toward Norway.

We Germans were still deeply desirous of a continuance of Norwegian neutrality and the *status quo.* However, we had no political, economic, or military means of influencing or compelling Norway's neutrality. We were dependent solely on the good will of the Norwegian Government for the maintenance of an unbiased neutrality. Unfortunately, in the *Altmark* case Norway had proved that she did not have the requisite firmness to resist British violations of her neutrality and did not intend to use her military forces to resist such encroachments. To trust that Norway could, or would, do anything more than make polite and ineffective protests against violations of her neutrality by the Allies would have been pure self-deception.

Undoubtedly it was both disturbing and infuriating to the British to see German ore ships from Narvik steaming unhindered through Norwegian waters. The British had not the slightest pretext under international law to stop the ships. Yet if they were to make their blockade effective, they would have to seal off this traffic, so essential to us. Hence a military occupation of Norway was more urgent for the British than for us. Granted that such an occupation would be made against the official wishes and protests of the Norwegian Government, still nothing more emphatic than protests could be expected. Norway would make no military resistance, and hence a move into Norway by England and her allies would entail no military risks worth mentioning. Once ashore there, they could hope to multiply their pressure on Germany from their new bases—something which was just beginning to seem especially urgent to the Allies, since they could almost certainly expect a big offensive by Germany in the west in the spring.

All this analysis boiled down to the simple fact that any defensive countermeasure we Germans might consider had to be put into effect in a hurry.

Naturally, as in any case involving preventive measures, the question had to be weighed as to whether any advantages gained might not be overbalanced by the disadvantages. Also discussed in the Naval War Staff was the proposal made by some that the English be allowed to make the initial landings, and then be thrown out by a vigorous counterattack. This was immediately ruled out as too hazardous: not only would this have established a new and unwelcome front in the north, but to drive up from southern Norway through the mountainous terrain against Allied troops already in position would have been an extremely difficult and tedious task. Furthermore, in any such operation, the Allies would find it much easier to keep their forces supplied and reinforced across the North

Sea, which they controlled, than we would in bringing up our supplies and troops from Germany.

As was later proved, the German occupation of Norway was accomplished only under extremely hard fighting, and probably could never have been accomplished if the German campaign in the west had not taxed the Allies to the utmost, preventing them from reinforcing their positions in northern Norway.

The one reasonable possibility was to forestall the British by moving into Norway first.

Any such operation, however, would compel the German Fleet to violate a fundamental rule of war by operating at a considerable distance from its home bases and across waters at that time more or less dominated by the enemy. That we would suffer heavy losses was inevitable. For the Naval War Staff, and for me personally, it was a bitter decision to have to make, but Germany had no other choice, and the only solution was to make the jump into Norway ahead of the enemy.

An occupation of Denmark had not even been considered by the Naval War Staff up until February 1940. Occupation of that country seemed neither necessary militarily nor useful politically, and in my most detailed reports to Hitler I did not even mention it, much less advocate it. Once we had occupied the strategic points on the Norwegian coast, I felt that we would automatically eliminate any English influence in Denmark. However, Marshal Göring's Air Force insisted that we have the use of the Danish airfields in Jutland because otherwise the flight from Germany to Norway would be long and unbroken. Therefore, Denmark was ultimately included in the occupation.

An important step in the planning was to select the most favorable time for the operation. Long, dark nights were essential for success, to avoid discovery of our transports and escorts on the long trip from Germany to Norway. This was particularly true in the case of the destroyers transporting General Dietl's mountain troops to their destination. I accordingly suggested to Hitler that the operation take place during the next period of the new moon, and recommended 7 April or thereabouts as the period which would best fill our requirements. On 2 April Hitler definitely ordered that Operation Weser be executed 9 April 1940.

The plans for the Norwegian landings brought about another disagreement with Hitler. He wanted the naval forces, after landing the troops, to remain in the Norwegian ports for some time to give continued support to the troops and to prevent the soldiers from feeling that they were being left isolated, cut off from the homeland. I had to insist on the contrary requirement—that all naval forces should retire toward home just as soon as they had refueled, so that they would not be lost in what would be a purely secondary task. I wanted the entire fleet kept ready to meet probable counteraction by the enemy as well as kept to maximum strength for future war at sea.

Hitler attached especial importance to the Navy's remaining to support the landings at Narvik and Drontheim, and I had great difficulty in persuading him differently as to Narvik. My warnings were fully borne out. The oil tanker which was to have refueled the destroyers at Narvik was sunk before these could get enough oil in their tanks for the return trip; they never got away as planned. Trapped by superior British forces in Narvik Fjord, they were all sent to the bottom, their incomparable leader, Commodore Bonte, dying with his ships. It was just what I had feared would happen if they were delayed in their departure. However, some 3,000 officers and men, the majority of the destroyers' crews, were rescued and joined General Dietl's troops ashore, where they formed an invaluable reinforcement. In the ensuing nip-and-tuck battle with Allied troops landed in that area, they contributed vitally to throwing back the enemy's attacks and putting an end to a most critical situation.

The German occupation of Norway was a highly successful operation. For the first time all three branches of the armed forces worked in close tactical cooperation, and the teamwork of officers and men was splendid. The Army and Air Force had originally been lukewarm toward the occupation of Norway, feeling that it might interfere with their great offensive in the west which they were planning, but finally the necessity for the Norwegian campaign was unanimously agreed to by all the officers of the three services who made up the special staff group to study the matter. The Navy representative on the staff, Captain Krancke, contributed especially to the joint agreement.

All three branches of the armed services were entitled to commendation for their distinctive parts in the successful operation.

In the opening phase—the swift transport and landing—the Navy had to bear the main burden of the battle. In view of the British domination of the North Sea, the Navy had to take extreme risks. The losses it suffered in doing its part weighed heavily upon it for the rest of the war. Still, the importance of the objective completely justified its use.

For its part, the Air Force largely wrecked British attempts to drive German forces out of Norway by a counteroffensive, and made it possible for our troops to hold out in a number of very critical situations. As to the Army, its troops far outclassed the enemy in the fighting in the extremely difficult northern terrain.

The occupation of Norway was of tremendous benefit to the German war effort. Shipment of Swedish ore from Narvik was assured, and remained practically uninterrupted for almost the entire war. England was all but completely cut off from access to northern ore and timber, the latter of which she particularly needed in her own mines. The German advance bases now established in Norway pushed German striking power much closer to Scotland and northern England. As a result the British, who had stretched a defense line across the exit from the North Sea between Norway and Scotland, were now pushed back to a line stretching from Scotland to Iceland—a 200-mile wide passage, much farther from British bases, and hence much harder to seal off. Any idea the British had of sealing off German's exit from the North Sea to the Atlantic by a continuous minefield now had to be dropped as the great depth of water off Iceland made such a minefield impracticable. To squeeze the Iceland exist passage for German ships as much as possible, the British forcibly occupied the Danish Faroe Islands and Iceland on 10 May 1940; but on the whole the German exit to the Atlantic was now infinitely easier than it had been before the occupation of Norway, as the British now had no chance of blocking off our submarines.

The German occupation of France took place shortly afterward. With it we acquired bases on the west coast of France. But the northern exit into the Atlantic from the North Sea still remained very important. Our ships and planes now operating out of the new northern bases could prevent Britain from concentrating enough forces to completely seal off the narrow Channel bottleneck at the Straits of Dover.

The supreme advantage accruing to Germany out of the occupation of Norway was that the British were prevented from gaining a foothold there. Thus the danger that the Allies might establish a third war front in the north was eliminated. The full value of the freedom of action thus won was not realized, however, until war between Germany and Russia broke out and the Allies started to ship great quantities of war supplies to their new ally through northern waters and the Russian port of Murmansk. From our new bases in Norway, our submarines, surface ships, and aircraft could make deadly attacks on the Allied convoys to Murmansk. This in turn tied up a large percentage of the British Fleet and enemy defensive forces generally, thus straining their war-making capabilities to a serious degree. These results had never entered into my calculations at the time of the occupation of Norway, as I had never anticipated a war with Russia.

Documents captured by our occupying troops from enemy personnel or seized elsewhere in Norway proved beyond the shadow of a doubt that not only had the British and French prepared to occupy Norway, but that the operation was already underway when we beat them to it. On the morning of 8 April 1940, even before our warships had entered Norwegian ports in order to land troops, Allied minecraft had laid mines in Norway's territorial waters. The Allied seizure of several bases on the Norwegian coast, which was to follow hard on the laying of the minefields, was abandoned only because our fleet was at sea ahead of the Allied naval forces of occupation, and was sighted and reported. The Allied ships that had the expedition's troops aboard returned to port and disembarked them for the time being.

The captured documents further showed that as far back as 5 February 1940 the Supreme Allied War Council, meeting in Paris, had decided to make ready an Anglo-French expeditionary force to land in Norway. On the very next day the British Foreign Minister had informed the Norwegian ambassador in London that England wanted to obtain certain bases along the Norwegian coast in order to stop the Germans from transporting ore from Narvik. On 28 March the Allied mining of Norwegian territorial waters had begun, and the actual landing of occupation troops in Norway was set for 5 April. Almost at the last minute, on 3 April, the date for the Allied operation had been postponed until 8 April. Only because of this incredibly lucky postponement of the Allied operation had we got a head start on the Allies by our own landing on 9 April.

At the trials of German leaders before the International Military Tribunal at Nürnberg at the end of the war, I was accused, among other things, of engaging in aggressive warfare because of my part in the German occupation of Norway. Evidence that the Allies not only had planned an identical operation in Norway, and had even set it in motion, was presented in my defense, based on the documents mentioned above; it was also shown that the Allied operation had been forestalled only because of the fortuitous last minute delay in the movement of the Allied forces. Nevertheless the International Military Tribunal held me guilty of conducting aggressive war against Norway, basing their judgment on "the basis of evidence at hand."

The judges who gave this verdict would have had no difficulty in establishing the actual facts in the case by simply questioning authoritative leaders on the Allied side. In his memoirs, published only a few years later, Winston Churchill, who, as First Lord of the British Admiralty and a member of the British Government at the time, was the leading force in the Allied move against Norway, admitted the Allied intentions fully and unblushingly. Official British histories and other documents fully confirm this, so that very soon the Nürnberg verdict had to be recognized as completely contradicted by the facts, though that did not have the slightest consequences as far as I personally was concerned.

After the unsuccessful attempt of the Allies to drive the German forces out of Norway had been abandoned, the Norwegian campaign ended with the surrender of the last Norwegian forces on 10 June 1940. The surrender terms were extremely liberal to the Norwegians, all war prisoners being freed and the Norwegian officers being allowed to retain their swords on condition of a declaration that they would take no further part in military or other hostile acts against Germany for the duration of the occupation of Norway.

Here was an excellent opporunity to make the occupation weigh as lightly as possible on the Norwegian people, and all orders issued by the armed forces to their personnel emphasized this requirement for correct behavior. As commander of the German naval forces in Norway, I had designated Admiral Boehm, whose firm yet understanding manner, I was sure, would insure a tactful and conciliatory policy toward the Norwegians—at least as far as the Navy was concerned.

Hitler had also declared his intention of following a conciliatory policy toward Norway—in fact, he had originally hoped to be able to negotiate the same peaceable arrangement with Norway that we achieved in the uncontested and limited occupation of Denmark. This hope, however, was frustrated by the flight to England of the Norwegian King and his Government, and their announced intention of continuing the war from British soil. Quisling then wanted to form a new Norwegian Government in order to restore law and order. Unfortunately this wish in turn was frustrated by the inapt conduct of one of Hitler's appointees, Under Secretary of State Habicht.

This individual had been sent to Norway both to report on the situation and to act as political adviser. But he misjudged the situation and the popular feeling completely, and, by unwarranted use of his authority, forced Quisling to resign. All this took place in the last three weeks of April. At the end of that month Hitler appointed Gauleiter Josef Terboven as German Commissioner in Norway.

Terboven himself told Admiral Boehm that Hitler, in giving him his parting instructions, had declared, "You can give me no greater pleasure than by winning the friendship of the Norwegian people!" What Terboven's manner and policy won from the Norwegian people was exactly the opposite.

Almost immediately the new Commissioner's actions brought on violent disagreements with Admiral Boehm. During the whole period of his duty in Norway Admiral Boehm carried out my instructions to present a warm and friendly attitude toward the Norwegians. But no sooner had the last Norwegian troops capitulated than Terboven informed General von Falkenhorst, General Stumpf, and Admiral Boehm, the commanders in chief of the three branches of the armed forces in Norway, that he intended a drastic change in policy. He intended, he said, to convene the Storting (the Norwegian Parliament) immediately and force it to depose not only the King and the whole Royal House, but the old government as well. He would make it clear to the political leaders and the president of the Storting, he added, that in case of their refusal, Norway would be deprived of all self-government and would be converted into a sort of German protectorate. Under this threat the Storting agreed to hold the necessary convention, but only after resisting to the extent of its ability.

Admiral Boehm immediately protested against this plan of the Commissioner, telling him that any such deposition would be ineffectual, as the whole people would realize that the Storting's action had been taken only under duress. He further informed Terboven that he felt it his duty to report the Commissioner's plan to the Commander in Chief of the Navy, as he knew I was very much interested.

I immediately laid Boehm's report before Hitler. After giving attention to all the various aspects, he gave his decision: There was to be no convening of the Storting, no such idiotic measure as deposing the King, but that all political parties except the National Samling should be dissolved, and that a state council should be made up of members of this party or else persons with no political affiliations whatsoever.

Hitler thus clearly disapproved of the policy of the German Commissioner in Norway; yet Terboven felt no obligation to resign his post nor did Hitler make any move to dismiss him. From that moment Terboven was in open conflict with me, and particularly with Boehm, whose dismissal by Hitler he sought by every possible means.

The ensuing developments in Norway were a sad blow to me. With information continuously supplied by Admiral Boehm I took every opportunity to persuade Hitler to remedy Terboven's mistakes. A people whose homeland is forcibly occupied will never forget it, but at least their resentment is lessened when they feel that restrictions on their freedom and independence are kept to the minimum of military requirements, that their honor is not attacked, and that their future as a nation is not threatened. Certainly we Germans, above every one else, should have had a sympathetic appreciation of the situation of the Norwegian people. We had suffered a forcible occupation of our Rhineland and had lived for many years under the harsh restrictions of the Versailles Treaty. It is still a mystery to me how a man like Terboven could not have learned anything from this, nor developed a humane outlook on the problems of the occupied land.

All these fatal errors of political policy, which Admiral Boehm had so ably described in his book, *Norway between England and Germany,* caused me constant anxiety. Many times, especially in 1942, I urged Hitler to conclude a definite treaty of peace with Norway. I proposed that as a preliminary assurance of a change in policy, he should replace German Commissioner Terboven with Admiral Boehm, who had expressed a willingness to take over the onerous office. But Hitler did not accept any of my suggestions. The impossibility to improve the relations between Germany and Norway was to be, eventually, one of my main reasons for resigning in 1943.

The Torpedo Crisis

Operation Weser had showed the Navy's efficiency in many ways: the initiative and fighting qualities of officers and men, the superb ability of independent units to adapt themselves to unexpected situations. This made the one real weakness—the numerous torpedo failures in the torpedoes fired by the submarines—all the more noticeable.

Some of our very best U-boat captains reported that they had repeatedly fired at enemy targets under most favorable conditions, and that what should have been certain hits had caused no damage. Thus they had missed many certain successes that could have had important effects on future naval operations. There could be no doubt that a considerable number of enemy ships, ranging from destroyers and transports to cruisers and battleships, would have been sunk if it had not been for the failure of our torpedoes.

This was a matter of most vital concern to the Navy, and immediate measures were taken to get at the bottom of the trouble.

Admiral Dönitz, Commander of the Submarine Forces, rightfully demanded a reliable torpedo if his units were to perform the tasks entrusted to them, and requested a speedy inquiry into the matter. Accordingly, on 20 April 1940, I appointed a special Torpedo Board of Inquiry, composed of leading men in both science and industry. These gentlemen, with their co-workers, gave us superb help in locating the causes of the failure, many of them dating far back.

For many years the Navy had conducted, at the torpedo testing station at Eckernförde, a torpedo design and development establishment to which many of its most experienced technicians and officers were assigned. Despite the scarcity of personnel and material in the postwar period, a number of advanced mechanisms had been developed here in the long years of peace. Most important of these, from the standpoint of the submarines, was the electric-propelled torpedo which left no giveaway wake on the surface in its passage, and likewise a method of expelling the torpedo from the underwater tubes that sent no revealing burst of gas or air bubbles to the surface upon discharge. Likewise there had been developed a magnetic type of "pistol" or firing mechanism which exploded the torpedo by the magnetic field of the enemy ship's hull when it passed underneath it. Compared to the ordinary impact type of exploder, which had to strike the target in order to set off the warhead, the torpedo equipped with the magnetic pistol could pass several feet underneath an enemy vessel and still destroy it by underwater explosion.

In the early days of the war, reports from ship commanders had cast doubts on the dependability of the magnetic pistol, as a result of which it had been temporarily displaced by the less effective impact pistol until the cause of failure could be found and remedied. Unfortunately, in the Norwegian campaign, even the torpedoes fitted with the impact exploder had registered a disturbing number of failures, from which it was evident that the depth regulator on the torpedo had not performed properly, allowing the torpedo to run at too great depth to damage the enemy.

The seriousness of the matter demanded immediate action, and all offices concerned with the design, development, construction, and testing of the torpedoes, whether within or without the Navy, were turned to on the problem. The study went on night and day—

a study in which the energetic Commander of the Submarine Forces aided invaluably. The result of the investigation established only too clearly that the German Navy's torpedo did not meet requirements either in its depth regulation mechanism or in its firing pistol.

The problem resolved itself into three parts: eliminating the causes of the failures, making continuous improvements based on the experiences of the war, and stepping up the mass production of torpedoes.

The first and most important step was finding and eliminating the causes of the failures. With understanding everywhere of the critical situation, both personnel and material facilities in the Navy's Torpedo Section were greatly expanded. University technical facilities, the laboratories of industry, and the Navy's own research organizations were put to work to their fullest capacity, utilizing even technicians brought back from the front for the emergency. Keen competition brought quick results, and before the end of the year the answers were found. Through the efficient leadership and administration of Vice Admiral Kummetz, the Chief of the Torpedo Section, dependable torpedoes were produced in sufficient quantities. New improvements in the torpedoes were of vast importance in the battle against the enemy's convoys. Most significant were the course-reversing torpedo, which steered itself repeatedly through a convoy until it found a target, and a target-homing torpedo which was steered toward its target by the noise of the enemy ship's own propellers.

The initial failure of the U-boat's best weapon was a damaging blow to our war effort in a material sense and also damaging in its psychological effect on the submarine crews. However, all hands—Ordnance Bureau, Torpedo Section, industry and science—recognized the urgency of the problem and worked wholeheartedly until it was solved. While recognizing that part of the cause for the failure could be laid to the shortage of men and money resulting from the restrictions of the Versailles Treaty, nevertheless there had been time to overcome this, and we could not avoid seeing that lack of initiative and faulty performance on the part of some individuals had to share the blame. To my regret, court-martial discipline had to be exercised in some cases, but the percentage was extremely small.

XVII

"Operation Sea Lion"—The Planned Invasion of England

THE SUCCESSFUL summer campaign in 1940 and the surrender of France had given us invaluable seaports on the Channel and, in western France, on the Atlantic itself. With this direct access to the open sea, where the war against the enemy's seaborne trade was being fought, our naval situation had improved tremendously.

No one had counted on such decisive results on the western front. The intelligence the Navy had received from the Army General of Armed Forces in the fall of 1939 had foretold the imminence of bloody battles, but it had indicated the offensive as requiring a long time. The first assumption was that we could reach the same advanced line that we had reached in the First World War and might even gain possession of ports on the French side of the Channel.

Regardless of this, the Naval War Staff had already been concentrating on how the war with England could be pressed after the end of the offensive in the west. Since in our prewar plans and preparations an armed conflict with Britain had not been considered, it was clear to us that studies should be made in case the developments of the war suddenly presented us with a new twist to the English problem.

Accordingly, in November 1939, I had set up a small special staff for this preliminary work. It was to study the possibilities of an invasion of England from the specific technical problem of transport, in addition to the over-all naval and military problems. Extreme care was taken to keep even the knowledge of such a study from any but a very few people.

I had good reason for this. Although the British people had been haunted from the first by the specter of invasion, there had not been the slightest thought of this on the German side. It was only natural, however, that this problem would one day be given attention by the armed forces command, and I wanted to have some soundly reasoned particulars on hand when that time came, so that the thinking could at least begin on a firm basis.

The Navy would be the first of the armed forces to be concerned with an invasion, since it would be a question of oversea transport on a colossal scale. We would be the ones who first had to determine whether, and under what conditions, it could be carried out. Since it would tax the Navy's resources to the utmost, our main task—the war on England's seaborne commerce—might have to suffer.

Up until now my main endeavor had been to convince Hitler and the armed forces command that this war on commerce should be carried on to the maximum extent of Germany's warpower and armament. Hence, any diversion of our already inadequate naval forces for some other objective would materially impair our naval campaign against the British enemy. Only if such a landing in England could be achieved without too much risk or too much difficulty—and that was highly improbable—should we deviate from our original plan.

All these aspects and fundamental hypotheses were laid down in the original study plan, with the studies themselves being made the responsibility of Vice Admiral Schniewind, Chief of Staff of the Naval War Staff, and Rear Admiral Fricke, Chief of the Operations Department, both of whom were among my most competent advisers.

From the winter of 1939 the western offensive had been repeatedly postponed right up until 10 May 1940. But when it did begin, the campaign in France developed so rapidly that within ten days it had reached the English Channel near Abbeville, and had driven a huge wedge between the British Army and the greater part of the French Army.

Now I was forced to bring our invasion study to Hitler's attention—for one reason, to forestall the invasion's being suggested first by some irresponsible person. In the latter case Hitler might jump at the idea, with the result that the Navy would be faced with impossible tasks. All my experience with Hitler had convinced me of the importance of giving him our own opinions of a situation before less qualified people could gain his ear.

Furthermore, we had just completed a most successful amphibious operation, over wide waters, against Norway, and many people might get the idea that a similar move could be equally successful against England.

At first glance, the jump across the Channel, whose opposite shore could be easily seen from France in good weather, would seem far less dangerous than the Norwegian landings. But any experienced naval leader would know that just the opposite was true. A long and careful preparation was absolutely necessary.

Such a landing would be extremely difficult and attended with the gravest risks. However, the development of the airplane for both combat and transport purposes had brought a new element not present in previous wars, and hence the possibilities of a successful invasion were not so infinitesimal as formerly. A powerful and effective Air Force *might* create conditions favorable for an invasion, whether it could was not in the Navy War Staff's province.

In my reports to Hitler on 21 May and 20 June 1940 I named absolute mastery over the Channel by our air forces as the first condition of any landing attempt. Furthermore, this German air superiority had not only to achieve mastery of the air, but also would have to damage the British Fleet tremendously even if it could not completely prevent its appearance on the scene. Anything less than this would make the risk too great and the invasion unjustified. The diversion of a huge percentage of Germany's ocean, coastal, and river shipping for transport of the invasion troops, I pointed out, would greatly impair Germany's domestic economy.

Hitler listened to all that I said, but expressed no views of his own at the time except to order that for the time being no preparations for a landing be made. But in any case Hitler had now been warned that any landing in England would have to be carefully studied first, and then just as carefully planned.

Heretofore, apparently, no one outside the Navy had given the matter any thought. But shortly after my second report of 20 June the Supreme Command of Armed Forces suddenly began to show an unexpected interest. After the fall of France it was obvious that it would be a pertinent question as to what *direction* the war should take now. The last Norwegian defenders capitulated on 10 June. Norway was now in our hands. On the same day Italy entered the war on our side, and with the signing of the armistice with France on 21 June the only opponent left was England.

Despite the change in the strategical situation, I was more than ever convinced that our surest and most effective weapon against England was our war on her commerce. Again I pleaded with Hitler for a priority for submarine construction over all other war measures. From the newly won bases on the Atlantic in France our submarines could act with increased effectiveness. If, from new airfields in northern France, we intensified air strikes against British shipping both at sea and in English harbors, and in addition strengthened our submarine arm by a speeded-up construction program, our resulting stepped-up war on England's commerce might have effects on England even to the point of decision. Any diversion from this might prove fatal.

I had presented the Navy's analysis and point of view to Hitler before the dazzling success in France led to any illustrations about any easy invasion and victory in England. That presentation had had some effect. The 2 July directive of the Supreme Command of Armed Forces, the first to mention a possible invasion of England, stated that "a landing in England can be considered only under definite conditions, the most important of which is the achievement of air superiority," and that the whole matter was still "only a plan on which no decision has been made." Hitler had as yet made no decision.

A few days later, on 11 July, I reiterated to Hitler my viewpoint that an invasion of England could be considered only as a last resort, in order to bring England to negotiate for peace. To achieve this last result I told him that in my opinion the most effective weapon was a stepped-up, effective U-boat campaign, and the next most effective means would be air attacks on convoys and other important targets, such as the port of Liverpool. In contrast to the Norwegian campaign, I could not recommend a landing in England. Aside from absolute mastery in the air, one further requisite was a dependable, absolutely mine-free zone for the troop transports. It was impossible to say how long the creation of such a mine-free channel would take, even if it could be done, or how it could then be kept free from the menace of fresh mines dropped by enemy planes. Furthermore, the flanks of the whole transport area would have to be protected by strong and effective minefields laid by ourselves.

Lastly, I called attention to the fact that the job of converting and readying ordinary shipping for troop transports and supply ships would be a long and tedious job, and would cause a serious stoppage in the ordinary waterborne traffic of Germany on which both our armament program and domestic economy depended. To go ahead with any real preparations before a definite decision had been made for the landing would be completely wrong. Hitler agreed. He stated that not only was mastery of the air an absolute prerequisite, but that a build-up of the submarine arm was also essential.

To my surprise on 15 July, the Naval War Staff was informed verbally that preparations for the operation were to be so expedited that it could be put in motion any day from 15 August on. On the very next day all three branches of the armed forces received a directive signed by Hitler, which ordered all-out preparations for an invasion of England. The directive indicated that the operation was to take the form of a surprise amphibious landing on a broad front, and the unexpectedly early date had obviously been selected because the Army General Staff knew that suitable weather could not be expected after the beginning of October.

A conference with Field Marshal von Brauchitsch two days later was very enlightening. I learned that the initial strong misgivings of the General Staff had been discarded, and that now the difficulties were considered relatively slight, or, at any rate, far from insurmountable.

I informed the Commander in Chief of the Army that, to the contrary, the operation entailed the greatest dangers. I pointed out that in the Norwegian landings the fate of the whole German Navy had been at stake, in this case there was a serious possibility that all the troops employed in the operation might be lost. And after two more days, on 19 July, the Naval War Staff delivered a detailed memorandum to the Supreme Command of Armed Forces in which it was stated that the task that would fall to the Navy was completely disproportionate to the Navy's actual strength—something which was not true of the tasks of the Army and Air Force.

The memorandum then explained in detail the difficulties involved in the operations: (1) The French ports from which the operation was to be mounted had been badly damaged by the recent fighting or were in other ways unsuitable; (2) The part of the Channel selected for the actual crossing presented great problems because of weather conditions, tides, and rough water; (3) The first wave of the invasion would have to be landed on the open English coast, and there were no suitable landing craft for such a landing; (4) The waters for the crossing could not be made or kept absolutely free of enemy mines; and (5) The vessels on which the troops and their supplies were to be embarked could not even be assembled in the embarkation ports until absolute mastery of the air had been achieved.

But the most important part of the memorandum was the emphatic reminder that up until now the British had never thrown the full power of their fleet into combat. However, a German invasion of England would be a matter of life and death for the British, and they would unhesitatingly commit their naval forces, to the last ship and the last man, into an all-out fight for survival. Our Air Force alone could not be counted on to guard our transports from the British Fleet, because their operations would be dependent upon the weather, if for no other reason. The Navy could support the movement by protecting the convoys to the maximum of its ability, and could, in addition, lay protective minefields and make diversionary attacks against the enemy. Any such minefields, however, would not offer absolute protection against such a desperate opponent; and even if the first landing wave got across and ashore successfully, the enemy would still be in position to drive into the amphibious area and cut off the advance wave from reinforcements.

We in the Navy doubted that we could establish conditions that would guarantee even reasonably safe protection for a crossing of the Channel by the invasion forces. Circumstances were entirely different from those in the Norway campaign. There, surprise had been a most important factor in the operation, and even though complete surprise had not been attained, the magnitude of the operation and the wide spread of the movement among so many ports, all occupied simultaneously, had been beyond the power of the enemy to anticipate.

But in the case of England, no such surprise was possible. The major part of the transport vessels we possessed were craft designed for our inland waterways and were not equal even to limited voyages in the open sea. Many, in fact, did not even have their own means of propulsion and had to be towed. To be ready in time, they would have to be assembled in the embarkation ports at the same time that the invasion troops were being assembled in the same localities. Such extensive movements could not be kept hidden from the enemy's air reconnaissance, not to speak of the very active intelligence agents he had throughout the whole occupied territory. Hence this powerful and desperate opponent, lying just across the Channel and knowing that his very existence was at stake, would not only have advance notice of the invasion, but would be able with great accuracy to figure out just where such a landing had to take place, and consequently to meet it with his entire defensive force.

It could not be expected that even for a brief period our Air Force could make up for our lack of naval supremacy. Yet if this most important requisite could not be fulfilled nor all of the others, then the Navy faced an impossible task.

Hitler was obviously impressed by the detailed arguments of the Naval War Staff. In his statements at a conference with the Commanders in Chief of the three branches of the armed forces on 21 July 1940 he admitted that the invasion of England would be an extremely daring enterprise. He agreed that we could not expect to effect a surprise landing, and that we would be facing a most resolute opponent who controlled the water area we had to cross. Also he conceded that to keep the invasion force of approximately 40 divisions supplied after they had landed would present the utmost difficulty. An absolute prerequisite for the whole operation would be complete supremacy in the air and an effective minefield protection along both flanks of the crossing channel, plus the added protection of a barrage from heavy guns installed on the French side of the Straits of Dover. He concluded by saying that owing to the lateness of the season, the main operation would have to be successfully completed by 16 September, and therefore if all preparations had not been completed in time for the landing to begin by the first of September, then other plans would have to be considered.

These admissions showed that Hitler had abated considerably from his original viewpoint. He had finally realized that the preparations would take far longer than had originally been expected and that surprise was out of the question. He was still firm in his view, however, that the study should be definitely continued and a conclusion reached as to whether a direct invasion could bring England to her knees.

Despite my views that a successful invasion of England was dependent on conditions which could scarcely be fulfilled, it is needless to say that the Navy did everything possible to accomplish the tasks assigned to it in the plans for "Operation Sea Lion," the code name assigned to the invasion of England. To obtain the necessary shipping space, we had to take over all the steamers, barges, lighters, tugs, and even motorboats and fishing craft operating on Germany's inland waters as well as out of the seaports themselves. After these vessels were converted for their intended task as transports they had to be brought to the embarkation ports along the Belgian and French Channel coasts. Some came through the canals, some by sea. In the assigned ports from Antwerp to Le Havre the Navy finally assembled 155 larger craft totalling 700,000 tons, plus 1,200 barges and lighters, almost 500 tugs, and over 1,100 motorboats. In addition, the Navy had ready approximately 30,000 mines, depth charges, and other material for sealing off the amphibious area from enemy assault. Lastly, the Navy, which was responsible for the country's coast defense works, mounted several heavy coastal batteries at Cape Gris-Nez and other points on the French coast opposite Dover.

It was manifestly going to be impossible to complete all these measures before the assigned date of 15 August, so on 30 July the Naval War Staff reported to the Supreme Command of Armed Forces that its preparations could not be finished before 15 September. That we could succeed in completing this multitude of jobs by that date was an accomplishment rendered possible only by the intensive work and loyal cooperation of the shipyards, the administrative offices, and the numerous naval commands.

Even before this, on 25 July, I had pointed out to Hitler that mid-September would be the earliest date the Navy could be ready, and in so doing called his attention also to the heavy burden the operation would place on Germany's ordinary water transportation, and also the tremendous load that would fall on the shipyards. Up till now, I insisted, there existed no German air supremacy. Furthermore, I emphasized the great difference of opinion between the Supreme Commanders of the Army and Navy concerning the strength of the invasion army and the extent of the landing area. The Army was demanding the transport of 13 landing divisions totalling some 260,000 men, and while this was considerably less than the originally planned 25 to 40 divisions, the Army was insisting that these be landed over a very broad stretch of coast. The Navy's strength was nowhere near great enough to guard this broad landing area demanded by the Army, and if this requirement was maintained, the transports on the east and west flanks would have to go without any effective protection. The Naval War Staff therefore had to make a counterdemand that the landing be spread over as narrow a coastal front as possible. Our choice was a limited area of coast on both sides of Dover.

In addition to these two opposite views as to size of forces and width of landing area, there were further differences of opinion as to the best time of day to make the actual landing.

From its viewpoint the Army was well justified in the demands it made. But the Navy could easily prove that not enough shipping could be assembled to make a crossing on such a broad scale. The Channel widened in the western half of the Army's proposed landing area so that the resulting distances that had to be covered were far too great for the Navy to protect the transports and supply ships here, or to insure the necessary flow of reinforcements and additional supplies.

On 31 July I again made a personal report to Hitler reiterating the Navy's position. In the presence of the Commander in Chief of the Army and the Chief of the General Staff I explained the difficulties, and called extra attention to the fact that the weather in the Channel got notoriously worse in the fall.

The British Fleet, I emphasized, undoubtedly would make its appearance. The safe transport of the troops was the most vital consideration. The Air Force could not effectively protect three beachheads stretching over some 100 kilometers of coastline. Therefore, I said, the landings should be restricted to the single area at Dover, and all the efforts of the Army and Air Force should be concentrated on this single narrow space. I concluded that the wisest thing would be to postpone the invasion until May 1941.

Hitler, however, decided that the attempt should be made, and set 15 September as the date for the landing. But the actual signal for the operation to commence was not to be given until after the Air Force had made concentrated attacks on the English southern coast for a whole week. If these showed powerful effects, the landing was to be carried out; otherwise, it was to be postponed until May 1941. In any case, however, despite the Navy's warnings, the preparations were to continue on the Army's plan for a broad invasion front.

This last point brought about violent quarrels again between the Army and the Navy. On 13 August I took the matter directly to Hitler, and requested his personal decision as to whether the invasion was to take place on the broad front envisioned by the Army or on the narrow front advocated by the Navy. I pointed out again my opinion that Operation Sea Lion should be regarded only as a last resort in case England could not be forced to negotiate for peace by any other means.

Hitler agreed, but wanted to speak again with the Commander in Chief of the Army, as the breadth of the invasion front might be a decisive factor in the whole ensuing land campaign. At this time the strength of the military forces in England was estimated to be in excess of a million and a half men. Of these, 300,000 were seasoned English, French, and Canadian troops rescued from Dunkirk and some 150,000 retrieved from other continental Channel ports. They had been rearmed. They would defend the island.

The opposing views of the Army and Navy as to the breadth of the landing front were reconciled temporarily by a compromise proposal of the Supreme Command of Armed Forces. Then Hitler made the final decision that the Army had to arrange its operations in accordance with what the Navy believed its own forces could achieve.

It was still an open question as to whether the Air Force would actually succeed in attaining complete mastery of the air. At the end of August, according to the reports of the Air Force, the prospects seemed very good. In reality, however, the German Air Force had attained no significant superiority over the Royal Air Force, and although some weakening of the enemy's defenses was apparent, the British fighters, bombers, and, most important, mine-laying planes, were still everywhere in the sky. Our own antiaircraft defense was not good enough to prevent continuous enemy air activity over the Channel ports, with the result that our congregating shipping and our embarkation areas were under steady observation and attack. On 13 September alone we lost 80 transport barges to enemy air attacks.

The Air Force had not achieved the air supremacy over the invasion area that the Navy considered a prerequisite for invasion. Instead of continuing to center his attention on preparation for the Channel crossing and landings, Göring was diverting his air forces more and more to an attack on London.

By the middle of September—the date presumably set for the invasion—the Naval War Staff recognized that the Air Force was making practically no effort against the units of the British Fleet that were operating in the Channel area, but was carrying on its own concept of total war quite apart from the plans for Sea Lion. Furthermore, Göring not only had failed in his task of making the Channel safe for the landing operation, but, with the heavy losses he was taking in the Battle of London, would not have the strength thereafter to do any better. Unquestionably, in the Navy's view, any possibility of successfully crossing the Channel had vanished.

Hitler himself had approved the change in the Air Force's role. Like Göring, he had cherished the hope that by all-out air blitzing of London he could succeed in bringing England to terms without having to accept the risks of an invasion.

To wean him from this view seemed hopeless to me. I would have had to argue for Sea Lion; and I had doubted the success of the planned invasion from the first.

On 17 September even Hitler admitted that the invasion could not be made at this time, and therefore would have to be postponed. However, because of the psychological effect on the English public, the decision for the postponement was not to be made public, and the threat of a landing, plus the air attacks on London, was to be kept up for its over-all effect.

I had to agree with the reasons Hitler gave, but the most satisfactory thing to me was that, with the landings postponed, the probability was that they would never be carried out. So outwardly all preparations were continued until 12 October, when Hitler privately informed us that the preparations were to be continued throughout the winter, but only in order to keep military and political pressure on England. If the movement was to be revived the following year, he said, he would give the necessary orders. To my mind this definitely buried any project for the invasion of England. From the first the Naval War Staff had never budged from its standpoint that an invasion across the Channel was so risky that it should be considered only as the ultimate operation in case all other measures against England failed.

Throughout all my disagreements with Hitler over Operation Sea Lion I never ceased emphasizing my contention that our war on Britain's seaborne commerce should be our first consideration, and for that reason a step-up in submarine construction was of utmost urgency. Diverting part of our industrial capacity to preparations for a landing in England could only rob us of part of our ability to carry on our U-boat warfare. Immediately after the victory in the west, I had argued, top priority should be given to the construction of more U-boats.

The Naval War Staff had conscientiously sought for every means that could make possible the English landings, but no matter how we looked at it, the risk was too overwhelming as long as the British Fleet remained in a position to intervene decisively. At no time since the beginning of the war had we felt so keenly as now the need for a German Fleet that could command the enemy's respect. The German Air Force could not possibly make up for the complete British superiority on the sea. I considered it extremely fortunate that the invasion project was not carried out, as the resulting setback would have been disastrous. That an overseas invasion on such a colossal scale cannot be improvised in weeks or even months was to be proved beyond a doubt by the difficulties met by the Allies in their Normandy landings in 1944. They had had two years for preparation. The operation was supported by the whole industrial capacity of the United States and had the advantage of amphibious techniques well tested in the Pacific. Yet the Normandy landings reached a critical state more than once—and that despite the undisputed supremacy the Allies then had at sea and in the air.

Hitler was never wholeheartedly in favor of Operation Sea Lion. By contrast with the driving force he put behind other operations, he was very sluggish in regard to the planning of the English invasion. It may be that he regarded the preparation as principally the means for bringing heavy moral and psychological pressure on the enemy. This, combined with the air blitzkrieg on the British capital, he counted on to bring England to negotiate for peace.

Be that as it may, the planning and preparations for the landing tied up important military and economic sinews urgently needed elsewhere. Wasted—and to no effect.

XVIII

"Operation Barbarossa"—The Campaign Against Russia

THE Navy had been vitally concerned in both the Norwegian campaign and the proposed invasion of England, because in each case the objective could be reached only by sea. Problems dealing with an essentially all-land campaign had no such close naval connotations.

The new bases we had secured on the Atlantic coast of France gave us extraordinary new advantages. Despite our lack of a striking fleet strong enough to contest the sea with Britain, we now had far better prospects of winning our war against British sea trade. Our battleships could make more effective sorties into the Atlantic. Our submarines would have less distance to cover going to and returning from their operating areas on the enemy's shipping routes; hence more of them could be in actual operation there, and they could stay on the attack longer. Thus, with the victory in France I hoped that Hitler would now carry out his oft-expressed intention of giving the priority to building up the Air Force and the Navy—the latter's submarine arm, especially.

In fact, when, at the beginning of June 1940, I complained to Hitler about the insufficient support for the submarine program, he assured me that once France was put out of the war, he was going to cut down the size of the Army, discharging all the older men and the technical specialists; then he would give precedence in materials and manpower to the Navy and the Air Force.

At that time, the question of an invasion of England was still open, it is true, and troops and transport shipping ostensibly assembled for the crossing. With the new bases we now had in France and Norway, the prospects for the Navy in its war on Britain's lifelines seemed brighter than ever.

It was therefore with deep surprise that, about August, I heard of a movement of large Army and Air Force units to our eastern border. When I asked Hitler what was the purpose of the movements, he said that they were just feints to camouflage the landing we planned in England. I could not think of any reason to doubt this, since the security of the German borders in the east was to me indispensable for our whole war effort. Hitler himself had often emphasized that our present favorable strategic situation was unique in our history in that we did not have to fight a war on two fronts.

To me it seemed vital that we should be free from any threatening enemy in our rear, to the east, regardless of what sacrifices we had to make to maintain it, for much of the reason for our defeat in World War I could be laid to this second front and second enemy in the east.

Moreover, even with France out of the war, the western front had not disappeared. England still faced us there, supported with all the resources of its world empire. To permit the rise of a second front now in the east was to me sheer madness.

Furthermore, the German Navy was enjoying particular benefits from the Russo-German Treaty, which had been signed just before the outbreak of the war in 1939. We were freed of any worry over the Baltic and our back door there, especially with the Polish naval forces eliminated, as they speedily had been. Our Baltic coast was free from threat. Our ore ships were safe in their passage from Sweden without our having to divert naval forces from the North Sea for their protection.

In addition, the Russians had granted us the use of their ice-free port of Polyarny on the Murmansk coast as a base for German naval forces, plus the right of transit through the Polar Sea passage to the Pacific Ocean. Being able to run into Polyarny had been a tremendous advantage to some of our merchant ships trying to return home from overseas during the first weeks and months of the war. In order to evade the British net, most of these had

had to take the far northern route along the edge of the ice pack, with a consequent battering from the northern storms; but at Polyarny they could make repairs and take on supplies for the rest of the run home through Norwegian waters. The fast liner *Bremen* had been one of the ships to make this trip, laying over in Polyarny for needed rest, repairs, and supplies, on its daring breakthrough. The German auxiliary cruiser, *Schiff 45,* had also taken off from this port in its passage to the Pacific in August 1940. Further, it was from Polyarny that had come the only tanker that had arrived at Narvik in time to be of help during our occupation of Norway.

Now, with our occupation of Norway, we did not need Polyarny any more. Nevertheless I had telegraphed my thanks to the Commander in Chief of the Russian Navy for the help given us.

It is true that our relations with the Russian Navy had not always gone off absolutely smoothly. The advance of the Russians in the Baltic, through occupying bases in the contiguous Baltic states, had strained relations somewhat, but our political leaders had done everything possible to avoid any actions to increase the strain. We had managed, without too great difficulty, to deliver the materials to the Russian Navy that we had promised in the Treaty. As for the two Navies themselves, they had sedulously carried out their agreements, and there had arisen no matters of major friction.

The first time that Hitler mentioned Russia to me in an unfriendly way had been on 9 March 1940, when I was discussing with him the advisability of occupying the Norwegian port of Tromsö, hoping that the Soviets would think we were refraining purely out of consideration for their interests. I even stated that it would be better to have Tromsö in Russian hands than to let the British establish a base there. Oddly enough, Admiral Darlan, the Commander in Chief of the French Navy, later told me that in December 1939 the Allies had actually discussed the occupation of Tromsö as well as Narvik in their plans to get control of the whole coast.

Hitler, however, demanded that our forces occupy Tromsö along with the other ports designated in our Norwegian occupation, and gave as his reason that he did "not intend to have the Russians so near."

At the time I did not attribute any real significance to Hitler's answer, as just then I was interested only in preventing the British from occupying Tromsö first. But in the light of later events, I am not sure that Hitler was not already thinking in terms of the later rupture with Russia.

Just when he began seriously to harbor the idea of a campaign against the Soviet Union, I cannot say, for, knowing how opposed I was to anything that would open up a front in the east, he carefully abstained from discussing anything like that with me. It is true that in a conference with the Commanders in Chief of the three armed services on 21 July 1940 he mentioned that England might be pinning her hopes on either a change in the policy of the United States or the entry of Russia into the war, but he mentioned the latter possibility as highly improbable and not in our interest, even if she entered the war on our side.

A few weeks later, on 6 September, when reviewing the war situation in a report to Hitler, I tried to get him to turn his thoughts to the Mediterranean as a promising theater of war. I pointed out to him the vital importance of Gibraltar and the Suez Canal in the British war strategy, and also the corresponding benefits that the port of Dakar, in French West Africa. would have for us if we could secure it.

Hitler made not the slightest reference to Russia in this conversation, either. But in the middle of September he admitted to me that he had certain intentions against Russia.

I immediately seized the opportunity to get in my own views on any such plans before they had been firmed up, and I repeated my statements in a similar report I made in a long private conference with him on 26 September. It had been a habit with me to request these private personal discussions with him when I had an especially important viewpoint that I wanted to urge upon him. On such occasions he was more easily approachable and would listen to arguments and objections more carefully than when other people were present.

I had brought a special memorandum prepared by the Naval

War Staff, and I used its details to support my own personal observations, as follows:

(1) The British still considered the Mediterranean as the strategic pivot of their world position, and were assembling strong naval forces there, as well as numerous troops from all their Empire.

(2) As a result of this impressive British buildup, Italy might soon find herself outclassed and in serious difficulties in the Mediterranean.

(3) To counterbalance this, we should bring our utmost strength to bear against England, before the United States entered the war actively on her side. Gibraltar, Suez, the Near East, the Canary Islands—all these were vital to the control of the Mediterranean, and any weakening of England's positon in these spots might be decisive.

I then went on to reiterate my constant theme: that we should concentrate all our efforts on beating England, the soul of the resistance. We could do this best by waging all-out naval war from our Atlantic bases, but at the same time we should extend our bases to the west coast of Africa if we could gain the acquiescence of France. If we could obtain the active cooperation of France, this, with the help of Italy, would enable us to dominate the Mediterranean as well as the African coastal area right up to the Suez Canal. England would be cut off from the Mediterranean route to India. At the same time we would incorporate North Africa into the European economic system, which vitally needed African supplies for the sustenance of Europe.

This advance in the Mediterranean, I pointed out, would also exert pressure on Russia to make her wary of doing anything hostile toward us, and thus eliminate any need for operations in the north against the Soviets.

I expressed myself as incredulous of any intent on his part to unleash a two-front war after his own constant denunciation of the stupidity of the Imperial Government in doing this identical thing in 1914. The Russo-German Treaty should not be violated and under no circumstances, since the treaty itself guarded us against a war on two fronts.

Finally, I pointed out that although a war with Russia would be primarily an Army and Air Force affair, the Navy would unavoidably be affected by it. Extension of the war to the Baltic would call for numbers of our lighter units—minesweepers, minelayers, motor torpedo boats, motor minesweepers, patrol craft, etc.—to be sent to that theater to protect our ports and our transports and escorts against Russian attacks. And we were already short of these craft, so badly needed to protect our new Atlantic bases which were essential to our decisive war on Britain's commerce. Any diversion of such craft to the Baltic would gravely weaken our own major efforts in the Atlantic. Under no circumstances should we go to war with Russia.

Apparently impressed at my detailed analysis, Hitler told his staff that from my unvarnished facts he could figure whether or not he was on the right course. It seemed that I had talked him out of the dangerous Russian gamble, for I heard nothing more about it for some time. And, despite some real conflicts of interest such as in the Baltic and Balkan areas, our relations with Soviet Russia seemed fairly smooth. That November, Molotov, the Soviet Foreign Minister, came to Berlin for several days of discussions. The day that he left, I was in Hitler's office on regular business. I seized the opportunity to urge him again to postpone any quarrel that he might have with Russia, pointing out that the Russians did not seem to be starting any trouble at the moment.

My admonitions and warnings were wasted. On 18 December 1940 Hitler informed the Commanders in Chief of all the armed services that he was irrevocably determined to attack Russia in 1941, to prevent its becoming a possible danger on the continent later.

Usually, in making declarations like this, Hitler set a deadline date after which Commanders in Chief were no longer allowed to argue the decision. But the 18 December directive for the attack on Russia—given the code name "Operation Barbarossa"—contained no such deadline date or prospective time for the operation to begin; it was just a preparatory directive. Nevertheless any prospect of dissuading Hitler now from his decision was exceedingly dim.

This shifting to a land campaign and the setting up of a second front in the east changed the whole picture for the Navy. If war against Russia really came, then any chance of stepping up the sea war against England in the near future was gone. To be sure, one heard a lot of talk about a short, swift campaign, and then victory. Just what sound military basis there was for such hopeful thinking was not apparent.

Then, at the end of December, the situation in the Eastern Mediterranean changed so drastically, and for the worse, that I again had to make urgent recommendations. During the fall the British had reinforced their Mediterranean Fleet under Admiral A. B. Cunningham, who surprised the Italian Fleet in Taranto harbor and severely damaged it with an air attack. The British had also managed to get needed ammunition, supplies, men, and aircraft through to besieged Malta, and themselves had smashed heavily at Italian convoys to Libya, sinking 21 ships in December alone. And American help was building up British strength all the time.

At this moment it was imperative to strangle England by cutting off her ocean traffic, and I warned Hitler that too little was being done to build up our submarine arm and expand our naval air force. Every effort should be made, I argued, to press the war against England—which meant, increased operations by the Navy and the Air Force. Any Russian campaign before we had defeated England would sorely weaken the war effort in the west, with possibly disastrous effects in the long run.

Hitler agreed that the U-boat construction program was too slow and too little, and said that he intended to build up the submarine arm to the greatest possible extent. However, he went on, the present political situation and Russia's tendency to mix into Balkan affairs made it necesary to eliminate this last enemy on the continent before he could "concentrate" on England. Therefore immediate priority had to be given to strengthening the Army. When that had been accomplished, it would be the Navy's and Air Force's turn next.

However, all the plans for the surprise attack on Russia had to be shelved for the time being because of Mussolini's ill-advised and unsuccessful attack on Greece. Instead of the quick success Mussolini had anticipated, the aroused Greeks not only hurled the Italian invasion force out of Greece but pursued them back over the border. Accordingly, at the beginning of April 1941, Hitler directed that the preparatory measures for the offensive against Russia be postponed until German troops rectified the situation in both Yugoslavia and Greece.

Early that spring the Japanese Foreign Minister, Matsuoka,

visited Berlin, and I knew that he must have expressed interest in the state of relations between Germany and Russia, which were becoming somewhat strained. When I asked Hitler, he told me that he had informed the Japanese Foreign Minister that "Russia will not be touched if she behaves in a friendly manner and in accordance with the Russo-German Treaty."

Nevertheless, on 22 June 1941, Hitler launched the Army and the Air Force in a surprise assault on Russia. His decision had been made—*in favor of the land war against Russia, not the sea war against England.*

In a long speech to all the senior officers of the armed force, on 15 June, he had elaborated on his reasons why Russia must be fought and defeated: The war was unavoidable; we must wage it now as a preventive measure rather than wait for the Russians to attack us later when they were better prepared and when we were tightly tied up elsewhere.

Knowing Hitler's method of argument, I was not so impressed as some members of my staff. But one thing was evident: probably the most important decision of the war had been made—and against my every advice and warning, *supported by all the facts and figures I could assemble.*

The directive which Hilter issued as the first one in the Russian campaign began with the statement: "The German Armed Forces must be prepared to defeat Soviet Russia in a swift campaign even before the war with England is terminated." As to the Navy's participation, it stated: "The main emphasis on the employment of the Navy still remains directed against England, even during the Eastern Campaign."

This was in complete accord with my own views, since now, as always, I held that England was our deadliest enemy. My one responsibility now was to see that as few of my units as possible were diverted to the Eastern Front, and that the battle against British ocean traffic should be pressed as vigorously as ever.

The Army made no request for any special support from the Navy; apparently such a rapid conquest of Russia was counted on that no real help was needed from the Navy. The orders we received specified that our primary task was to prevent enemy forces from breaking out of the Baltic.

"Since, after we reach Leningrad, the Russian Baltic Fleet will lose its last base and be in a hopeless situation," the directive read, "previous large-scale naval operations are to be avoided. After the Russian Fleet is eliminated, the Navy's essential task will be the safeguarding of water traffic in the Baltic, including ships carrying supplies for the northern flank of the Army.

In other words, our main job would be minelaying and mine-sweeping.

As a first measure of defense against the Russian Fleet, we began to lay thick minefields in the western part of the Gulf of Finland to block Russian naval forces from sortieing into the Baltic from their home ports. As a result, the Soviet ships soon retired from their bases at Hango and Reval, suffering quite heavy losses before they reached the protection of Kronstadt and Leningrad. This withdrawal was a great relief to me, as the Russian surface ships could have made it very unpleasant for us if they had attacked our Baltic trade, especially the ore carriers coming down from the Swedish port of Lulea.

After a short time we discovered that the Soviet battleships had reached Leningrad in a badly damaged condition, so there was no necessity for us to bring in major fleet units to prevent their sortieing. We also learned that the Russian submarines had suffered so heavily in our minefields that they no longer represented real threats; in fact, as it proved, they never managed to break through into the Baltic again except in very limited numbers, and then they obtained no successes worth mentioning.

The main objective of our warfare in the Baltic—protection of our own Baltic seaports and our Baltic trade—was completely realized by the daring and aggressive actions of our light forces. Our cruisers *Leipzig, Emden,* and *Köln,* in company with many patrol and minecraft, took important parts in the capture of the Russian-held island of Ösel, Moon, and Dagö, in the Baltic. Not until Finland dropped out of the war and we had to retreat by land in the fall of 1944, did we lose the control we thus gained in the Baltic.

The Baltic was not the only new sea front we got through the war with Russia: the Black Sea, in the southeast, and the Arctic

Ocean, in the north, were waters that were destined to see exploding mines and torpedoes and bursting shells and bombs.

In the Black Sea, the Russians had a battleship, several cruisers, and a great number of destroyers and torpedo boats. The forces with which our ally, Rumania, could face them were very small, and support by our Navy was urgently needed. We set up naval shore defenses at important points along the Rumanian coast, and in addition we sent a considerable number of small submarines, motor torpedo boats, and motor minesweepers to the Black Sea. These craft were transported from Germany part way over the *autobahn* and then the rest of the way via the Danube. This improvised and highly ingenious measure was the result of splendid cooperative effort by the various departments, officials, and civilian industries involved.

The third theater of the naval war against Russia—the waters of the northern North Sea and the Arctic Ocean—was to see operations of greater importance. In these operations the bases we had acquired in Norway were invaluable. I would have liked to occupy the port of Polyarny, on the Murmansk coast, but we had not the forces to spare. Consequently we could attack Russian naval forces in the Arctic, as well as the Allied convoys which soon began rushing materials to Russia, only from our bases in northern Norway. But even so, our naval and air forces exerted constant pressure against the enemy from these bases.

The Allies were using three routes to transport much needed munitions and supplies to their Russian comrade-in-arms. Part of the shipments went by rail from the eastern U. S. industrial areas across the American continent, and then by ship across the Pacific to the Russian ports in Siberia. This route was long and inefficient, but it had the advantage that it was out of reach of our attacks. Other shipments went by sea to the ports of Iran, which the British and Soviet troops had forcibly occupied in August of 1941, compelling the Shah to abdicate and the new Iranian Government to cooperate in their efforts against Germany. After occupying the country, the Allies had expanded the Iranian rail and road systems, thus opening a second supply route to Russia. This route, too, was beyond range of any really serious attacks by us.

The third route, from the Atlantic ports of the United States, through the North Atlantic and the Arctic Ocean to the Russian port of Murmansk, was not so invulnerable. Connected to Leningrad by the Murman Railroad, it was far shorter and more efficient than the other two routes. However, it also led right through an area of naval warfare well within range of our Norwegian bases and airfields. And from these Norwegian bases we kept a number of U-boats constantly operating, as well as strong surface forces and air forces. As a result of attacks by these, the enemy had to route his supply ships far to the north—a circuitous and time-consuming route—in order to stay out of range as far as possible. When he bunched this shipping into convoys for better protection, he had to escort them with heavy fleet units in order to guard them from possible attack by our own major units. To form his escorts, he had to withdraw some of his best ships from the main Atlantic theater. But even in spite of his bulked-up escorts, he suffered heavy losses on the "Murmansk Run." One striking case was Allied Convoy *PQ-17,* from Iceland to Archangel, in the summer of 1942. Approaching continental waters in early July, the 33 ships of the convoy were harassed for over three weeks by U-boat wolf packs and by air attacks so deadly that only 11 vessels finally staggered into Russian ports, the other 22 having been sent to the bottom with the loss of innumerable lives and millions of dollars worth of cargo.

Here was verification of our contention that we could never have afforded to let the Allies establish bases in Norway. With such bases, the flow of desperately needed Allied supplies to Russia would have been vastly increased, and at little cost in lives and ships. But because of the constant attacks from our naval and air forces operating from Norwegian bases, no tremendous stream of supplies flowed steadily to the Russian front. Instead, what Allied ships did win through came in only at long intervals, and only after great attrition.

These convoy battles in the Arctic Ocean took place under greatly varying conditions. In the summer, the long hours of daylight aided our attacks and increased our percentage of successes. In the grim winter months, the almost constant darkness, the violent storms, and the bitter cold brought severe hardships to our sailors and flyers, but they brought as bad or worse to the enemy also. The tenacity with which the battles were fought attested to the importance of this Allied supply route in maintaining the battle strength of the Russian front. It also demonstrated the increased effectiveness which the Norwegian bases lent to our U-boats and surface units.

It is one of the odd features of the war that it was just this question of the employment of our heavy forces in the far north that became the major causes of the decisive quarrel between Hitler and me.

XIX

The War at Sea—1941-1942

As GREATLY as the occupation of Norway had improved our strategic position, it had cost us heavily, particularly in destroyers sunk, as well as in heavy damage for a number of our larger ships. Also, during this campaign, our U-boats were necessarily partly withdrawn from the Battle of the Atlantic. Nevertheless the Naval War Staff held firmly to our first contention: that the oversea trade of the British Empire was its most vulnerable point, and we should strike there with all possible means in order to make the enemy scatter his naval forces and exhaust them through sheer wearisome patrols at sea. With his forces thus scattered, he could not concentrate them at any critical place for a dangerous attack on us.

Being the numerically weaker force, we had to make up for this by constantly developing new ideas. This demanded boldness and a zest for action not only among the members of the Naval War Staff, but to an even greater degree among the naval leaders and commanders of the individual ships. The goal of all our operations was to sink as much enemy merchant tonnage as possible, thus depriving him not only of finished war equipment but also of indispensable raw materials for his armament industries.

But the success of the commerce-destroying operations would be measured not only by actual enemy tonnage sunk but by their effect in tying up the enemy's naval forces and in the disruption of his whole economic system. These secondary effects could not always be appraised immediately, but they were unmistakable in many ways.

For instance, in order to combat our surface and undersea

raiders, the enemy had to keep broad areas of the Atlantic under continuous and ever-expanding surveillance. The planes he used for this purpose—principally long-range craft—were thus not available for such offensive operations as bombing German cities. The percentage of the enemy's air forces that our submarines tied up over the Atlantic relieved the homefront incalculably.

All of our naval forces operating in the open seas sailed under one basic directive: their goal was the enemy's seaborne commerce, *and not the enemy fleet.* Battle with stronger enemy warships was to be avoided at all costs. My quarrel with Hitler after the end of the pocket battleship *Admiral Graf Spee* had moved me to examine this question again from all angles, but I returned to the same conclusion I had always had.

To conduct war over the whole wide surface of the oceans required that the command be centralized under one authority, and that authority the Naval War Staff itself. It alone possessed the necessary sources of information—all the particulars, the political intelligence, the knowledge of the enemy's radio communications—and it alone had the facilities to operate the necessary widespread overseas supply system. We had already put into service a number of fast supply ships—oil tankers, ammunition carriers, and the like—to service our U-boats and surface raiders overseas so they would not have to put back to home bases before renewing their activities. As just one aspect that required careful planning, we had to make arrangements that the crews of captured enemy merchantmen could be transferred to cartel ships from time to time, in order that acceptable and hygienic living conditions could be maintained for the personnel on our own ships.

We naturally could not predict the exact measure of success that we could achieve in this type of warfare, but at least it gave us the initiative and did not force us to strive vainly to counter the enemy's offensive tactics. That freedom of action it was imperative to maintain for as long as possible.

Naturally my staff and I had never had any illusions from the very beginning that the enormous superiority of the enemy, and his concentrated efforts to defend his lifelines against our attacks, would not one day put an end to our surface raids. Sooner or later our raiders would inevitably wear out, and their importance in the war picture wane. But I hoped that by that time our submarines would be strong enough to take their place against the enemy with even greater effect.

Hence, our effort was to organize these operations by our surface raiders to obtain the maximum results for as long a time as possible—especially in view of the feeling by both the political leadership and the Naval War Staff that the entry of the United States into the war against us was only a question of time and opportunity.

From the very first, the anti-German bias of the American president, Franklin D. Roosevelt, had been obvious, and his desire to support the Allies unmistakable. Despite all the efforts of the German Government to maintain tolerable relations with the United States, and despite the prohibition on official intervention imposed under the American Neutrality Laws, support of our enemies was evident, especially in the conduct of American naval forces.

As an example, the republics of North and South America, meeting in a convention at Panama at the end of September 1939, had created the concept of a "Neutrality Zone," extending to 300 or 1,000 miles offshore from the American continent, depending upon geographical location. Within this zone the warring powers were not to carry on combat operations. One of the main objectives, of course, was to limit the activities of both our surface raiders and our submarines, whose most favorable operational theaters were in the zone thus barred off. As "neutrality patrols" by United States naval forces were set up within this Neutrality Zone, it was almost impossible for German blockade runners to break through this Neutrality Zone without being sighted. It being the practice of the United States naval patrols, immediately upon sighting one of our ships, to broadcast its description and position over the air, the result was that a number of our merchant ships were intercepted and sunk by the enemy.

Then, in September of 1940, in the famous "destroyer-base" deal, the United States Government turned over to Britain 50 overage but very serviceable destroyers which the British Navy desperately needed in their convoy protection against our U-boats in the North Atlantic. Damaged British warships were also being repaired in American shipyards. And from April 1941 on, United States naval and air forces reported the position of all German or Italian ships sighted by open, uncoded radio broadcasts.

Recognizing these sympathies of the United States Government, both the German political leadership and the German Naval War Staff had from the very first issued the strictest orders to avoid any incidents with American ships. Although the Pan-American Neutrality Zone was, of course, not officially recognized by us, in actual practice all our combat ships and submarines received strict orders to abstain from warlike operations within the Zone. Our ship commanders all realized that such incidents, even if brought about through no fault of theirs, could only lead to serious political involvements with the United States. Every one knew that it was important to postpone the entry of America into the war as long as possible, even if it was not possible to avoid it entirely. Yet in spite of all our efforts, a series of incidents did occur.

Needless to say the Naval War Staff viewed the possibility of the United States entering the war with the gravest concern. That it would undoubtedly have an adverse effect on our warfare in the Atlantic was one of our first considerations. Thus it was important for us to obtain all possible success there before the whole weight of American seapower was thrown on the side of the enemy.

Fortunately, our operations against British shipping in the Atlantic had benefited tremendously from the bases we had gained in Norway and France in 1940. Also, the first of our specially designed auxiliary cruisers had just been completed. Converted from merchant ships, with all the improvements we had developed from our experiences in the previous war, these were the first specially designed ships that we were able to put into service for the long-range projects of the Naval War Staff.

To command these surface raiders which would be operating independently in distant seas, we selected men who, in addition to being skilled seamen with good common sense and a zest for action, could plan operations on their own responsibility and who, above all, could inspire their hundreds of officers and men, confined as they would be to narrow shipboard quarters for long and wearisome months of cruising. It was a tribute to our system of selection that, without a single exception, these cruiser commanders proved admirably their fitness for these assignments.

In acknowledgment of their unusual responsibilities we permitted these captains almost a completely free hand in the selection of their personnel, and they, by their performance, in turn demonstrated the wisdom of their selection. As a further assistance to the commanders of these cruiser raiders in their unique assignments, each of them was given an experienced merchant marine officer who could give expert advice on the customs and procedures of the merchant marine of all nations.

The value of these measures was proved by the fact that in the years from 1940 to 1942, these auxiliary cruisers succeeded in sinking almost a million tons. In addition to actual tonnage sunk, these cruisers disrupted the enemy's merchant shipping to such an extent that he had to tie up innumerable naval units and other facilities in the effort to protect his commerce.

The operations of these auxiliary cruisers formed a glorious chapter in the naval history of the war. To their captains and crews, as well as to the captains and crews of the supply ships and oil tankers that serviced them, and to the men who designed them, as well as to all the officers and specialists in the Naval High Command who cooperated in their creation and operations, should go full recognition of a great service heroically performed.

The acquistion of bases on the Atlantic coast of western France had brought with it one additional new asset in our warfare on the seas: these bases would be excellent ports of departure and return for the merchant ships we were outfitting as blockade runners.

These blockade runners were urgently needed to bring in critical strategic materials vitally needed for our war and domestic economy. As early as 1940, the Naval War Staff had inaugurated the import of raw rubber from Asia. This, and other strategic materials, was collected in Japanese ports, whence it was brought home on suitable German ships.

Up to the beginning of the war with Russia, we had imported much of this vitally needed raw material via land route through Russia, but after June of 1941, this route was closed and all subsequent shipments had to be brought in by sea.

Raw rubber was almost as vital to our war economy as Swedish ore, and if the supply failed, the effect on our war-making potential would be serious. Therefore the Naval War Staff determined to use all possible German and Italian ships in Pacific ports for the transport of rubber to our bases in western France, and to increase the number of these carriers by ships especially sent out to the Far East.

The pattern had been set by the motor ship *Weserland,* under command of Captain Krage, which had set out at the end of December 1940 from Kobe and reached Bordeaux safely on 4 April 1941. Despite some losses, quite a number of resourceful German and Italian merchantmen succeeded in slipping through the British cordon and reaching the French coast with their valuable cargoes. In 1941, four German ships slipped through, and, in the following year, eight German and four Italian freighters succeeded in running the blockade.

While our auxiliary cruisers and submarines were making it tough everywhere for British commerce, and our own blockade runners were attempting to bring in vitally needed cargoes, our major naval units were not idle.

The first of our larger ships to operate in the Atlantic after the scuttling of the *Admiral Graf Spee* was the pocket battleship *Admiral Scheer,* commanded by Captain Krancke. Going out by the roundabout way north of Iceland and then down through the Denmark Strait, she operated daringly and successfully from October 1940 to March 1941 in both the Atlantic and Indian oceans.

The pocket battleships had proved their exceptional worth in this type of operations. But the *Admiral Hipper,* putting to sea about the same time for the same sort of raid, revealed a disturbing weakness in long-range operations. She consumed an excessive amount of fuel. Going out also by the northern route and down through Denmark Strait, she could remain on station only for about a month, from the end of November 1940 until her return to Brest at the end of December.

While the pocket battleship *Admiral Scheer* was still at sea, the battleships *Gneisenau* and *Scharnhorst,* making up a task force under direct command of Admiral Lütjens, Commander in Chief of the Fleet, had put out from Kiel at the end of January 1941. Although enemy patrols were encountered east of Iceland, the force skilfully evaded them and succeeded in breaking through into the open Atlantic. After a most rewarding cruise under the superb leadership of the capable Admiral Lütjens, the undamaged force triumphantly returned to Brest on 22 March 1941.

However, it quickly and painfully became evident that the antiaircraft defenses of Brest were not equal to the occasion, and repeated enemy air attacks on the ships brought damage that required extensive repairs. Shifting the *Scharnhorst* to the port of La Pallice, on the Bay of Biscay, was no improvement. It was evident that the battleships were being made special priority targets by the British.

The only answer was a strengthening of antiaircraft defenses in the target areas. Insofar as this lay within the cognizance of the Navy, this was done by increasing the number of antiaircraft batteries, setting up smokescreen facilities, and adding camouflage. But our great lack was in a special protective cover force of our own fighter planes. The seriousnes of the problem reinforced us in our conviction that the weight of our Air Force should have been thrown principally against our main enemy, Britain, instead of our new opponent, Russia.

As part of the over-all operational concept embracing the two battleships, the heavy cruiser *Admiral Hipper* left Brest again in the middle of February, under command of the adept Captain Meisel, and shortly thereafter destroyed seven steamships out of an enemy convoy in the vicinity of the Azores. Returning to Brest after this success, she put out again into the Atlantic, and returned by way of the Denmark Strait to Kiel, which she reached in April of 1941. The readiness with which these vessels had cruised the Atlantic demonstrated that surface ships, used in conjunction with submarines, could not only inflict heavy damage upon the enemy convoys, but also could force him to wide-spread dispersion of his naval forces in order to protect his shipping routes.

In the meantime the great battleship *Bismarck* was nearing completion, and after commissioning on 24 August 1940, she was soon ready to take her part in the combat. We consequently put

Prinz Eugen on her dash through the English Channel.

WILHELMSHAVEN AFTER THE WAR

PRINZ EUGEN WITH EMERGENCY RUDDER

our best thoughts into planning the strategy where she could prove most valuable.

Because of her extraordinary fighting power and her sturdy armor and almost unsinkable compartmentation, she was, ship for ship, far superior to anything the enemy could throw against her. However, in common with all our other naval units, she suffered under one great disadvantage which the enemy did not share: she would have no accompanying, integrated air forces to protect her. On the other hand the enemy, with his numerous aircraft carriers and airfields, could project his air strikes against us wherever our ships might be.

This was recognizably a terrific handicap, yet, with no aircraft carriers of our own, there was nothing we could do about it. In limited areas near the French and Norwegian coasts, some air support could be given, depending upon the cooperation of the German Air Force planes stationed at the airbases there. We faced the bitter realization again that it is impossible, in a few short years, to build up a fleet with all the combat strength that must go with a modern navy. Ever since 1935 we had included a carrier in our plans, and construction on one had actually begun, only to be permanently postponed when the war began, because the Air Force had not developed suitable planes to operate from it.

In all our strategy for the *Bismarck* we had to face the realization of this critical weakness, and the fact that the only remedy for it would have to be the battleship's own extraordinary sturdiness and fighting power. We could not permit this knowledge, however, to dissuade us from use of the ship in our naval offensive. The real question that we debated, was whether to send her to sea at once, or wait until her sister ship, the *Tirpitz,* was ready to go to sea in concerted action.

This, however, would not be until the late fall or winter of 1941-1942. Moreover, our recent experiences with operation at sea—notably, the successful cruises of the *Admiral Hipper* and the *Admiral Scheer*—had demonstrated that even single heavy units could perform brilliantly in the Atlantic. This ability would decrease automatically in proportion to the increase in the enemy's defense measures, particularly his air patrols. And the inevitable entry of the United States into the war in the near future was staring us in the face; once that occurred, our chances for successful operations in the Atlantic would drastically diminish.

All these seemed to us cogent reasons for not postponing employment of the *Bismarck* until an uncertain future date, but to send her out, in company with the new cruiser *Prinz Eugen,* for a telling offensive in the Atlantic as soon as possible. As part of the same over-all operation, we planned to send out the *Scharnhorst* and *Gneisenau* from Brest in a simultaneous movement, and to bulk the whole with numerous submarines. To service all these forces at sea, a widespread organization of tankers and supply ships was set up. After pushing her operations to the maximum extent, the *Bismarck* was to return, not to a French base, but to a home port in Germany.

An important part of this strategical and tactical concept was frustrated by engine trouble on the *Scharnhorst,* which put that ship out of commission for several months. Then, on 6 April 1941, the *Gneisenau* received an enemy torpedo-plane hit, and, a few days later, four bombs, all of which damaged her to such an extent that she would have to lay up for some time for repairs.

Despite the fact that the *Scharnhorst* and *Gneisenau* were now definitely removed from participation, I still considered it advisable to proceed with the operation in order not to lose valuable time that probably could never be made up. As the *Prinz Eugen* unluckily struck a mine and had to go into dock temporarily for repairs, the operation had to be delayed until the middle of May.

Accordingly, on 25 April, I took advantage of the delay to hold a detailed conference with Admiral Lütjens, who was to be in active command of the *Bismarck* force. In the discussion we took up the question as to whether, in light of the circumstances that had arisen, it would be advisable, or perhaps actually necessary, to postpone the departure of the *Bismarck* and *Prinz Eugen* for the time being. In reply to my questions, Admiral Lütjens gave his opinion in favor of delaying the operation until the *Scharnhorst,* at least, was ready for action again, or even until the *Tirpitz* was ready for sea.

It speaks much for Lütjens as a man that he so frankly expressed this view to me.

I then tried to make him understand the reasons why I took

the opposite stand, that the operation should not be delayed. Even though Admiral Lütjens probably was not completely convinced of the correctness of my view, the discussion ended in complete mutual understanding.

The decision to send out the *Bismarck* was one of the most difficult decisions I personally had to make during the war. For one thing, the premises with which the Naval War Staff had begun consideration of the operation were no longer applicable. The sortie of the *Bismarck,* originally planned as but one part of a vast over-all offensive, had now become an individual, isolated undertaking. The enemy could afford to concentrate all his naval forces against this one small task group, thus making the risk immeasurably greater.

On the other hand, wars do not wait, and the general strategical situation did not permit our deliberately withholding such a strong combat unit. If we delayed until the *Scharnhorst* and *Gneisenau* were ready for action again, it might mean forever renouncing the opportunity to use the new battleship in the Atlantic, since the *Scharnhorst* and *Gneisenau* were under constant British air attacks in their exposed French berths, and there was no telling when they would be in fighting shape again. (As it later turned out, neither of these ships actually put to sea again until their dash home through the Channel in February of the next year.) And if the undertaking was postponed until the *Tirpitz* was ready for sea, it would mean at least a half-year's inactivity—a half year in which the unneutral attitude of the United States might change to outright hostility.

One strong psychological factor in my decision was my unbounded confidence in Admiral Lütjens' leadership. His knowledge of naval warfare and his mastery of tactics was superb. Even as a very young officer in the First World War, he had commanded a torpedo boat squadron. After that he had risen progressively to flotilla commander, then captain of a cruiser, and then Commander of the Torpedo Boat Forces. He had also had sound experience in staff work, and as my Chief of Personnel he had won by special confidence in years of close association. During part of the Norwegian campaign he had commanded the heavy forces in place of the Commander in Chief of the Fleet, who was ill. Finally, in the recent sortie of the *Scharnhorst* and *Gneisenau* he had proved his great ability in every respect.

Among the unexpected difficulties I faced in making my decision was Hitler's personal attitude. When I informed him of the planned operation, he did not positively reject the plans, but his attitude showed that he was not in full agreement with them. However, he left the decision up to me. Then, at the beginning of May, Admiral Lütjens had a long personal discussion with Hitler in Gotenhafen, during which he not only recounted in detail his experiences with the *Scharnhorst* and *Gneisenau* in the Atlantic, but also explained his views on the tactical use of the *Bismarck.* He also covered the danger from enemy carriers to which the battleship would be exposed.

Only after careful assessment of all the circumstances involved did I finally give the orders for the operation to be carried out, and 21 May saw the beginning of that dramatic and pulse-tingling sortie.

The *Bismarck,* captained by Ernst Lindemann, and the *Prinz Eugen,* under Captain Helmuth Brinkmann, and all under the over-all command of Admiral Lütjens, took the roundabout route to the north of Iceland, skirted the ice fields, and broke through the British cordon of patrols stretched across the Denmark Strait between Iceland and Greenland. Turning southward in the Atlantic, they encountered an intercepting force consisting of the new British battleship *Prince of Wales* and the old battle cruiser *Hood,* with screening destroyers, and, just before six o'clock on the morning of 24 May, gave battle in a contest that was to be as short as it was decisive. Within bare minutes the *Bismarck* dropped a couple of salvos of 38-cm. shells on the *Hood,* which blew up with the loss of all but three of her crew. The *Prince of Wales* suffered such damage from the accurate fire of the *Bismarck* and the *Prinz Eugen* that she broke off the engagement and retired under cover of a smoke screen.

The *Bismarck* and *Prinz Eugen,* however, had not been without casualties themselves, the *Bismarck's* worst injury being a shell hit which opened a leak in one of her fuel tanks as well as contaminating other tanks with salt water. Admiral Lütjens therefore determined to shorten his cruise and head immediately for St. Nazaire, on the French Atlantic coast.

Meanwhile the British, upon first sighting the *Bismarck* group in the Denmark Strait, had summoned their strongest units in the whole northern and eastern Atlantic—aircraft carriers, battleships, cruisers, and destroyers. From the British Isles they came, and from Halifax convoys, and from as far away as Gibraltar, all hurrying toward the place where the *Bismarck* was expected to be. That night of 24 May, torpedo bombers from the British aircraft carrier *Victorious* attacked the battleship and made one torpedo hit, but it only cut down the sturdy *Bismarck's* speed slightly. Then Admiral Lütjens, taking advantage of stormy weather and low visibility, shook off the pursuit and lost himself in the wide Atlantic. But realizing that his own ship had lost its cruising range, he detached the *Prinz Eugen* to operate independently in the sea lanes.

From early morning of 25 May until almost noon of the 26th, the *Bismarck* eluded her pursuers. Only the fortuitous sighting of her by a lone long-range British Catalina plane, flying the southernmost of the Bay of Biscay patrols, brought her under enemy surveillance again. She was at that time within less than 700 miles of Brest, and even closer than that to the area where she could have come under the protection of the Luftwaffe's heavy bombers. And within a couple of hundred miles she would have passed inside the protection of a barrier line of half a dozen U-boats, specifically assigned beforehand to post themselves across any prospective line of enemy pursuit. As a matter of fact, the British Admiral Tovey had already decided that the pursuit should be abandoned if the *Bismarck* were not overtaken by midnight of the 26th.

The sighting by the Catalina changed all that. Over the air went out the orders bringing in every British man-of-war that could possibly reach the scene. And just before dusk a swarm of British torpedo planes from the nearest carrier swooped down over the *Bismarck*.

The battleship's gunfire was hampered by rain clouds, strong winds, stormy seas, and fading daylight, but she set up a barrage of antiaircraft fire against the attack. Despite continuing strikes for over half an hour, the attackers managed to get home with only two torpedoes. One of these, striking the armor belt, damaged the *Bismarck* little more than had the first torpedo the previous night; the other, however, struck her right aft, damaging her propellers and jamming her rudders, so that she was helpless to maneuver.

Still steaming but now crippled, the *Bismarck* fought off torpedo attacks through a good part of the night, but at daylight two of Britain's most powerful battleships, the brand new *King George V* and the *Rodney,* took up the most favorable positions that could be secured, and opened fire at 16,000 yards with their 14-inch and 16-inch batteries. Unable to maneuver for position, almost out of ammunition, and swept by a hurricane of armor-piercing shells, the *Bismarck's* fire was finally beaten down and her turrets silenced, while flames swept her decks. Closing now to almost point-blank range, the enemy still poured in their fire, yet no one on the *Bismarck* made a move to surrender. Finally the enemy cruiser moved in to give her the *coup de grâce* with torpedoes, and the *Bismarck* went down at half past ten in the morning, with her flag still flying. Only 110 of her crew of over 2,000 officers and men survived, the rest all going down with the ship. These included Admiral Lütjens and practically all of the officers.

The *Prinz Eugen,* after refueling in the mid-Atlantic, developed engine trouble and had to return to Brest, which she reached safely on 1 June.

Most of the details of the *Bismarck's* cruise and her last battle had to be pieced together long afterward from enemy sources and from the lips of the survivors, as of necessity the group had exercised radio silence for most of the cruise in order to prevent detection by the enemy. And each hour from the moment she departed was a strain upon my heart, for I alone bore the responsibility for sending her out to sea, just as I bore the sole responsibility for all the naval operations that took place during my term as Commander in Chief of the Navy. No one had compelled me to send her out; the decision was mine alone, based upon my conviction that the enemy had to be fought with every means possible, and my personal concept of how best to use our forces for that purpose.

When, on 22 May, I had personally reported the departure of the *Bismarck* force to Hitler, he had expressed considerable doubt and anxiety. I tried to allay his fears and explained to him the favorable effects we hoped to obtain from the operations, and so succeeded in obtaining his acquiescence for the continuation of the sortie.

At first it seemed that events would justify my decision, When the *Bismarck* had engaged the enemy forces, she naturally had been able to open her radio circuits, since her location was now known, and her report of the sinking of the *Hood* and defeat of the *Prince of Wales* was received with keen delight by Hitler, who personally congratulated me on this success. However, I pointed out to Hitler that our worries were not yet over, for, from the *Bismarck's* reports before she lost touch with the enemy and resumed radio silence, we knew that she had suffered damaging hits and that her cruising efficiency was impaired.

At this point I had to make the second of the difficult personal decisions involved in the *Bismarck's* sortie. Should the Naval War Staff recall the *Bismarck* group now after the success over the *Hood,* or should the decision as to further operations be left to the Commander in Chief of the Fleet, Admiral Lütjens?

At this time I considered the break out of the restricted northern waters through Denmark Strait into the main Atlantic the most difficult part of the whole operation. To order the Commander in Chief of the Fleet to break off the operation and to return through the narrow and dangerous waters off the coast of Iceland seemed to me an unwarranted assumption of a decision that should be left entirely to Admiral Lütjens. As the commander on the spot, and the only one able to appraise the tactical situation in light of his own damage and its effect on further operations, he was the one who should have the say-so. And knowing Admiral Lütjens for these many years, I felt sure that any decision he might make under the circumstances would be the wisest one.

With the *Bismarck* observing radio silence again, all we knew was that Admiral Lütjens had forced his way open to the whole Atlantic. Then, through enemy radio messages monitored by our intelligence officers, we discovered that the regular contact signals of the shadowing British cruisers had ceased. We deduced that they had lost contact and that Admiral Lütjens was free and unobserved in the open sea.

The full scope of the reasons that impelled Admiral Lütjens to decide on an immediate return to St. Nazaire we can not know, for he and the captain of the *Bismarck,* as well as all their staffs and almost every other officer aboard, went down with the ship. Hence when the final report on the *Bismarck's* end came from enemy sources, all I could give Hitler were my own conjectures.

From a climax of glee over the sinking of the *Hood* Hitler was thus, within little more than three days, dropped to the depths of despondency, and his anger was in proportion. I am convinced Admiral Lütjens, who was distinguished for his brilliance and fighting spirit and who thoroughly understood my plan and desires, had made decisions that were correct, based as they would be on his knowledge of the tactical situation and the condition of his ship. I had planned and ordered the sortie of the *Bismarck* group, and therefore was the one entirely responsible for all that had happened.

The sinking of the *Bismarck,* however, was to have lasting effects upon the whole naval warfare for the rest of the war. Hitler's attitude toward any suggestions or proposals advocated by me was now completely different. Where before this he had given me a relatively free hand as long as government policies or the other armed services were not involved, he now became extremely critical and very apt to insist on agreement with his own personal views. He had previously preferred not to be worried with too much advance briefing about the sorties of the larger ships, as he always felt anxious about them, but now he issued directives to me that radically restricted the movements of these major units. He forbade their sorties into the Atlantic. The success we had had even with our inferior forces through bold initiative and the taking of calculated risks was to be a thing of the past. For us the naval war was given an entirely new face.

Our fears in the Naval War Staff that favorable opportunities in the Battle of the Atlantic would diminish rather than improve soon proved justified. Immediately after the sinking of the *Bismarck,* the British Admiralty instituted an extensive search operation designed to locate and destroy every unit of the effective supply organization we had built up in the Atlantic. In quick succession no fewer than six German supply ships were caught and sunk. And with the increasing network of enemy air reconnaissance over the ocean, we found it impossible to repair the losses or even to maintain the units that we had. Even so, we did not abandon efforts to stage offensive operations in the nearer waters of the Atlantic. In June 1941 the pocket battleship *Lützow* was scheduled to proceed to an advance base in Norway as the first stop on a planned raid into the ocean lanes. However, she was hit by a torpedo in an enemy air attack before she even got there, and had to go to a repair yard instead, where she remained for a long time.

The prospects of staging raids with the battleships *Scharnhorst* and *Gneisenau,* which still lay in Brest undergoing repairs, also had deteriorated; in fact their very stay in the French port was endangered. Exposed to constant enemy air attacks, their repairs dropped from slow to almost a standstill. It was only a matter of time until they would inevitably be forced to return to Germany.

However, Hitler was obsessed with fear at this time that the British were making plans for a major reentry into Norway. He had received this impression from a number of small commando raids the British were making on scattered Norwegian coastal facilities, and was sure that they were planning a major attack on Narvik. Nobody in the Naval War Staff shared this view, but Hitler asserted that Norway was not sufficiently protected from a British attack, and he demanded that we send all our available ships—including the *Scharnhorst* and *Gneisenau*—to Norway to strengthen our positions there.

In mid-November of 1941 I analyzed for Hitler our remaining possibilities in the Battle of the Atlantic, as I saw them. I would not send the *Tirpitz,* which should be ready for service the following month, into the Atlantic—not only because of our severe shortage of fuel oil but also because deteriorating conditions there were not favorable for an effective sortie by a ship the size of the *Tirpitz.* However, in two or three months the *Scharnhorst* and *Gneisenau* should be ready and would be available for short offensives in the Atlantic, especially against the British convoys from Gibraltar.

Unfortunately, after their long stay in the shipyards, the crews of both ships were in sad need of battle training. This training they could only get by short training cruises out to sea where they would undoubtedly be exposed to heavy air attacks, especially by torpedo planes. To return the ships to a Norwegian or German port would be difficult and would involve great danger, but by taking advantage of exceptional weather conditions, they could perhaps get home by the roundabout passage north of Iceland. The *Prinz Eugen,* I added, should have good chances of returning home by a swift surprise dash through the English Channel.

The possibilities of getting the *Scharnhorst* and *Gneisenau* back to Germany by a quick surprise dash up the Channel had been the subject of intense study by the Naval War Staff. From the beginning I had been against any such undertaking. From reports of his intelligence agents and other sources, the enemy could keep advised of the state of readiness of the ships at any time, and calculate accurately their time of sailing, and thus have his entire naval and air forces alerted to stop them. In addition, the danger from mines in the narrow waters was serious.

Hitler, nevertheless, insisted on the return of the ships through the English Channel. Since surprise was the great essential to such a successful dash, he was willing to accept a low state of combat readiness on the ships and forego any training cruises at sea that might tip off the enemy.

Some of the plans which we had already worked on called for the ships to break out of port for the up-Channel dash and to pass the narrow Straits of Dover in board daylight. I presented this and all the other plans to Hitler at a conference attended also by the principal commanders who would actively participate: Vice Admiral Otto Ciliax, Commander of the battleship group, Commodore Ruge, head of the minesweepers, and Colonel Galland, who was to command the fighter planes that would provide the air cover. Hitler approved the plan for the daylight breakthrough.

The decision to risk the ships in a Channel dash was absolutely at variance with my views. If the enemy were even reasonably alert and prepared, I did not see how the dash could succeed. Hitler was adamant. He stated unequivocally that if I rejected the Channel breakthrough, he would have the ships decommissioned in Brest and the guns taken off them.

The operation took place during the two days and intervening night of 11-12 February, and was a decided success. Because of a combination of unusual circumstances we had achieved complete surprise: the enemy's usually effective air reconnaissance had fortuitously broken down; the Royal Air Force had been temporarily concentrated on other objectives; weather conditions had been unusually favorable for us; and there had been confusion in command jurisdiction on the enemy's side.

On our side, we were correspondingly elated, Hitler himself being especially so, since now he would no longer have to worry over the exposed position of the two ships. The one fly in the ointment was that the *Gneisenau* struck an enemy mine during the dash and had to lay up for repairs in the Kiel shipyard. There she was presently so badly damaged by a night bombing raid from Britain that she was rendered *hors-de-combat* for the remainder of the war.

Tactically, the dash up the Channel was a great success. Strategically, it was an outright retreat. Withdrawing the most powerful part of our fleet from ports looking onto the Atlantic, and transferring our strength to Norwegian waters to protect Norway, ended the "Battle of the Atlantic" for all practical purposes. It amounted to giving up the offensive in that extremely important sea of operations.

But while we would no longer be able to menace the enemy with sorties of strong surface units against his thin-spread lines of communication in the Atlantic, the Naval War Staff had no intention of abandoning the war on the enemy's commerce completely. The increasing stream of Allied supply vessels transporting war material to hard-pressed Russia offered opportunities for attacks by our ships lying in northern Norway. In January 1942 the superbattleship *Tirpitz,* and, a few weeks later, the pocket battleships *Admiral Scheer* and *Lützow,* along with the cruisers *Admiral Hipper* and *Köln* and a squadron of destroyers, were sent north to prevent any possible enemy landings in northern Norwegian fjords. The presence of these ships there was an ever-present threat to the Allied convoys to Murmansk. The air forces in northern Norway were reinforced, giving them greater power to locate and attack enemy convoys. But it was the U-boat forces that were responsible for most of the sinkings there.

Also, our submarines were still able to operate effectively in the

Atlantic, and in 1942 their successes mounted steadily. We were able to keep an increased number of submarines actually operating at the front despite the fact that our new construction was still far below what our U-boat construction program called for. My best efforts all these years had not availed to secure the needed additional workers and additional material, and even within the Navy the importance of repairs and new construction did not seem to me to be sufficiently recognized. The completion of the *Bismarck, Tirpitz,* and *Prinz Eugen,* as well as the extensive battle-damage repairs on the battleships and cruisers, had been first priority in the shipyards at the expense of the submarines.

That the U-boats achieved increased successes despite all this was due mainly to the fighting spirit of their crews and the able leadership of Admiral Dönitz, Commander of the Submarine Forces. What peacetime operations had indicated, the U-boats in the Atlantic now proved: that not only the actual direction of U-boat activities at the front, but the training belonged in the hands of the Commander of the Submarine Forces.

In the training field, the initial preparation of the crews of new submarines for their participation in the war was under the immediate supervision of Rear Admiral von Friedeburg, Deputy Commander of Submarines. For the training of the individual boats, he assigned battle-tested skippers right from the front so that they could pass on to the new captains and crews the benefit of their own battle knowledge and experience.

In the Atlantic, the greatest successes were obtained by submarines acting together in whole groups, or "wolf packs," some of whose running battles with convoys often lasted for days. Such continuous battle demanded the all-out efforts of both skippers and crews, and the bravery and tenacity they demonstrated under the most difficult conditions cannot be praised too highly.

Both Admiral Dönitz and I were in complete agreement that in the long run the U-boat arm alone could have a decisive effect on the war, although he differed with me in my view that the surface forces could have significant effect, too. Also, Admiral Dönitz thought that the submarine construction program would be advanced by its being turned over to Minister of Armaments Speer—a viewpoint directly contrary to that of all the technical experts on my staff.

Despite these divergences of opinion, however, Admiral Dönitz never championed anything but a well-considered, objective strategy. It must have been surprising to Hitler later, after his break with me, to find that Dönitz supported my views instead of Hitler's, in opposition to the decommissioning of the remaining large ships. In his capacity of Commander of Submarines, Dönitz naturally and rightfully often made demands on me which unfortunately I could not always fulfill to the extent he wished, so that he thought he had just cause to complain that his requests were not being given proper consideration. Still this was just the complaint I myself often had against Hitler. Regardless of all such disagreements, however, our objective cooperation did not suffer, nor did I ever lose any of my high opinion of Dönitz's ability and performance as wartime leader of the U-boat forces. Subsequently, during our common ordeal in the Nürnberg trials and our subsequent long years of imprisonment in Spandau, I came to appreciate even more his sterling worth as a man.

But while the Naval War Staff was occupied with the war in the Atlantic, we suddenly found ourselves involved in a whole new theater of war as well. Japan's entry into the war through the sudden attack on the American Fleet in Pearl Harbor was of the greatest importance strategically.

Neither I nor any other member of the Naval War Staff had any advance warning of this step. News of the Japanese attack on 7 December 1941 came as a complete surprise to us, even though on 5 March the Supreme Commander of Armed Forces had issued a directive suggesting the possibility that Japan might enter the war on our side. In this directive the statement was made that the capture of Singapore, England's key base in the Far East, would operate decisively for ultimate victory in the global war.

Since that time I had argued that if Japan did enter the war, she should advance against Singapore rather than against Vladivostok, as some military circles advocated. The choice of Vladivostok as an objective I thought would be a bad mistake; Japan's target should first of all be Britain's strong point in the Far East. Also I had the private hope that a Japanese capture of Singapore might scare the United States out of entering the war herself.

There had been no real study or even detailed discussions of a possible change of the strategical situation before Japan actually entered the war, and even after that there was never any really effective cooperation between her and the other two Axis partners.

Had the situation been considered from a broader viewpoint, the Japanese success in Southeast Asia, combined with an energetic offensive of our own into the Mediterranean, together with the safeguarding of North Africa—if the French could have been influenced to cooperate—all this could have led to a notable strengthening of our postion in the conflict. But any such possibilities were deprived of any chance of realization by Hitler's northern campaign, which tied down all our available forces in Russia. And, contrary to the expectations of the optimistic, this had turned out to be a campaign of long duration.

The year 1942 also brought a radical change in the Mediterranean. During the early spring, the situation there had considerably improved for us as the result of a German air corps being sent to Sicily and a number of U-boats into the Mediterranean.

At this time the island of Malta was the main base for the British in their attacks on the Italo-German communication lines leading to North Africa, but its usefulness as a base had been considerably reduced by continuous bombing from the air and by successful naval and air attacks on the British convoys that were supplying Malta. As a result, the stream of supplies and reinforcements of Field Marshal Rommel's Army in North Africa, which previously had been seriously curtailed by British attacks, now flowed almost uninterrupted. But these communication lines would never be completely secure until we eliminated the British wasp nest at Malta.

Field Marshal Kesselring, the Commander in Chief South, and the Italian High Command were in thorough agreement with me on this point. In the opinion of the Naval War Staff as well as of Vice Admiral Weichold, our liaison officer with the Italian Navy, the time was ripe for a successful move against Malta. Accordingly, in my conferences with Hitler I repeatedly urged the occupation of Malta.

A combined German-Italian staff was set to work to draw up the necessary plans. Under these, Marshal Rommel's tank army was to begin the operation by a strong offensive toward Cairo whose purpose would be to push the English airfields in North Africa so far back from the coast that they would not be able to fly off planes that could interfere with the assault on Malta.

This drive by Rommel was at first very successful—so much so that it seemed as if it might reach the Suez, the supreme goal of all the operations in North Africa—and Marshal Rommel received authorization to drive on and take the Suez. Concomitantly, the original plan to take Malta first and drive for the Suez afterward was reversed, and the Suez was given priority.

This proved a fatal mistake, because the offensive died down with Rommel's increasing distance from his supply ports, and the air forces, including an Italian paratroop division which had been assigned for the attack on Malta, had to be used instead to support Rommel's tank army in North Africa. The British took advantage of the opportunity to pour men and planes and supplies into Malta, even at cost of severe losses in the resupply convoys. Thus the exceptionally favorable opportunity for a successful attack on Malta passed forever.

From the first the Naval War Staff had urged the attack on Malta because strategically it was Britain's most important point in the Mediterranean, only later did we too hope that Suez would fall to Rommel's offensive. However, Hitler had never seemed deeply interested in the attack on Malta or in other phases of the Mediterranean problem whose importance seemed to me so evident. For him, the Mediterranean was only a secondary battlefield, and he was quite willing to leave the command there to the Italians, and to commit only our weaker forces to the battle there. With the great demands which the war in Russia was now placing on the Army and Air Force, it was probably impossible to spare any really strong reinforcement of troops or air squadrons for the Mediterranean front. But it was just this that I had feared all along—just this that had impelled me to my original warning against any campaign in the east.

On the other hand, the Mediterranean has always been for England "the sea of decision." Upon the maintenance of her position in

Gibraltar, Malta, and Suez might depend the whole fate of the British Empire.

But there was another Empire with a strong stake in the Mediterranean—France, with her metropolitan territory on one side, and her colonies on the African side. I had repeatedly pointed this out to Hitler. Toward France, as toward Norway, I had always held that a positive policy for peace was necessary and possible as well. And there were good reasons why France might be favorable to such an approach. For, on 3 July 1940, a British Fleet under Admiral Somerville, upon rejection of a demand on the French naval forces that they either reenter the war on Britain's side or submit to internment, had opened fire on the unprepared French ships in Oran and all but annhilated them. Over a thousand Frenchmen lost their lives, and popular indignation in France rose to a high peak against this action by their former ally. There were even circles in France which favored an alliance with Germany and were prepared to help her fight England.

One of those most indignant was the Commander in Chief of the French Navy, Admiral Darlan, who was also a member of the French Government at Vichy and possessed great personal influence. On 28 January 1942 I had a long, detailed discussion with him in Paris. This meeting had been arranged by General Admiral Schultze, commanding all our naval forces in France; no witnesses were present.

Admiral Darlan's attitude was that of a dedicated French patriot. He made no bones about freely admitting to me his dislike for the British, and he was strongly in favor of a rapprochement between Germany and France. Naturally his country's interests held first place in his heart, and his one goal was the restoration of peace and the security of the French Colonial Empire.

I reported this conversation to Hitler in detail, and could only regret that German policy never found a way to reach an understanding with the French. Certainly the friendly cooperation of the French Colonial Empire would have been an invaluable safeguard against the Allied attack on us that came later via French Northwest Africa.

Our fears of what would happen in the Mediteranean theater if Malta was not eliminated were soon confirmed. At the end of October 1942 Field Marshal Montgomery's great British offensive against Rommel's army got underway. With his supply lines to Italy and Germany almost choked off, Rommel was compelled to fall back to Tunis, thus abandoning Italian North Africa to the enemy. On 8 November British and American troops under the over-all command of General Eisenhower made a surprise landing in Morocco and Algeria. From the position where their transports were first sighted, we drew the erroneous conclusion that the attack was to be made farther east, and consequently our countermeasures came too late. Although our U-boats and planes succeeded in sinking quite a few enemy ships, the British-American landings had already proceeded too far to be crushed.

Thus the enemy had established the first foothold for his ultimate offensive against Germany's "Fortress Europe" and scored an important success. The knell of the German-Italian operations in North Africa was sounding. In the spring of 1942, when the proposals had first been advanced for an assault on Malta, that key to the mid-Mediterranean could not have withstood a determined attack by the Axis Powers. But that opportunity had been lost by default. The situation in the Mediterranean, where for a time there was every prospect of success, had now changed to the exact opposite.

XX

The Final Break With Hitler

IN THE WEST, we had never deviated from our plan to use the German forces in northern Norway to inflict damage upon the enemy whenever opportunity presented. In March 1942 the *Tirpitz* put to sea to attack an Allied convoy, but missed contact because of blinding storm and fog. But the presence of the superbattleship in northern Norway forced the Allies to add two American battleships to their convoy escorts in order to guard against possible attack by the *Tirpitz.*

Combined operations in which submarines, planes, and destroyers all participated led to notable results in the following months. On 30 April the British cruiser *Edinburgh* was torpedoed by the *U-456,* under Lieutenant Commander Max-Martin Teichert, and two days later received the *coup de grâce* from a German destroyer squadron commanded by Captain Alfred Schulze-Hinrichs. In July an enemy convoy north of North Cape was dispersed by orders of the British Admiralty when it was reported that the *Tirpitz, Scheer,* and eight destroyers were at sea. This convoy, the Allied *PQ-17,* already mentioned, was screened by two battleships, an aircraft carrier, seven cruisers, and approximately twenty destroyers. Yet our U-boats and planes succeeded in sinking no fewer than 22 out of the 33 ships with which the convoy had started out.

Results would have been even greater if the German heavy forces had not been required to return to their bases in accordance with orders. As an aftermath of the *Bismarck's* loss, Hitler had issued strict instructions that our heavy ships should accept battle only after the enemy carriers had been crippled. Nevertheless, the heavy losses which the enemy convoys regularly suffered on the northern route led to the Allies' discontinuing the Murmansk run for the whole ensuing summer.

When, in the fall, the Allies resumed the run, they often sent out single ships. However, in the last days of December a large enemy convoy protected by a strong cruiser and destroyer escort, essayed the dangerous route again.

A German naval task force went out to intercept it: the heavy cruiser *Admiral Hipper,* the pocket battleship *Lützow,* and four destroyers, all under the tactical command of Vice Admiral Kummetz, Commander of Cruisers.

The intercepting force closed the convoy in time to make one attack before the twilight gave way to the long Arctic winter night. In the encounter with the convoy's escort, several enemy destroyers were severely damaged; two sank later. On our side one destroyer was sunk and the *Admiral Hipper* received a hit in the boilerroom which cut down its speed considerably.

As the enemy convoy was strongly screened by destroyers, Admiral Kummetz very wisely broke off action, since in the dark the torpedoes of the British destroyers offered a dangerous threat to our heavy ships. With so few of these left, it was not sound tactics to risk them in the uncertain visibility of an Arctic winter night, especially in light of the standing order that Admiral Kummetz had received not to risk his ships under conditions unfavorable to him. With his flagship already damaged and the darkness affording the enemy an unusual opportunity to get home with a torpedo attack, Vice Admiral Kummetz withdrew his ships to Alta Fjord.

It was an action which was to have unexpected consequences.

During the engagement itself, Admiral Kummetz had kept his radio as silent as possible. From the few short tactical messages he sent out it was impossible for us at headquarters to get any clear picture of what was happening. However, from a German U-boat in the vicinity there came a few code signals which gave the Naval War Staff and the Führer's General Headquarters the impression that Admiral Kummetz's heavy ships had actually got the enemy convoy under the guns of the *Hipper* and *Lützow.* Hitler jumped with joy as he waited for the confirming word that the enemy convoy had been annihilated.

But no confirming word—in fact no word at all—came from Admiral Kummetz, even after he arrived at Alta Fjord. The reason was that he did not wish to send out broadcast signals that enemy intelligence officers might monitor and decipher. He put his report on the land wire from Norway.

Unfortunately there had been a breakdown in the land wires in northern Norway. Instead of receiving the joyful word of the resounding success which he expected, the first details Hitler received came from the British broadcast communique, which stated that the German ships had been driven off after an unsuccessful attack, and that the convoy had got through unscathed.

Hitler thereupon flew in an uncontrolled rage, unjustifiably claiming that information had been deliberately withheld from him. He announced his intentions of immediately having all the heavy ships laid up, and recorded in the War Diary his view that the heavy ships were utterly useless—an entry made so that his opinion on the matter should be on record in black and white. He would not listen to any explanations by Vice Admiral Krancke, my personal representative at his headquarters, but ordered me by telephone to report to him immediately.

I requested time to obtain the necessary, accurate details, but it was some time before the Naval War Staff was able to get the full report of the operation from Admiral Kummetz in northern Norway. It was 6 January before I had the full picture of what had happened.

By then Hitler had recovered some self-control, but it was immediately clear to me that he would probably request my resignation.

For one whole hour Hitler, in the presence of Field Marshal Keitel, gave me a thorough dressing down. He reiterated his complaint about getting insufficient information. He went on to attack the Navy in a vicious and impertinent way. He disparaged its founding, belittled its every role since 1864, and stated that except for the submarines the entire history of the German Navy had been one of futility.

Göring's hand and influence was evident in everything Hitler said. Heretofore the heavy ships had been Hitler's special pride and interest. Now he damned them as being utterly worthless, needing the Air Force and the smaller ships to protect them every time they went to sea. He added, further, that in case of any Allied attack on Norway, the Air Force could be put to better use attacking the British Fleet than flying air cover for our ships. Next, he stated that the large ships no longer had any operational value, and that they should be laid up so that their guns could be put to use elsewhere —ashore, where guns were so urgently needed. Lastly he even criticized the scuttling of the German Fleet at Scapa Flow and attacked the spirit and morale of the Navy, which, up to then, he had always praised. It was glaringly obvious that this whole diatribe against the Navy which I commanded was intended for but one thing—to insult me personally. Hitler concluded by inviting me to hand in a memorandum in which I would be permitted to explain any views to the contrary that I might have as to the role of the heavy ships.

Throughout his remarks I had exerted my utmost self-control to keep silent. I felt it beneath the dignity of the senior officer of the Navy to attempt to contradict in detail such utterly prejudiced statements.

When he finished speaking, I quietly asked to be allowed to speak to him by myself. Field Marshal Keitel and the two stenographers left the room.

For ten long years I had advised Hitler in connection with the affairs of the Navy. He had not been a disinterested listener. He had had a lively interest in the ships and in naval problems. He had often expressed appreciation of the steadiness of the Navy, and of its accomplishments, and of its leadership. In my position it had been incumbent upon me to warn him time and again of the danger of any policy that might bring us into conflict with British seapower. Each time Hitler had assured me that he would never permit such a conflict to occur. Then when, contrary to his assurances, Germany had become involved in war with England and France, I had emphasized that England was the dangerous opponent and that all our greatest efforts should be directed against her. But in each case he had gone his own, and different, way.

The influence I had had on Hitler, I realized, was now on the wane. Perhaps my personal handling of the matter had been wrong, though in actuality our arguments had always been objective, never personal. Beginning with the Norwegian occupation, however, he had disregarded my suggestions. He had not been able to bring himself to remove Reich Commissioner Terboven, because the Commissioner had been an old member of the Nazi party, even though he knew Terboven's actions were harmful to the government. He had gone to war with Russia against my earnest protests. He had sympathized with me—but not helped me—in my efforts to obtain a bigger share of materials and manpower for the Navy, and especially for the U-boat building program. The strategical and tactical handling of the heavy ships by the Naval High Command had been at times too bold for Hitler; at other times, he had thought them too timid.

Now our disagreements had become more and more frequent, our points of agreement fewer and fewer. And the biting words he had just used to me, the uncontrollable anger he had permitted himself toward me, showed me that he did not regard this present disagreement as merely one of impersonal difference of opinion.

It was time for a parting of the ways.

For one thing, it was different now from the earlier times when I had considered resigning my post. Now, other, younger admirals had been coming along, gaining the necessary experience and proving their capability to command. I could ask to be relieved without having any fears that such an action might be detrimental to the service. Perhaps a new Commander in Chief might be able to obtain better support from Hitler than I had been obtaining of late.

Very quietly, then, I requested Hitler to relieve me from my position as Commander in Chief of the Navy, since in his remarks he had indicated that he was dissatisfied, no longer had confidence in me. Without this confidence I could not continue in office. Furthermore, I stated, I was now almost 67 years of age, and my health not of the best. It was time for a younger man to take over.

Hitler, as he always did when faced with firmness, began to calm down and try to smooth over his remarks. He said he had not meant to condemn the Navy as a whole, but only the heavy ships. Age was no drawback in a commander, as he had often proved by his selections. He begged me to realize that at this critical time—it was just before the fall of Stalingrad—my resignation would throw one more heavy responsibility on him. And he was already under criticism for having dismissed so many generals from their Army commands.

I repeated what I had said, that after today's discussion I could not possibly continue in office, since my authority was in question. However, in order not to allow the outside world to know of our disagreements, and to make the change of command as undisturbing as possible on the Navy, I would be happy to have my relief take place under whatever circumstances would be easiest for Hitler. If he wished to avoid giving the impression that a break had occurred, he could give me some more or less honorary assignment which would indicate that I was still actively connected with the Navy.

For the date of my relief, I suggested 30 January 1943, as that would be the tenth anniversary of my service as Commander in Chief of the Navy under his government, and the selection of this date would therefore make my relief understandable to the public.

Hitler realized from my words that my decision to resign was irrevocable, and he finally agreed. Before I left, he asked me to recommend, in writing, two officers from whom to select my successor.

The first name on the memorandum I handed Hitler was that of General Admiral Carls, who also was the senior of the two. Admiral Carls was Naval Group Commander North, and I thought his character and his vast knowledge of administration and the problems of naval warfare made him ideally suited for the post.

The second name on my list was that of Admiral Dönitz, Commander of the Submarine Force of the German Navy ever since I had appointed him to that position in 1935. He was without doubt our greatest authority on submarines and undersea warfare. If Hitler intended to give the U-boats the pre-eminent position in the German naval forces hereafter, then Admiral Dönitz would be the choice for Commander in Chief of the Navy.

Admiral Dönitz was Hitler's selection for the post.

At our conference on 6 January, Hitler had asked me to give him a memorandum containing my views on the function of battleships and cruisers, as well as why they were essential. This memorandum I handed him on 15 January. The entire Naval War Staff had cooperated in its preparation, and I had carefully checked it in detail. In unmistakable terms it stated that the scrapping of the heavy ships, such as Hitler intended, would be a clear-cut victory for our opponents and one which they would gain without the slightest risk or effort on their part. It would not only be accepted everywhere as a sign of weakness, but, considering the importance of naval warfare in the approaching final stages of the war, would be completely senseless. "England, whose whole warfare stands or falls with its control of its sea communications," the memorandum declared, "will consider the war as good as won if Germany scraps her ships."

On 30 January Hitler received me in my farewell call. He accepted my resignation in the friendliest terms, so phrased that the outside world could not know that it occurred over an unbridgeable difference of opinion. As a parting gesture I was given the title of Inspector General of the Navy—a post which had no active duty connected with it. If it had had, I would not have accepted it, as I wished above everything else to avoid anything that might make my successor's task more difficult.

As I had thought might be possible, Dönitz even succeeded in persuading Hitler by the end of February to abandon his plan to lay up the heavy ships, as he had vowed he would in his talk with me on 6 January—and he succeeded in doing this without any help from me. It was a personal victory for Dönitz, and gave me great satisfaction, too, in that he thus supported the view I had always championed as to the important mission of the heavy ships.

At the time of my farewell, Hitler had assured me that he intended to take full advantage in the future of my advice and counsel. This never happened. Only twice did he call upon me to do anything. The first occasion was when I was appointed to head the government delegation at the funeral of King Boris of Bulgaria, in Sofia, at the end of August. The second occasion was my designation to go to Budapest and present a motor boat to the Regent of Hungary, Admiral Miklos von Horthy, as a gift from Hitler.

On both occasions I went to the Führer's Headquarters beforehand to receive the necessary instructions for the task.

However, Hitler evidently thought it very important for everyone to think that we were still on the best of terms. Though I had retired to a quiet existence in the small suburb of Babelsberg, an officer from the Supreme Naval Command was appointed as my aide, and, in addition, an officer from each of the three branches of the armed services came every three or four weeks to brief me on the general war situation. And my comrades of the Navy did not forget me.

This quiet existence continued for a year and a half, during which time I devoted myself mainly to trying to get back my health after the constant strain and work from which I had had no relief since the beginning of World War I, almost. But though I kept carefully out of public life and scrupulously abstained from any political activities whatsoever, I found myself suddenly and dangerously involved when the attempt was made to assassinate Hitler on 20 July 1944.

I was so completely innocent of any complicity that the first I knew of the attempt was when I read the newspapers the next day, as neither my wife nor I had listened to the radio the night before. And the first I knew that I was a suspect was when an acquaintance asked me if I knew that I was reported to have taken part in the attempt.

Having been completely ignorant of even any plans on Hitler's life, I could only assume that someone had maliciously started rumors of my participation. I did not put it beyond the circles around Göring or Himmler to have started these rumors, knowing haw unfriendly was the feeling there toward me—but I also knew equally well that even such rumors could have exceedingly unpleasant consequences for me.

Therefore I telephoned to Rear Admiral Wagner, in the Führer's Headquarters, and asked for permission to call on Hitler at once. The next morning, 22 July, I flew to the Führer's Headquarters, where I first called on General Guderian, who had just been designated as Chief of the General Staff. The usual conference on the general war situation was about to begin, and though I greeted Hitler personally, it was in the middle of the rather large group gathered for the discussion.

Every one at the conference recognized that the situation on the Eastern Front was desperate. The front had been completely split apart by the Russians, and there were not enough reserves to close the gap. Göring's behavior at the discussion was deplorable. He sat next to Hitler and pretended to be giving extremely important suggestions and advice, to which Hitler paid not the slightest attention. In particular, Göring seemed anxious to make a good case for his "Hermann Göring Division" in the rapidly developing catastrophe.

After the conference I had lunch with Hitler, who then told me all about the attempt of his life, and later took me to see the actual scene of the attempt.

The blast of the assassination bomb had been so terrific that it seemed a miracle that every one present had not died in the explosion. Hitler himself had been only slightly wounded. Berger, the stenographer, had had both his legs blown off, and both Colonel Brand and General Korten, Chief of the General Staff of the Air Force, had been mortally wounded. General Jodl, along with Rear Admiral von Puttkamer and Captain Assmann, had suffered burns and other injuries. General Schmundt had received wounds in which tetanus afterwards developed, resulting in his death.

When I told Hitler goodby, he could surmise that I was very much concerned over the deterioration in the war situation, and he told me he was confident that the battleline in the east would soon be restored.

During the whole time at Headquarters I had had a loaded pistol in my pocket in case I should have any need for it. But apparently my prompt and unexpected appearance right at Hitler's Headquarters had so startled my enemies that they had hurriedly abandoned any ideas they might have had of trying to incriminate me in either the planning or the attempt on Hitler's life. I heard no more of it, and in a personal note to Hitler, Dr. Goerdeer vouched for my complete dissociation from anything political.

The details that now came to light about the assassination attempt and the organization behind it (to which quite a number of military leaders belonged) were a complete surprise to me. In all the years of my career no one had every approached me to influence me to any action against the State, nor had any one ventured to sound me out. Nor had Admiral Canaris, Chief of the Intelligence Section of the Joint Armed Forces Staff, ever reported to me the slightest suspicion that such a group had come into being.

Naturally, I knew that many people, including some in the armed services, were not in agreement with Hitler's policies or his taking Germany into war. I myself was among those who had often disagreed with Hitler. But it had never occurred to me to try to make my views respected in any other way than by open discussion, man to man, and throughout all my period in office I had often felt obligated to convey to Hitler my personal advices, remonstrances, or warnings.

For me, too, as for others, there existed a limit beyond which I would not have consented to follow Hitler. This had been made clear to him many times during the years of peace, and decisively so in 1943 when he had issued orders for the Navy which I could not accept. If war had not come, I probably would have asked to be relieved from my post at the end of 1939, or in 1940 at latest. But with the advent of the war I considered it my duty, as it was that of every other German, to aid in the country's defense as long as I could be of use. This is the natural and patriotic instinct of human beings everywhere. But to engage in a conspiracy or a *coup d'état* was something so contrary to my nature that it never crossed my mind.

On the political side, I had never required anyone to accept the National Socialist view unconditionally; on the contrary, I insisted always on the preservation of our old military traditions and values. But so long as I headed the Navy I would not have tolerated agitation or conspiracy by anyone against the Navy's discipline or its loyalty to the State which it had nurtured and sustained since 1921. The Navy had fulfilled its duties to the utmost that any nation could demand of its soldiers or sailors. In the Navy there existed no condition conducive to political action such as a *coup d'état*. The Navy, and I as its leader, could follow no course except that of loyalty to the government—the same loyalty we had given to the Weimer Republic under Presidents Ebert and Hindenburg.

But from the facts that became public after the attempt on Hitler's life, and the speeches and articles engendered by it, it was evident that a deep cleft had opened up in the mass of the German people. The popular joy in the peacetime foreign policy successes of Hitler had disappeared with the prolongation of the war. Apart from the understandable desire for a speedy end of hostilities, there existed in many circles a deep dissatisfaction with Hitler's leadership.

One great factor in this feeling was that by interference, dismissals, court-martial, and other measures, Hitler had undermined the esteem and public confidence which the military leaders had always enjoyed in the country. Then the war situation, which had initially seemed so promising with all the brilliant early victories, had now deteriorated so that hope for a victorious conclusion of the war had sadly faded. The German people had always had great faith in its regular armed forces, but now special military organizations such as the SS and the "Hermann Göring Division" were being formed outside the Army, and this many people did not approve of. While the members of these units did their military duty well at all times, the political roles which their leaders played placed their reputation as military commanders under wide suspicion.

The Army, which had always been considered the senior service in Germany, was bitter over the fact that Hitler himself had personally assumed the position of Commander in Chief after Field Marshal von Brauchitsch's resignation in the spring of 1942. They felt that one of the regular service generals, who had already proved their capabilities in numerous battles, should have been made head of the Army. That Hitler, in addition to his duties as Head of the State, took unto himself at the same time the command of the Army was thought by many to be an inefficient combination of administrative duties. To have a service with the vast tradition and reputation of the German Army, and one with numerous distinguished generals, dominated by an overburdened politician with no military accomplishments whatsoever rankled.

In contradistinction to the Navy, with its single, tight command structure, the Army was not under the concentrated control of one single responsible individual. Here were numerous functions, each under its own general, and many of them co-equal in status, so that Hitler had to deal directly with many generals instead of just one. This resulted in his being burdened with innumerable individual problems requiring continuous discussions and individual decisions when the Commander in Chief should have been able to restrict himself to major problems and policies only. The imposition of a political leader at the top of the Army's command structure was an unnatural condition which undermined confidence in the top command and the directives issuing from it. Senior generals received often conflicting and frequently impracticable orders which resulted in confusion and conflicts, to the great detriment of unified, effective operations.

Feeling at the time that Hitler's taking over in person the command of the Army was a fatal mistake, I had deliberated as to whether tactful suggestions might induce him to forego the arrangement. But before I could offer any argument, I would naturally have to have an answer ready in case he asked me whom I would then recommend for the position.

The first names that came to my mind were those of Field Marshal von Rundstedt and Field Marshal von Mannstein. If Hitler thought von Rundstedt's age was against him, then von Mannstein, whom I regarded as the most capable of the senior generals, would be a suitable man. However, Hitler had had personal disagreements with von Mannstein which might make cooperation between the two impossible.

I mentioned my views to General Schmundt, who was in Hitler's confidence. I told General Schmundt that I thought each of the great fighting Fronts—the eastern and the western—ought to have its own general in command over all the armies on that front, and that one of these two senior commanders ought also to be Commander in Chief of the Army as a whole. However, the suggestion never got anywhere, as, for one reason, there was too much difference of opinion in the Army itself as to which general was best fitted for the supreme role.

The net result of everything—the war casualties, the reduced standard of living, and other domestic difficulties—was that a number of important people, including some very high military officers, came to believe that the only way out of Germany's ever more critical situation was to get rid of the Head of the State through a *coup d'état*.

It is not within my capabilities or desires to attempt to judge men who felt it necessary to tread a different path from mine. If a man in a responsible position, with a knowledge of the whole complex situation, feels compelled by his conscience and the interests of the Fatherland to take extraordinary measures, then he must justify his actions to his conscience alone. If his motives are irreproachable, and if in his concern for Germany he considers it necessary, right, and also feasible, by a *coup d'état* to ward off the danger threatening his people, then I cannot refuse him my compassionate respect.

Of the men involved in the occurrence of 20 July—the attack on Hitler's life—I knew only a few intimately. General Beck, with whom I had been acquainted for many years, I knew to be of unimpeachable character. There were others, I am convinced, who, with honest hearts and impeccable motives, felt themselves obliged to do what they did. I respect the decision of their own consciences. They bear the responsibility for it before history and the German people, just as I bear mine.

I am convinced that none of the men whom I have described above had any other intention than that of replacing a bad government with a better one, and of bringing the war to a tolerable end. Whether this last would have been possible is a question that can scarcely be answered, since the revolt was not successful. It is doubtful, however, that our enemies would have departed from the demand for Germany's unconditional surrender, which had been jointly decided upon by them as their war aim in their Casablanca Conference of January 1943.

After the war it became known that there were some individuals among those opposed to the government who actually aided and abetted the enemy by giving them plans and details of future operations of our forces. With such men I can find nothing in common. Whoever, in wartime, supports the enemies of his country and thereby betrays his own Fatherland to injury stands on another ground than I.

The events which followed the revolt and the attempt on Hitler's life represent an especially unhappy chapter for me. Despite my personal attitude toward *coups d'état,* I had no sympathy with the form of justice which the government subsequently imposed upon the participants and their accessories. It is but natural that after an attempted *coup d'état* the government acts with vigor, digging deep into not only the facts of the conspiracy but the reasons behind it as well. However, a circus type of trial, like that conducted by the People's Court, under Dr. Freisler as presiding judge, is not judicial procedure. The methods with which the trials were carried out can but impair the respect which all citizens should have for the instruments of their government. In addition, I had personal experience in the case of former Minister of Defense Gessler, with the persecutions thus visited upon suspected people.

Dr. Gessler had had the important portfolio of Minister of Defense of Germany in the cabinet from 1920 to 1928. A member of the German Democratic Party, he had earned my esteem not only because of his abilities as a statesman but also because of his frank and upright convictions. I had kept in contact with him after his retirement to a small farm in the Allgäu district of Bavaria. In 1943 Dr. Gessler wrote me that he would like to get in touch with some of the higher Nazi leaders, as he was seriously concerned with the reaction of the people in Bavaria and Württemberg toward some of the things that were happening. He wanted to advocate a change in the sort of propaganda the government was putting out in those areas.

When I went to receive my instructions just before leaving for my visit to Admiral Horthy in Hungary in 1943, I took advantage of the opportunity to inform Hitler of Dr. Gessler's request, and to ask him to appoint a suitable person to discuss these political affairs with Dr. Gessler. On this occasion Hitler of his own volition praised Dr. Gessler as a person of loyal and irreproachable character. Accordingly Himmler was directed to send a high official of the police to see Dr. Gessler. Dr. Gessler then advised this officer of the dissatisfaction of the Bavarian population and the revival of a separationist movement there, none of which was being remedied any by the mishandling of the public information officers. Dr. Gessler's action in this matter had been that of a conscientious and loyal patriot.

Hence it was a shock to me when, a little after 20 July 1944, I received a letter from Dr. Gessler bearing the postmark of a prison camp near Fürstenburg, in Mecklenburg. In it he told me that despite his long government service and his loyal actions of 1943, he had been accused of being involved with the attempted *coup d'état* against Hitler. The charge was based solely upon a trip he had made to former Minister Fehr, of the Center Party, and a meeting with former Minister Hermes, occurring about the time of the attempt on Hitler's life. What Dr. Gessler wished was for me to arrange an immediate audience for him with Hitler wherein to prove his innocence, which both Hitler and I were convinced of anyway.

I lost no time in telephoning Admiral Wagner, of Hitler's staff, as a result of which Hitler ordered that Dr. Gessler be questioned at once. I immediately informed Dr. Gessler of this by letter both to him and his wife. (These letters, I heard later, were never delivered.) Consequently I was astounded when, two weeks later, Admiral Wagner told me that he had been informed by an SS representative at the Führer's Headquarters that Dr. Gessler had confessed before an investigative body that he had not only known beforehand of the attempt on Hitler's life but had been involved in it.

I naturally assumed that the agency which had investigated Dr. Gessler's conduct had told the truth. To attempt to do anything further would be hopeless on my part, and I wrote Dr. Gessler and his wife to that effect. These letters, too, I later learned, never reached their destinations.

All these events took place in the fall of 1944. In March 1945 I received a telephone call from Director Schmidt of the Engine Plant at Augsburg-Nürnberg. He told me that Dr. Gessler had just been released from concentration camp and was now in Hedwig Hospital in Berlin, trying to regain his health sufficiently to make the rest of the journey home.

I visited the hospital right away and found Dr. Gessler lying in bed, broken both mentally and physically. I asked him to tell me what had happened.

He told me he had not received my letters—neither the second nor the first, in which I had told him that I was sure his actions of November 1943 would prove to Hitler, without a doubt, his integrity and loyalty. He then told me the almost unbelievable story of his treatment at the concentration camp.

At first this treatment had been very bad, but then had improved somewhat, evidently after receipt of Hitler's orders for an immediate hearing. This hearing, however, had been nothing but a torture session. Sharp wedges had been driven between his fingers, causing excruciating pain—so much so that he had to be given injections to bring him back to consciousness. I myself saw the scars of the wedges between Dr. Gessler's fingers. When Dr. Gessler

Grand Admiral Raeder reading a statement to the court.

AT WILHELMSHAVEN MEMORIAL

Grand Admiral Dönitz, Naval Chaplain Ronneberger, Grand Admiral Raeder, and Mrs. Raeder leaving the Memorial Church after its dedication on June 2, 1957.

protested against the torture, he had been informed that it had been given by Hitler's specific orders.

All the documents in his case, he told me, had later been sent to the People's Court in Berlin, where the Court found nothing criminal or even blameworthy in them. Only then, after close confinement for more then six months, had he been released, although his innocence should have been established from the first.

I telephoned Dr. Gessler's wife the glad news that he had been released, and then with Director Schmidt's help I arranged for him to be taken back to his home.

This story, with its brutal details, Dr. Gessler told me with the greatest reluctance, begging me even then to tell it to no one else because he was "so ashamed for Germany." I wished to bring the matter directly to Hitler's attention. He begged me not to do that either, as one of the conditions upon which he had obtained his release was his written promise not to reveal any of the happenings during the period of his confinement in the camp.

That such a thing could happen in Germany, and to an innocent person like Dr. Gessler, made me so bitter that that very same day I took off the gold Party emblem that Hitler had personally conferred upon me in 1937, and I ground it to bits. I had never been a member of the Nazi Party—something generally forbidden to officers of the regular services—and had accepted the emblem only as a mark of honor conferred upon me personally by the Head of the State. From now on I could never again regard it as a mark of honor.

Like Dr. Gessler, I was ashamed that such things were possible in Germany.

XXI

National and Personal

WHEN Germany capitulated on 7 May 1945 I was in Babelsberg Hospital.

Hitler had died by his own hand just one week before.

Out of the hospital 16 May, I immediately visited Colonel Pimenow, head of the Russian Kommandantur which had been set up in Potsdam. Colonel Pimenow assured me that guards would be posted at my house to provide protection for my family.

Before the guards arrived, however, I was taken by truck to Caputh, near Potsdam, where a Russian Intelligence Group had evidently been established. That was on 17 May. That evening Colonel Pimenow intervened directly for my release. I was released with a personal security guard.

Three days later Colonel Pimenow visited me, bringing with him a general on the staff of Marshal Schokow. They asked what I intended to do now. I replied that I wanted to write a book about my career similar to the one I had written about cruiser warfare in World War I.

That same evening I had another physical breakdown, a heart attack. The draft and the jolting I had been exposed to in my Russian truck ride to Caputh had been rough on me. For several days my condition was critical, and for weeks after that I was confined to bed.

Colonel Pimenow sent me special food on several occasions to aid in my recovery. On 23 June he sent word that he would like me to report to a certain general's office. The discussion, he said, would not last more than an hour and a half, but he added that I would probably be required to go to Moscow in the near future.

I was taken not to any general's headquarters, but to Lichtenberg Prison. There I was incarcerated in a single cell under the strict custody of a general who obviously was a member of the OGPU, the Russian state police. My jailer told me that I was a prisoner of war, and that after a week or two at Lichtenberg I would be taken to Moscow. As a consolation he stated that I could continue the writing which I had already begun at home. A few days later my wife managed to prevail on the authorities to let her reside in Lichtenberg also to take care of me, as my health had gotten worse. While she was with me, our house in Babelsberg was plundered from top to bottom.

Around 8 July my wife and I were flown to Moscow, under a most hostile set of guards, and for twenty-four hours were not given a mouthful of food.

It was not until after we were received by the two highest generals of the Commissariat of the Interior that our situation improved. We were then put up in a well-furnished country house just outside Moscow, with one or two officers in constant attendance. The two generals from the Commissariat of the Interior visited us often and engaged me in long conversations, asking interestedly about the state of my notes, but never giving any definite word as to when my hearing would take place.

My stay in Moscow lasted three months, during which time I made quite a collection of notes, partly at the suggestion of the Russians and partly of my own volition. With good food and medical attention now, my rundown physical condition improved. But the unhappy end of the war and my harrowing experiences of recent years and months threw me into a deep emotional depression.

Inevitably my notes, which I had to prepare without any reference material available, and with only my memory to rely on, suffered. I tried to recreate as many experiences and problems of the past as possible in order to give them an orderly analysis when I began the actual writing. These notes were later taken from me. My prosecutors tried to use them against me at the Nürnberg trials, making no allowance for the fact that these were rough notes intended for my private use alone and representing neither final judgments nor definitive evaluations. This was particularly true of my descriptions of several public figures.

At six o'clock on the morning of 17 October 1945 I was taken from the house without advance warning. My wife, who was left behind, was told that I was merely going to Moscow for a few hours' questioning. But once outside, they told me I was being taken to Berlin, instead, though I would return in a few days. My new escort, a general I did not know, took me first to the Commissariat of the Interior and then to the airport.

During the flight and, afterward, in Berlin, I was in the custody of a lieutenant colonel and one other Russian officer. They kept close watch over me in the house in Babelsberg, where I was quartered along with the journalist Hans Fritzche. He had been under arrest in Lubjanka Prison, and had been brought from Moscow on the same plane with me. Here at Babelsberg we were given copies of the indictment which had been brought against us by the Allied International Military Tribunal for the trial of war criminals.

This was the first time I had heard of war crimes.

As I would need my Moscow notes for my defense, I asked that they be sent to me. A few days later the notes were given to me, along with a deposition I was to sign. When I examined the notes and deposition, however, I refused to sign such a statement since it was a fabricated jumble of excerpts from my notes, taken out of context, erroneously translated, and generally misleading. By such cunning excerpting out of context and misleading translations the Tribunal had compiled a document which, if I had been foolish enough to sign it, would have taken on the appearance of a confession.

I wrote a full explanation of the inaccuracies and misrepresentations in the deposition to the General Secretary of the International Military Tribunal. I never heard what became of my explanation. My notes were taken from me again, and a few days later Fritzsche and I were taken by automobile from Berlin to Nürnberg, where we arrived on a bleak November night. Like the other defendants who had preceded us or who came after us, we were incarcerated in individual cells of the Nürnberg Criminal Prison, under glaring electric lights.

The Nürnberg trials began on 20 November 1945. Among the defendants, Admiral Dönitz and I were accused as war criminals in naval warfare.

We were given scant time to prepare for our defense. For my personal counsel I had chosen the well-known Hamburg lawyer, Dr. Siemers, while Admiral Dönitz chose Fleet Judge Kranzbühler, who had won an enviable reputation in the Navy for his splendid capabilities and high standard of conduct. In the technical field of naval warfare Fleet Judge Kranzbühler supervised the defense of both of us.

I had not previously known Dr. Siemers except by reputation, but in my opinion this was an advantage rather than a disadvantage; having no personal ties, he would bring to the trial an absolutely impersonal, unbiased attitude and thus would be able to analyze all points of the accusation. This was important because the defendants were not being accused merely as individuals but as representatives of the services and the German people themselves. Dr. Siemers' conduct of this phase of the indictments was dignified, yet brilliant to an extent for which I shall always feel indebted to him.

For the phase of the trial dealing with operations at sea, and, in fact, for the conduct of the naval warfare as a whole, Fleet Judge Kranzbühler conducted a defense that could not have been excelled. Not only did he have vast professional and factual knowledge, and an intuitive appreciation of what was relevant, but in addition he had a tremendously engaging personality.

The charges against me were conduct of naval warfare contrary to the rules of civilized warfare, and preparing the German Navy for aggressive war and then actually conducting aggressive war by the naval operations against Norway. Admiral Dönitz was similarly accused, except for the charge of preparing for a war of aggression.

The Nürnberg trials were unique in that the victors sat as judges on the conquered, and the actions of the vanquished only were on trial while those of the victors were not open to question at all.

Such a limited procedure can not result in justice, for while the accused were being tried and judged on points which had never existed in international law before, the actions of the victors were held unimpeachable.

It is universally recognized that, in every war, the actions of any nation are influenced substantially by the behavior of its opponent. Hence any verdict handed down by a victor over his vanquished foe must lose in credibility and acceptance if the same rules do not apply to the victor also. And the judges at Nürnberg, the International Military Tribunal, adopted as a basic clause in their procedures that no mention should be allowed in court of any Allied actions or crimes. Furthermore, even the Versailles Treaty was not permitted to be introduced except insofar as Germans and Germany were accused of violating it. The decisive part it had played in all the developments in Germany since 1920 was not allowed to be mentioned.

It soon became evident in other respects, too, that the Nürnberg trials were not a court of justice in the usual sense. Instead, they had developed solely out of the political considerations of our opponents, and their main purpose was a political one—that of damning the whole German nation as an international outlaw. It was not merely Hitler or the National Socialist Government, but the German people as a whole who were to be indicted as the sole criminals, guilty of waging a malevolent war of aggression. In this way the Allies were going to vindicate before the world, as justified and necessary, their own war measures against Germany and the severity of their long continuing occupation policy. This vindictive attitude is revealed by the fact that this sort of Military Tribunal was set up only in the cases of Germany and Japan, and not in the case of Italy, the third member of the Axis.

After the First World War, an acknowledgment that Germany had been responsible for the war was inserted as one of the clauses in the Versailles Treaty, and Germany had had to sign this before she could secure peace. When this citation of guilt had begun to be questioned later, as it inevitably would be, the very foundations of the Versailles Treaty were shaken.

The Allies, this time, were going to avoid any such development again. In place of a flimsy confession obviously forced from Germany at gunpoint, there was to be an extensive public trial in which the guilt of Germany for the whole war as well as its consequences was to be proved before the world.

Instead, I think the trial proved beyond question that there was no conspiracy of the German people, or of any definite segment of them, against the peace of the world. Similarly, the prosecution's thesis that a regular group of military personalities existed whose purpose was to instigate a war of aggression has been utterly refuted. The prosecution's indictment of so-called criminal groups wherein charges were lodged against the 3,000,000 leading members of the Nazi Party, the 500,000 members of the SS and an equal number of the SD, and the 2,000,000 members of the SA, all fell flat. Even the accusation against the 50,000 members of the Gestapo failed. In every case the Court held that membership in such a group was not grounds for prosecution; the actual crime had to be proved against the individual.

In this one respect, at least, truly democratic concepts of justice validated themselves. The broad, all inclusive accusations with which the trial began soon were so substantially reduced by the testimony presented and the decisions rendered, that no longer was there even any attempt to pin the badge of collective guilt on the German people.

This was an extremely important conclusion, and was evidence that the court refused in some cases to be bound to a purely political viewpoint. At the same time, in the field of criminal jurisdiction, the trial produced indisputable evidence that numerous crimes, many of the most horrible type, had been penetrated by certain National Socialists. Yet, aside from the perpetrators, no one in Germany had the slightest presentiment that any such things were going on.

For me this was the most depressing part of the whole trial. Public knowledge of the crimes in the concentration camps and elsewhere had been sealed off by the impenetrable wall of silence the perpetrators had thrown around the scene of their crimes. From the evidence of the former Prussian Minister of the Interior, Severing, as well as from the testimony of some of the numerous military figures who were heard at the trial, it developed that isolated individual cases had occasionally come to light, but the huge extent of the crimes, as well as their horrible nature, came as a complete shock to the vast majority of Germans. The shock was the greater in that it was not just one group of criminal political elements that was involved, but the head of the State, Hitler himself, had been in many cases not only an accessory, but even the instigator of the crimes. To most of Germany, Hitler's true face came to light for the first time at the Nürnberg trials.

Thus the trials developed along two distinctly separate lines: the political, of which every German could feel ashamed, and the military, which was quite a different matter. On the whole, in the military field the progress of the trial produced a picture quite different from the one the prosecutor had presented at the start. The biased line which the trials in the military zone took was the result not only of the political roots in which they had originated, but also of the two completely different systems of justice under which the prosecution and the defense had grown up. In Anglo-Saxon court procedure, which was the system under which the trials were largely conducted, a trial is a sort of all-out contest between prosecution and defense, after which the court hands down a verdict. The prosecution does not try, in its part, simply to get at the unconditional truth, but endeavors to win its case against the accused by any and all available means. Similarly, the defense contests the prosecution at all points, regardless of where truth and justice may lie. This was completely the opposite of the legal system of Germany, where both sides are committed primarily to establish the truth or falsity of the matter. The Anglo-Saxon system was both new and outlandish to the German defendants and their counsel, and hence made the presentation of our side of the case more difficult. The way in which our counsel adapted themselves to the Anglo-Saxon methods of legal procedure, and their success in presenting our case, was beyond praise.

Through a long and honorable history the Anglo-Saxon trial procedure has proved itself worthy, but it can not result in justice unless both prosecution and defense have equal opportunities to function. This was not the case at Nürnberg.

The prosecutors had had many months to prepare their bills of indictment. They had seized all archives and documents known to exist, and had ransacked them for incriminating evidence. Since all the German archives had fallen into enemy hands, the number of records and papers available to the prosecution was unlimited. From this mass of documents, prejudicial items had been gathered, often completely out of context, and the whole welded into a weapon against the accused.

On the other hand, the counsel for the accused were not allowed access to this wealth of documents in Allied hands. They were allowed only such material as the prosecution was willing to give them. Anything else that might go to exonerate the accused could be obtained only with the greatest difficulty, in the most roundabout ways, in the most incomplete form. A natural result was that only evidence from German sources was available for the defense counsel. To ascertain certain relevant facts, like the Allied intent and plan for attacking Norway, for example, it would have been necessary to look into foreign archives; this was never permitted.

In another way, also, the defense was at a decided disadvantage in preparing its case. Witnesses for the defense had to be brought in from all parts of Germany to bombed-out Nürnberg and had the most extreme difficulty in finding lodgings, and defense counsel similarly had the same trouble finding even the most primitive working space. Owing to the rigid nature of the confinement in which the defendants were held, it was impossible for their counsels to confer confidentially with their clients.

Finally, the whole atmosphere under which the trials were held was completely hostile. All newspapers, all radio broadcasting stations, were under direct supervision of the Allies, and hence put out only news items prejudicial to the accused. The fact that the defense counsels, particularly my own, were so successful with their limited facilities while the prosecution's advantages were so overwhelming, is proof of the exceptional capabilities of our defenders.

As my chief witnesses I had called Vice Admiral Schulte Mönting, my aide for many years and later my Chief of Staff; and former Minister of the Interior Severing.

Severing's calm and assured appearance in giving testimony on the stand was most impressive. He refrained from any propagandistic or polemical utterances, confining himself entirely and objectively to the areas on which he was intimately informed, such as the early rearmament of the Navy, in particular. The warmth with which he defended me moved me deeply. He testified that it was at the direction of the German Government that the Navy's expansion after 1928, contrary to the restrictive terms of the Versailles Treaty, had taken place. He also testified that he had heard of the mass murders of the Jews and others only after the collapse of the Hitler regime. In answer to questioning by my counsel as to whether he and his friends in the Social Democrat Party during the Nazi regime had had support from abroad, his reply was both frank and courageous.

"If you are asking me," he said, "whether my political friends, in their fight against the Hitler regime, even by so much as protest, found support from foreigners whom you might call Anti-Fascists, I must answer no! Unfortunately, no! We were shocked when members of Britain's Labor Party who had no status as government delegates, accepted Hitler's hospitality, and then, back in England, praised Chancellor Hitler as a friend of peace. And in this respect I name Philip Snowden, former Labor Cabinet Minister, and George Lansbury, leader of the Labour Party."

At this the president of the court silenced Severing and would admit no further testimony on this point. This was the sort of evidence they were determined should not be heard.

Vice Admiral Schulte Mönting was cross-examined long and minutely, both by the counsel for the defense and the prosecution. His excellent memory, the clarity of his answers, and the effectiveness of his analysis of the Navy's problems, both in peace and war, made an obvious impression on his hearers.

Very effective also was the testimony of Baron von Weizsäcker, the former Secretary of the Foreign Office. At the time of the Norwegian operation, he stated, he had not agreed with me that the Allies were already planning Norway's occupation themselves, but now he knew that I had been quite right. He also testified that the German naval forces stationed in Norway during the occupation had always enjoyed an excellent reputation among the Norwegians, as affirmed by many of the latter personally to Baron von Weizsäcker.

The numerous witnesses who provided testimony, not only in

person before the court, but in affidavits, letters, and other documents sent from all sections of the country, have earned my eternal gratitude, especially as numbers of these were not even known to me personally. In general, all the witnesses who testified for Admiral Dönitz and me through their bearing and appearance impressed everyone most favorably with the German Navy, even though many of them had been brought directly from Allied prison camps. By comparison with the straightforward, convincing testimony of these witnesses, the evidence presented by the prosecution, and especially its written documentation and affidavits, appeared both feeble and biased.

For my own part, during my long and trying appearance on the stand, I tried to give a clear and conscientious account of everything that I had been connected with, both before and during the war, to the best of my recollection. For, except for a few documents and parts of my notes which our counsel had been able to obtain despite tremendous difficulties, my memory was all I had to go on.

From the very beginning Admiral Dönitz and I had been in agreement on one thing: the important thing here at stake was the historical justification of German naval warfare. The indictment of the way the German Navy had conducted the war, and especially its submarine operations, was more important to us than any charge brought against us personally. Compared to the good name of the German Navy, what happened to us as individuals was of no consequence.

As a mere matter of course, both Admiral Dönitz and I considered that ours was the full responsibility for everything that had occurred during the years in which we respectively were at the head of the Navy. This was a view which German military leaders had always held. Hence I emphatically held that any charges made against Admiral Dönitz in connection with the U-boat warfare while I was Commander in Chief of the Navy were utterly unjustified.

It was our conduct of submarine warfare that was the principal subject of attack by the prosecution. But it was just in this sphere that we had moved most carefully. Before any policies or directives were issued in connection with our U-boats, we had had each step carefully checked by the legal division of the Naval War Staff so that we could be sure that we were taking every precaution against any violation of the rules of international law in regard to war at sea. It had been Admiral Dönitz's determination, as well as mine, that no actions should be taken, no orders or directives issued, which could lead to a violation of the moral law of the sea as it is recognized by all civilized peoples. I knew positively that Admiral Dönitz, as Commander of the Submarine Forces, had on several occasions deliberately put some of our U-boats and their crews in positions of utmost danger from enemy attack in order to insure the safety of surviving crew members of torpedoed ships.

Despite this, the prosecution was determined to prove us guilty by use of every means possible. In contrast to this was the attitude shown by the written depositions of the British Admiralty and of Admiral Nimitz, American Naval Commander in Chief in the Pacific, in our favor.

This was the one instance in which the court relaxed its prohibition on our obtaining access to the confiscated German archives for our defense, or on our obtaining evidence in foreign papers or from foreign witnesses. In the case of naval warfare, however, Fleet Judge Kranzbühler had succeeded, after repeated attempts, in obtaining permission for one of our assistant defenders, Junior Captain Meckel, to sift through and to evaluate the documents on German naval warfare which had been sequestered in London. In addition the court granted Kranzbühler's request for permission to question officers and functionaries of the British and American Navies.

With the assistance of Dr. Siemers, Fleet Judge Kranzbühler prepared and submitted a questionnaire to both of these organizations, and received answers in due time.

From the answers of the British Admiralty, it was established, and accepted by the court, that at the very beginning of the war the British Navy had begun arming British merchant ships in accordance with directives already laid down in 1938 in their *Handbook for the Merchant Marines*. It had also sent ships out under armed escort. British merchant ships had orders to report all submarines they sighted, and for this purpose were made part of the British Navy's reconnaissance and warning system. On 1 October

1939 the British Navy had directed British merchant ships to ram German submarines whenever possible. And on 8 May 1940 the British naval forces had received orders to sink, *without warning,* any ship encountered at night in the Skagerrak.

Admiral Nimitz was equally frank and helpful in his answer to the questionnaire. Immediately upon outbreak of the war with Japan, he avouched, the United States Government had declared the whole Pacific Ocean a war zone, and had ordered all-out war against Japan. In this war zone, the largest ocean area in the world, United States submarines had authority to attack, without warning, all merchant ships sighted. Hospital ships, and other vessels proceeding under security protection for humanitarian purposes, were the only ships exempted from this directive.

The crucial question on the questionnaire sent to Admiral Nimitz was this: "Were American submarines forbidden, either by specific order or recognized practice, to take measures for rescue of the passengers and crews of ships sunk without warning *if the safety of the submarines themselves were endangered by these measures?"*

The unequivocal reply of the United States admiral was as follows:

"In general practice, the United States submarines did not rescue enemy survivors if such an attempt meant an unusual additional risk, or if the submarine was thereby endangered in the further execution of its tasks."

The information from the highest, most authoritative officers in the two great navies with whom we had been at war was of utmost significance in arriving at any just appraisal of the conduct of war operations by the German Navy. It proved to the Nürnberg court that the German Navy had conducted its own naval warface in accordance with the same rules and customs that were observed by the two largest seapowers with whom it was engaged. As a result, the International Military Tribunal completely vindicated the German Navy in its methods of warfare, certifying that such warfare had been conducted in full accord with the rules of international law. Thus Admiral Dönitz and I obtained a victory in what was to us the most important part of the trial. And the acquittal was the more significant in that it had been achieved through the substantial support of our former enemies, particularly those whose forces had most vigorously opposed us in the hardfought submarine war.

Fleet Judge Kranzbühler's arguments in rebuttal to the prosecution in connection with German naval warfare were dignified, yet convincing. In his own final summation advocating my acquittal, Dr. Siemers refuted the prosecution's charges at all points. In his brilliant pleading he concerned himself particularly with the charges against us in connection with the Norwegian operations, bringing the Allies' plans and intentions in for comparison.

Primarily on this charge of conducting aggressive war, the court did not agree fully with Dr. Siemers' rebuttal, and eventually brought in a verdict against me "on the basis of the evidence now available."

This basis for the verdict and sentence against me was incomprehensible to me, since the court itself had limited the amount of material presented as evidence when it rejected the request of our counsel to introduce the official British papers and directives and documents dealing with their side of the Norwegian operations. When this documentation was later made public, particularly in Prime Minister Winston Churchill's own memoirs, any grounds for the Nürnberg court's verdict and sentence against us in connection with the occupation of Norway were completely demolished.

In my own final appearance before the court, I made a brief summation:

"The conclusion of this trial, after all the witnesses have testified, brings a *dénouement* favorable to Germany, but unexpected by the prosecution. Unimpeachable testimony has acquitted the German people—and with them all others under the same accusations as I—of the frightful guilt of knowingly acquiescing in the murder of millions of Jews and other people, if not actually participating in it. Despite the prosecution's knowledge of the truth gained from previous hearings, its attempt, in moralist guise, to defame the whole German people through all these accusations, indictments, and cross-examinations, has completely collapsed.

"Another result, almost equally important to me, is that the legality and honorable nature of the German Navy's conduct of war has been publicly proved in this trial. The Navy stands before this court and before the world with a clean escutcheon and an unspotted flag. The attempts in Shawcross's[1] arguments to place the U-boat war on the same plane as the terrible atrocities elsewhere, we can conscientiously and emphatically reject. They are not tenable for a moment in the light of the undisputed testimony. The charge that the Navy 'never intended to live up to the laws of naval warfare' is completely refuted. Refuted also is the charge that the Naval War Staff and its Chief showed 'contempt for international law'; instead it has been proved that from the first to the last they honestly sought to bring modern naval warfare into accord with the requirements of international law and of humanity, on the same basis as our enemies.

"I regret that the prosecution tried repeatedly to defame me and the Navy, as evidenced by its presenting a second and amended trial brief, which, however, differed from the first only in the number and sharpness of its insulting deformations. The obvious explanation is that the prosecution itself recognized the weakness of its accusations.

"I also feel that the British and American charges did their own navies a disservice when they depicted, as inferior in morale and spirit, the German Navy which gave the Allied naval forces such stern and honorable opposition at sea for so many years. I am convinced, however, that the Allied Admiralties understand me, and know that they did not fight against a criminal.

"I can, therefore, account for the attitude of the prosecution only by my recognition of the fact that they, and their representatives, showed little understanding of the fundamental principles of military conduct and the profession of arms. Consequently they would seem scarcely qualified to pass judgment on military honor.

"In summary, I wish to state that I did my duty as a soldier because it was my conviction that I could thus serve the German people and the Fatherland, for which I lived and for which I am ready at any time to give my life. The only ground on which anyone could even have suspected me of being guilty would be the mistaken belief that I had gone outside of my military duties to

[1] Sir Hartley Shawcross was the British representative on the staff of the prosecution.

involve myself to some extent in political affairs. This does not take into consideration the fact that my position was purely military, and, furthermore, that such political involvement would have been contrary to my whole career as well as to the traditions of the German armed forces. Any such activity would have been a moral guilt to the German people, but could never, never stamp me as a war criminal. Such guilt can never be established before a criminal court of man, but only before God."

The verdict of the court, and the sentences, were handed down on 30 September and 1 October 1946. To me they were in many respects a great surprise, not insofar as they related to me, but as they related to others of the defendants.

From the moment when I saw how the trial was to be conducted, I fully expected that I would receive some sentence. Although acquitted of the charge of "committing crimes against humanity," I was held guilty of preparing for and waging a war of aggression, this latter based upon the Norwegian operation. I received a sentence of imprisonment for life. Admiral Dönitz was similarly sentenced for his part in the Norwegian operations, but received a lesser prison term of ten years on the grounds that what he had done had only been in a "professional status."

This verdict and sentence against Admiral Dönitz was to me completely incomprehensible, because all the accusations against him had been practically disproved, and the reasons given for his punishment were absolutely insufficient.

But the thing that really shocked me was the sentencing of Field Marshal Keitel and Colonel General Jodl to die by hanging. I had not thought that any court of military origin could inflict this particularly disgraceful form of death on high ranking military officers, for whom the customary forms of execution even when proven guilty of common crimes, has been shooting by a military firing squad.

The adjudication of this disgraceful form of death was apparently distasteful to many of our opponents: The American generals who were present rose and left the room before the death sentences of the German generals were pronounced.

The close relationship in which the two generals had been tied to Hitler through their official positions was decidedly prejudicial to their defense. As Hitler's daily co-workers they were charged with the responsibility of all the military commands and orders Hitler had issued, even though they had often used their high positions and even run great personal risks to oppose some of the immoral things that occurred.

I had always had a very high opinion of General Jodl, with whom my military position often brought me into personal contact. As Supreme Commander of Armed Forces, he was distinguished by his intelligence, his quick grasp of a situation, and his ability to think and act in the light of the broad over-all picture, even in affairs that did not lie within his special province. A brilliant and capable General Staff officer, he was also a man of firm and upright character. He did not hesitate to take issue with Hitler and to stand up for his own convictions even at great personal risk. In Nürnberg he demonstrated his mastery of the theory and practices of war, and refuted the biased charges of the prosecution by the cold, clear logic of his answers.

Field Marshal Keitel had been even more unfortunately associated with Hitler through his position as head of the Joint Armed Forces Staff. Doubtless he had not always resisted with sufficient firmness and resolution, and had let his better nature be submerged by Hitler's stronger personality. He should have realized this and made way for a more indomitable successor. But I believe that he strove tirelessly and selflessly to do his duty.

Between the sentence and the executions, the defendants were allowed to visit each other in the prison cells. I visited Keitel first, in order to show my sympathy for him in his ordeal.

From the middle of October 1945, when I had been separated from my wife in Moscow and flown to Berlin and later, to Nürnberg for the trials. I had been greatly concerned for her. I heard nothing at all until, quite a while later, I heard that she was being held under shameful conditions in a Russian prison camp near Berlin.

In the middle of September 1946, after all the evidence in the trials had been heard and before the verdicts were handed down, the immediate families of all the accused were given permission to visit them. My daughter and son visited me in Nürnberg, but every effort of my counsel, as well as of Lord Justice Lawrence, presiding judge of the Nürnberg court, failed to obtain permission for my wife to come. Telegrams sent to her came back as "undeliverable." Attempts of my counsel to get in touch with her through the Soviet representatives in Nürnberg brought promises, nothing else. When I wrote Lord Justice Lawrence to this effect, he personally took up the matter with the Allied Control Council for Germany—an effort for which I shall ever be grateful to him—but even he had no better success. When I next saw my wife, it was through the tiny metal grille in Spandau Prison, in March 1950, more than four years after we had been separated in Moscow. She had finally been released from the Russian prison camp.

The only crime charged against her was that of being my wife.

My sentence to life imprisonment meant that I would have to pass the rest of my life behind prison walls—a cause for humiliation and anxiety with my family. Against the protests of my counsel, I resolved to petition the Control Council for clemency—death by shooting. I did not wish at my age to be a continual mental burden on my family. But my petition was refused.

During the Nürnberg proceedings I was put under a debt of gratitude by a number of former admirals of the old German Imperial Navy, well-known in England, who sent a petition to the British Navy, interceding for Grand Admiral Dönitz and me. Numerous German naval officers who had been captured and were held in British and American prison camps also handed in mass petitions for our pardon. Among other things, they stated that they felt it an obligation to defend the honor of their wounded and fallen comrades, and that they could not believe the officers of the Allied Navies would accept the charge that the German Navy had operated as pirates.

Present in the Nürnberg courtroom when the sentences were pronounced was Admiral Lord Andrew B. Cunningham, at that time First Sea Lord of the British Admiralty. A few days later Dönitz's counsel spoke to him about the petitions that had been organized for the pardon of the German naval officers. Lord Cunningham advised him to hand the petitions directly to the British admiral on the

Allied Control Council, and to inform the latter that he, Lord Cunningham, had specifically advised this action. One could only read in this Admiral Lord Cunningham's support of these petitions.

Admiral Cunningham had come to Berlin in December 1938 as one of the British naval representatives appointed to negotiate with the German Naval Command in connection with changes in the original Anglo-German Naval Agreement of 1935. We had informed the British Admiralty, in accordance with the stipulations of the agreement, that we intended to construct two cruisers and to build our submarine arm up to 100 per cent parity with the British submarine arm, as permitted in the agreement. The negotiations went off without a hitch. After they were over both Admiral Cunningham and I expressed hopes that war between our two navies would never again occur. I am convinced that he meant it as sincerely as I did.

Unfortunately our mutual wish was never to be fulfilled. When the war broke out, only eight months later, Admiral Cunningham, one of Britain's most distinguished naval officers, fought for his country—as I did for mine.

XXII

Spandau—and Homecoming

ALMOST AS SOON as the International Military Tribunal in Nürnberg had pronounced our sentences, these were put into execution. If the restrictions on me during the trial had been rigid, they were even more severe now. To speak to my counsel, Dr. Siemers, I was taken to the conference room handcuffed by the right arm to my soldier guard. If during the conference it became necessary for me to write anything, the guard had to move his hand back and forth with mine to permit me to write. Like all the others who had been given prison terms, I had my hair shaved off and was garbed in prison clothes.

I had already passed my seventieth birthday.

Then on 18 July 1947, along with my co-prisoners, Baron von Neurath, Admiral Dönitz, Rudolf Hess, the former deputy to Hitler, Walther Funk, former president of the Reichsbank, Munitions Minister Speer, and Reich Youth Leader von Schirach, I was brought to Spandau, the military prison of the Four Allied Powers.

Life at Spandau was utterly different from life in that outside world from which we were now completely cut off. Once a month we were permitted to write one short letter, subject to censorship; we could also receive one short letter—and that too was subject to censorship. Oftentimes the letters from outside were not given to us at all, or else were delivered mutilated through large parts having been cut out. The letters we wrote were often delivered to the post office too late to allow our families to send replies in time for the censorship day.

Every second month we were allowed to receive a visit from a member of our families—and that visit was limited to fifteen minutes' duration. My wife's first visit was on 15 March 1950. As I mentioned, she had not been released from concentration camp —at first in Sachsenhausen and then in Oberursel—until 1 September 1949. Why she and my son, Hans, had never been allowed to visit me in Spandau until March 1950 no one ever explained.

At Spandau the prisoner was kept separated from his visitor by a double thickness of close metal grille. Even then interpreters were seated on the prisoner's right and left, and in addition the conversation was closely observed by officers of the Four Powers, who often interrupted it.

Inside the prison we prisoners were not allowed to communicate with one another, and until the summer of 1954 any exchange of words even during such common prison occupations as cleaning, or making paper bags, or working in the prison garden, was prohibited.

I would prefer not to describe in detail the prison life at Spandau as long as other Germans are still incarcerated there. But I wish to say that I cherish no animosity toward the British, French, American and Russian soldiers who guarded us; they were only carrying out the orders of their military superiors and their governments. And neither the western democracies nor the Soviet Union permit a soldier to refuse military orders. The medical officers assigned to duty at the prison performed their medical duties correctly and without any personal bias, as far as I could learn. The French prison chaplains particularly earned our gratitude for the humanity with which they carried out their functions within the narrow leeway allowed them. However, since we were not allowed to converse with them, it was impossible to obtain spiritual advice and counsel from them.

The International Military Tribunal at Nürnberg had been an oddity in the whole history of jurisprudence. Unlike any court in any western country, it had above it no authority for revision nor any court of appeals. Even the Allied Control Council for Germany had no such supremacy. It was allowed to grant a lightening of a sentence, but could not make one more severe. This was why, when I requested the clemency of being shot in preference to dragging out my life in prison, my request was refused. Even at that the Control Council soon ceased to "control," and for all practical purposes no longer existed. Spandau Prison and its supervisory organization, set up in military form to receive the prisoners after the Nürnberg trials, was the only activity of the Four Powers that continued to exist. It formed a unique contrast to the split that had occurred everywhere else between the East and the West. But since there was no higher authority to which one could appeal—though such was to have been provided for by the directives of the Nürnberg court—conditions in the prison often became more arduous.

Prison walls and the quietness of an individual cell, such as we knew at Spandau, give a man both the opportunity and the incentive to reflect. In those long, dragging years I often thought with thankfulness of my parents and my teachers, who had given me a firm Christian faith to support me in my life. That faith now kept me from despair, for I was conscious of no guilt before mankind.

My thoughts, too, turned constantly to my wife and my son, about whom I felt much anxiety. I was grateful that my Hans faced the world and his daily work dutifully and unfalteringly, though my fate loaded him with many burdens. Our true friends all stood by him. Because any progress in the field of agriculture was impossible under the conditions he faced, he had to give up his chosen profession of farmer, a profession in which he had already demonstrated exceptional aptitude on large estates both in Silesia and in Schleswig-Holstein, after having graduated from an agricultural college in Schleswig. But through the kindness of an old friend, Dr. Röpke, he obtained a very promising position in the metals industry at Lippstadt, Westphalia, and could look again to the future with confidence. It was a great consolation to me when he was able to rejoin my wife. But his early death destroyed all my hopes there too.

In Spandau we were permitted to read as long as the electric lights were on and we had no other duties to perform. Hess had received some books sent him from England, and others of us received books sent to us by faithful friends. These formed the nucleus of a small lending library, which was placed in my charge. Various Berlin libraries added volumes, also, but all political or military books were carefully excluded by the prison authorities. Aside from the monthly letter to our families, no personal writing was permitted any of the prisoners.

Later, when restrictions were somewhat relaxed among the prisoners, we had many interesting discussions. In these I found myself on common ground with Baron von Neurath and Dönitz most of all.

Neurath was three years older than I, and his wealth of information in Foreign Affairs, going back all the way to 1914 when he had been German ambassador in Constantinople, provided endless topics. Although he was in poor health, he never for a moment lost his natural dignity and bearing, and his calm acceptance of his situation was an example to everyone. But it moved me deeply to observe how his years were bearing down more heavily and his strength visibly ebbing. When he was finally released in 1954, he could scarcely stand erect, and within two years he passed away quietly at his home.

It was only natural that I saw a great deal of Dönitz, since we had been together in the Navy for so long and had been joint defendants at Nürnberg. He read a great deal, occupied himself, as he always had, with problems in all fields, and had a firm and steadfast bearing, although his health, too, was not of the best.

As my sentence had been for life while Dönitz's had been for only ten years, we naturally expected that he would be the first one of us to be released. It was a great surprise to me, then, when I was released first and had to leave my old comrade in prison, where he was forced to serve out his entire term. But when he was released, we had a moving reunion.

It was only long after I was released that I learned that numbers of men and women had worked untiringly all those years, not only to lighten the conditions of my imprisonment but to obtain my complete release. These unselfish friends came not only from all ranks of my old service comrades, but from prominent personages both in Germany and abroad, including many who had been former enemies during the war. A profound feeling of gratitude sweeps over me when I think of this, and their friendly humanity takes much of the bitterness from my memories of the more recent past.

Never having had any other thought than that I would see the end of my life in Spandau, I had come to regard the idea with resignation. What troubled me most was the thought that not only was I unable to help my family, but by my very imprisonment was burdening them with a constant worry. My son Hans died in Lippstadt, on 17 January 1953, from an illness resulting from his war service. Though my wife and numerous other people, some of them personages in high positions, endeavored to obtain a short leave for me to see him before he died, I was not even allowed to attend his funeral. In fact, I did not learn of his death until the French chaplain broke the news to me two days afterward. It is incomprehensible to me even today why it was thought necessary for the prison directors—four colonels—to be present on this sad occasion when I received the distressing news.

I was not to escape the maladies of old age, which began to creep up on me, too. I was hospitalized for a while, and by 1955—my eightieth summer—I had become so crippled that I could barely walk, and then only with the aid of two canes.

Probably the state of my health was responsible for my completely unexpected release. On 26 September 1955 the British army doctor took me out of my cell with the casual statement that he wanted to given me an examination. Instead, he took me to the visitors' reception room, where I found my clothes all laid out—the same clothes which I had exchanged for prison garb almost ten years before. A short time later my wife came to get me. A closed car was waiting at the prison gate, and to my great joy the person at the wheel was my old driver, Rudolf Schulze, and in attendance was also my old house steward, Adolf Palzer. These two faithful friends would not hear of anyone bringing me out of prison but themselves. Through the kindness of other friends, including German officials, I was able to reach Lippstadt, our temporary residence, by car and plane that same day. Mr. Bunker, the chief of the traffic bureau in Lippstadt, had smoothed out all transportation problems, and Dr. Röpke had placed his own car, driven by his son, at my disposal.

As there were some doubts as to how my health would stand up to the trip, Dr. Hoffmann, the head doctor of the Lippstadt

Lutheran Hospital, had come to Hannover, where the plane was to land, in order to look after me.

Arrived at the house, I found a large group of friends and acquaintances waiting to receive me. They had decorated the whole house with flowers. My former aide, Admiral Baltzer, was the first to step forward to shake my hand. Such a reception, and the wealth of good wishes that arrived by telegram, letter, or were delivered in person, quite overwhelmed me. Here and now I express my heartfelt thanks to all those who welcomed me home and had kept my memory green.

The Germany I found in 1955, however, was utterly different from the one I remembered ten years back, before my isolation in Moscow, Nürnberg, and Spandau. I was not completely unprepared for the change, since during the last year in Spandau we had been allowed to receive German newspapers—though, to be sure, whole pieces were often cut out of the pages. What impressed me most now was the division of Germany into two parts, the constant influx of the dispossessed and the fugitives, the consolidation of West Germany under a firm leadership deeply conscious of its democratic goal—and the altered attitude of our former western enemies toward us. What they had refused the Weimar Republic, back in the days following World War I, they now freely granted the new West Germany—international equality, both internally and externally.

Even so, it seems to me that the burden of a divided Germany which the present German people bear is heavier than all the burden imposed upon my generation by the Versailles Treaty. The task of the men whom the people have confidently intrusted with the government of Germany today, therefore, is in many respects more difficult than the task we had then.

I am confident, however, that if we Germans on both sides of the East-West dividing line have the firm desire to reunite, union too will come to pass in good time. The internal strength that resides in the German people—the strength that has proved itself in the political and economic revival of the past decade—must not be wasted. The first and foremost obligation of every German national must be devoted to the welfare of the country as a whole, not the personal gratification of the individual. We must profit from the lessons of the past—lessons which will be many and varied, depending upon the experiences and moral character of the people. All our history has showed that great accomplishments are attainable only when the overwhelming majority of the people have one common goal in view. Before us, in the coming years, lie tasks of impressive magnitude and difficulty. In facing them no one should hesitate or hold back, for it is the common fatherland for which we strive.

It is only natural that I should feel a compelling interest in the Navy of the West German Republic. Because of the changed world situation, and, especially, the changed position of Germany in Europe and the world, the new Navy's tasks and objectives are markedly different from those of the old Navy, just as its personnel, its ships, and its procedures differ from those of former times. On the one hand, it has to its advantage the lessons and experiences of two wars, as well as the model of the buildup of the new Navy after 1918; on the other hand, its course in the future will lie along entirely new lines.

And it is not in imitation, but in recreating from the old that the value of tradition lies. In the days of the Weimar Republic, when we had then, as now, the task of building a Navy anew out of the ruins, we did not simply follow after the old traditional procedures and customs, but put all our thought and effort into producing something new and better in place of that which had been outmoded or which had not proved worthwhile. Regardless of then or now, the basic principles of the military services are unchangeable. Courage and candor, obedience and comradeship, love of fatherland and loyalty to the State: these are ever the distinguishing characteristics of the soldier and sailor. Building character through intelligent training and education is always the first and greatest goal.

A most important factor in Germany's future development will be the extent to which the German people understand the nature and problems of the sea. Germany has extensive land borders to the east, in the center of Europe. At the same time she is a nation built on industry and trade, and therefore inseparably linked to the world beyond the European continent. Under present world conditions, no nation can any longer isolate itself economically, politically, or even militarily. Least of all can Germany do this—a nation whose economy and industry are dependent on import and export, whose ties are not only with her neighbors but also across the sea, and whose shipping and fishing industries are among the most important of her enterprises. One of Germany's tragedies is that large segments of her population, including her leading classes, have not recognized this fact in the past and hence have failed to seize Germany's special situation.

Both before and during World War I, our political and military leaders failed to grasp the significance of the weapon of seapower which was opposed to us, and ignored the advantages the enemy held through his unlimited mastery of the ocean routes. Despite the collapse of Russia, the greatest land power opposed to us, we were brought to our knees in 1918 by the pressure of the naval blockade, and were starved out by lack of food and raw materials.

After World War I the leaders of the National Socialist State failed to read the all too clear lessons of that decisive conflict. In the second great world war, we, a central, continental nation with only weak weapons at sea, were unable to burst through the cordon that the great sea powers drew around us. By the ocean, that most efficient of all transport routes, gigantic convoys of goods and foodstuffs crossed from America to England, and indispensable war materials went to hard-pressed Russia. By the sea the Allied armies landed in North Africa and, later, in Italy and Normandy, for the final assault on "Fortress Europe."

The lessons of seapower we learned in those two wars were bitter, but plain. I believe that Germans can now recognize and understand them. In this age of air traffic, radio and television, and all other means of speedy communication, the boundaries separating one people from another have largely vanished. Unless artificially reinforced, boundary posts and national boundaries no longer constitute a significant barrier. The things that bind together the lands and peoples of the West, the things they have in common, are more important than the things that separate them. Even we are beginning to abandon the narrowness of our previous continental viewpoint and to look out beyond our coastal and land boundaries. We are a member of the Free World, to which we naturally belong, and thus find ourselves in close community with the great sea powers. Opposed to, and vanquished by, them in two wars, we now move beside them into a new future. The seapower embodied by the Atlantic nations, among whom we now take our place, will give us security and, I fervently hope, peace. A generation ago Grand Admiral von Tirpitz first used the expression, "The German people have never understood the sea." Today I hope that bitter experience has given us the knowledge we lacked, and that it will henceforth become an integral part of our thinking.

Looking back on the decade and a half in which I was at the head of the Navy, I feel deep and lasting gratitude to all those who served under me so loyally and ably. Each contributed to the best of his ability toward the building up and operation of the Navy. For things uncompleted, or poorly done, I take all the responsibility. Under my command the Navy sincerely welcomed Hitler's agreement with England as to the relative strengths of the two fleets. The great majority of the Navy, accepting my assurance, believed up until the very last moment that war with England would never occur. When that war did break out all unexpectedly, the Navy embarked upon it with a heavy heart and without malice, but with the firm determination to contribute its best efforts and to maintain its loyalty and discipline to the end.

Of all the results achieved by the Navy in the buildup years from 1918 to 1939, the inner loyalties among its personnel were the most important. With the great influx of raw recruits from civilian life, and with the great expansion in ships and shore activities, it was inevitable that the Navy's organization and the caliber of its personnel would change. Despite this, loyalty and discipline and comradeship within the Navy remained fully alive right to the end of the war—sure proof of the soundness of our development in peacetime; sure proof that the traditional Navy virtues were not limited to the professional Navy alone, but could equally well inspire the civilian who was simply fulfilling his duty for the duration of hostilities. Certainly, between the regular career Navy and these volunteers, there was no difference in the degree of their dedication. They were all united in a common cause.

The accomplishments which the Navy, in cooperation with the other armed services, achieved in the Second World War cannot be fairly appraised at this short distance. But the basis of all those accomplishments was the innate devotion of every German to the fatherland, and the bravery which has been characteristic of him throughout all history. The test of the individual in wartime is far different from that in peacetime. That the German people unconsciously tend to look up to their soldiers and sailors, especially those on the fighting front in wartime, is a worthy tribute and forms a common spiritual bond among citizens in time of stress.

It is not my province to thank the personnel of the Navy for their devotion and courageous efforts under the stern tests of war; it is for the German people as a whole to do that. In so doing, Germany will have to include also those who wore the uniform of the other branches of the armed services, as well as the men and women everywhere who risked their lives just as devotedly in other forms of service to the country.

Human greatness is not measured by whether it reveals itself through victory or defeat, or whether the political direction of a war is approved or disapproved. It can be measured only in terms of the principle of character from which conduct stems. When the stresses and shadows of the immediate present are lifted from the German people, it is my firm belief that the human greatness exhibited by the many individuals in their different roles during the war will shine through the darker shadows of that period and take its rightful place in the nation's traditions and history.

Service in the Navy was for all of us a matter not only of duty to the fatherland, but also a contribution from the heart. Many of our closest friends and shipmates gave their blood and their lives for Germany, in peace as well as war, but the things for which they fought and died did not perish with their ships or go down in the wreckage. The eternal sea has closed over the fallen; the memorial wreaths which their surviving comrades strew upon the waters float but for a little time before they too sink from sight. But indestructible and eternal is the legacy which the dead have left to future generations: that comradeship which has typified the German Navy since time immemorial, and which forms not only the bridge between the old and the young, and the past and the future, but also between the men of all the navies who sail the seas of all the world.

This book, now finished, I lay in the hands of my wife, who has shared my life in joy and in sorrow; who, with our son, fought tirelessly for my liberation through all those darkest years; and who gallantly stood in lonely grief at the deathbed and the grave of that only son. For her boundless loving-kindness I ask her, my best comrade, to accept, from the deepest wellspring of my being, my thanks.

Appendix

(Letter from Captain Fritz Boie (Ret.) to Admiral Erich Förste)

THE LATE Captain Baron von Harsdorf and Enderndorf, who was an aide on the flagship *Seydlitz* from 1914 to 1916 and who stood beside the Commander of the Battle Cruiser Forces at his station during the Dogger Bank action, has made the following report to me:

I was near Raeder during this whole period, and especially during the engagement on the Dogger Bank. Raeder's capacity and talent for work were remarkable. Always alert and tireless, he arrived at decisions immediately and had all necessary details ever present in his head. When unexpected circumstances arose, Raeder had solutions ready immediately for his beloved commander. Admiral Hipper in turn had a high opinion of the energy and keen judgment of his senior staff adviser—so high, in fact, that he almost invariably and immediately accepted the proffered solution. This mutual confidence proved invaluable in battle. Sometimes all that was needed was a glance or a wave of the hand to pass on important orders. Everyone who had the opportunity to observe the teamwork between these two was impressed by the modesty of Raeder, who always kept in the background, behind his commander, and who tactfully diverted special recognition—from the *Seydlitz* skipper, Captain Egidy, for instance—to his admiral.

(Letter from Admiral von Hipper to his former Chief of Staff on 31 May 1919)

My dear Raeder:

This day—a day filled with proud yet melancholy memories—must not end without my thinking gratefully of you and your many years of devoted service as chief of my staff.

Whatever was granted to me in this war, whatever I have received in the way of honors and distinction, I owe to your clear, energetic, and sympathetic support. I shall never cease to be aware of it. You were my good star, and it turned pale when you left me.

(Letter from Admiral von Hipper to his former Chief of Staff on 30 March 1926)

My dear Raeder:

Remembering the stirring events of ten years ago, my thoughts today turn to my most faithful helper and adviser, and I recall with the deepest gratitude all that you and your co-workers meant to me, not merely during the battle, but during the entire war.

Today, when throughout the nation the battle anniversary is celebrated and the deeds of the battle cruisers and scouting ships are remembered warmly, you can proudly say that it was all your achievement; that it was due to your unceasing alertness and attention that the battle cruisers arrived at such a high peak of training that they were able to pass their ordeal by fire with flying colors.

Again and again I feel a debt to the fate that put you at my side, and a thankfulness, also, that I could keep you throughout the entire war—something granted to no other unit commander. Five years, almost, of close association, and that during such a critical period—that is the only such case that I know of in the Navy. For this most memorable period of my life I shall be ever thankful.

(Excerpt from the Kieler Neueste Nachrichten *of 2 June 1926.)*

SKAGERRAK CELEBRATIONS IN KIEL

Vice Admiral Raeder Granted Honorary Doctor's Degree

Vice Admiral Erich Raeder, Commander of the Baltic Naval District, has been granted the honorary degree of Doctor of Philosophy by Christian Albrecht University in Kiel. The citation, which the Dean of the Department of Philosophy, Dr. Walther Kossel, presented to him at his home, read as follows:

"The Department of Philosophy of Christian Albrecht University, through its Dean, Dr. Walther Kossel, Professor of Theoretical Physics, confers the honorary degree of Doctor of Philosophy upon the Commander of the Baltic Naval District, Vice Admiral Erich Raeder, distinguished historian of German cruiser warfare. Admiral Raeder recounted the cruise of the cruiser squadron under Count von Spee, both in its victory and its doom, in all its tragic majesty. He recreated before our eyes the death cruises of the light cruisers *Emden, Königsberg,* and *Karlsruhe,* demonstrating their influence on the over-all war situation and portraying their incredible struggle against their inevitable fate. With keen historical insight, he viewed the events not only as a whole but also in all their parts. The very simplicity of his style molds the historic events to heroic stature.

"Done at Kiel on 31 May 1926 during the tenure of Dr. Leonhard Jores, Professor of Pathological Anatomy, as Rector.

(s) WALTHER KOSSEL, PH.D., DEAN"

(Transcript)

Weiler, Allgau
11 April 1946

Sworn Deposition by Dr. Otto Gessler
Reichsminister (Ret.) in Lindenberg.

I, Otto Gessler, have known the former Grand Admiral Dr. Raeder personally since about the middle of the twenties, when I was German Minster of Defense. Raeder was at that time Inspector of Education in the Navy. I learned to know Raeder as a man always of blameless, courageous disposition, and a person with a keen sense of duty.

On the subject of the accusation I know only this little:

When I was lying in the Hedwig Hospital in Berlin, after my release from imprisonment by the Gestapo in March 1945, Raeder visited me often. He also exerted himself to have me brought home, since I was ill and completely exhausted. At this time I told him of the mistreatment, and particularly of the torture, to which I had been subjected.

He was both shocked and indignant at the news, and said he would report it to the Führer. I begged him not to do this, for I had been told, before the torture, that this treatment was being given me by Hitler's express command. Too, I knew that the only result would be that I would be immediately re-arrested, since at my release I had had to sign the customary declaration to observe silence about all that had happened and would not even be able to get confirmation of my imprisonment in order to obtain a railroad ticket home.

When the Nationalist Socialist regime came into office, I was ignored by some members of my former department, and coldly snubbed by others. Dr. Raeder was one of the few exceptions to this. Three times prior to 1939 he invited me, with other guests, to visit abroad the cruiser *Nürnberg*, although I refused the invitation on two occasions. When I did go aboard in June 1939, he himself came to Kiel to receive me personally.

At that time we discussed the political situation, and I expressed my fears that the invasion of Poland would bring on a war of all Europe. Raeder told me positively that he considered it impossible that Hitler would attack Poland. When the war came anyway, a little later, I thought that Hitler had been in the dark because Hitler delighted in presenting the highest military leaders with a *fait accompli.*

(*signed*) DR. OTTO GESSLER,
Reichsminister (Ret.)

(Transcript)

Frankfurt, Main
Niedenau 54
28 October 1950

Deposition by Rear Admiral Karl Kühlenthal (Ret.)

Herewith do I, Karl Kühlenthal, Rear Admiral (Ret.), of Niedenau 54, Frankfurt, Main, declare the following in lieu of oath:

I avouch that I am aware of the significance of a statement made in lieu of an oath, especially the fact that a false statement is punishable by law. I agree that my declaration may be put in evidence before foreign or domestic authorities or courts.

Up until the year 1920, I was an officer in the old German Navy, and have been a close friend and comrade of Grand Admiral Dr. h.c. Erich Raeder since the year 1901.

I am half Jewish, and have a Jewish wife. Consequently, in accordance with the Nürnberg laws, my two sons and I were treated as fullblooded Jews. Thus my family and I were delivered to the worst of fates.

To free myself from this horrible situation, I asked Grand Admiral Raeder to secure, from Adolf Hitler, an exemption for my family and me from the crushing restrictions of the Nürnberg Laws.

Although Raeder was fully aware of Hitler's merciless anti-Semitic attitude, and the serious and unpleasant consequences his intercession might bring upon himself, he loyally used the full power of his office in interceding, and demanded from Hitler the exemption for which I had asked.

At first Hitler sharply refused. But despite this refusal, Raeder repeated his intercession when the persecution of the Jews became progressively worse. By stubborn insistence he finally did obtain for us a certain measure of relief in that we were spared unbearable calumny, and in that, above all, my wife escaped the horrible fate of being dragged into one of the notorious concentration camps. In particular, Raeder obtained for me an exemption signed by Hitler's own hand which protected my wife and me from further persecution. I not only continued to receive my pension, but our property, including our apartment, was insured to us.

Courageously and in disregard of his own personal safety, Grand Admiral Raeder resisted the damnable principles of National Socialism and stood by a comrade and friend who had fallen under the persecution of the National Socialist laws. He deserves to be called a noble champion of humanity.

I can cite another insurance of his noble character.

The wife of a Navy friend of mine was imprisoned because of her membership in the Christian Science Church. Since he was familiar with her beliefs, Dr. Friedrich Krebs, the former chief burgomaster of Frankfurt-am-Main, intervened in her behalf. Traveling to Berlin, he reported the incident to Grand Admiral Raeder. The latter immediately got in touch with Heydrich, the head of the Gestapo, and demanded her release forthwith. It was only through this intervention that a comrade's wife was thus freed after a month in prison, and was thereafter spared any further persecution.

In my intercession here I should like to express my eternal thanks to Grand Admiral Raeder, and to ask that my full statements be used in his favor.

(*signed*) KARL KÜHLENTHAL,
Rear Admiral (Ret.)

(Transcript)

Hamburg,
26 February 1946

Guenter Jacobsen
Sierichstr. 20
Hamburg 39

To Dr. Walter Siemers,
Maximilian str. 23, bei Müller
Nürnberg

Subject: Grand Admiral Raeder.

From the newspapers I have learned that you have undertaken the defense of Grand Admiral Raeder. I consider it my self-evident duty to point out that Raeder freed my Jewish uncle and my Jewish father from the concentration camp.

Raeder is well acquainted with my father's family, who come from the same town of Grünberg, in Silesia. In 1935, when my grandmother died, Grand Admiral Raeder expressed his most heartfelt sympathy to my uncle, Fritz Jacobsen, retired counsellor of the district court in Berlin, although my uncle is a full Jew. And in 1938, when my uncle was thrown into the Oranienburg concentration camp, his release was obtained through Raeder's intercession.

The case of my father, Erwin Jacobsen, M.D., was similar. Though acquitted of the charge of racial dishonor, my father was thrown into the concentration camp at Fuhlsbüttel. In May 1939 my father was released from the concentration camp through Raeder's intercession, and permitted to emigrate to England. He was interned there as an enemy alien from 1940 to 1943, and since then has resided in Appleby, Westmoreland.

Thus Admiral Raeder saved my father's life. When my father left the concentration camp, a Gestapo official asked him if he were related to Raeder, since Raeder had worked so hard in his behalf.

It goes without saying that I am ready to confirm this testimony under oath.

Most respectfully yours,
(*signed*) GUENTER JACOBSEN

(Transcript)

Starnberg
18 February 1946

Solemn Affirmation by Konrad Lotter,
Managing Director in Unterbrunn,
above Starnberg, Upper Bavaria.

I served in the Navy from 1914 to 1918, and again from 1944 through 1945, in the last war. Previously, from 1907 through 1909 I served on board the SMS *Yorck,* where I became acquainted with the navigation officer, later Grand Admiral Raeder.

Grand Admiral Raeder has always seemed to me to embody in himself the best traditons of the old Imperial Navy. This was especially true in connection with his outlook on world affairs and his philosophy of life. As a man and as an officer he was a model of the best.

In the year 1941, when the anti-Christian policy of the Hitler regime started up in full force in Bavaria, when the monasteries and convents were closed, and when the youth were being indoctrinated with the utmost intolerance of every religious faith, I sent Grand Admiral Raeder a 12-page memorandum in which I detailed my objections to this policy.

Grand Admiral Raeder took up the matter immediately. Through his offices I was summoned to meet Gauleiter Wagner, at that time Bavarian Minister of the Interior, in Munich. After a number of conferences, agreement was reached that prayers and the display of the crucifix should still be permitted in the schools. In addition, fifty-nine ministers and priests, who had been fined 500 marks each, were pardoned.

Even the suppression of the monasteries and convents was halted for the time being. Gauleiter Wagner had to go to Berlin to answer for the failure of his policy, and he shifted the blame onto "overzealous district leaders."

All of this would have been impossible without the initiative of Grand Admiral Raeder. To set everything straight, I would like to add that I, as an opponent of the Hitler regime, was subjected to various plots of the Gestapo, and was imprisoned as a consequence.

I believe, therefore, that I can be accepted as a trustworthy witness. With this letter I assert, in lieu of an oath, that all of my above statements are true and correct, and have conscientiously been made in accordance with my best knowledge.

(*signed*) KONRAD LOTTER.

Index

F

G

Trimmed size: 6 x 9 inches
Type page: 25 x 43 picas
Type face: Intertype Garamond
Type size: 12 point on 13
Chapter title: 24 pt. Weiss
Paper: 50 lb. White Winnebago Eggshell and 70 lb. White Woodbine Enamel
Jacket: 70 lb. White Crestline Offset
Cloth: Roxite LS51275 Vellum

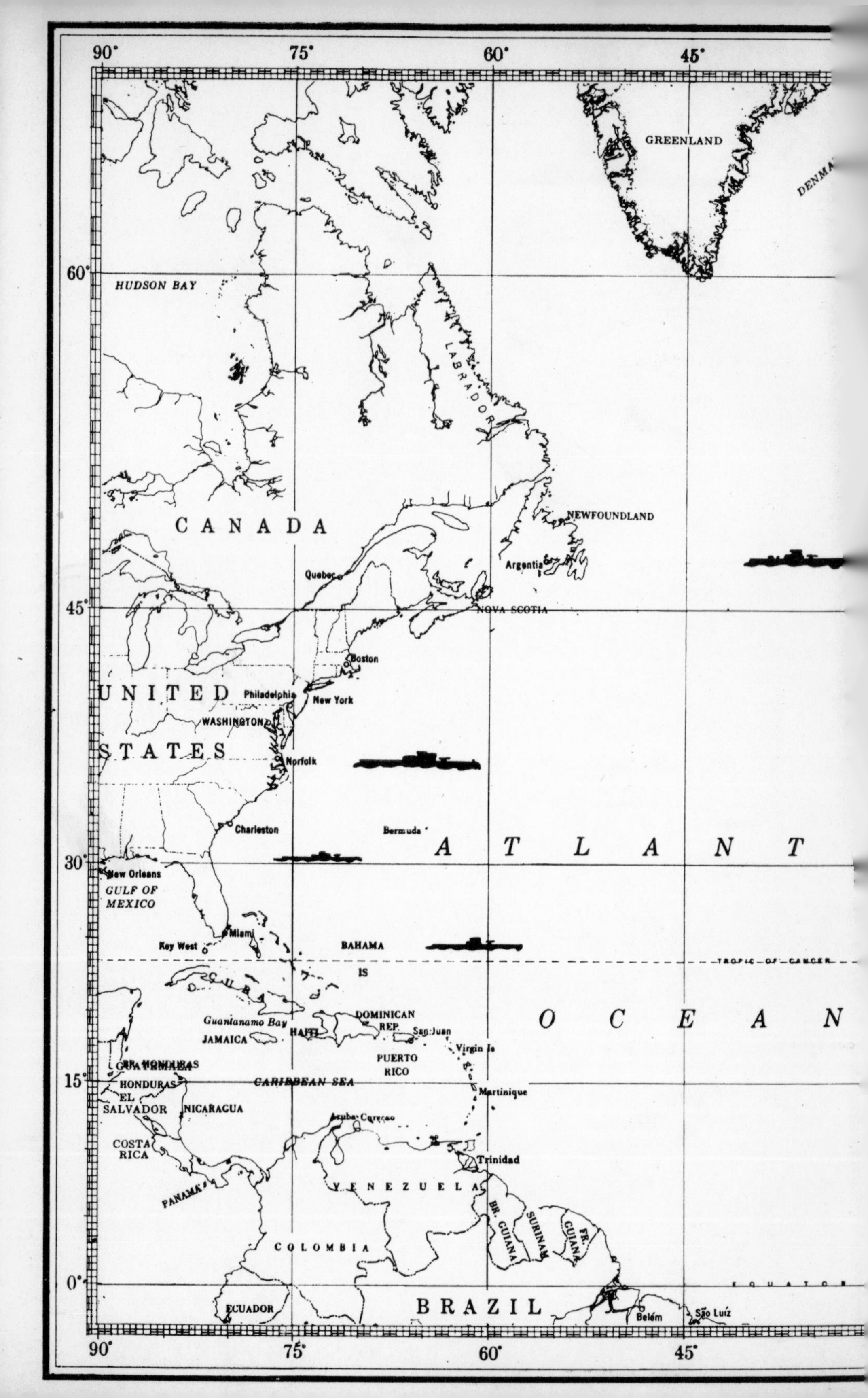

90°
75°
60°
45°
GREENLAND
HUDSON BAY
LABRADOR
CANADA
NEWFOUNDLAND
Argentia
Quebec
NOVA SCOTIA
Boston
UNITED
STATES
Philadelphia
New York
WASHINGTON
Norfolk
Charleston
Bermuda
ATLANTIC
New Orleans
GULF OF
MEXICO
Miami
Key West
BAHAMA
IS
TROPIC OF CANCER
CUBA
Guantanamo Bay
DOMINICAN
REP.
HAITI
JAMAICA
San Juan
Virgin Is
PUERTO
RICO
OCEAN
HONDURAS
CARIBBEAN SEA
Martinique
EL
SALVADOR
NICARAGUA
Aruba
Curaçao
COSTA
RICA
Trinidad
PANAMA
VENEZUELA
BR. GUIANA
SURINAM
FR. GUIANA
COLOMBIA
ECUADOR
BRAZIL
Belém
São Luiz
30°
15°
0°